4 Week Loan

This book is due for return on or before the last date shown below

University of Cumbria
24/7 renewals Tel:0845 602 6124

MARKETING PROFESSIONAL SERVICES

SECOND EDITION

Forward-Thinking Strategies for Boosting Your Business, Your Image, and Your Profits

PHILIP KOTLER PH.D.

Thomas Hayes Ph.D. / Paul N. Bloom Ph.D.

PRENTICE HALL PRESS

Library of Congress Cataloging-in-Publication Data
Kotler, Philip.
    Marketing professional services / Philip Kotler, Paul Bloom, Thomas Hayes.—2nd ed.
        p. cm.
    Includes bibliographical references and indexes.
    ISBN 0-7352-0179-X
        1. Professions—Marketing. I. Bloom, Paul N. II. Hayes, Thomas J. (Thomas Joseph)
    1953- III. Title.

    HD8038.A1 K67 2002
    658.8—dc21   2001056024

Senior Editor: Tom Power
Production Editor: Jacqueline Roulette
Formatting: Inkwell Publishing Services

*This publication is designed to provide accurate and authoritative information in regard
to the subject matter covered. It is sold with the understanding that the publisher is not
engaged in rendering legal, accounting, or other professional service. If legal advice or
other expert assistance is required, the services of a competent professional person should
be sought.*
                        —From a Declaration of Principles jointly adopted by a Committee of the
                        American Bar Association and a Committee of Publishers and Associations.

Printed in the United States of America
10 9 8 7 6 5 4 3 2

ISBN 0-73520179-X

ATTENTION: CORPORATIONS AND SCHOOLS

Prentice Hall Press books are available at quantity discounts with bulk purchase for
educational, business, or sales promotional use. For information, please write to:
Prentice Hall Press Special Sales, 240 Frisch Court, Paramus, NJ 07652. Please supply: title of book, ISBN, quantity, how the book will be used, date needed.

PRENTICE HALL

http://www.phpress.com

To Jordan, Jamie, Ellie, and Abby Heifetz and
to Olivia and Sam Schwartz, our future professionals
—Philip Kotler

To Mag, Sarah, John, and Devin, my sources of happiness
—Tom Hayes

In memory of my parents,
Frieda and Joseph Bloom
—Paul Bloom

....

About the Authors

Philip Kotler (M.A., University of Chicago; Ph.D., M.I.T.) is the S. C. Johnson Distinguished Professor of International Marketing at the Kellogg Graduate School of Management, Northwestern University, Evanston, Illinois. He has published *Marketing Management* (10th edition), twenty other books as well as more than a hundred articles in leading journals. His research spans strategic marketing, consumer marketing, business marketing, services marketing, and e-marketing. He has been a consultant to IBM, Bank of America, Merck, General Electric, Honeywell, and many other companies. He has received honorary doctorate degrees from nine major universities in the United States and abroad.

Tom Hayes is a Professor in the Department of Marketing at Xavier University where he has taught for the last twenty-five years. He has also served as Chair of the Department for thirteen years and as the Director of Institutional Advancement. Before taking on the responsibilities of Chair of the department, he served as Vice President of Research Services at Qualitative Associates, Inc., a full-service qualitative research firm in Cincinnati. He is presently president of VisionQuest Marketing Strategy, a full-service marketing consulting agency. He was the founder of the American Marketing Association's Symposium on the Marketing of Higher Education and is co-editor of *The Journal of Marketing for Higher Education*. He is a nationally recognized expert in services marketing, the marketing of higher education, and the development of ideas for new products and services, and consults in these areas on a national and international basis. Dr. Hayes received a Bachelor's degree in Psychology as well as an M.B.A. in Marketing at Xavier University. He also received an M.B.A. in Organization Behavior and a Ph.D. in Marketing from the University of Cincinnati. Dr. Hayes sat on the Board of the Cincinnati Chapter of the American Marketing Association for ten years, including serving as its President in 1989-1990 and was voted Member of the Year for the period of 1991-1992. Tom served as Vice President of the Services Division of the American Marketing Association in 1994. He served as Vice President of the Marketing Management Council of the AMA in 1997-1998.

Paul N. Bloom is Professor of Marketing at the Kenan-Flagler Business School of the University of North Carolina at Chapel Hill. He holds a Ph.D. in Marketing from the Kellogg School of Northwestern University and earned an M.B.A. at the Wharton School of the University of Pennsylvania. He is a frequent contributor to marketing journals on topics related to services marketing, consumer protection, antitrust, and social marketing. One of his articles won the award for the outstanding article published in the *Journal of Public Policy & Marketing* for 1987 to 1991. Bloom's previous books include *Knowledge Development in Marketing: The MSI Experience*, and he is a co-editor of *The Handbook of Marketing and Society*. He has served on a variety of editorial review boards and in leadership roles within the American Marketing Association and the Association for Consumer Research. He was a member of the American Marketing Association's Task Force on the Development of Marketing Thought and served as Chair of the Marketing and Society Special Interest Group of the American Marketing Association. He formerly held posts as a visiting scholar at the Marketing Science Institute and on the faculty of the University of Maryland at College Park.

Preface

We have spent our entire professional careers—a combined total of almost one hundred years—teaching, writing, and consulting in the field of marketing. As close observers of developments in this field, we have witnessed an enormous surge of interest in marketing over the last two decades, even from sectors of our society that formerly ignored or disdained marketing, such as hospitals, educational institutions, and government agencies. But nowhere in our experience have we seen the acceptance and adoption of marketing occur as rapidly and as massively as it has in the professions. Accountants, lawyers, management consultants, architects, engineers, doctors, and other professionals are turning to marketing with great enthusiasm and commitment. And marketing, in turn, is creating fundamental and lasting changes in their professions.

In spite of the great enthusiasm and commitment that professionals have shown toward marketing, there have been only very limited amounts of resource materials made available to guide the adoption and implementation of professional service marketing programs. We have been constantly told by professionals that an increasing need exists for written materials that recognize the distinctive problems of marketing professional services (versus more conventional goods and services) and provide sound, in-depth advice on how to deal with those problems. This book is intended to satisfy such a need.

Like the preceding edition, this second edition of *Marketing Professional Services* carefully explains how marketing concepts can be applied to the problems commonly faced by professional service organizations when they seek to improve their practice-development programs. In this book, we provide guidance on how to think *strategically* and *analytically* about marketing in professional service settings. We have gone beyond the offering of a collection of marketing tips and ideas and sought to integrate the thinking of numerous individuals into a resource that teaches both the *how* and the *why* of various professional services marketing approaches. In other words, rather than just writing a "how-to" book or a book that focuses on the theoretical and impractical, we attempt to give the professional a solid grounding in *usable* marketing principles and theories that can readily be applied with profitable results.

One other feature of this book is the use of examples from a wide variety of professions. Although we recognize that each profession faces certain unique circumstances, we do not treat the marketing problems of each profession separately. We believe that the various professions have a considerable amount in common when it comes to marketing problems. Practitioners in one profession can gain helpful insights into their own problems by reading and learning about the problems of practitioners in other professions. Although for convenience we use the term "clients" throughout the book to refer to organizations and individuals served by professionals, the book is intended to have value for all types of professionals and practices, including those whose clients are typically called "patients."

A book like this can only be written with the help and guidance of numerous people. We would first like to thank the many practicing professionals who have freely discussed their marketing problems and programs with us over the last few years. We especially appreciate the ideas offered by Suzanne Lowe (Expertise Marketing LLC) and Bruce Marcus (The Marcus Letter [www.marcusletter.com]).

In addition, we appreciate the careful reviews of earlier drafts by Raghu Tadepalli (Xavier University). Furthermore, this book would not exist without the patience and dedication of Izola White, who has seen and improved more reviews than we can count. The encouragement and support of our Prentice Hall editor, Tom Power, is also deeply appreciated. Finally, our families (Mag Gajus, Sarah, John, and Devin Hayes; Nancy, Amy, Melissa, and Jessica Kotler; and Shelly Bloom) deserve considerable thanks for allowing us the time to pursue this endeavor.

Contents

The origin of professional services can be traced all the way back to the Middle Ages, and in particular, to the profession of law. At that time, gentlemen were assumed to have the ability to live a life of leisure without actively working. Professions in law, the church, and the army provided the aristocracy a socially acceptable way of making a living. Members of these professions were given high individual status and lived the life of gentlemen, which was synonymous with the concept of being a professional. The expansion of professional services occurred during the 16th century when a newer set of occupational professions, including medicine and accounting, developed as a result of the growth of capitalism and the expansion of industrial technology. The traditional professions fought to defend their positions by developing and promoting attributes that they felt set them apart from other workers. These included "a dislike of competition, advertising, and profit, a belief in the principle of payments in order to work, rather than working for pay, and a belief in the superiority of the service motive." Over the centuries professionals worked to separate themselves further from other lines of work. They created exclusionary practices to protect themselves from market competition. They organized their own training and credentialing and policed their occupations through rigorous barriers to entry. They believed they held a special position in society and possessed values that set them apart from more common workers. These professions developed codes of ethics that members were required to uphold, which further elevated their position in society. The professional market operated under the credo of *caveat emptor, credot emptor*, which means "let the buyer beware, let the consumer trust." The professions had developed a privileged place in society within a regulated market with no requirement for competitive practices. It had become what one marketing manager of a legal practice described as "survival of the existing with no need to be the fittest."[1]

Contents

1 | The Marketing of Professional Services

"The times, they are a'changin'"
BOB DYLAN
American song writer

In this new millennium, the concept of "survival of the existing" no longer applies to professional services. Major transformations in the environments of all the professions are leading many professional service organizations down new paths. Traditional professions are facing major competition not only from within, but among one another as well. Some of the major changes facing professionals in the recent years have been:

1. A CONTINUED REVISION OF THE LEGAL AND ETHICAL CLIMATES. Restrictions against the use of advertising, solicitations, competitive bids, and promotional tools have essentially disappeared in the last 20 years. Ever since the classic *Bates* v. *The State of Arizona* case that allowed attorneys to advertise, former barriers of professional practice have come tumbling down. Restrictions on how professions do business have been eliminated from both professional codes of ethics and state statutes. Professionals are essentially free today to promote their services whenever and wherever they want, as long as they don't make any deceptive or misleading claims. This new-found freedom has sparked intensifying promotional and competitive activity in almost every profession. Many

1

The origin of professional services can be traced all the way back to the Middle Ages, and in particular, to the profession of law. At that time, gentlemen were assumed to have the ability to live a life of leisure without actively working. Professions in law, the church, and the army provided the aristocracy a socially acceptable way of making a living. Members of these professions were given high individual status and lived the life of gentlemen, which was synonymous with the concept of being a professional. The expansion of professional services occurred during the 16th century when a newer set of occupational professions, including medicine and accounting, developed as a result of the growth of capitalism and the expansion of industrial technology. The traditional professions fought to defend their positions by developing and promoting attributes that they felt set them apart from other workers. These included "a dislike of competition, advertising, and profit, a belief in the principle of payments in order to work, rather than working for pay, and a belief in the superiority of the service motive." Over the centuries professionals worked to separate themselves further from other lines of work. They created exclusionary practices to protect themselves from market competition. They organized their own training and credentialing and policed their occupations through rigorous barriers to entry. They believed they held a special position in society and possessed values that set them apart from more common workers. These professions developed codes of ethics that members were required to uphold, which further elevated their position in society. The professional market operated under the credo of *caveat emptor, credot emptor,* which means "let the buyer beware, let the consumer trust." The professions had developed a privileged place in society within a regulated market with no requirement for competitive practices. It had become what one marketing manager of a legal practice described as "survival of the existing with no need to be the fittest."[1]

professional service organizations are finding their survival hinging on being able to compete in this new climate.

2. AN OVERSUPPLY OF PROFESSIONALS. The legal, medical, architectural, and management consulting professions are facing oversupply conditions. This is most easily seen in the number of practicing lawyers in the United States, which in the 1990s alone increased almost 25 percent, reaching the one-million mark for the first time in 1999. The United States has the highest per capita number of lawyers of any country in the world.[2]

NUMBER OF PRACTICING LAWYERS

1990	755,694
1991	777,119
1992	799,760
1993	846,036
1994	865,614
1995	896,140
1996	946,499
1997	953,260
1998	985,921
1999	1,000,440
2000	1,022,462
2001	1,048,903

This oversupply within certain professions is intensifying further because of the addition of paraprofessionals into the fields (for example, paralegals and midwives), who provide services previously only provided by licensed professionals. When supply exceeds demand, there will be more vigorous competition for customers. Insufficient demand for their services is leading many professionals to intensify their marketing efforts to attract clients.

3. THE BLURRING OF BOUNDARIES AMONG PROFESSIONALS. Not only are certain professions competing heavily internally, they are also facing new sources of competition from outside their traditional boundaries. Major public accounting houses have moved heavily into management consulting; some accounting firms employ more lawyers than the large legal firms; and some divorce attorneys are aligning themselves with profes-

sional social workers in order to help their clients. The result is that many professional service organizations, rather than being distinct entities of accountants or management consultants, are positioning themselves as one-stop-shopping service providers for their clients.

4. INCREASING DISSATISFACTION WITH PROFESSIONALS. Members of professions no longer enjoy the high esteem they received in the past. Substantial numbers of people see lawyers as ambulance chasers, accountants as tax loophole finders, architects as avant garde elitists, and physicians as overpriced mechanics. Influenced by unflattering portrayals of professions in the media and in best-selling books, clients are much more likely to question the judgment of professionals or to offer strong complaints against them. Consumers have become more aggressive in challenging the position of professionals through malpractice suits and, in some cases, taking a do-it-yourself approach in order to save money. Visit any bookstore and you can find law books for lay people and small-business owners with forms for conducting much of their legal activities without engaging a lawyer. The Internet has also increased the knowledge of many clients of professional services, making them much more savvy users. Clearly, professionals need to take actions to improve client satisfaction and enhance their public image.

5. RAPIDLY CHANGING TECHNOLOGIES. The advances in technology during the past 20 years have changed the way in which professionals can and should do business. The widespread use of the Internet has created new opportunities to communicate with clients every day. Although the rapid changes in technology have given professional service providers new opportunities to serve their clients better, these changes also pose new threats. On the one hand, new technologies allow physicians to provide safer, less obtrusive and less painful forms of medical care; data bases allow management consultants to better understand the environments in which their clients are competing; Web sites allow legal firms to provide more information and more immediate access to their clients. On the other hand, the use of technology requires the professional services to update their investments in technology and to acquire new skills. The Internet increases the consumer's ability to provide self help—whether through the hundreds of sites that deal with medical conditions or with

potential legal problems and their solutions—often eliminating the consumer's need to pay a professional for the same information or services. As a result of these changes, many professions find themselves in an intensified competitive environment. It is not surprising that more and more professional service practitioners are turning to marketing as a way to ensure their survival in this environment.

But what exactly is marketing? Why have so many professionals who formerly disdained marketing become so attracted to its potential? What are the core components of marketing and how can they help a professional service organization reach and satisfy its clients? How is the marketing of professional services different from marketing tangible goods like cars or soap? Finally, what are the distinctive problems associated with marketing professional services that can prevent marketing from achieving what its newly won advocates expect from it? These major questions are the focus of this chapter, and in answering them, we will introduce several basic concepts and topics that will receive extended discussion throughout the book.

WHAT IS MARKETING?

Marketing has been maligned and misunderstood for most of its existence. Some people see marketing as manipulative, wasteful, intrusive, and unprofessional. Take a random poll of lawyers, doctors, consultants, and accountants and ask them what marketing is and you are likely to hear that it is either advertising or selling. This perception continues to make it difficult for marketing to be effectively implemented outside the conventional business world. While it is increasingly difficult to find a hospital, educational institution, or non-profit organization that does not discuss marketing, it is still rather difficult to find one that implements it properly. Marketing is only a tool, not a panacea that will solve all of an organization's problems. As a tool it can be used well or poorly. And although marketing is sometimes used as an aid in manipulating or implementing high-pressure and hard-sales techniques, it is also possible for a sound marketing program to make only minimal use of advertising and selling, relying, instead, on the careful design of professional services, pricing, and distribution to achieve profitable results. As well-known management theorist Peter Drucker noted, "The aim of marketing is to make selling superfluous."

Marketing can be done with as much professionalism as the work of a lawyer, CPA, or doctor. The professional marketer is skilled at understanding, creating, and managing client demand and knows how to conduct research to understand the needs of those with whom he seeks to establish relationships; how to design a valued offering to meet these needs; how to communicate the offer effectively; and how to present it at the right time and place.

A more precise definition of marketing is as follows:

> **Marketing** is a social and managerial process by which individuals and groups obtain what they need and want through the creating and exchanging of products/services of value with others.[3]

The following points should be noted about this definition of marketing.

First, marketing is a managerial process that manifests itself in carefully formulated programs—not just haphazard actions—designed to achieve desired responses. If the managing partner of an accounting firm simply urges all partners to spend more time finding more clients, this is not a program that's bound to produce results. The partners are not given any direction on whom to call, what they should say about the firm, or even how to follow up. They are being asked to sell something without the benefit of a marketing program to support them. It is important to understand that marketing takes place before any selling takes place and involves the development of carefully designed and formulated programs.

Second, marketing is based on the needs, wants, and demands of a chosen customer group. Human needs are states of felt deprivation. They could include physical needs such as food, clothing, or warmth; social needs such as belonging or affection; or individual needs such as self-actualization. These needs are not invented by marketers, they are a basic part of the human makeup. Wants, on the other hand, are the form taken by human needs shaped by culture and individual personality. In the

Amazon, an individual in need of medical attention might seek out a shaman; in the United States, a sick person may seek out a physician. Wants are described by people in terms of objects that will satisfy their needs. While one might want the best doctor to help with his or her medical condition, the reality is that most individuals have limited resources. They, therefore, will choose services that provide the most value and satisfaction for the money they have available. When backed by buying power, wants become demands. The clients will actively seek out the physicians who can satisfy their needs—physical, psychological, and monetary—in the best fashion. Professional marketers go to great lengths to learn about and understand customers' and clients' needs, wants, and demands. Marketers conduct consumer research about customer likes and dislikes and analyze their behavior. They observe customers using their own and competing products and they train their personnel to be on the lookout for unfulfilled customer needs. Understanding customer needs, wants, and demands in detail provides important insights for designing marketing strategies.

Third, central to the definition of marketing is the concept of exchange, or the act of obtaining a desired object or service from someone by offering something in return. In other words, consumers get something of value for something of value. Value is the difference between the benefits consumers get from using or purchasing a service versus the costs of obtaining that service. Benefits can simply be described as the solution to a problem. For example, a corporation may wish to develop a corporate headquarters that is both functional and at the same time establishes a strong image in the minds of its clients and potential clients. In order to obtain such a structure, the corporation's management may be willing to pay a professional architect a certain sum of money to design and oversee the construction of the company's headquarters. At the same time, the architect must realize that besides money, other costs to his or her client may be the time and convenience and ease of doing business with the architectural firm. In order for value to occur and the exchange process to be equitable, all these factors must be taken into account.

Fourth, marketing means the choosing of target markets rather than a haphazard attempt to serve all markets and all needs. Marketers routinely distinguish among possible market segments and decide which ones to serve on the basis of market size, profit potential, firm mission, or some other basis. A divorce lawyer is not likely to actively seek out clients interested in finalizing an international business transaction or conducting a malpractice suit against a hospital. Rather, the lawyer will go with the clients possessing narrowly defined geographic, size, or other relevant characteristics.

Fifth, effective marketing is client oriented, not seller oriented. Marketing relies on designing the organization's offerings in terms of the target market's needs and desires, rather than in terms of the personal seller's tastes. According to this view of marketing, efforts that try to impose on a market an offering that is not matched to its needs and wants are likely to fail. Thus, a management consulting firm that recommends the same organizational structure for all of its clients regardless of their unique needs is likely to fail.

Sixth, long-term marketing success is found in providing satisfaction to the clients that one wishes to serve. Customer satisfaction can be defined as the difference between a client's expectations of a service versus the service that the client actually received. For example, a client seeking the help of a tax accountant may expect the accountant to help prepare the client's tax return in an efficient and accurate fashion for a reasonable price. If the client's experience matches this expectation, he or she will be satisfied. If, however, the client finds that the tax return has errors that attract the unwanted scrutiny of the IRS, the client's level of satisfaction is likely to be greatly diminished. In today's competitive world of professional services, clients simply have too many choices. If they are not satisfied, they will go elsewhere; and even if they are satisfied, they still may!

Seventh, a major component for long-term customer satisfaction lies in the development of relationships with clients. Rather than focusing on short-term transactions, the professional marketer needs to build long-term relationships with valued customers, distributors, and suppliers, as well as strong economic and social ties by promising and consistently delivering high-quality service at a fair price. If, and when possible, the marketer would like to take this further, he or she will work to develop structural ties as well. The goal is to develop a relationship that is both equitable and positive for both parties. Developing and maintaining relationships with valued customers and clients where both parties are truly committed to one another's success can help to ensure long-term survival and profitability for both.

MANAGING THE MARKETING EFFORT

The key to long-term profitability for any professional is the creation of a service that satisfies the needs and wants of one's clients and facilitates the exchange of those services in such a manner that provides value and satisfaction to the client. One creates these services through the combination and blend of a set of tools that are referred to as the marketing mix. We define the marketing mix as a set of controllable, tactical marketing tools that the firm blends to produce the result it wants in the target market. It might be helpful to use the analogy of a combination lock. In a typical combination lock, you need to know the pattern of three numbers to successfully open the lock. In marketing a firm's products or services, we

Table 1-1. The Seven Ps of Marketing.

Product	Price	Place	Promotion
• Quality • Features • Options • Style • Packaging • Sizes • Services • Warranties • Returns • Brand	• List Price • Discounts • Allowances • Payment Period • Credit Terms	• Channels • Coverage • Location • Inventory • Transport	• Advertising • Personal Selling • Sales Promotion • Publicity
Physical Evidence	**Processes**	**People**	

• Arrangement of objects
• Materials used
• Shapes/lines
• Lighting/shadows
• Color
• Temperature
• Noise
	• Policies &
	  procedures
	• Factory/delivery
	  cycle time
	• Training &
	  rewarding systems
		• Service provider
		• Customer being serviced
		• Other employees and
		  customers	

attempt to take everything that the firm can do to influence the demand for its products or services and organize them in such a manner that best meets the needs, wants, and desires of the customer. Many combinations are possible with marketing's controllable variables, known as the Seven Ps. (See Table 1-1 on pg. 9.) These Ps are the product, price, place, promotion, physical evidence, processes, and people.[4]

Product means the good or service combination that the company offers to the target markets in order to satisfy its needs. For example, Accenture (formerly Andersen Consulting) may provide a combination of different levels of services, plus a higher level of expertise and the security of a well-known name. All of these together represent the "product" the client is buying from Accenture.

Price consists of the amount of money the customer has to pay to obtain the product, along with any non-financial costs such as time, hassle, and convenience, among others. A physician may list a given price for an office visit. Clients, however, may pay less if the cost is partly borne by an insurer. At the same time, patients may have other costs besides the out-of-pocket dollars. For example, there may be a time-cost of driving across town to get to the doctor. They may have to sit in a crowded waiting room for an extended period of time and fill out a number of complicated forms. In the consumer's mind, all these factors increase the costs of using that physician.

Place includes everything the organization does to make its services available to the target consumer. To a legal firm, this might mean having law offices in all the major cities in which its clients do business. At the same time, the firm might make its legal practice more accessible by having extended hours of operation, having 800 numbers to enable clients to call at a lower price, or even providing a Web site that allows clients to download information 24 hours a day, 7 days a week.

Promotion refers to those activities that communicate the merits of the service and persuade target markets to purchase it. For example, an accounting firm might employ traditional advertising on television or in selected magazines; it may choose to sponsor cultural events where it believes its target market might be exposed to the message; it may choose to offer public seminars on basic tax preparation or investments. The key is to ensure that the forms of promotion are properly integrated so that they all communicate the same image and core messages.

Physical evidence makes up for the fact that services are inherently intangible and therefore cannot be seen, touched, or felt, as in the case of a management consulting firm or a law firm. In such cases, customers tend to look for other clues to the quality of the service they wish to obtain. Many times the most immediate clue is the physical evidence of a firm's building and furnishings. One would not expect a legal firm that is targeting large corporations to have its office located in a strip mall and its office furniture composed of plastic chairs with subscriptions to *People* magazine strewn about. The message that the potential clients would receive would not be in line with their needs to facilitate a major corporate transaction, such as a corporate merger.

Processes refer to the ways in which an organization does business. Processes can be highly complicated or simple, highly divergent or very consistent. For example, x-ray technologists perform relatively few steps when x-raying a potentially broken wrist, and there is high consistency from one to another. On the other hand, if you visit a physician and complain of heartburn and shortness of breath, there are a number of levels of diagnoses that might be taken to help determine the problem, and one physician might treat you entirely differently from another.

People matter, particularly in the marketing of services, because services are intangible and clients are looking for tangible cues to determine their value or quality. An obvious cue is the people associated with that service, such as the physician, the nurse, the lawyer, or the consultant. But it might also come from observing other clients. For example, some patients prefer to use doctors who care only for individuals they perceive to be similar to themselves. Thus, a female patient may prefer a female physician who sees only women in her practice, because the patient may view this as an indication that this particular physician is highly attuned to her needs.

Professional marketers must design the right combination of these seven Ps to satisfy their target customer. They must employ marketing research to gain the insight and knowledge to find the right combination of the Seven Ps. However, the real challenge in a competitive environment is that once marketers discover the right combination, it is likely to change. Competitors may introduce processes, features, or prices that change client expectations. The implication is that professional service providers must constantly improve their service offerings.

HOW SERVICES DIFFER FROM PRODUCTS

The marketing of services, while sharing some similarities with physical goods, has some inherent differences. The professional service providers must fully understand these differences and how they affect their organizations. The characteristics of a service that set it apart from physical goods are intangibility, inseparability, variability, and perishability. Further, the criterion for satisfaction is different and the customer participates in the process.

Intangibility

Service intangibility means that services cannot be seen, tasted, felt, heard, or smelled before they are bought. For example, people undergoing cosmetic surgery cannot fully see the results before the purchase and an individual involved in a lawsuit cannot know the outcome before the end of a trial. An individual hiring an architect doesn't have the completed plans before agreeing to the transaction. As a result, the clients attempt to reduce uncertainty by looking for "signals" of service quality. They draw conclusions about service quality from the physical evidence, equipment used, people involved, or the communications they have been exposed to. The service professional needs to provide a tangible representation that communicates the likely service process and outcome.

Inseparability

Because the service cannot be separated from the service provider, how that individual is perceived—his or her professionalism, appearance, and demeanor—will all be used in judging the quality of the service firm. This inseparability carries over to those individuals who answer the phones for the organization or occupy the receptionist's desk. They often provide the first impressions prospective clients get of the service organization.

Variability

Because service is inseparable from people, the quality of the services delivered to clients can vary. The best lawyer can make a mistake; the best accountant can miss a number; the best doctor can have a bad day. The implications of variability in services are twofold. Because we know that mistakes can happen, we can develop processes that attempt to minimize these mistakes. For example, accountants can use software packages that minimize the potential mistakes in tallying income returns and architects can use computer simulations to test for structural problems before a building is built. However, even with the best preventive systems, mistakes can occur. Thus, the professional service provider should anticipate where mistakes are most likely to occur and have recovery measures in place to maintain the trust of the client who experiences the mistake.

Perishability

Perishability of services means that they cannot be stored for later sale or use. Some doctors charge patients for missed appointments because the service value existed only at that time and disappeared when the patient did not show up. The perishability of services also has certain implications. One of these is that the service provider is basically selling performance. For example, although knowing that your physician has performed one thousand open-heart surgeries is reassuring, what's really essential is the physician's ability to safely perform yours. Another implication of perishability is the fluctuation of demand. When demand is steady, it may be relatively easy to perform on a consistent basis; when demand fluctuates wildly, it may become more difficult to maintain consistency. In the case of a physician, for example, it may be difficult to give every patient time and personal attention in the middle of a flu epidemic.

Criterion for Satisfaction Is Different

Before buying a product, a customer can assess what he or she is buying. For example, before purchasing an automobile, a customer can test drive it. But services are different. They are first sold, then produced and consumed at the same time. One cannot be sure that an architect grasps a client's needs until the construction drawings come back. In some cases, the client will never know how good the service he or she received really was. For example, a person who hurts his or her knee in a skiing accident and has surgery will not know whether physical rehabilitation would have been a better solution. Similarly, if a lawyer suggests settling out of court versus going to trial, the client will never know what results the other option would have yielded.

The Customer Participates in the Process

When customers purchase a physical product, they don't take into account the factory in which it was produced, nor the individuals working in that factory. However, when purchasing services, customers are "in the factory," observing the entire process. Each experience creates an impression about the service, known as a "moment of truth." A service provider must properly manage each moment of truth to provide a consistent message about the quality of the service.

TEN DISTINCTIVE PROBLEMS IN MARKETING PROFESSIONAL SERVICES

Just as marketing services are different from marketing physical goods, the professional service provider cannot assume that marketing approaches and techniques that have worked in other industries will automatically work for his or her business. We have identified the following ten distinctive problems that make marketing of professional services different, and often more difficult.

Problem 1: Third-Party Accountability

Sound marketing involves making a strong commitment to serving the needs and desires of target markets. Yet professional service providers face some constraints. Professionals typically cannot go to quite as great lengths to produce satisfied "customers" as conventional commercial marketers can. A CPA cannot offer to overlook a client's financial irregularities; a doctor cannot continuously prescribe addictive narcotics to a patient; and an engineer cannot accede to cost-cutting pressures of clients and use unsafe building materials. Professionals should always recognize that in serving one type of client, they are also serving other third-party "clients" such as investors, insurance companies, government regulatory agencies, and the members of their own profession. To go overboard in serving one type of client could lead to a loss of trust with important third parties—and a loss of the legal certification or licensing that allows one to be a professional in the first place.

Problem 2: Client Uncertainty

People face uncertainty in all types of buying situations, but this uncertainty is particularly high for buyers of professional services because, as we've already mentioned, buyers of professional services face difficulty in evaluating a service offering due to its intangibility. Even after the fact, clients frequently still have difficulty knowing the service quality. This level of uncertainty results in client anxiety, sometimes known as cognitive dissonance, before, and certainly after the purchase decision. It is therefore imperative that the professional service provider work to relieve this anxiety and assure the client that his or her choice was the correct one. The three ways of providing this assurance are client education, immediate follow up after the client's purchase decision, and providing guarantees.

High levels of client uncertainty create unique challenges for professional service providers; therefore, client education must play a bigger role in the marketing of professional services than the marketing of other offerings. Clients must be educated about what criteria to use in evaluating professionals and how to employ professionals productively. In some cases, people must even be educated about what they need to seek out in the services of a professional.

After making any type of important decision, a person is likely to experience cognitive dissonance. As a result of this, clients will question whether they made the right decision in choosing a particular professional service provider. They may be looking for some kind of verification that they made the right decision. To relieve some of the uncertainty that the client will be experiencing, the professional service provider must provide assurance and support through follow-up contact.

Finally, a professional service provider may provide some type of guarantee to allow clients to make the decision in a more confident manner. For example, tax accountants may guarantee their work in tax preparation by offering to pay any fines or penalties that were a result of their efforts; lawyers can work on a contingency fee basis where they do not get paid unless they win the case for their clients.

Problem 3: Experience Is Essential

Although buyers of professional services are frequently uncertain about the criteria to use in selecting a professional, one criterion is almost always prominently considered: the professional's prior experience with similar situations. People prefer to use accountants and management consultants who have worked in their industry before, lawyers who have litigated cases just like theirs, architects who have built buildings like the one they want to build, and surgeons who have successfully performed the surgical procedure they need hundreds of times.

The need to demonstrate their experience to obtain clients produces problems for many professional service organizations. Firms with expertise in limited areas often find it difficult to diversify into new lines of work. And inexperienced professionals often find it difficult to find any work at all. "Newness" cannot be readily promoted as a favorable attribute in most professions, as might be done with a new car model or coffee beverage. This situation makes it especially important for professionals to do extensive marketing planning to help them determine the future market potential associated with the different specialized services they are considering providing.

Problem 4: Limited Differentiability

Marketers typically attempt to differentiate their offerings from those of their competitors. They desire to have target markets perceive their offerings as having certain unique and superior characteristics. Differentiation is carried out by actually producing an offering with unique characteristics and/or by persuading buyers through advertising and selling that the offering possesses unique characteristics.

The differentiation of offerings is difficult for most marketers to achieve, and especially difficult for marketers of professional services. It is hard to differentiate an accounting audit, a title search, and an eye examination. Additionally, even if a service is provided that really is different from competing services, it may be difficult to get clients, who may be experiencing great uncertainty, to perceive and recognize the real differences.

Problem 5: Maintaining Quality Control

Keeping high-quality control levels is a challenging task for service marketers in general, and for professional service providers in particular. Services do not come off production lines where statistical sampling can be done to check on levels of quality. Instead of fine-tuning a machine to maintain quality, people-intensive service organizations must emphasize finding good people and exhorting them to work conscientiously.

Many professional service organizations have to contend with the additional problem that the quality of their service often depends on the behavior of their clients. A consultant's or doctor's services will usually be more helpful to those clients who follow the professional's advice. Uncooperative clients can, unfortunately, produce poor results and a poor track record for the professional.

Problem 6: Making Doers into Sellers

Before "buying" professional services, people like to meet and become acquainted with the professionals who will be serving them. It is a way for them to reduce their uncertainty. The use of only salespersons or full-time presenters to sell the services of unseen professionals is therefore ill advised. The professionals who will be the "doers" of certain kinds of work need to become involved with the selling of that work. But convincing many professionals that they should become actively involved with selling their own services can be exceedingly difficult. And teaching these people improved selling skills can be even more difficult. Many lawyers, accountants, architects, doctors, and other professionals simply do not want to have anything to do with selling, and many others do not have personal characteristics that would make them good at selling.

Problem 7: Allocating Professionals' Time to Marketing

Because professionals bill clients for their time, but cannot bill anyone for time they spend marketing their services, many firms are reluctant to allocate much professional time to marketing. Moreover, even if professionals devote substantial time to marketing, decisions must still be made about how much of this time to devote to existing clients, new prospects, and more general public relations work. And in some firms a problem can arise when certain key people spend too much time with marketing— accepting every speaking invitation and proposal-writing opportunity— and not enough time being a doer and helping to maintain the firm's quality control. Clearly, the need for professionals to be both doers and marketers creates many time-management problems.

Problem 8: Pressure to React Rather than Proact

Another problem related to time allocation has to do with the constant demands many professionals face to provide services on short notice. Clients tend to want their work done for them "yesterday," and this can frequently cut into time that has been set aside for marketing planning. Being a proactive marketer while dealing with existing clients' demands can be quite difficult.

Problem 9: Conflicting Views about Advertising

Even though it's been more than 20 years since the landmark case of *Bates* vs. *Arizona* that allowed attorneys to advertise, the advertising issue is still hotly debated among professionals themselves. Each professional service firm must decide whether to advertise and, if so, to what extent. While one physician may believe that advertising medical services is unprofessional, many others, particularly in the field of plastic surgery, rely heavily on very sophisticated advertisements as a means to attracting clients. Similarly, advertisements in the legal profession range from simply listing the name of the firm in the Yellow Pages to full-page ads, billboards, and television commercials complete with ambulance sirens. The decision to advertise, as well as the extent and type of advertising a particular professional service firm chooses, depends on many issues, such as its target markets, the image the firm wants to project, and the level of competition it is experiencing.

Problem 10: A Limited Marketing Knowledge Base

Many professional service providers do not have knowledge available to guide them in making their marketing decisions. Professional schools did not provide instruction in business practices where professional service providers might learn about fields such as marketing. This is especially true for lawyers and physicians. It may also be true for management consultants in highly technical areas. As a result, many professionals need to learn about marketing on their own time by attending conferences, reading books like this, or sharing insights and information with one another. Others have hired professional marketing managers to deal with their marketing problems. While this solution may address strategic issues, it still does not address the fact that services are inseparable from the individuals delivering them. So the architect, the doctor, and the lawyer must still have some type of rudimentary understanding of marketing because they, not their marketing managers, ultimately create the image of their organizations.

DEVELOPING A CLIENT ORIENTATION

Regardless of how a firm markets its services, its success in marketing will be directly related to its level of client orientation. The development of such an orientation is so important that it should be the very first mission of any professional service organization seeking to become effective at marketing. This task involves much more than introducing the marketing function and appointing a marketing director. Marketing is not something someone does following directions as in a cookbook. Marketing is more a way of thinking and an approach to the marketplace and the customer. A firm that is client centered can be described as having an outside-in perspective versus an inside-out perspective. The latter implies that the firm's first focus is on itself and that its offerings are typically based on what members of the firm are good at or interested in, rather than on the needs of its clients or potential clients. It expects its customers to respond to the firm, rather than the firm responding to its customers. On the other hand, the outside-in perspective starts with well-defined markets, focuses on customer needs, coordinates all the marketing activities affecting customers and clients, and makes profits by creating long-term customer relationships based upon customer value and satisfaction. Obtaining this client-focused orientation in an organization is hard work. The firm must systematically study clients' needs, wants, perceptions, preferences, and satisfactions using marketing research. The organization must act on the information to consistently and constantly improve its services to meet its clients' needs better. The professional staff must be well selected and trained to feel that they are working for the client (rather than the boss). A client orientation will express itself in the friendliness in which the organization's telephone operators answer the phone and the helpfulness of various staff members in solving client problems. Members of professional service organizations that are client-centered will work *with* clients rather than *on* clients.

SUMMARY

Professional service organizations have changed dramatically over the years. Professionals have to cope with increasing competition, greater public dissatisfaction with professionals, rapidly changing technologies, and other changes in their external environments. One tool that they are turning to as a way to ensure their survival in this unpredictable environment is marketing. They are finding that marketing is not inherently unethical or manipulative nor is it defined by the field of advertising. Indeed, professional service firms are discovering that marketing can be carried on with as much professionalism as the work of a lawyer, CPA, or doctor. The successful marketer of professional services is skilled at understanding, creating, and managing exchanges. He or she uses a marketing mix involving the right combination of service, price, place, promotion, physical evidence, processes, and people to achieve voluntary exchanges with target markets.

Professional services are intangible, inseparable, variable, and perishable. Professional service providers face some distinctive problems not faced by other types of service organizations and must deal with high levels of client uncertainty, limited service differentiability, quality control difficulties, and several other obstacles to mounting a successful marketing effort.

The development of a client orientation should be the very first mission of a professional service organization seeking to become proficient at marketing. Such an orientation involves having the entire organization give primary attention to serving the needs and wants of its clients .

NOTES

[1] Adapted from "Relationship in Marketing and Corporate Legal Services," *The Service Industries Journal*, July 1998, Susan Hart and Gillian Hogg.

[2] American Bar Association. Chicago, IL, 2000.

[3] Kotler, Philip and Armstrong, Gary. *Principles of Marketing*. Upper Saddle River, NJ: Prentice Hall, 2001.

[4] Booms, Bernard H. and Bitner, Mary Jo. "Marketing Strategies and Organizational Structures for Service Firms," in *Marketing of Services*, eds. James H. Donnelly and William R. George, editors (Chicago: American Marketing Association, 1981), p47-51.

2 Twelve Keys to Effective Professional Services Marketing

....

*"Some men succeed by what they know; some by
what they do; and a few by what they are."*

ELBERT HUBBARD

This chapter introduces 12 keys to effective professional services marketing. The keys turn the theory and knowledge of marketing into
practical guidelines for the professional service firm. The two main objectives of these marketing keys are:

1. To highlight important marketing issues that are particularly relevant to professional services.

2. To inspire the professional service firm to review and audit its
   own marketing assumptions and actions in order to improve its
   performance.

A professional service has the following characteristics:

- A professional service is qualified, advisory, and problem solving
  even though it may also encompass some routine work for
  clients.

- Professionals involved have a common identity and are regulated
  by traditions and codes of ethics.[1]

- Professional services involve a high degree of customization.

Eleven Deadly Assumptions that Kill Your Marketing Program[2]

Deadly assumption #1: "My prospects and clients know the services I offer."

If you assume prospects and clients know the services you offer, you will start losing clients to other service professionals who make their offering of specific services crystal clear. Many lawyers have had the experience of losing a client to another lawyer because the client did not know the first lawyer would provide the same service.

Deadly assumption #2: "My referral sources will send me all the new clients I need."

It won't happen. You may, in fact, get referrals from time to time, but if you believe that all your new business will be a result of referrals, 99 percent of the time you will be mistaken. You must develop a marketing program that will attract clients directly to you.

Deadly assumption #3: "When prospects or clients have questions, they will call me."

Not true. This is especially the case with clients with whom you have not yet established a strong relationship. People often hesitate to call unless they know their calls are welcome.

Deadly assumption #4: "It makes no difference whether my photo appears in my marketing materials."

Your photograph is worth 2,000 words and can help establish the sense of a friendly, trusting relationship with your reader and increase your reader's comfort. Prospects do not really care what you look like, but they feel better when they know.

Deadly assumption #5: "The more I interact with prospects, the more time I waste."

The truth is, the more time you spend interacting with clients, the more opportunities you have to explain how you can help them.

Deadly assumption #6: "I have to be careful not to repeat myself when talking with prospects."

It is important that people understand what you say, and selective redundancy gives you the opportunity to get your points across from two or three different perspectives.

Deadly assumption #7: "My prospects understand what I say because they are in business and know the jargon."

Always put your communications in a language that your client will understand. When you assume that your prospects have basic knowledge or understand the jargon you use internally in your service firm, you are usually wrong.

Deadly assumption #8: "Marketing methods don't work as well today as they used to."

If your marketing techniques do not work, it's probably due to poor, inadequate, or incomplete marketing research, planning, and execution.

Deadly assumption #9: "The more complicated my message, the more prospects and clients will understand the need for my services."

Clients constantly suffer from information overload. Keep your messages simple, easily understood, and straight to the point.

Deadly assumption #10: "How an advertisement looks is not as important as what the ad says."

A powerful message is important, but without the proper graphics your prospect may never see your communication, meaning you have wasted your money.

Deadly assumption #11: "Prospects and clients do not mind when I'm slow to return phone calls; they understand that I'm busy."

Everybody is busy. When you return phone calls promptly, you make a powerful, positive impression. Prospects and clients cannot easily evaluate the depth of your knowledge or experience. One thing they can evaluate is how responsive you are by whether you promptly return phone calls.

- Professional service providers typically have a strong component of face-to-face interaction with their clients. This has major implications on the definitions of quality and service.[3]

This book will primarily focus on professionals in the fields of law, medicine, management consulting, architecture, and engineering. However, the same principles are equally applicable to other professional service fields, such as advertising agencies, public relation consultants, and marketing research companies.

TWELVE KEYS TO EFFECTIVE PROFESSIONAL SERVICES MARKETING

Marketing professional services successfully involves the right mix of various elements, including the following 12 keys.

Key 1: Quality Is King

Individuals belonging to the professions are likely to enjoy a certain level of respect from the general public based upon their years of education and specialized knowledge. However, there is a difference between how smart or educated someone is and what the person does with that intelligence. In the competitive world of professional services, a person's educational background is merely the "ticket to the dance." What becomes important is the quality level that clients experience when dealing with the professional.

At a basic level, the client seeks a successful outcome of the problem that he or she brings to the professional. At another level, the client will also evaluate the process by which the service was delivered. In order to market services successfully, the professional service provider must understand how clients evaluate the quality of both outcomes and processes.

In this book we define quality as "the delivery of a service at a superior level relative to the client's expectations." This definition makes two key points. First, professional service organizations must try to deliver a higher level of quality than their clients expected. The reason is that even satisfied clients are at risk. While they may be satisfied and have every intention of doing business with a particular firm again, the reality is they may not. This could be due to changes in their circumstances or needs, new offerings by competitors, recommendations by acquaintances, or lapses in responsiveness or accessibility of the firm when clients need services.

The second point highlights the fact that a client's perception of service quality is directly related to the service expectations the client has going into the relationship. The professional service provider must be aware of those variables that affect client expectations. They include the service professional's promises, the client's past experiences, and word of mouth.

Research has shown that there are primarily five indicators of service quality from the clients' perspective. These are reliability, responsiveness, assurance, empathy, and tangibles such as the physical appearance of the firm's offices. (These will be examined in greater detail later in the book.)

Service professionals understand that despite their best intentions and hard work, service breakdowns are likely to occur. When this happens, it is important to recover customer goodwill. This can be done by providing an apology, rectifying the situation quickly, making amends for the inconvenience, and finding the root cause for the problem and correcting it so the problem is less likely to occur in the future.

Key 2: Building the Marketing Organization

The question is not whether a professional service firm will undertake marketing activities, but rather how they will implement the marketing process. Many professional firms don't like to think that they must carry on marketing, so they give it different names. Attending the "right" social events, playing golf with important clients, or sponsoring the symphony are all examples of marketing, whether one calls them marketing or not. Many firms resist the more visible forms of marketing. A law firm may complain about advertisements that perpetuate the image of lawyers as "ambulance chasers," identifying them as an example of all that is wrong with marketing. A physician may point to the heavy use of advertising by chiropractors as the distinction between "real" medicine and quackery. What the professional service provider must realize is that these behaviors are just different points on a continuum.

Marketing is about creating equitable exchanges and building long-term relationships. The professional services organization cannot be effective unless it is committed to understanding its clients' needs and desires at a level that allows the firm to create services that meet and exceed clients' expectations. This requires learning and using marketing techniques and principles.

The professional service firm must decide which marketing activities to outsource and which to produce internally. For those that will be produced internally, the next decision is how to organize these activities. The responsibility for marketing may be given to a committee, a marketing director, or senior management.

The presence and use of formal marketing, however, does not mean that the firm as a whole is market-oriented. There will be some professionals and staff members who do not exhibit client skills or attitudes. Truly creating a customer-centered firm requires top management support, an effective organizational design, and the facilitation and reward of marketing-oriented behavior, among other variables. (How to use these points as an aid to building effective marketing within the firm will be covered in Chapter 4.)

Key 3: Knowledge Is Power

Ask the average professional service practitioner to define marketing and he or she is likely to answer "advertising or personal selling." This perception is so pervasive that when a professional service firm hires a marketing professional, typically one of the first assignments is to create a brochure or a Web page. There is little thought as to who the audience for these promotional materials is, what is important to them, how they go about selecting a professional service firm, what they think of the firm being represented versus the competitors, their language, or even what the objective of the brochure is. Equating marketing with promotion is a common and serious mistake.

Information is the basis for building a solid marketing program. Every professional service firm must identify the clients it wishes to serve and the subsequent marketing issues that revolve around them by thoroughly and methodically conducting and analyzing market research, and then using the information it gathers to guide its marketing activities. (The importance of market research will be examined in greater detail in Chapter 5.)

Key 4: Charting the Course

To paraphrase Lewis Carroll's *Alice in Wonderland*, "If you don't know where you're going, any path is fine."

No organization likes to waste time and money and risk its future due to missed opportunities and poor choices. Strategic planning is an important tool in adapting to a changing competitive environment. A solid strategic planning process provides structure, direction, and meaning to a firm's efforts and energies. It seeks to create a strategic fit between the institution's goals and capabilities and its changing marketing environment. It may mean the difference between success and failure or real growth and mere existence. Strategic planning is very much front-loaded in the sense that the greatest amount of work may be performed at the outset. The task starts with environmental analysis in which the organization researches its internal environment, market environment, public environment, competitive environment, and macro environment. Following the environmental analysis, the professional service firm proceeds to identify its major strengths and weaknesses, as well as opportunities and threats, to guide its subsequent decision making. This information aids in developing the firm's mission and goals.

Following the goal formulation, the firm can create a broad strategy for achieving its goals, starting with the choice of tactics to guide its daily operations.

The driving force behind developing marketing strategies is to create sustainable competitive advantages that set a professional service firm apart from its competitors. (Marketing strategies will be examined in greater detail in Chapter 6.)

Key 5: The Firm Can't Be All Things to All People

In a competitive environment, attempting to serve everyone with one standard service offering would be equivalent to a death wish for any professional firm. More focused competitors will nibble away at the firm's customer base, each searching for the least satisfied clients and developing a service offering that is designed for their particular wants and needs.

On the other hand, it would be equally difficult to develop separate marketing strategies for every possible market segment. This would require tremendous resources; therefore, the professional service firm must identify the market segments it can best serve based on its expertise and resources. The firm must then find out as much about the target market as possible, including:

- What types of services does the target segment buy?
- How do they buy? (That is, what process do they go through?)
- Who influences their buying decisions?
- What are their stages of buying behavior?

(Segmenting, selecting, and appealing to market segments and understanding the individual consumers within the chosen segments will be examined more closely in Chapters 7 and 8.)

Key 6: Making an Offer Clients Can't Refuse

Marketing is in essence an exchange process. One provides something of value in exchange for something of value. As long as both sides see the exchange as equitable, there is the opportunity for further exchanges. If a professional service firm's clients believe the exchange is more than equitable and exceeds their expectations, the exchanges are more likely to continue. For this reason a professional service firm must identify and develop service offerings that its clients "can't refuse." The offering includes the perceived quality level of the service, brand promise, service time, and the process by which the service is delivered.

It is also important to understand that no offer will remain viable forever. Services pass through stages beginning with their introduction and ending as a result of lack of continuing need. Managing service offerings at different stages of their life cycles requires different marketing strategies. Each stage presents new marketing challenges and requires adjustments in the target market and marketing mix.

Finally, as consumer and client needs and desires change, the firm must develop new services. (The steps and challenges in the creation of a firm's service offerings will be explained in Chapter 9.)

Key 7: Pricing for Success

Professional service firms must not only develop attractive service offerings but also price them appropriately. Customers evaluate pricing for services differently from goods. They often have inaccurate or limited references for prices for services. There are also non-monetary costs in obtaining a service. Furthermore, price is a key signal to quality in a client's mind. If a client believes that "you get what you pay for," a low fee structure can actually be a detriment to the client's perception of the firm's professional services.

(In Chapter 10, we will discuss how to determine the price clients will be willing to pay for services, as well as different fee presentation approaches, such as time and expense, contingency retainer, and performance-based along with fee negotiations, changes, and collection systems.)

Key 8: Accessibility, Accessibility, Accessibility

Although location, location, location is still important to the success of the professional service firm, it is not the final consideration when determining client access and acceptability toward the service firm. Clients are increasingly demanding services based upon their needs and time schedules. Professional service firms may provide greater access to their organization through the use of the Internet, telephone system, expanded hours of operation, and the use of non-traditional points of access.

The physical evidence that a service firm presents to a client will affect the customer's ability to mentally access an organization. This holds true with both the physical location and the Web site.

Key 9: You Cannot *Not* Communicate

Everything the organization says, is, and does communicates. The challenge is to make sure that the communications are consistent, clear, and effective. Service professionals can use many different tools to communicate with their clients: advertising, personal selling, sales promotion, publicity, and direct marketing. The tools have different strengths and limitations. Furthermore, each tool may be controlled by different people within the organization. The professional service firm must work hard to ensure that everyone in the firm is "on the same page" when it comes to deciding what the firm wants to say, to whom, how, and with what intended effect. Given the many communication options, this can best be achieved by appointing a marketing communications manager who has responsibility for the overall communication efforts and who will coordinate the use, timing, expenditures, and effectiveness of the communication tools.

For most professional service organizations, personal selling through personal contact is probably the most important of all tools available within the promotional mix. Through personal contact, the professional can persuade and reassure existing and potential clients.

Key 10: Riding the E-Train

In the future the Internet will be viewed as just another communication improvement following the likes of language, the printing press, newspapers, mail, telegraph, telephone, television, and the fax machine. Today, it represents one of the most exciting and challenging opportunities facing professional service firms in their efforts to provide superior client-based services. E-commerce and the Internet offer ever-expanding possibilities for serving clients, including the ability to expand from national to international markets; decrease the costs of creating, processing, distributing, storing, and retrieving paper-based information such as brochures or catalogs; improving the efficiencies of service systems; building brand awareness and brand equity; and even helping build stronger relationships with clients.

The Internet represents challenges to the professional service firm primarily because it is so new. It is still in its infancy and is very likely to undergo rapid and dramatic changes, requiring the professional service firm to continuously invest in newer software that will maximize its effectiveness.

(In Chapter 13, we will take a closer look at doing business via the Internet, including such issues as ensuring client or patient privacy and the importance of face-to-face interaction.)

Key 11: Building Meaningful Relationships

Most people take comfort and enjoyment in the presence of others and yearn for the ability to connect with others and develop meaningful relationships. Meaningful relationships give us comfort and peace of mind and make our lives richer and simpler.

The desire for relationships in business is no different from what it is in people's personal lives. A strong business relationship between a professional service firm and a client is mutually rewarding and simplifies the lives of both parties. To the professional service firm, the relationship is rewarding both on a professional and financial basis. It is rewarding to the client because it provides peace of mind about that particular aspect of the client's life. Strong business relationships simplify both parties' lives by reducing the need or the desire to constantly seek out, evaluate, choose, and develop new relationships. (This will be further explored in Chapter 14.)

Key 12: The Future Is Now

Any student of military strategy understands that there are three essential components for winning the battle, and ultimately the war. First, one must be aware of history, because as George Santana once said, "He who does not know history, is doomed to repeat it." By understanding the firm and its industry as well as the firm's relationship with its clients and being able to view it in a historical context, the professional service marketer will be better able to anticipate and respond to future events. Second, one must have a thorough understanding of the environment in which he finds himself. Members of the firm must understand the firm's external environment (competition, clients, economy, social/political shifts) as well as its internal environment (organizational strengths and weaknesses, expertise, capital needs, and financial resources).

Finally, to succeed one must create strategies that include multiple plans based upon multiple scenarios. Plan A rarely ever works perfectly. Clients change, competition changes, the environment changes, all potentially interfering with the organization's strategic initiatives. It is far better to develop Plans A, B, C, D, and so forth based upon scenarios that have a pre-determined probability of occurring. This will allow for seamless and smooth transitions as the environment in which the firm operates changes.

(In Chapter 15, we will cover nine trends that may influence the future business operations and ultimate success of professional service firms. Awareness of these trends will help the professional service marketer to understand and anticipate how these trends may affect his or her firm, and develop strategic initiatives that allow the firm to capitalize on the trends rather than be made obsolete by them.)

SUMMARY

Professional service firms are defined as having four characteristics: (1) being qualified, advisory in nature, and problem-solving in their focus; (2) having a common identity regulated by traditions, codes, or ethics; (3) involving a high degree of customization in their work; and (4) having a strong component of face-to-face interactions with clients.

The 12 keys to effective professional services marketing are: quality is king; building the marketing organization; knowledge is power; charting the course; the firm can't be all things to all people; making an offer clients can't refuse; pricing for success; accessibility, accessibility, accessibility; you cannot *not* communicate; riding the e-train; building meaningful relationships; and the future is now.

NOTES

[1] Gummesson, Evert. "The Marketing of Professional Services—25 Propositions," in *Marketing of Services*, James H. Donnelly and William R. George, editors (Chicago: American Marketing Assocation, 1981).

[2] Adapted from *Eleven Deadly Assumptions That Kill Your Marketing Program*, Trey Ryder, 1999. Used with permission.

[3] See Gummesson, Evert.

3 | Delivering Quality Service

*"Quality is remembered long after price
is forgotten."*
GUCCI FAMILY SLOGAN

WHAT IS QUALITY?

Anyone browsing through the business section of a bookstore is likely to find a plethora of books on the subject of quality. Although the definition of quality may vary from one text to another, there are some basic elements the various definitions are likely to agree upon. First, quality is in the eye of the beholder—the client, in the case of a professional service firm. Second, it's difficult to know how customers define quality without asking them. As in the example of HLW and Skansa on page 38, a professional service firm may have to do some preliminary work to identify what clients expect of it and how well its performance met those expectations.

Among the definitions of quality one might find are those by Edward Deming and Philip Crosby. Deming's definition of quality was "Zero Defects." This definition implies that quality is what is left when all the problems are taken out. In the world of manufacturing, where Deming spent most of his career, this definition might work quite nicely. If one is mass producing a certain size bolt to be used in building automobiles, they must be a certain length, width, have a given number of

37

Betting Your Profits on Quality[1]

How do you define quality and would you bet your profits on it? The architectural firm of HLW International along with its contractor, Sordoni Skansa Construction Co., took the challenge when building Ciba Geigy Corporation's Martin Dexter Laboratory. When bidding on the $39-million project, the firms emphasized their commitment to quality as part of their pitch. Traditionally, this meant they would meet their schedule and stay on budget. This time, however, they were challenged to risk a portion of their profits on user satisfaction, a very subjective and personal concept. The firms accepted the challenge.

As a beginning point, HLW and Skansa worked with Dexter employees to eliminate as much subjectivity from the process by establishing quality standards that could be measured. In order to ensure they could create measurable goals from what appeared to be subjective criteria (for example, user friendliness), Dexter's future employees were engaged in each phase of the project. This involvement began with the drafting of a post-occupancy survey of employees to be given at the end of the project. If the survey's composite score did not total more than 70 percent, HLW and Skansa agreed to forfeit one-third of their profits. The survey covered the following criteria: HVAC (heating and air conditioning), acoustics, odor control, vibration, lighting, fume-hood performance, quality of construction (finishes), building appearance, and user friendliness. Specifications were determined for as many criteria as possible. In one case, a mock lab was created and end-users were invited to tour it. Questionnaires were then given out to determine where modifications might need to be made.

The results were that the project came in below budget and three months early. The building quality scores were well over 70 percent on all items except for temperature, which needed to be reset because of the impact of employee furniture in the building. This was easily fixed. High scores in other areas, including a 100-percent approval score for building appearance, easily offset the slightly low score for temperature.

This is an example of putting your money where your mouth is! Quality was promised and delivered.

rings and be able to withstand a specified level of stress. If the customer ordered 10,000 of these bolts and 25 percent of them were defective in some way, the supplier would obviously not be considered a source of quality components. On the other hand, if all 10,000 bolts were usable, it would be a different story.

This definition does not, however, readily apply to professional services, because as we've already established, services by their nature are variable. People are incapable of performing like machines, and there will be breakdowns. Furthermore, the definition of "Zero Defects" does not include an orientation to the customer.

Crosby's definition of quality is "Conformance to specifications." This definition is of more use to the professional service firm. In line with our opening story about HLW, the professional service provider can ask what the client wants and can then provide it. This definition of quality is also in line with client-centeredness.

THE SECURE CUSTOMER

Even when the professional service provider provides quality services, retaining clients can still be a challenge. Clients who are given what they want are likely to be satisfied; however, there is some indication that even a satisfied client may leave for another service provider. According to Burke Customer Satisfaction Associates of Burke Inc., one of the largest market research firms in the United States, the only secure client is one who has had his or her expectations exceeded, not just satisfied.[2] Burke developed the "Secure Customer Index." (See Exhibit 3-1.) This index is based on Burke's research, which shows that in order to feel comfortable with the loyalty of a client, the professional service provider must understand how his or her clients score on at least three measures. These are:

- Overall satisfaction with the firm
- Likelihood to continue to do business with the firm
- Likelihood to recommend the firm to others

Exhibit 3-1. Gauging Customer Security.

The following questions are designed to gauge customer retention among management consultants, but can be used to gauge client satisfaction with any professional service provider or firm. How do you think your clients would respond?

1) Overall, how satisfied were you with the services of ABC Consulting Associates?

    ___ very satisfied

    ___ somewhat satisfied

    ___ somewhat dissatisfied

    ___ very dissatisfied

2) How likely are you to choose ABC Consulting Associates the next time you are in need of management consulting services?

    ___ definitely will

    ___ probably will

    ___ might or might not

    ___ probably will not

    ___ definitely will not

3) If a friend or associate was in need of management consulting services, how likely would you be to recommend they use ABC Consulting Associates?

    ___ definitely would

    ___ probably would

    ___ might or might not

    ___ probably would not

    ___ definitely would not

In order to be considered a "secure" customer, the client would have had to check:

• very satisfied with the services of ABC

• definitely will choose ABC again

• definitely would recommend ABC to a friend or associate

Figure 3-1. Performance-Attitude-Behavior Model.

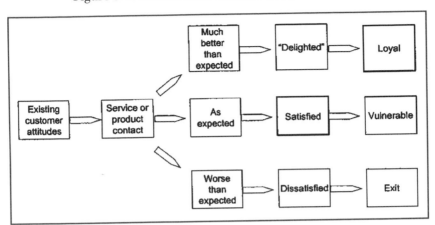

If the client does not give the firm the highest rating possible in any or all of the measures, he or she is at a significantly high risk of leaving the firm for a competitor.

Other elements of customer security that might be measured are:

- Customer perceived value
- Willingness to consider/switch to a competitor
- Confidence in the firm's ability to handle problems
- Firm's relative quality to competition position

UNDERSTANDING CLIENT BEHAVIOR

Why would an individual who is satisfied with a firm's service leave it for another? Common reasons can include the following.

Change in needs or circumstances. The reasons the client came to the firm in the first place may not exist any more. For example, someone may originally employ the services of a lawyer to draft a will or to work out a divorce agreement. Once the service is completed, the lawyer's help is no longer needed. The person may have no need of further legal services or perceive the law firm as not having expertise in another area in which he or she needs legal assistance. To keep the client, one lawyer in the firm must be willing to "hand off" the client to another lawyer in the firm better suited to address his or her needs. While this might be difficult because it reduces the first lawyer's income, it is better to keep the client in the firm than to lose the client completely.

In the case of a medical provider, the ability to retain patients may be beyond the provider's control, because patients' HMOs and networks of providers may change as they change employers. Doctors lament that they provide quality care but lose patients because of insurance reasons. Nevertheless, providing quality service can still be an effective way of building a patient base, because as other doctors lose patients for similar reasons, the positive word-of-mouth will help attract some of those patients, offsetting or even overcoming previous loss of patients.

New developments by competition. Between the time that a client used a firm's services and the time he or she may need additional services, the competition may have done something in the marketplace to attract the client's attention. This might include the addition of new services that complement the customer's particular needs, it may be new locations that make it more convenient for the client to do work with the competition, it might be the fact that the client noticed and positively responded to a competitor's advertisement. For example, in the plastic surgery field, many plastic surgeons provide finance packages to make their services more accessible. This may lure clients away from plastic surgeons who don't offer this option.

References from others. Even though a firm's client may be perfectly satisfied, a reference from a friend, co-worker, or colleague may make the client switch to a competitor. Clients may think they are missing out on something because they are not as enthusiastic about the services you provide as other people are about the services they receive elsewhere.

Insufficient responsiveness. A firm may lose clients or patients simply because it did not respond fast enough to their needs. This is especially likely to occur in times of high demand for a particular type of professional service. Clients may be in a state of high-perceived need of a particular service, complete with the anxiety that goes along with that perceived need. If new or existing clients' calls to a service firm's office go unreturned, they are likely to turn elsewhere, either as a result of a desire to get faster service, or because they may perceive the unresponsiveness as a lack of interest in their business. However, there are occasions when clients will respond positively to the appearance of extreme busy-ness, seeing this as an indication of a professional service provider's success, and thereby, his or her competence. Most clients like it when a busy professional can "make time for them."

Accessibility issues. A professional service provider may lose a client as a result of not having convenient hours of operation or because the practice's physical location is inconvenient. Although many professionals may like to have office hours from nine to five Monday through Friday, in times of high employment, dual-career marriages, and single-parent households, the marketplace dictates otherwise. Saturday mornings and/or extended weekday hours may be necessary to make it easy for actual and potential clients to do business with a firm. In addition, the firm's location must be within a reasonable distance of the people it is intended to serve.

TAKING QUALITY SERVICE TO THE NEXT LEVEL

As pointed out earlier, a service provider should seek to exceed client expectations, not merely satisfy them, by providing quality service, which we define as: *The delivery of a superior level of service in relation to client expectations.*

A central point of this definition is client expectations. The professional service provider needs to be aware of how his or her clients' expectations are created, and in particular, the source of those expectations. Marketing researchers Zeithaml, Berry, and Parasuraman have done some of the seminal work in identifying the bases of client and patient expectations. They have identified no less than 11 factors that affect an individual's expectations of a professional service provider. We will briefly explain nine of these.[3] (See Exhibit 3-2 on p. 47.)

1. EXPLICIT SERVICE PROMISES. The clients' expectations will obviously be affected by what they are told they can expect. If a plastic surgeon offers a free consultation in an ad, the client will obviously expect that to be the case. What the patient would not expect is to find that the free consultation is only free if he or she agrees to have the plastic surgery. If a lawyer advertises low-cost, legal help with routine transactions such as wills, the prospective client will expect it to be true. Because such explicit promises create specific expectations, a service provider must be careful to make only realistic and accurate promises to prospective clients.

2. IMPLICIT SERVICE PROMISES. Because services are intangible, clients will look for some other clues as to the potential quality of the service. They will look at the physical evidence provided by the professional service provider and the price they will be charged for services. An office furnished with Persian rugs, etched glass, and fine art may communicate that a professional service provider is successful, and also expensive. Because there is an implied price-quality relationship, a higher price implies a higher quality. Thus, clients who are willing to pay higher fees do so because they expect a greater amount of attention and a more positive outcome.

3. ENDURING SERVICE INTENSIFIERS. Sometimes client expectation is actually driven by the expectations of the client's own clients. This is also known as derived demand. For example, if a management consultant is hired by the marketing director of a given firm, the consultant must realize that the marketing director *and* his boss are expecting a certain level of performance. The consultant's job is "to make his client—the marketing director—look good" in his own eyes and in the eyes of his boss.

4. PERSONAL NEEDS. Professional service providers must be aware of the personal needs and desires of their clients. For example, if a client looking for an architect to design an addition on her house specifically communicates to three architects her desire to preserve the beveled ceilings of a room, and only one of the three architects addresses this concern in his or her drawings, which architect is most likely to get the job? The architect who does address the client's specific requests is aware of her personal needs, and therefore is the one the client is most likely to select.

5. TRANSITORY SERVICE INTENSIFIERS. Client expectations can shift as a result of the circumstances surrounding the need. For example, the par-

ent of a sick child having symptoms of flu who brings that child to the doctor's office may be willing to wait a reasonable time, say 20 minutes, especially if there were other children with the same condition crowding the doctor's waiting room. On the other hand, if that same parent's child fell off a swing and cut his head and had serious bleeding, the parent will expect immediate attention.

6. PERCEIVED SERVICE ALTERNATIVES. The more competitors a professional service provider has and the more clients are aware of their existence, the greater the expectations of quality service. Clients are not likely to put up with poor service when they perceive they can get better attention across the street.

7. SELF-PERCEIVED SERVICE ROLES. In many cases clients' expectations will be affected by their perceptions of how well they played their part in helping the service to be delivered. For example, it might be very difficult for a doctor to deliver quality medical care to a patient who does not communicate his symptoms. When the patient believes that he has done everything to provide the necessary information, he will have higher expectations of the doctor.

8. WORD OF MOUTH. While a professional service provider cannot directly control what one client tells another, he or she can influence it. For example, if an optometrist gains a new patient as a result of a personal reference from an existing customer, the optometrist can send the referring customer a note of thanks, thereby encouraging such positive word of mouth. In addition, a professional service provider can attempt to stimulate word of mouth through the use of testimonials in communications and advertisements.

9. PAST EXPERIENCE. It makes perfect sense that one's expectations of future service will be based, at least partially, on his or her past experiences with the service provider or competitors. The professional should keep a log of past experiences and problems with the client in the hope of exceeding past performance.

One final point should be made about customer expectations, and that is, they change. As J. Willard Marriott, Sr., founder of the Marriott Corporation, said many years ago, "Success is never final." While a professional service provider may presently be doing a very good job of delivering and exceeding clients' expectations, there is no guarantee that the service provider will do so in the future. Customer expectations can shift with changes in their conditions or as a result of competitors' moves; therefore, a professional service provider must continuously monitor clients' expectations.

Client expectations of professional services are probably a bit different from those one would have of a hotel or some other type of service. Most people would expect that doctors, lawyers, and consultants know more about the basis of the clients' problems than the clients do. Indeed, that is why they are using them in the first place! Given this, a client is walking in the door expecting a certain level of quality care and/or advice based solely on the prestige or assumed competence of the professional. This implies that much of the expectations of a professional, and resulting perception of quality, may be centered on process quality rather than outcome quality. The assumption may be made that the lawyer or consultant did everything possible to ensure a positive outcome but, because this is difficult to judge, one will look at how the service was delivered in order to judge the level of quality. (See Exhibit 3-2.)

WHAT IS QUALITY? REVISITED

Earlier we defined quality service as a delivery of a service at a superior level relative to client expectations. Now we will examine how one's clients judge quality, with a special focus on two key issues: (1) the distinction between process quality and outcome quality, and (2) the five dimensions of service quality.

Process vs. Outcome Quality

When a client contracts with a professional service provider, such as a management consultant for assistance, the client judges the quality of the service on two levels. The first level has to do with the outcome. For example, the client will ask, "Did the consultant's recommendations improve the operation?" And "Did the consultant deliver each phase of the project on time?" The second level has to do with the client's overall perceptions of the quality of the process. If the outcome was successful but the process was unpleasant—for example, the consultant was difficult

Exhibit 3-2. Strategies to Influence Client Expectations.

Controllable factors	Possible influence strategies
Explicit service promises	Make realistic and accurate promises that reflect the service actually delivered rather than an idealized version of the service.
	Ask contact people for feedback on the accuracy of promises made in advertising and personal selling.
	Avoid engaging in price or advertising wars with competitors because they take the focus off customers and escalate promises beyond the level at which they can be met.
	Formalize service promises through a service guarantee that focuses company employees on the promises and that provides feedback on the number of times promises are not fulfilled.
Implicit service promises	Ensure that service tangibles accurately reflect the type and level of service provided.
	Ensure that price premiums can be justified by higher levels of performance by the company on important customer attributes.

Less controllable factors	Possible influence strategies
Enduring service intensifiers	Use market research to determine sources of derived service expectations and their requirements. Focus advertising and marketing strategy on ways the service allows the focal customer to satisfy the requirements of the influencing customer.
Personal needs	Educate customers on ways the service addresses their needs.
Transitory service intensifiers	Increase service intensifiers delivery during peak periods or in emergencies.
Perceived service alternatives	Be fully aware of competitive offerings and, where possible and appropriate, match them.
Self-perceived service role	Educate customers to understand their roles and perform them better.

Exhibit 3-2. Strategies to Influence Client Expectations (*cont.*)

Word-of-mouth communications	Stimulate word of mouth in advertising by using testimonials and opinion leaders.
	Identify influencers and opinion leaders for the service and concentrate marketing efforts on them.
	Use incentives with existing customers to encourage them to say positive things about the service.
Past experience	Do research on customers' previous experience with similar services.

to work with—the client may not hire that consultant again. On the other hand, if it is difficult to judge the outcome, then the consultant's process will be more important. If clients feel that the service provider was responsive, easy to work with, and fulfilled all his or her other promises, they are more likely to believe that the outcome was at a similar level of quality.

Five Service Quality Dimensions

Zeithaml, Berry, and Parasuraman found that the customer's perception of quality is not a uni-dimensional concept. They identified five dimensions that a client considers in his or her assessment of service quality.[4] They are shown in Exhibit 3-3.

Exhibit 3-3. Five Service Quality Dimensions.

Reliability:	Ability to perform the promised service dependably and accurately.
Responsiveness:	Willingness to help customers and provide prompt service.
Assurance:	Knowledgeable and courteous attitude inspires trust and
Empathy:	confidence. Caring, individualized attention given to customers.
Tangibles:	Appearance of physical facilities, equipment, personnel, and written materials.

Reliability. Of the five dimensions, the researchers found reliability to be the most important determinant of perception of quality service. Reliability deals with the consistent, dependability of the professional services firm, and its honoring of its promises. It is important for the professional service firm or provider not to overpromise. Honoring promises is especially important with the core service being provided. For example, a CPA hired to perform a yearly audit is expected to complete the core service—the audit—in an accurate fashion each and every year.

Reliability also has a great deal to do with the process of delivering the service. Because consumers participate in the service process, they are exposed to many moments of truth. If the moments of truth are erratic, it becomes very difficult for clients to trust that the outcome will be a good one. It creates client anxiety because they cannot be certain what to expect next. Their anxiety and uncertainty may hinge on such questions as "Will a scheduled meeting take place?" "Will the service provider call when promised?" "Will the legal papers be delivered on time?" If a client has to worry about this, the service provider's reliability is in question.

Responsiveness. Responsiveness deals with the appearance, readiness, and willingness of the service provider to help. This dimension takes into account the openness and speed with which the service professional addresses client concerns, needs, questions, or complaints. This dimension also deals with the service provider's flexibility to adapt to a client's particular needs or changing conditions.

The professional's level of client centeredness has a great deal to do with success along this dimension. The ability to look at problems from the client's, rather than the firm's, perspective helps ensure client satisfaction. Further, clients of professional service providers tend to be fairly astute at being able to discern whether their service provider "can't" do something or merely "won't" do something. The latter attitude will create an impression of unresponsiveness. An experienced architect, for example, not only must be open to changes in the design of a building, but should probably expect them. The concept of responsiveness not only applies to the professional but also to his or her staff. For example, the receptionist's willingness to listen to the client's concerns can have a big impact on the client's overall perceptions of the firm. All staff members must be trained in the importance of being responsive to client's needs and emotions.

Assurance. Given the inability of many clients to be certain of outcome quality, trust becomes extremely important. This is especially important in professional services where the customer perceives a particularly high risk. In a 1998 study on legal services, the belief that clients have been given quality legal advice was clearly the most important feature of determining the relationship between a lawyer and client. Clients needed to be able to trust the lawyers to provide sound legal advice, because the information is outside the clients' sphere of knowledge. In line with the previously mentioned concept of responsiveness, the accessibility of the lawyer was rated as the second most important aspect in evaluating the strength of the relationship between client and lawyer.[5]

The deepest level of trust is one that is earned over time. If a professional such as a management consultant has served a client well over the years, the trust level will be high. The greater the level of reliability, the greater the level of assurance. Problems develop when the client does not have the experience and the history to fall back on. So how does the professional service provider develop trust with a client who does not have experience with the firm?

There are a number of ways. The first is to convey assurance through the corporate image. In this regard, well-known corporations have an edge over those less-established.

A second way to instill trust is through credentialing. Physicians regularly use board certification to distinguish themselves from other physicians. Prominently displaying diplomas or awards helps convey an image of professionalism and confidence. Another approach is to list in brochures and other client communications important clients that the firm or the professional has served.

A third way to develop assurance and trust is by highlighting one's experience in the field. Where possible, a professional service provider should reference his or her years in the field or the number of satisfied clients. A client will have more trust in a professional with 20 years of experience than one who just entered the field. In some instances, an organization may not have an impressive number of years of individual experience and therefore may promote the firm's combined experience in a given area. One law firm we know advertises its more than one hundred years of combined experience. Most of those one hundred years can be attributed to one senior partner who is in semi-retirement. The rest of the lawyers at the firm are relatively young, and therefore have little individual experience to promote.

Empathy. Everyone likes to be treated like he or she is important. The ability to make each client feel unique, special, and important is the crux of what empathy is all about. As in the theme song of the popular television sitcom 1980's "Cheers," one wants to go where "everyone knows your name." To foster feelings of empathy, the service practitioner must learn and remember the details of a client's needs and wants. The professional service firm must therefore develop systems that capture, retain, and display the information about individual clients and their backgrounds. Custom Research, Inc., a marketing research firm and a Malcolm Baldrige Quality Award winner, uses the following technique. They assign each client to a designated team that remains consistent throughout their relationship. Each team is responsible for developing a customer notebook that profiles the client's preference, history, and any relevant personal data. This notebook is constantly updated and as new members join the team, it becomes part of their training so that they can instantly relate to their clients. The client, at the same time, does not find it necessary to re-educate the service provider every time there is a change of staff.

Developing empathy does not necessarily require sophisticated data processing. A management consultant we are familiar with regularly subscribes to multiple magazines and journals that relate to the fields of his clients. Once a month, the consultant goes through the magazines looking for articles that relate to his customers. When he finds one, he attaches a note that says "Saw this article, thought of you. Hope you find it interesting," and signs his name and sends it to the client. The client knows that even when the consultant is not working on a project for him, he is still thinking of him and paying attention to his needs. A physician can develop rapport and empathy with clients by making a notation in the patient's record that briefly outlines any topics of conversation that were non-medical in nature; in this way, the provider can later be reminded and will be able to refer to their last conversation when meeting the patient again. It is these little things that help a client or patient feel that the service provider is taking a personal interest.

Tangibles. It is important to re-emphasize that because services are intangible, customers will look for physical cues as an indication of quality. Professional service providers must be certain that their physical facilities, equipment, personnel, and communication materials convey the desired image. Lawyers for years have kept their volumes of books containing federal and state statutes in plain view of clientele to create confidence. It is probably equally important that the lawyer, as well as other service professionals, displays an updated computer system somewhere in sight as well. Other intangibles that clients use to determine the quality of service include the contents of written communications and the quality of materials on which they are presented. For example, if a consultant's proposal to a client is full of misspellings, poor grammar, and is submitted on cheap paper, it will be difficult to trust the abilities of that consultant to pay attention to detail.

RECOVERING FROM A QUALITY BREAKDOWN

Things do not always go as well as we would like or as well as we had planned. Even with the best intentions and skills, a service provider is likely to fail in the delivery of service to one or more of his or her clients. Even though systems are in place to avoid errors, it is impossible to avoid them all. For example, perhaps a client was promised a set of architectural drawings by a certain date and didn't receive them, or was promised a return call within a given time but didn't receive one. When this happens, the likelihood of the client being vocal and not afraid to tell the service provider that he or she is dissatisfied with some aspect of the work is minimal. Research shows that 96 percent of unhappy customers do not bother to tell the service provider. People may not complain about their dissatisfaction for a number of reasons. They may feel that the service provider won't care, they may wish to avoid confrontation, or they feel they can go elsewhere for the same service. On the positive side, those who do complain are more likely to do future business with the service provider if he or she fixes the problem to their satisfaction.

The techniques used in recovering from a failure with a client are basically the same as those a person would use in his or her personal life. For example, someone who forgot a birthday or an anniversary is likely to apologize and try to remedy the situation as quickly as possible, make amends for the hurt feelings, and try to figure out a way to keep from making the same mistake again. These same guidelines should be used in professional shortcomings as well.

When things go wrong, how quickly the service provider makes them right again is of utmost importance. If the quality of service your firm provided to a customer is less than satisfactory, take the following steps.

Apologize. When you make a mistake, the first thing you should do is provide a heartfelt apology and take responsibility for the error. Don't attempt to shift the blame. Don't attempt to explain it away. Most important, don't attempt to ignore it. Remember that the objective is to maintain the client's trust. As long as service failures are the exceptions rather than the rule, a client is likely to believe and accept an apology.

Fix it quickly. The faster the service provider recovers and the faster he or she solves a service failure, the better. The speed and attention given to rectifying problems is an indication of the professional's level of commitment to the client. The client will expect the service provider to give a service failure his or her immediate attention. Any delay or lack of responsiveness will only further deteriorate the relationship.

Make up for the inconvenience. It is important to search for ways to make up for the error. This could mean providing some additional service free of charge or sending the client a token of appreciation for his or her business and expressing regret over the inconvenience caused. This token can be something as simple as a gift of dinner at a local restaurant or tickets to a sports event.

Find the root cause. It is not enough to apologize and fix the problem quickly. The prudent service professional will attempt to identify what caused the service breakdown and rectify the problem there. The goal is to ensure that the problem will never occur again. Just as you would not keep replacing tires that wear out prematurely without finding out why this is happening, it would not make sense to address the problem when it happens without fixing the cause of the problem. There is a saying: "Your system is perfectly designed for the results you are getting; if you want different results, you have to change the system." While changing the system may require time and energy, the long-term retention of your clients will be worth it.

SUMMARY

In business books and journals there are myriad definitions of quality. These range from "Zero Defects" to the definition we have endorsed of "the delivery of a service at a superior level relative to clients' expectations."

Even satisfied customers are at risk. This could be due to changes in their circumstances or needs, new developments by competition, references by colleagues, or lack of responsiveness or accessibility on the part of the service provider. A client's perception of service quality is directly related to his or her service expectations. The professional service provider must monitor variables that affect client expectations, which include explicit or implicit service promises, the client's past experiences and personal needs, the number of service provider alternatives, and transitory service intensifiers. Service quality is also determined by the client's perceptions of the service process and outcome. How the service is delivered and the end result are both important in the client's assessment of quality. Research has shown that the following five indicators of service quality are particularly important: reliability, responsiveness, assurance, empathy, and tangibles.

Even with the most conscientious service provider, mistakes are likely to happen. When service breakdowns occur, it is important to recover in a manner that rebuilds the client's trust and confidence in the service firm. This is accomplished by providing an apology, rectifying the situation as quickly as possible, making amends for the inconvenience, and finding the root cause of the problem and correcting it so that the problem is less likely to occur again.

NOTES

[1]   Adapted from "Fee Not So Simple," *Building Design and Construction* (August 1997), v 38, p 30.

[2]   Burke, Inc., Cincinnati, OH 45202. Used with permission.

[3]   Zeithaml, V. A., Berry, L. L., and Parasuraman, A. "The Nature and Determinants of Customer Expectations of Service," *Journal of the Academy of Marketing Science*, 21:1 (1993), p1-12.

[4]   Parasuraman, A., Zeithaml, V. A., and Berry, L. "Servcal: A Multiple Item Scale for Measuring Consumer Perceptions of Service Quality," *Journal of Retailing* (Spring 1988), p12-70.

[5]   Hart, Susan and Hogg, Gillian. "Relationship Marketing in Corporate Legal Services," *The Service Industries Journal* (July 1998), p55-69.

4 | Building and Reinforcing the Firm's Marketing Efforts

"The System is the Solution"
AT&T ADVERTISEMENT

In today's competitive environment, marketing expertise is essential for keeping a professional service firm busy or growing. A professional service provider's first inclination might be to seek outside help or to borrow marketing expertise from sources like management consultants, professional associations, or a local college, but it will quickly become evident that constantly going out for marketing expertise may be inefficient, a waste of resources, and may result in not having the marketing expertise at the time it's needed. Frequently, a professional service firm may best be served by bringing marketing inside. In this chapter we will look at ways the professional service firm can create an organization proficient at marketing itself. We will consider the following questions:

- Does a professional service organization need a formal marketing person or office in order to be effective in marketing itself?

- If an organization decides to establish a formal marketing office, what should be its level and job description?

- What can the marketing director do to accomplish results quickly?

- How can this marketing function be elaborated over time?

Six Dysfunctional Marketing Programs[1]

1. THE SQUEAKY-WHEEL MARKETING PROGRAM
Defining Characteristic: Those who demand the marketing resources get them

In the absence of any type of common objectives, marketing resources are provided on the basis of demand. As a result, money might be spent on ineffective professionals and activities. Individual service providers use the firm's resources to build their own practices and visibility.

2. THE FLAVOR-OF-THE-MONTH MARKETING PROGRAM
Defining Characteristic: Something more "sexy" or interesting always comes along to capture the attention of the marketing effort.

In these programs, the attention span of the marketing director, marketing committee, or marketing partner is relatively short and new ideas receive immediate endorsement. One month it's a client survey, the next a Web page, the next an image advertising program, with no commitment to any direction or strategy. The result is that the firm fails to achieve long-term marketing objectives.

3. THE MONKEY-SEES-MONKEY-DOES MARKETING PROGRAM
Defining Characteristic: The firm copies the marketing efforts of its competitors or other firms in its market.

Many professional service firms simply imitate the marketing activities of their competitors. This results in two potential problems. First, if the competitors are using the flavor of the month marketing program, imitating them will result in aimless marketing just like theirs, with possibly even less effectiveness. Second, if the competitors actually know what they are doing, mimicking marketing strategies and programs that are built upon their strengths and opportunities will result in ineffective marketing for the strengths and opportunities of the firm.

4. THE PASS-THE-BUCK MARKETING PROGRAM
Defining Characteristic: Something or someone else is always holding things up in marketing.

In this situation, marketing plans and programs are never effective because no one ever takes responsibility for initiating or implementing the marketing ideas. For example, the lawyers within a firm blame the ineffective marketing on the management committee who did not respond to a proposed strategy, on a marketing director who never sets up a meeting, or on an out-of-date brochure.

5. THE GRASS-IS-ALWAYS-GREENER MARKETING PROGRAM
Defining Characteristic: Other firms' clients are a lot more attractive than the ones we have.

This program is usually the result of a compensation program that rewards finding new clients rather than maintaining old ones. As a result, the firm is chasing new business while existing, hard-earned clients slip away.

6. THE EVERY-MAN/WOMAN-FOR-HIM/HERSELF MARKETING PROGRAM
Defining Characteristic: Everyone in the firm gets equal time and resources for marketing.

In this situation, every professional in the firm warrants the same resources regardless of his or her skills or of marketing opportunities. The result is internal competitiveness and lack of coordination rather than collaboration in taking advantage of collected contacts and ideas. Individuals within the firm may even be pursuing conflicting opportunities.

Conclusions
There are many professional service firms whose primary goal is just getting staff members to undertake marketing activities, regardless of the quality or degree of the effectiveness of the activities. And the last thing a firm should do is construct what the staff members perceive to be barriers to marketing, such as processes, controls, or approvals. Still, without a better system for making decisions about marketing strategies and resources, many professional service firms will find their levels of activity and expense rising appreciably without a corresponding increase in results.

- What steps can be taken to make the whole organization more responsive and marketing oriented?

ASSESSING THE NEED FOR MARKETING

The issue of whether a professional service organization should create a formal marketing office is not the issue of whether it should do marketing. All organizations do marketing whether or not they organize it in a formal way or call it marketing, business development, or practice development. Many different people carry out the marketing work of a professional service firm. Some staff members may identify prospects while others convert them into clients; still others may do marketing analysis to determine new markets, and so on. While the marketing office (if it exists) is totally involved in marketing work, the marketing function is larger than the work occurring within the marketing office. The marketing office carries only a small part of the total marketing efforts taking place in a professional service firm.

Many professional service organizations might prefer to operate without a formal marketing position at all. They would like their reputations to draw in all the clients, eliminating the need to spend any time or money on marketing. However, according to Bruce Marcus, a leading consultant in the area of marketing legal services, the idea that reputation sells is one of the great myths that impede the marketing success of professional service firms. The only reputation that comes close to selling is a reputation for a specific capability. For example, a firm with the reputation for integrity and skill in human resources cannot depend on using that reputation to sell its risk management or actuarial abilities. Marcus points out that the reputation is not what sells, it's the platform on which selling takes place. In addition, reputations are a fragile thing.[2]

All professional service firms would be well advised to establish some type of formal marketing function. This is especially important for firms that face (1) target markets in which the firm has no reputation and limited experience, (2) active marketing efforts by competitors, and (3) unpredictable and demanding clients. Unfortunately, the installation of formal marketing responsibilities will have to either add to a firm's overhead expenses or cut down on the billable hours of its professionals. This will make it even more imperative to find highly profitable projects to compensate for the overhead and non-billable hours that will be spent on marketing. However, if too many highly profitable projects are pursued, service quality levels could suffer as senior people might become less involved with the work. Take, for example, a small law firm consisting of three partners who all recognize a need to get more involved with marketing. These partners may be reluctant to cut back any of their own billable hours—or, alternatively, to hire someone permanently to perform marketing tasks—because of a concern about having to compensate for this move by obtaining more ongoing business and by having more of the work done by the firm's young associates and paralegals. They may fear a decline in quality in the firm's work. Or they may fear that clients will feel mistreated (even if quality is unaffected) by not having as much contact with the partners. This could damage a firm's reputation and its ability to attract future clients. A fear of these possible developments often contributes to a professional service firm's resistance to establishing formal marketing responsibilities.

Makeshift Marketing Approaches

Firms that reject the creation of a formal marketing office can still take some concrete actions to improve their marketing resources, including:

- Sending key people to marketing seminars and workshops to learn marketing so that they can apply what they learn to their normal responsibilities.
- Inviting help from the marketing faculty of a business school, such as using a marketing research class to research a problem the firm is facing.
- Hiring a marketing consulting firm, marketing research firm, advertising agency, or public relations firm to do specific projects when needed.
- Relying on marketing support and assistance provided by a professional association.

Although these makeshift ways of acquiring marketing services will not do the full job of creating a marketing-oriented organization, they will often produce good value in the short term and allow a firm to move gradually closer to installing a formal marketing function. Nevertheless, in using these approaches, the expected results should be realistic. Seminars and workshops should be seen as a way to provide a very brief introduction to marketing; they cannot take the place of years of real-world marketing experience or semesters of course work in marketing and will not turn people into marketing experts overnight. Similarly, one cannot expect unusually perceptive advice to come from students' projects, because students typically have limited relevant experience upon which to base their recommendations. And while this may suggest that the advice of an outside marketing firm with years of experience may be invaluable, the reality is that even in this case the results may be only average. There are numerous factors that may affect the results an outside marketing firm may yield. For example, even though it may have years of experience, that experience may have been in industries that bear little resemblance to the relevant profession. Moreover, experienced marketers vary in quality. The good ones will talk about doing research on markets and building strong long-term relationships with clients. The poor ones will recommend quick-hitting advertising or public relations campaigns and growth for growth's sake.

Taking Marketing Inside

Although using a makeshift marketing approach may suffice for a while, the professional service organization may eventually determine that a formal marketing office within the firm would best serve its needs. Perhaps the makeshift use of outside marketing resources turned out to be too costly or unreliable, or maybe the firm's marketing needs are extensive enough to hire a full-time marketing person, or at least have someone devote a substantial amount of time each week to marketing. A key upside to developing a formal marketing position may be that the firm can position itself as being proactive rather than reactive. The proactive firm implements a formal marketing process because it sees the market changing and wishes to stay ahead of competition, whereas a reactive firm establishes a marketing office because everyone else has.

Although establishing a formal marketing position within the firm has many advantages, it can also pose some risks, particularly if some members of the organization are resistant to the plan, or if the new appointee is not given sufficient marketing authority to carry out his or her responsibilities. Once the organization decides to move forward, it must address the following issues: (1) Will they establish marketing on a lower level with shared responsibilities in the form of a marketing committee, (2) will they hire an individual specifically to perform marketing activities, (3) at what level should this person be hired, (4) what should be the job description, and (5) how should they go about selecting or recruiting this individual.

Marketing Committee. A marketing committee is made up of individuals from different sections of the professional service firm. These individuals may represent different departments or practice areas. The committee may exist in place of a formal marketing director and typically has the overall responsibility of encouraging, organizing, and coordinating the firm's business development activities.

Joel A. Rose, a management consultant, explains the roles a marketing committee would have in a law firm. These guidelines are also applicable to other professional service firms.

"The committee will: (1) Work within the firm from the top down and within practice areas in an environment that is conducive to practice development. (2) Ensure that the firm's policies and practices governing lawyer compensation and production standards do not serve as a disincentive for lawyers to participate in marketing activities, including selling the services of the practice areas and individual lawyers. (3) Establish and maintain lines of communication within the firm with substantive practice areas and among attorneys in different practice areas. These communications should keep everyone informed about the expertise, accomplishments, and opportunities for enhancing the synergy within the firm generally and within and between practice areas. Without this knowledge, cross-selling of the firm's specialties by lawyers in other practice areas will not occur to the extent desired. (4) Monitor the overall implementation of lawyers' development plans for the firm in the substantive practice areas and by individual lawyers. (5) Maintain communication with the partnership and the heads of practice areas with respect to successful business development activities. Such communications should be concerned with methods to enhance the synergy within the practice and between practice areas."[3]

To this list, we would add a sixth role that should be performed by a marketing committee: To oversee market research projects and ensure that plans are on target, making refinements where necessary, and identifying new opportunities.

While marketing committees can be effective for many firms, they are not without their drawbacks, which include:

- **No formal power.** Marketing committees typically report to a senior partner or a management committee. As such, their ability to get things done may be more related to individuals on the committee and their personal skills than to formal lines of authority.

- **No ultimate responsibility.** Because no one is formally responsible for marketing, controversial yet important tasks may go undone simply because no one on the committee may be willing to assume responsibility for the task's completion. This might be especially true in circumstances where the task might be politically charged or out of line with the organization's culture.

- **A slower pace.** Committees, based on their size or perhaps organizational structure, tend to move slowly. Because various functions or specialties are represented on the committee, it may be necessary to gain consensus before taking action. This results in a committee that tends to have a "bias toward reflection" rather than a "bias toward action."

- **Too many masters.** An unfortunate characteristic of many committees is that rather than focusing on a common goal, members of the committee tend to focus on the goals of their own constituents. Unless the committee is truly acting as a team with its own shared mission and shared values, it can be difficult for the individual members to forget they do not represent their own little corner of the firm, but rather the firm as a total entity.

Membership Means Non-billable Hours. Another reality of marketing committees within professional organizations is that time devoted to marketing activities is time not devoted to billable hours. Therefore, unless the firm adjusts its compensation systems to allow for marketing activities, marketing activities will always receive stepchild treatment in favor of those activities that pay the bills.

The Marketing Director. Because of the difficulties of working with a marketing committee, many professional service firms prefer to hire a marketing director. Once this decision is made, the question that must be addressed is "Where on the organizational chart should this position be placed?" Selection of a marketing director as a mid-level manager means not designating him or her as a partner or principal. This person would basically act as a resource person or internal marketing consultant to other personnel in the organization who need marketing services, and to a marketing committee. This mid-level marketer would help define marketing problems, arrange for marketing research, and hire advertising agencies as needed. A job description for the mid-level director of marketing services is provided in Exhibit 4-1.

Alternatively, an organization could hire or appoint an upper-level person to lead the marketing effort. This person would be given partner or principal status and would hold a position with more scope, authority, or influence with a title such as "Partner in Charge of Marketing" or "Vice President of Marketing" and would not only coordinate and supply marketing services for others, but would also participate in the setting of policy and direction for the organization. An upper-level marketing director would also be responsible for planning and managing relations with all the organization's clients.

Which position should an organization choose? Some organizations prefer to appoint a mid-level person on the idea that the position costs less, its value can be tested, and if the person proves effective, he or she can be promoted to an upper-level post. Other organizations feel that the middle-level person cannot be very effective, because he or she would not have the ear of the most influential people and would not participate in making important strategic decisions. The Legal Marketing Association's 1998 survey of senior legal marketing directors points out that "the marketing direc-

Exhibit 4-1. Sample Marketing Director Position Description.[4]

- Although the position reports to the managing partner, this position has dotted-line relationships with the five other partners. Budget is projected at $200,000 with spending authority, within this amount, of $2,000.

- Responsible for the design, execution, and analysis of all marketing research activities. This would entail hiring the appropriate outside marketing research support, developing profiles of present and potential clients, and conducting issue and image studies and client satisfaction research among other potential research projects.

- Assisting in the development and execution of strategic planning for the firm. This entails the ability to transform both marketing research data and internal data bases into information capable of outlining appropriate strategic plans and initiatives. Particular emphasis will be placed on strategies that enhance the firm's ability to recruit and retain profitable clients.

- Managing direct mail, networking, and seminar programs. Reports to managing partner. Responsible for one part-time subordinate. Position is considered middle management. This means that the director is to make most decisions, but is to keep the partner fully informed.

- Direct mail responsibilities include the selection of prospects; collection of reply cards; dissemination of leads to partners; and follow-up results monitoring and preparing for reports on program successes.

- Networking responsibilities include attending social and professional functions, selecting those that complement the business interests of the firm; matching seniors, managers, and partners to organizations; training partners and associates in efficient networking techniques, monitoring their activities, and supporting their efforts with follow-up mailings and oppotunities for further interaction.

- Seminar program responsibilities include identifying prospect interests, selecting sites, negotiating with hotel properties, selecting presenters, training presenters, editing materials, arranging for print and visual support, supervising rehearsals, preparing invitations, following up to ensure prospect attendance, determining reactions, managing follow-up activities, and ensuring long-term personal contact.

- Overseeing on-line activities of the firm. This includes management of Web site that projects a positive image of the firm and facilitates communication internally and between the firm and its present and potential clients.

tor is one of the few senior non-attorney non-administrative positions" at a firm. As such, if a firm hires a non-professional it may indicate that it is not taking marketing seriously and, consequently, neither will its professional staff. The firm's marketer should have the experience, credentials, and advanced degrees to be considered a "fellow professional."[5] Our view is that the upper-level option should be adopted initially, because among other things, this approach makes it easier to accomplish the necessary task of transforming the thinking of key people into a marketing mode.

Suppose, however, that the organization decides to initially appoint a mid-level director of marketing services to occupy a position like the one described in Exhibit 4-1. For years it was difficult for professional service firms to find someone ideally suited to perform this task. Typically, one of two problems existed. Either the person had a strong knowledge of the field, but no marketing training, or the likely candidate had a great deal of marketing training, typically in package goods, but no knowledge of the professional service field for which he or she was applying. Today, many of these difficulties have disappeared. With the advent of joint MBA/JD degrees, legal firms have the ability to recruit people not only trained in the law but who also understand business. The new 150-hour requirement for the CPA has resulted in many business schools combining the MBA with a five-year accountancy program. The MBA has long been the pedigree of choice of management consultants, but many of today's business schools are finding their Executive MBA programs brimming with physicians. Furthermore, credentialing organizations, such as the American College of Physician Executives, provide extensive training to professional members desiring to become more adept in business practices such as marketing. (See Exhibit 4-2.)

Marketing the Concept of Marketing

A newly appointed marketing director, marketing vice president, or other top marketing executive will want to demonstrate quickly that marketing thinking can contribute value to the professional service organization. However, it is likely that many members of the organization will be critical of marketing, arguing that it is inappropriate or a waste of money; others will be puzzled about what marketing is or does. Only a few will see it as a strong opportunity for the organization.

Exhibit 4-2. How Serious Are You about Marketing?[6]

A marketing professional cannot be effective without the total support of top management and senior partners. Before you hire someone to handle your marketing activities, answer the following questions. If you can answer yes to all of them, you are ready to begin your search for a marketing professional.

- *Do our partners believe marketing is a necessary business function that requires the same level of attention and resources as client service, billings, employee recruitment?* If your partners consider marketing a necessary evil—little more than an administrative function—then that is *all* it ever will be. Your firm must view marketing as a logical extension of its mission and goals—a tool for helping it achieve long-term growth and improve profitability.

- *Do we recognize that a skillful marketing professional will study every aspect of the firm, seeking to make changes that will make it more client- and service-centered?* A good marketing professional will analyze every aspect of your firm in order to improve client satisfaction. He or she may recommend change in areas as diverse as client billing, hallway lighting, and print advertising. You need to be ready to listen and, when appropriate, make change.

- *Is our managing partner (or the partner in charge of marketing) prepared to guide the marketing professional's efforts?* To be successful, a marketing pro requires the insights, leadership, and support that only the managing partner can provide. Does your firm's already overburdened managing partner have the time?

- *Do we have a clear sense of what we want to accomplish? Do we have a marketing vision?* Some would argue that they need to hire a marketing professional to help them through the marketing planning process. But suppose the process reveals that what you really need is an entry-level person who can help you produce client communications materials. Your marketing pro will need to understand your own marketing vision, which comes from you. So, come up with the vision first and then let the pro help you develop it with a plan.

- *Are we prepared to invest the time, money, and resources necessary to hire a marketing professional and to fund his or her programs?* Once you hire a marketing professional, your expenditures will extend beyond his or her salary and compensation. The programs dictated by your marketing plan will require capital outlays and administrative support, such as a full-time secretary, office space, and computer.

Exhibit 4-2. How Serious Are You about Marketing? (*cont.*)

• *Do we all recognize that our marketing professional will not contribute to bottom-line profits overnight?* Realistically, most expenditures are long-term investments in the future of the firm. Everyone in the firm, especially the partners, must appreciate and accept this fact. This does not mean you shouldn't scrutinize marketing outlays or ask for a statement about the return on investment. However, you cannot expect the pro to make a direct contribution to the bottom line until he or she has been in place for at least six months to one year.

In the face of this skepticism, the new director must carefully choose initial projects that can, if successfully executed, demonstrate the value of marketing. The marketing director must, in essence, market marketing, and should therefore spend considerable effort determining what other people in the organization think and feel about various marketing projects. Rather than assuming he or she knows what others want, the director should conduct interviews and group discussions to get opinions and ideas about projects.

Obtaining feedback about possible projects will build goodwill and understanding with various people in the organization and lead to many project ideas—often more than a single marketing director operating with a small budget can handle. The director should not commit to any project until he or she reviews all the possible projects and chooses the best ones. The best early projects to undertake have four characteristics:

1. a high likelihood of making money or saving money for the organization

2. a relatively small cost to carry out

3. a short period of time for completion

4. a high visibility potential if successful

Projects possessing these characteristics will vary by organization and by profession. For some organizations, the best initial projects might involve exercises in introspection for top management, where the organization's mission and the clients it should be targeting are carefully examined. For other organizations, the best initial projects will involve small, narrowly targeted promotional efforts, such as sending a reprint of a journal article written by someone in the organization to prospective clients who are likely to be facing the problems discussed in the article.

Whatever the project, the marketing officer should ensure that everyone understands the project's objectives. Is it to find new clients, improve client retention, or gain share of mind? Whatever the objective, one of the most difficult tasks for the new marketing officer is to communicate that achieving a marketing orientation and its benefits is only accomplished over time. Patience may be one of the first marketing lessons to be taught to other professionals in the organization.

BUILDING A COMMITMENT TO MARKETING

Whether a professional service organization pursues marketing by relying on outside marketing resources or by building an internal formal marketing structure, achieving excellence in marketing requires the total commitment of the firm. A marketing structure alone does not ensure a marketing-oriented or client-centered organization. It is crucial that the departments and key managers and staff have the proper philosophy. Inculcating this philosophy may be the marketing manager's most important task. The marketing manager has a limited influence on how others in the organization think and behave towards customers and other public. The marketing officer in an architectural firm, for example, cannot insist that its architects show a stronger interest in their clients. A physician may ask the staff to be more courteous to patients, but it is the staff who decides. The marketing manager must work patiently to build everyone's commitment to the client. Any attempt to re-orient an organization requires a plan based on sound principles. A plan to achieve a marketing orientation calls for several measures, including the following.

Top Management Support

Phil Marriott of the Marriott Corporation once said, "As a CEO, if you're not generating excitement, you're not generating much." An organization is not likely to develop a strong marketing orientation until its chief exec-

The Changing Role of the Law Firm Marketing Director

In 1995 a survey was conducted for the National Law Firm Marketing Association (NALFMA) to determine the roles and responsibilities of the law firm marketing director. The author, Charles Maddock of Altman Weil, identified a number of interesting points.[7] Among them were:

- Marketing directors claimed to have lead responsibility for the following activities within the law firm.

    Arranging for presentation skills training

    External communications such as:

    > brochures

    > newsletters

    > advertising

    > public relations

    > image programs

- Marketing directors share responsibility with lawyers in the areas of:

    strategic planning

    cross-selling activities

    practice area planning

    proposal writing

    client relations

The report predicted that marketing directors would report more and more to the managing partner or chairperson, rather than an executive committee or client relations committee. Furthermore, the report states:

"For the marketing function to succeed within the firm, the in-house marketing director must be a cheerleader, a motivator, and a human tickler file—in short, a non-stop advocate of the importance of marketing a promotion."

utive officer believes in it, understands it, wants it, and wins the support of other high-level executives for building this mindset. The CEO is the organization's highest "marketing executive," and has to create the climate for marketing by talking about it and advocating for it. This is especially true in professional service organizations. This requires that the CEO formulate and articulate a vision of the future based upon a marketing orientation and communicate personal commitment to the vision by acting as a role model for others within the organization.

One example is the Arbor Consulting Group, Inc., which in 1998 won a special tribute award as a progressive work place. Joan E. Moore, the organization's leader, identified ten strategies:

1. LINK UNDERLYING PRINCIPLES TO VISION.

2. WALK THE TALK. The employees' perceptions of a CEO's actions become their reality in viewing how consistently the CEO follows his or her own stated philosophy.

3. BE STRATEGIC ABOUT YOUR CULTURE. Your culture needs to support your vision's value of work and ways in which you need to interact. Build a culture that supports market orientation.

4. INSTITUTIONALIZE LEARNING. In a learning organization, the value and importance of learning must be stressed as an important part of day-to-day business activities at all levels.

5. STRIVE FOR CONTINUOUS IMPROVEMENT. A commitment to continuous improvement is critical to remaining competitive in the market place and responsive to clients and customers.

6. WORK FOR RETENTION. Support the well-being of your employees as an effective retention strategy.

7. STRESS COLLABORATIVE DECISION MAKING AND INNOVATIVE PROBLEM SOLVING. Provide incentives and resources to allow for collaboration such as investment in technology that enables shared information systems, channels for open communications, and rewards for innovation.

8. ENCOURAGE BOUNDARY-LESS POSITIONS. This means all employees need to feel ownership and responsibility for the success of the organization. Make "it's not my job" an unacceptable attitude or response.

9. GIVE BACK TO THE COMMUNITY. Encourage and support employees in community outreach efforts.

10. MAKE IT FUN! Build fun into the workplace, with employee-empowered reward and recognition programs, wellness incentives, and even company-sponsored events all designed around the needs and likes of your employee population.

Effective Organizational Design

The CEO cannot do the whole marketing job and neither can a marketing director. It is the CEO's responsibility to create an organizational design that is conducive to supporting the marketing director. Characteristics of such an organization include structuring the operation around processes and not tasks, managing information in a manner that employs marketing research, and encourages upward and downward communication throughout the organization, and where the CEO spends time in the field with the firm's clients.

Better Employee Hiring Practices

Training can only go so far in inculcating the right attitudes in employees. For example, architects who have spent most of their careers working on highly technical matters and talking mostly to one another will not easily adopt marketing and selling skills. The organization should gradually hire more client-centered professionals. Some individuals are naturally more service minded and friendlier than others and this can be included as a criteria for hiring.

The Ivey Business School of the University of Western Ontario conducted research to determine what attributes clients sought in management consultants.[8] These characteristics can serve as a guide to a professional service firm in screening and hiring professionals. The most highly regarded included:

- *Trust.* Virtually all management consulting involves mission-critical assignments and the stakes are often very high; therefore, it follows that companies place enormous trust in their consultants.

Trust was the first and most important attribute management consulting clients mentioned. A good management consultant, therefore, must be able to make the client trust in his or her abilities and experience. That's the quality that will get them in the door.

- *Ability to discern clients' needs and objectives.* Once inside the client's door, the best consultants help the organization discern its true needs as opposed to stated wants. They move with the client's leaders from uncertainty and ambiguity to focus and confidence around the well-defined strategy.

- *Inspirational and motivational.* The best consultants are able to generate energy, confidence, and focus that allow both parties to contribute to a solution that would not have occurred otherwise. While their demonstrated trust and expertise got them in the door, what keeps them there is the ability to inspire others to buy into a chain of process.

- *Challenge oriented.* The best consultants are not motivated by money and power; what really motivates them is the profound sense of accomplishment of being an instrument of meaningful change. They are self-confident, a little impatient, and always seeking a new challenge. They build, but don't inhabit. They move on to build again.

- *Collaborators.* Good consultants don't work *for* clients, they work *with* them.

- *The ability to create a favorable future.* A consultant creates this future by helping clients define it and then deploy resources—human, financial, technological, and natural—to realize it.

In-House Marketing Training

Marketing training should consist of initial training sessions and subsequent reinforcement training sessions, first for top managers and partners. Their understanding and support are essential if marketing is to work within the organization. The training may take place at the firm's headquarters, but may work best in an off-site location where participants will be less distracted. The training program should consist of highly professional presentations of marketing concepts, cases, and planning exercises. From there, further presentations can be made to other staff members. These presentations should cover marketing opportunity identification, market segmentation, targeting and positioning, marketing planning and control, as well as pricing, sales, and communication skills. Subsequent marketing training sessions should sustain earlier lessons and reinforce issues central to the firm's long-term health, such as client development and retention. They may also be focused on new initiatives and programs that the organization is undertaking.

Creating an Employee-Friendly Environment

Successful professional service organizations focus their attention on both *their customers and their employees.* They understand the concept of the *service profit chain* that links service firm profits with employee and customer satisfaction. This chain consists of the following links:[9]

- *Internal service quality.* This begins with superior employee selection and training, and a quality work environment where employees are treated with respect, and given a sense of empowerment, and where there is strong support for those dealing with the customers. This in turn results in . . .

- *Satisfied and productive service employees.* The more satisfied the employees, the more loyal they become, resulting in long-term employee retention, which in turn results in . . .

- *More effective and efficient customer value creation and service delivery.* Because the service environment has resulted in long-term retention of employees, the employees gain the opportunity to get to know their clients and customers better and develop the long-term relationships necessary for the organization to prosper. This results in . . .

- *Satisfied and loyal customers.* Satisfied customers who remain loyal purchase again and refer others, which results in . . .

- *Healthy profits and growth*

Clearly, reaching service profits and growth will begin with taking care of those who take care of the customers.

Rewarding Marketing-Oriented Employees

One way for top management to convince everyone in the organization of the importance of marketing-oriented attitudes is to reward those who demonstrate those attitudes. An organization should identify and reward employees who have done an outstanding job of servicing customers. Hopefully, other employees will be motivated to emulate this behavior. As an added incentive to all employees, compensation and bonuses could be tied to creating high customer satisfaction.

Improving Planning Systems

One of the most effective ways to build a demand for strong marketing is to improve the organization's planning system. Suppose an accounting firm has neither strong marketing nor strong planning. The organization might first design and implement an organization planning system. To make the system work, strong marketing and data analysis are necessary. Those responsible for planning will see that organization plans must begin with an analysis of the market. This will require strengthening the organization's marketing function. Top management will see that organization planning is largely an empty gesture without good marketing and data analysis.

SUMMARY

The question is not whether a professional service firm will be involved in marketing activities; instead, the question is how well will the firm implement marketing processes? Organizations can draw on marketing resources in a number of ways: through hiring outside marketing firms such as advertising agencies, marketing research firms, or consultants, or sending their staff to marketing seminars. At some point, the organization is likely to decide that it is ready to establish a formal marketing function. Many times this takes the form of a marketing committee in place of a formal line position. The marketing committee is typically made up of department participants representing different specialties within the service firm. However, marketing committees have several disadvantages, including a lack of formal power, no one is ultimately responsible for marketing, they have a tendency to move slower, their meetings detract from participants' billable hours, and committee members may represent their own constituents more than the firm's interests. The service firm also might hire a middle-level marketing services director whose job is to supply marketing assistance and services to others in the organization, or it can hire an upper-level vice president of marketing whose job is to participate with management in strategy and policy formulation. The level of the appointment and the extent of the appointee's responsibility will vary depending upon the firm. Regardless of which marketing solution a firm chooses, the presence of a marketing committee or department does not mean that the organization as a whole is marketing oriented, because the marketing personnel may have limited influence. To create a truly marketing-oriented organization requires top management support, effective organizational design, improved hiring practices, in-house marketing training, an employee-friendly environment, the facilitation and reward of marketing-oriented behavior, and, finally, planning system improvement.

NOTES

[1] Adapted from "Do You Recognize Your Marketing Program?" by Sally J. Schmidt, Fall 1995, Schmidt Marketing, Inc., www.schmidt-marketing.com. Used with permission.

[2] Marcus, Bruce, "The Marcus Newsletter," www.marcusletter. com.

[3] LoCurto, Ellen Grayce. "A Buyer's Guide to Hiring a Marketing Director or Coordinator," *The Marketing Advantage: How to Get and Keep the Clients You Want*, Collette Nassutti (ed.), AICPA (1998) and *Journal of Accountancy* (January 1999).

[4]   Adapted from *How to Hire a Marketing Director and Make It Work,* by the Association for Accounting Marketing (AAM) (1996). Issued by the American Institute of Certified Public Accountants (AICPA).

[5]   MacDonagh, Catherine Alman. "Business Development and Client Services: Law Firm Marketing: Why Should You Hire a Professional?" *Law Firm Partnership and Benefit Report,* New York Law Publishing Corp. (October 1998).

[6]   Source: "A Buyer's Guide to Hiring a Marketing Director or Coordinator," by Ellen Grayce LoCurto, CAE. *The Marketing Advantage: How to Get and Keep the Clients You Want,* edited by Collette Nassutti. Published by the AICPA Management of an Accounting Practice Committee.

[7]   Adapted from "The Changing Role of the Law Firm Marketing Director," by Charles Maddock and Norm Rubenstein. Altman Weil Publication, Inc. (October 1996). Law Firm Management Web site at: lawfirmmanagement/asked/asked038.htm.

[8]   Adapted from "Maintaining Excellence in Management Consulting," by Lawrence G. Tapp. *Ivey Business Quarterly* (Winter 1997) v62, n2, p15(3).

[9]   Kotler, Philip and Armstrong, Gary. *Principles of Marketing,* Upper Saddle River, NJ: Prentice Hall, 2001.

5 | Acquiring and Using Marketing Information

....

"On the whole, knowing is better than not knowing."
KARL ALBRECHT
Author and consultant

Information is the basis for a solid marketing program. However, in professional services, where most practitioners are far more educated than the average individual, lawyers', doctors', or accountants' "knowledge" may be one of their largest barriers to success. It's not what they know that is the problem; it's what they "think" they know.

In marketing, presuming to know what the customer is thinking is akin to mortal sin. The professional service provider is not representative of his or her average customer, and does not think like the average customer.

Let us provide you a simple quiz. Please try to answer these questions to yourself as honestly as you can. The questions are:

1. How many years of education do you have?

2. Did you receive training in your organization when you began there?

3. How many hours a week do you work?

4. On your way into work in the morning, do you think about what is waiting on your desk?

One of the trends in professional service marketing has been the synergy between professions. For example, accountants have long looked at law firms as sources of referrals. According to Judith R. Trepeck, of Trepeck Consulting Group in Southfield, Michigan, representing law firms as a consultant offers an excellent opportunity for accountants to expand their practice. Ms. Trepeck, who is a CPA, works with lawyers in planning a firm's growth and development. She believes that the accountant's management and consulting strengths must focus on accountability, policy and procedure, performance-based compensation systems, rainmaking, training, team building, human resources, budgeting, forecasting, and tracking time. When Trepeck takes on a legal firm as an accountant, her first move is to analyze the firm. She plunges into a number of areas with the express goal of completing what she terms the "operations assessment" of the firm. She works to get answers from the partners to such questions as:

- Why do clients come to this firm? Why do they stay? Why do they leave?

- What is your greatest contribution to the success of the firm?

- What stops you or gets in your way of getting your work out the door?

- If you could change one aspect of the firm-wide management practices and policies that affect the success of the firm, what would it be?

- If you could invest $100,000 in the next year with the goal of improving the competitiveness of the firm and make its future more secure, how would you spend it?

The answers provide her group with a snapshot of the company, its strengths and talents as well as its weaknesses and obstacles to growth and profitability. Trepeck then works with the particular firm to create and implement an action plan. Particular areas she reviews and develops include a financial analysis, firm management, technology, marketing/client-focused issues, human resources, employee relations, and operations.

Ms. Trepeck clearly recognizes the need for obtaining market information in order to better serve her clients by better understanding them and the environment in which they operate.[1]

5. When you get in your car or ride the train home in the evening, do you think about what was left on your desk at the end of the day?

6. When you go on a week's vacation, what day of the week is it when you quit thinking about the messages, projects, and the reports that are left back on your desk, and what day of the week is it when you start thinking about them again?

In the United States only about 22 percent of those old enough to have a four-year college degree have one. Professional service providers are obviously in this minority, and typically have multiple college degrees, whether it's a JD, MD, or MBA, not to mention other levels of professional certification. This puts them in an even smaller minority. In addition, professionals typically receive training specific to their professional organization, whether formal or informal. At this training, during an introduction to the firm, a professional is likely to be exposed to the way that firm "does things": the firm's mission, values, and day-to-day procedures. Even in the absence of formal training programs, a member of a professional organization probably learns how things are done around the organization by observation or through subtle rewards and punishments.

According to *USA Today*, the average man in the United States works 48.6 hours per week, the average woman works 43.8 hours per week. The odds are that professionals routinely exceed these averages. It is not unusual for surgeons to work 80-hour weeks. And chances are that even on vacation, the professional service provider thinks about work quite a bit, and perhaps even checks in by phone a couple of times.

What all this means is that not only are the members of the professions probably more educated than the average individual, but the area in which they are educated will have an impact on how they think. An accountant probably processes information differently from a psychologist. A lawyer, due to rigorous training, probably has more advanced analytical capabilities than someone who is not in a professional field. Furthermore, the training professionals receive within their organization as well as its culture will have an additional impact on how they think.

All this formal and informal education, combined with their above-average dedication to their professions, diminishes the professional service providers' ability to think objectively about their clients or to see things from their perspective. What a professional service provider knows about his or her firm and its capabilities is not likely to be known by the firm's clients (unless they are told). Of course, even if they know a great deal about the firm, they still may not care. The fact that a firm is the oldest, largest firm or has the smartest employees will not mean much unless it can be related to clients' needs. To reach clients in a manner that appeals to them, the professional service provider must first understand what drives them, what their needs are, and what their expectations are. In this chapter we will describe the marketing tools the professional service firm must employ in order to better understand its customers and communicate with them in terms meaningful to them. We will explore the need for and value of a formal system of collecting, analyzing, and acting on marketing information. We will develop the components of a strong marketing information system: the internal records system, marketing intelligence system, marketing research system, and analytical marketing systems. We will also look at developing a customer satisfaction measurement program that is integral to serving customers better.

ASSESSING INFORMATION NEEDS

Most professionals recognize the value of information gathering in managing their business. Yet they attach less importance to conducting formal research. Many fall prey to the "just talk to people" syndrome. Although no one would argue that professionals should be talking with current and prospective customers, there are serious problems in relying on this method of gathering "information." First, the individuals they speak to may not be representative of their customer group. And because we all have a tendency to talk to people who are similar to us, the information that is collected by "just talking to people" is likely to support the person's preconceptions. This approach also typically is characterized by biased interviewing techniques. Finally, there are likely to be inconsistencies between how individuals are asked questions. A well-planned research program should eliminate these problems.

A good marketing information system should balance the information that managers would like to have against what they really need. The ideal first step is to interview managers to find out what they generally need to know. The costs of obtaining, processing, storing, and delivering information must be factored in. The firm must decide whether the benefits of having additional information are worth the costs of obtaining it. By itself, information has no worth; its value comes from its use. Collecting additional information that is not used is a waste of money and resources no matter how little one paid for it.

DEVELOPING MARKETING INFORMATION

The components of a firm's marketing information system (MIS) are illustrated in Figure 5-1. At the bottom of the chart is the marketing environment that an institution or organization must monitor—specifically target markets, marketing channels, competitors, publics, and key trends external to the firm. Using the firm's records and other data sources and conducting new research studies as needed, the firm develops analyses to

Figure 5-1. The Marketing Information System.

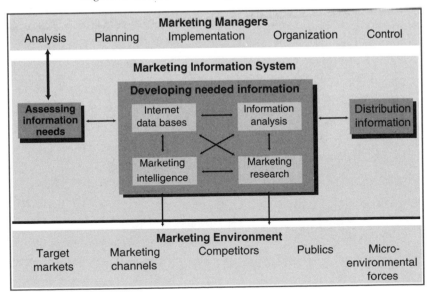

guide decision-making. This information then flows to the appropriate partners or managing directors to help them in marketing analysis, planning, implementation, organizing, and control. The resulting decisions and communications then flow back to the marketing environment, which must be continuously monitored.

Many professional service firms fail to see that internal records and marketing intelligence can play an important role in helping to identify and resolve marketing problems. Formal marketing research projects ideally build on a base of existing data and marketing intelligence, rather than starting from scratch.

Internal Data

The most basic information system is the organization's internal records system. Many firms have built extensive internal data bases, computerized collections of information obtained from data sources within the company. Those responsible for marketing should be able to readily access and work with information in the data base to identify marketing opportunities and problems, plan programs, and evaluate performance.

The internal records system should provide information on the organization's marketing efforts, including the number of phone calls, mailings, advertisements, meetings, proposals, presentations, and so on. Information should also be available about the responses to marketing actions, such as:

- The number of inquiries received
- The number of "short lists" made
- The number of new clients obtained
- The amount of new work obtained from old clients
- The number of communications received that express satisfaction or dissatisfaction with services
- The amount of billing generated

These data can be organized by type of client, supplying information that can be useful for deciding how to segment markets and how to choose targets. The data bases should also retain information about existing clients, such as their past history, the way they came to the organization, the club and association memberships they have, the names of other professionals they use, their ongoing and current problems, their activities and hobbies. Such information can prove valuable in trying to maintain their loyalty, in designing new services for them, and in deciding how to market toward others just like them.

The internal records system must be designed to serve the information needs of decision-makers in a timely and cost-effective way. One way to help design a needs-oriented MIS is to conduct periodic surveys of decision-makers to ascertain their perceived information needs. Once their opinions are gathered, the information system designers can design a system that reconciles (1) what decision-makers think they need, (2) what decision-makers really need, and (3) what is economically feasible. Table 5-1 provides a sampling of questions that can be asked of marketing decision-makers.

Table 5-1. Questionnaire for determining information needs of marketing decision-makers.

1. What types of decisions are you regularly called upon to make?
2. What types of information do you need to make these decisions?
3. What types of information do you regularly get?
4. What types of special studies do you periodically request?
5. What types of information would you like to get that you are not now getting?
6. What information would you want daily? weekly? monthly? yearly?
7. What magazines and reports would you like to see routed to you on a regular basis?
8. What specific topics would you like to be kept informed of?
9. What types of data analysis programs would you like to see made available?
10. What do you think would be the four most helpful improvements that could be made in the present marketing information system?

Gathering Marketing Intelligence

Whereas the internal records systems supply the decision-makers with information on the past, the marketing intelligence system supplies them with information on current happenings and emerging trends. We define a marketing intelligence system as follows:

> The *marketing intelligence system* is the set of sources and procedures by which managers obtain their everyday information about developments in the environment beyond their firm.

Gathering marketing intelligence is not a cloak-and-dagger operation. Most useful information is readily available. According to one specialist in intelligence for business corporations, 95 percent of the information companies need to make business decisions is available and accessible to the public.[2] Among the ways to learn about competitors are accessing public data bases, looking up financial statistics, reading company reports and public records, attending trade shows, and observing competitors' activities in the marketplace.

Most professional service organizations collect marketing intelligence in an informal way by having high-level people read trade and other publications and through having them carry on regular discussions with well-informed intermediaries, experts, and with clients themselves. Important developments are frequently identified through these procedures. However, an informal approach to intelligence-gathering can result in incomplete information or learning too late of some important developments, such as a new business opportunity with a large client or a pending shift in competitive strategy by a rival firm.

An organization can take some concrete steps to improve the quality of marketing intelligence available to its top people. First, the organization must "sell" its entire professional staff on the importance of gathering marketing intelligence and passing it on to others in the organization. Designing information forms that are easy to fill out and circulate can facilitate intelligence gathering. Examples of some forms are found in Exhibits 5-1 to 5-3.

Exhibit 5-1. Prospective Client Data Form.

BACKGROUND

Name of Prospect: _____

Company: _____

Address and Telephone Number: _____

_____

Classification code for industry, etc.
   (SIC or other): _____

Growth potential of industry: _____

Major products/services: _____

_____

Sales: _____

Number of employees: _____

Financial condition: _____

Major strengths: _____

Major weaknesses: _____

Major competitors: _____

Other key developments: _____

DECISION-MAKERS

Names	**Title**	**Affiliations**	**Our contact**
Managers:			
_____	_____	_____	_____
_____	_____	_____	_____
_____	_____	_____	_____
_____	_____	_____	_____

Board Members/Major Stockholders:

_____	_____	_____	_____
_____	_____	_____	_____

Bankers/Professionals Used:

_____	_____	_____	_____
_____	_____	_____	_____
_____	_____	_____	_____

Exhibit 5-1. Prospective Client Data Form (*cont.*)

POTENTIAL

Volume of Service Currently Being Used:

Type of Service	Yearly Hours	Professionals Used	Satisfaction
_____	_____	_____	_____
_____	_____	_____	_____
_____	_____	_____	_____

Potential Volume of Service per Year:

Type of Service	Yearly Hours
_____	_____
_____	_____
_____	_____

Competitors for this work: _____

_____

_____

OUR MARKETING PROGRAM

Our In-House Contact Person: _____

Needed Frequency of Contact: _____

_____

Core Marketing Strategy: _____

_____

_____

_____

_____

_____

_____

_____

_____

_____

_____

Exhibit 5-2. Key Intermediary Data Form.

Name of Intermediary: _____

Company: _____

Address and Telephone: _____

_____

Profession/Position: _____

_____

Our Previous Experience with Person:

Situation	Our Contact	Outcome

Ties to Prospective Client:

Client	Nature of Relation

Club-Association Affiliations:

Club Association	Our Contact

Our Person in Charge: _____

Needed Frequency of Contact: _____

Exhibit 5-3. Competitor Data Form.

Name of Competitor: _____

Address and Telephone: _____

_____

Number Partners/Staff: _____

_____

Stongest Markets:

Market   Major Clients

_____   _____

_____   _____

_____   _____

Directing Competing Services: _____

New Services or Areas Being Developed: _____

Reputation/Image: _____

Key Personnel:

Name   Title

_____   _____

_____   _____

_____   _____

Key Club/Association Memberships: _____

Major Strengths: _____

Major Weaknesses: _____

Fee Strategy and Hourly Rates: _____

Major Marketing and Promotion Activities: _____

Other Developments: _____

Our Person in Charge of Monitoring: _____

Intelligence-gathering can also be improved by setting up an individual or an office to coordinate and manage the activity. The coordinator would be responsible for (1) encouraging people in the organization to fill in their forms, (2) scanning major publications, with the help of the Internet, for news about competitors, clients, and relevant government actions, (3) soliciting suggestions and complaints about marketing from staff members, and (4) organizing a filing system for intelligence that will make the retrieval of past and current information relatively easy. The performance of these and other tasks would greatly enhance the quality of information available to marketing decision-makers.

Marketing Research

We define marketing research as follows:

> The systematic design, collection, analysis, and reporting of data relevant to a specific marketing situation facing an organization.

A professional service firm will occasionally need to commission specific qualitative or quantitative marketing research. Qualitative research is designed to be exploratory in nature and is not projectionable to a larger population (focus groups). Quantitative research is typically based on a random sample and is projectionable to a larger population (surveys). For example, a physician group may want to know its patients' attitudes toward its practice, or an architectural firm may want to determine its image among construction companies. Many studies can prove helpful to the firm in such cases, but the firm must know how to choose the marketing research projects carefully, design them efficiently, and implement the results effectively, especially when working with a limited budget.

The responsibilities of marketing researchers include carrying out studies of market potential, market share, customer satisfaction, and purchase behavior. Although having an on-staff marketing research professional offers certain advantages, very few professional service organizations have a full-service market research function. Instead, a person within the firm responsible for marketing research typically acts as liaison between the firm and research firms that have the capabilities of designing and executing the research.

Working with external marketing research firms has several advantages, including gaining access to a level of expertise that is not available within the professional firm, and they may be able to maintain objectivity in conducting research studies. Their expertise and objectivity can lead to higher response rates in surveys, more valid findings, and more creative interpretation of results.

Employing a marketing research firm can be done directly or indirectly. Indirectly, a consultant or advertising agency that has already been brought in to work on a particular project may suggest a research firm and coordinate its work. There are a few drawbacks to the indirect approach. Allowing a consultant or ad agency to contract with a marketing research firm adds on another layer of expenses for the professional service firm. Also, if the advertising agency has contracted with a marketing research company, it is likely that the solution to the problem under study is promotionally based. It may be more expedient to hire a marketing research firm directly. Information about outside marketing research firms is available from a number of sources, including the annual research issue of the weekly trade journal *Advertising Age;* the *Green Book*, published by the New York Chapter of the American Marketing Association; or the annual issue of *Marketing News*, known as Honemichal's 50. You can also find outside marketing research firms simply through networking within your own professional associations.

In choosing a marketing research firm, the most important criteria is "comfort."[3] The professional service firm must be comfortable with many facets of a relationship with a market research firm, including:

- How well the research firm understands the professional organization's issues and requirements.
- How well they answer questions.
- Their organization's resources.
- The way they do research—for example, do they have a proactive approach or a defined process?
- How innovative they are.
- How easy they are to do business with. Are they responsive and flexible?

- Overall costs, including the cost of the program development, implementation costs, and the cost of the professional service firm's reputation in the industry.

- Personal chemistry.

MARKETING RESEARCH PROCESS

Figure 5-2 shows the four basic steps in a sound marketing research project.

Figure 5-2. The Marketing Research Process.

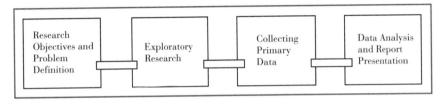

Research objectives and problem definition

The first step in research is to state the research objectives and define the problem they are intended to address. The overall objective may be to learn about a market and determine the most attractive program to offer in that market, or to measure the effect of a communication program. In any case, the problem guiding the research must be clearly specified. If the problem statement is vague, if the wrong problem is defined, or if the uses of the research are unclear, the research results may be useless or even misleading. Identifying the problem is more difficult than it seems. For example, stating that the firm's problem is that "its client retention rate is low" is not defining the problem; this is just a symptom of a problem. The problem may be that client satisfaction with some level of your service is poor, such as timeliness of service or responsiveness to questions. It could be a reliability issue that resulted from promising more than the firm delivered, or it could be related to costs in relation to competitors. To come up with useful answers, a problem must be clearly identified. One way to clarify the research objectives in advance is to use "backward" marketing research, shown in Figure 5-3. Alan Andreasen, developer of this approach, urges researchers and decision-makers to determine what decisions need to be made and what the final research report will look like *before* the research process is launched.

Exploratory Research

Before carrying out a formal research study, researchers often review secondary data, conduct observational research, and interview individuals in groups informally to arrive at a better understanding of the current situation.

Analysis of secondary data. Marketing researchers typically begin by gathering and reviewing secondary data if any exists. Secondary data has usually been collected for another purpose and is normally quicker and less expensive to obtain and is a good way for the researcher to determine a starting point. After analyzing the secondary data, the researcher can gather *primary data*, namely, original data collected to address the specific problem.

There are numerous sources of existing (or secondary) data:

1. INTERNAL RECORDS. The organization's internal record system should first be examined to identify relevant data. These might include information on existing or prospective clients, old proposals or reports, past marketing activities, and so on.

2. GOVERNMENT. The federal government publishes more marketing data than any other source in the country. Data found in the *Census of Population, Census of Housing, Census of Business, Census of Manufacturers, Census of Agriculture, Census of Minerals*, and *Census of Governments*, and special research reports issued at all levels of government, can prove to be invaluable sources of information.

3. TRADE PROFESSIONAL AND BUSINESS ASSOCIATIONS. Hundreds of associations regularly collect information about their members and about topics that interest their members. A professional service organization can often obtain valuable information about target markets and competitors' activities from its own associations. Additional valuable information can often be obtained by

Figure 5-3. The Process of "Backward" Marketing Research.

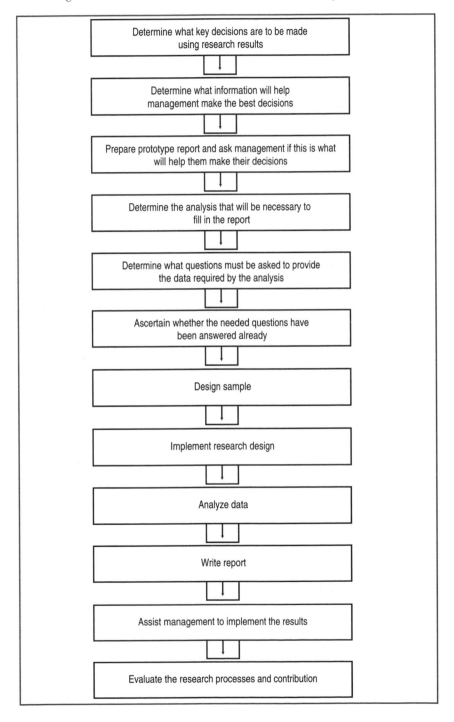

contacting and working with the associations of targeted clients. Thus, an engineering firm interested in obtaining clients from the coal industry would want to monitor and perhaps become involved with the activities of that industry's associations.

4. COMPETITORS AND OTHER PRIVATE ORGANIZATIONS. Although direct competitors will not make available their marketing research studies, it might be possible to obtain studies from less direct competitors, such as firms located in other regions or serving very different market segments. Moreover, professional service organizations might be willing to share old data on markets of mutual interest. Additional data can be obtained from large banks, which often publish studies on the economic prospects of their clients' businesses.

5. MARKETING FIRMS. Marketing research firms, advertising agencies, and media firms may possess old studies or syndicated data having considerable value.

6. UNIVERSITIES, RESEARCH ORGANIZATIONS, AND FOUNDATIONS. The range of issues and industries that have been examined by researchers in the more "intellectual" organizations is enormous. Such organizations can often be worthwhile sources of market data.

7. PUBLISHED SOURCES. Both the scholarly literature and the general business press can be helpful. Scholarly journals like the *Journal of Marketing, Journal of Marketing Research,* and *Journal of Consumer Research* are useful for obtaining general ideas about marketing strategy and marketing research methods. Trade and business periodicals like *Business Week, Advertising Age,* and *Fortune* also provide general ideas. More specialized magazines focusing on specific industries can stimulate thinking about more focused strategies and tactics.

8. ON-LINE DATA BASES AND INTERNET DATA SOURCES. By using commercial on-line data bases, marketing researchers can conduct their own searches of secondary data sources. A recent survey of marketing researchers found that 81 percent used such on-line services for conducting research.[4] Readily available on-line data bases exist to fill almost any marketing information need. For

example, a law firm that has a client interested in creating a con-
tractual agreement with a German company can check out
CompuServe's *German Company Library of Financial and
Product Information* covering more than 48,000 German-owned
firms. Just about any information a marketer might
need—demographic data, today's Associated Press news wire
reports, a list of active U.S. trademarks is available in on-line
data bases. See Exhibit 5.4 for more on on-line data bases.

Exhibit 5-4. On-line Data Base Services.

DIALOG offers several services, including ABI/INFORM, which provides information on business management and administration from more
than 800 publications. The site also provides access to full text reports and
newsletters from 50 industries and a collection of U.S. public opinion surveys. In addition, subscribers can view Dun & Bradstreet data, such as census statistics and business directories, by searching through Donnelly
Demographics and Dun's Electronic Business Directory.

LEXIS-NEXIS, in addition to providing access to articles from a wide
range of business magazines and journals, features in-depth research reports
from research firms, SEC filings, Standard & Poor's, and worldwide investment banks, and also provides access to legal information, statutes, etc.
Users can also access information from consumer goods and marketing trade
publications. The service also includes PROMT/PLUS, which tracks competitors and industries, identifies trends, and evaluates advertising and promotion techniques.

CompuServ provides a variety of on-line data base services. For example, its *Business Demographics* files summarize statistics on state employees
by industry codes and categorizes retail trade businesses by employee
counts. By mining the *Neighborhood Report*, a user can access summaries of
the demographics of any ZIP Code in the U.S. Other CompuServ data bases
offer full-text articles, news releases, and market and industry research
report indices. The service also provides access to an additional 850 data
bases ranging from newspapers and newsletters to government reports and
patent records.

Dow Jones News Retrieval specializes in providing in-depth financial,
historical, and operational information on public and private companies.
The site offers Standard & Poor's profiles as well as Dun & Bradstreet and
company reports. In addition, the service compares stock price, volume, and
data on companies and industries, and summarizes same-day business and
financial stories from both the United States and Japan.

In spite of the abundance of secondary data, there are limitations. First, the specific information the marketing researcher needs may not exist. Second, the secondary data must be carefully evaluated to make sure it's relevant, accurate, current, and impartial. It often becomes necessary to move beyond secondary data and collect exploratory primary data. Typically this is done through observational research or qualitative interviewing

Collecting Primary Data

Observational Research. One way to collect primary data is by carrying out personal observation in various situations. Office staff members might observe patients in the waiting room to ascertain their comfort level, how they spend their time waiting, or even whether the physical layout is conducive to minimizing the waiting time. An architect might visit a client's present office spaces to observe how the client's employees work, interact, and function. This information may help him or her design the client's new office space more efficiently. Observational research is done to suggest issues to explore in more depth as well as qualitative interviews for more formal research studies.

Qualitative Interviewing. Researchers often need to conduct some interviews during the exploratory stage of a marketing research project. Interviewing should be aimed at uncovering new qualitative information rather than obtaining quantifiable results. Exploratory interviews are typically open-ended to stimulate respondents to share their thoughts and feelings regarding the issue being studied.

Qualitative research can be used (1) to probe deeply into consumers' underlying needs, perceptions, preferences, and level of satisfaction; (2) to gain greater understanding of marketing problems the causes of which are not known; and (3) to develop ideas that can be further investigated through quantitative research. Qualitative research is not only a desirable first step, it is sometimes the only step permitted by limited budgets, and it can often reveal important insights that help sharpen the market researcher's understanding of important issues. Quantitative research, on the other hand, seeks to produce statistically reliable estimates of particular market or consumer characteristics, and usually entails interviewing or surveying a much larger number of people than does qualitative research, and it assumes that the interviewer knows in advance what specific questions to ask.

When seeking information about individuals, the researcher could conduct individual interviews or group interviews. *Individual interviewing* can be done in person or over the telephone. One-on-one interviews can be used to probe very deeply and are especially useful when the subject can be emotionally charged, because group conformity could bias the responses. In-depth individual interviews are also ideal for soliciting the viewpoints or insights of experts because they allow for spending more time with each.

Group interviewing consists of inviting a focus group of eight to ten people to gather for a few hours with a trained interviewer to discuss a program, service, or institution. The group interviewer needs objectivity, some knowledge of the subject matter of the study, and an understanding of group dynamics and consumer behavior; otherwise, the results can be worthless or misleading.

Group interviews are typically held in pleasant surroundings—a hotel meeting room or a home, for example—and refreshments are served to increase the informality. Sometimes representatives of the commissioning organization will observe the focus group from behind one-way glass, but this requires use of a special facility.

The interviewer starts the group interview with a broad question related to the research theme. For example, in a study of the changing role of accounting, clients might be asked, "What services does the ideal accounting firm provide?" Questions would then move to the subject of how well accountants in a given firm do in providing certain services, other services they might provide, and so on.

The interviewer must encourage free and easy discussion among the participants, hoping that the group dynamic will bring out real feelings and thoughts. At the same time, the interviewer "focuses" the discussion (hence the name *focus group interviewing*). The focus group's comments must be recorded through note-taking or tape-recording, and then studied to understand the participants' attitudes.

Focus group interviewing had long been one of the major marketing research tools for gaining insight into customer thoughts and feelings.

In many cases, the results of focus group interviews are used to guide the development of survey instruments or marketing experiments.

In spite of the significant value of focus group research, we would not recommend developing a marketing strategy based on the information from focus groups alone. Participants in focus groups are not necessarily representative of the target market, and because they are typically paid for their time, fed, and find the process entertaining, they may be in a more positive frame of mind and thereby give more favorable answers than they otherwise would give.

Survey Research. Many marketing managers take an overly simplistic view of survey work. They think that it consists of writing a few obvious questions and finding an adequate number of people in the target market to answer them. Yet amateur research is liable to produce many errors that can waste anywhere from $5,000 to $50,000 of the organization's funds. Designing a reliable survey is the job of a professional marketing researcher. Here we will describe the main things that users of marketing research should know about developing the research instrument, the sampling plan, and the fieldwork.

There are a number of different types of market research studies the professional service firm may wish to consider. Among these are:

- Perception or image studies (probing how the firm is viewed by current, past, and prospective clients).

- Competitive positioning studies (comparing the firm with competing firms on a range of quantitative and qualitative criteria by current, past, and prospective clients).

- Performance evaluations (analyzing current and past clients' experience with the firm).

- Issues studies (examining clients' viewpoints regarding specific issues, such as billings and collections, in-house engineering, and evaluation of key managers).

- Reference checks (verifying what past clients say to prospective clients).

- Market demand/supply studies or trends analysis (investigating potential services for the firm).

- Geographic studies (identifying locations for regional offices).

- Acquisition/merger/teaming research (identifying and evaluating prospective firms for strategic alliances).[5]

How this information is collected will be examined later in the chapter.

The main survey instrument is the questionnaire. The construction of good questionnaires calls for considerable skill. Every questionnaire should be pretested on a pilot sample of individuals before being used on a large scale. A professional marketing researcher can usually spot several errors in a casually prepared questionnaire. (See Exhibit 5-5.) One of the most common errors in survey questionnaires occurs in the *types of questions asked*. For example, often questions that cannot be answered, would not be answered, or need not be answered are included in the questionnaire, and other questions that should be answered are omitted. Each question should be checked to determine whether it is necessary in terms of the research objectives. Questions that are just interesting should be dropped (except for one or two to start the interview) because they lengthen the time required to complete the survey and try the respondent's patience.

Survey questions can be either open-ended or closed-ended, and the type of questions asked can make a substantial difference to the response. An *open-ended question* is one in which the respondent is free to answer in his or her own words. An example would be "What is your opinion of engineering consulting firms?" The problem with open-ended questions is that the answers can be quite diverse, making it difficult to classify results and summarize findings. This is not a problem with *closed-ended questions*. But closed-ended questions can be too leading, putting ideas for responses in people's minds that might not have arisen with an open-ended question. Closed-ended questions can also force people into responding with answers that do not truly reflect their feelings. Some of these problems can be alleviated by conducting telephone surveys where the respondent does not see the list of potential responses and allowing for the respondent to provide an answer not on the list. However, in this instance the researcher must balance the cost of adding an open response to the potential value of the answer. Some examples of types of open-ended questions are in Table 5-2. Examples of closed-ended questions are in Table 5-3.

Exhibit 5-5. A Questionable Questionnaire.

Suppose a child psychologist had prepared the following questionnaire to use in interviewing the parents of a new patient. How would they address each question?

1. What is your income to the nearest one hundred dollars?

   People don't usually know their income to the nearest one hundred dollars, nor do they want to reveal their income that closely. Moreover, a researcher would never open with such a personal question.

2. Are you a strong or weak supporter of "time out" intervention?

   What does strong or weak mean?

3. Does your child behave himself well at home?

   Yes   No

   Behave is a relative term. Furthermore, are yes and no the best options for this answer?

4. How many temper tantrums has your child had in the last year?

   Who can answer this?

5. What are the most salient and determinant attributes in your evaluation of your child's behavior?

   What are "salient" and "determinant" attributes? Don't use big words!

6. Do you think it's right to deprive your child of the opportunity to grow into a mature, healthy person through therapy?

   A loaded question, given the bias, how can anyone say "yes"?

Table 5-2. Open-Ended Questions.

1. What is your most important criteria for choosing a lawyer and why do you feel this way?
2. What is your decision process when choosing an accounting firm?
3. What motivated you to switch physicians?
4. What impact, if any, does having CPA accreditation have on your choice of an accountant?
5. Why are you considering plastic surgery?

Table 5-3. Closed-Ended Questions.

Name	Description	Example
Dichotomous	A question offering two answer choices.	"My firm plans on expanding its facilities in the next five years." Yes ❑ No ❑
Multiple choice	A question offering three or more answer choices.	"What sources did you use in choosing a physician?" ____ No one ____ Family member ____ Friend ____ HMO list Advertisement ____ Other_____
Likert scale	A statement with which the respondent shows the amount of agreement/ disagreement.	"Women physicians are more empathetic to the needs of female patients than male physicians." Strongly disagree 1 Disagree 2 Neither agree nor disagree 3 Agree 4 Strongly agree 5
Semantic differential	A scale is inscribed between bipolar words, and the respondent selects the point that represents the direction and intensity of his or her feelings.	"Smith Consulting is" Large . . . . Small Expensive . . . . . .Inexpensive Global in scope . . . . Domestic in scope
Importance scale	A scale calling for rating the importance of some attribute from "not at all important" to "extremely important."	"For me, having a law firm with international offices is" Extremely Important 1 Very Important 2 Somewhat Important 3 Not Very Important 4 Not at all important 5
Rating scale	A scale calling for rating some attribute from "poor" to "excellent"	"The law firm of Smith Smith and Jones legal staff is:" Excellent 1 Very good 2 Good 3 Fair 4 Poor 5

The *choice of words* used in a survey questionnaire also calls for considerable care. The researcher should strive for simple, direct, unambiguous, and unbiased wording. Other "do's" and "don'ts" arise in connection with the *sequencing of questions* in the questionnaire. The lead questions should create interest, if possible. Open-ended questions are usually better here. Difficult, sensitive, or personal questions should be introduced toward the end of the interview, in order not to create an emotional reaction that may affect subsequent answers or cause the respondent to break off the interview. The questions should be asked in as logical an order as possible in order to avoid confusing the respondent. Classificatory data on the respondents—such as the size of their firm or the number of years they have been working in their present position—are usually asked last.

Questionnaires have to be tailored to the specific research problems facing an organization. There is no single questionnaire that will obtain desired data for all professional service organizations. However, Exhibit 5-6 contains a sample questionnaire that could be adapted by many accounting, law, consulting, or architectural engineering firms to obtain valuable information about prospective clients.

The other element of research design in conducting a survey is creating a sampling plan, which calls for four decisions.

1. *Sampling unit.* Who is to be surveyed? The proper sampling unit is not always obvious from the nature of the information sought. Should it be the usual initiator, influencer, decider, user, purchaser, or someone else? For example, in choosing a pediatrician, whose opinions or influence will probably be the most important? Is it the mother's, the father's, perhaps the mother-in-law's, or is it a joint decision?

2. *Sample size.* How many people should be surveyed? Large samples obviously give more reliable results than small samples. However, it is not necessary to sample the entire market or even a substantial part of it to achieve satisfactory precision. Samples amounting to less than a fraction of one percent of a population can often provide good reliability, given a creditable sampling procedure. To determine sample size, it is important to know exactly what the objectives are and the possible relationship between sample units, among other things. Researchers often use too large of a sample because they have not adequately analyzed the situation.

Exhibit 5-6. Client Behavior Questionnaire.

Hello, my name is _____ and I'm helping to conduct a research project for _____ on the way _____ professional services are searched for and used by people like yourself. This is purely a research study designed to obtain the kind of information about client decision-making that will allow _____ to continue serving its clients well in the future. We are sampling only a small, randomly selected group of persons and pledge to keep all their responses strictly confidential. If I could have no more than 10 minutes of your time to ask a few short questions, it could make a valuable contribution to our study. Most people find our questions to be interesting and enjoyable to answer. Would this be a convenient time?

I.   GENERAL OPINIONS
   1. In general, what is your opinion of _____ (lawyers, CPAs, etc.)?

   2. Please tell me how much you agree with each of the several statements I will read to you. Do you STRONGLY AGREE, AGREE, NEITHER AGREE NOR DISAGREE, DISAGREE, or STRONGLY DISAGREE with each of the following statements:
      a. _____ (lawyers, CPAs, etc.) vary greatly in their skills.
      b. It is difficult to find a good _____.
      c. _____ generally charge too much for their services.
      d. _____ rarely finish a project by the time they have promised.
      e. _____ should be allowed to advertise.

II. PRIOR EXPERIENCES
   1. Have you or your organization used the services of a (lawyer, CPA, etc.) during the last 12 months?
      a. Yes   b. No (Go to Section III.)
   2. Were all the _____ you used ones you had used in previous years?
      a. Yes   b. No
   3. Was this the first time you have ever used a _____?
      a. Yes   b. No
   4. What first stimulated you to seek the services of a _____?
      a. An advertisement
      b. An article you read
      c. A comment by a friend or business associate
      d. An uninvited call or visit by a _____
      e. Other (please specify)

Exhibit 5-6. Client Behavior Questionnaire (*cont.*).

5. What first led you to consider using the services of a new or different _____ during the last 12 months?
   a. A desire to pay lower fees
   b. A desire to obtain better quality service
   c. A desire to obtain more prompt services
   d. A desire to find a more friendly _____
   e. Simply a desire for a change
   f. Other (please specify)
6. How satisfied overall are you with the services you have received
   during the last 12 months from _____?
   a. Very Satisfied
   b. Satisfied
   c. Neutral
   d. Dissatisfied
   e. Very Dissatisfied

III. CURRENT PRACTICES
   1. Please give the titles of the people in your organization who tend to
      (or would tend to) become involved in decisions using _____
      (lawyers, CPAs, etc.).
   2. How important would the following attributes be in any future
      choices you might make among _____? Please answer by stating
      VERY IMPORTANT, IMPORTANT, OF SLIGHT IMPORTANCE, or
      NOT IMPORTANT AT ALL.

a. Reputation	VI	I	OSI	NIAA
b. Fees	VI	I	OSI	NIAA
c. Location	VI	I	OSI	NIAA
d. Experience with problems similar to yours	VI	I	OSI	NIAA
e. Size of firm	VI	I	OSI	NIAA

   3. How many hours of a _____'s time do you expect to require
      over the next 12 months?
      a. None
      b. Less than 20
      c. 21 to 50
      d. 51 to 100
      e. More than 100 (please specify amount) _____
   4. For what types of projects are you most likely to require a _____'s
      services over the next 12 months? Over the next 3 years?

Exhibit 5-6. Client Behavior Questionnaire (*cont.*).

IV. SPECIFIC OPINIONS
    1. Have you ever heard of the following _____ (lawyers, CPAs, etc.)?
        a. Firm A
        b. Firm B
        c. Firm C
        d. Firm D
    2. How do you feel Firm A rates on the following attributes? Would you say that it rates VERY GOOD, GOOD, NEITHER GOOD NOR BAD, BAD, or VERY BAD on each attribute?

a. Reputation	VG	G	N	B	VB
b. Fees	VG	G	N	D	VB
c. Location	VG	G	N	B	VB
d. Experience with problems similar to yours	VG	G	N	B	VB
e. Size of firm	VG	G	N	B	VB

    3. How do you feel Firm B rates on the following attributes? (Repeat sequence)

V. CLASSIFICATION DATA
I'll conclude with just a few questions about you and your organization that we need answered in order to classify responses into groups. Let me remind you that all information will be kept strictly confidential.
    1. Which category does your organization fall into in terms of its annual sales volume?
        a. Under $100,000
        b. $100,000 to $500,000
        c. $500,001 to $750,000
        d. $750,001 to $1,000,000
        e. Over $1,000,000
    2. Which category does your organization fall into in terms of its number of employees?
        a. Under 20
        b. 20-100
        c. 101-500
        d. Over 500
    3. What are the major products and services sold by your organization?
    4. What is your position in the organization?
That completes the interview. Thank you very much for your help.

3. *Sampling procedure.* How should the respondents be chosen? To draw valid and reliable inferences about the target market, a random probability sample of the population should be drawn. Probability, or random, sampling allows the calculation of confidence limits for sampling error. However, probability sampling is almost always more costly than non-probability sampling. Some marketing researchers feel that the extra expenditure for probability sampling could be put to better use, such as designing better questionnaires and hiring better interviewers to reduce response and non-probability sampling errors. (See Table 5-4.)

4. *Means of contact.* How should the subjects be contacted? The choices are telephone, mail, or personal interviews. *Telephone interviewing* stands out as the best method for gathering information quickly. It also permits the interviewer to clarify questions if they are not understood. The main drawback of telephone interviewing is that only relatively short, rather impersonal, interviews can be carried out. The *mail questionnaire* may be the best way to reach persons who would not give personal interviews or who might be biased by interviewers. On the other

Table 5-4. Types of Samples.

A. PROBABILITY SAMPLES:

Simple random sample. Every member of the population has a known and equal chance of selection.

Stratified random sample. The population is divided into mutually exclusive groups (such as age groups), and random samples are drawn from each group.

Cluster (area) sample. The population is divided into mutually exclusive groups (such as city blocks), and the researcher draws a sample of the groups to interview.

B. NON-PROBABILITY SAMPLES:

Convenience sample. The researcher selects the easiest, most available members of the population from whom to obtain information.

Judgment sample. The researcher uses his or her judgment to select population members who are good prospects for relevant information.

Quota sample. The researcher finds and interviews a prescribed number of people in each of several categories (e.g., age, sex, education level).

hand, mail questionnaires require simple and clearly worded questions, and the return rate is usually low and/or slow. *Personal interviewing* is the most versatile of the three methods. The personal interviewer can ask more questions and can supplement the interview with personal observations. Personal interviewing is the most expensive method and requires more technical and administrative planning and supervision.

Experimental Research. The experimental research method is being increasingly recognized in marketing circles as the most rigorous and conclusive one to use in collecting primary data if the proper controls can be exercised and the cost afforded. The method requires selecting matched groups of subjects, giving them different treatments, controlling extraneous variables, and checking on whether observed differences are statistically significant. To the extent that the design and execution of the experiment eliminates alternative hypotheses that might explain the same results, the researcher and marketing manager can have confidence in the conclusions.

Experiments could be used in many ways, such as

1. To test the effectiveness of different direct-mail pieces by sending them to different, matched groups of subjects.
2. To test the effectiveness of different advertisements by running them in different regional editions of the same publication.
3. To test the effectiveness of different ways of requesting cooperation with a survey by making different requests to different matched groups of subjects.

Data Analysis and Report Presentation

The final step in the marketing research process is to develop meaningful information and findings to present to the decision-maker who requested the study. The words *meaningful information* are key here. Consider the following thoughts:

The difference between data and information is that while data are crudely aggregated collections of raw facts, information represents the selective organization of those facts. . . . Good data about customers, converted meaningfully into good information, have the power to improve strategic decisions in the right directions.[6]

In analyzing primary data, keep in mind the following points:

1. The analysis plan should be developed before any customer data are gathered. How the data will be analyzed will depend on what information is being sought and will have a great impact on the types of questions that should be asked.

2. In order to determine how the data will be analyzed and the type of data that must be collected, these key questions must be answered by the marketing researcher prior to collecting customer data.

   What decisions must be made and/or action taken based on the results?

   Who will make these decisions?

   What information will be required to support the preceding decisions/actions?

   What data must be gathered and how can these data be transformed into actionable information?

   These are all examples of the type of "backward" research we discussed earlier. Again, identifying these answers will give us a better idea on how to construct our overall research.

3. In any type of research project there are typically four approaches to analyzing the data. The first summarizes characteristics of a measure or set of data. For example, *What's the average size of a firm that employs our accounting agency?* The second way of analyzing data is to compare two or more measures or sets of data. An example of this would be a physician's office comparing satisfaction scores between their male patients and female patients. The third approach to analyzing data is to determine the association or relationship between two or more measures and/or sets of data. For example, an architectural firm may want to know if there is a relationship between individual

satisfaction scores after a project and one's overall satisfaction level with the firm. The last approach to analyzing data is to make projections about one measure or set of data based upon at least one other measure or set of data. Can a legal firm make projections about the amount of money their clients will spend with them in the following year based upon their customer satisfaction scores this year? Most issues addressed through analysis will require two or more of the preceding approaches.

The researcher's purpose is not to overwhelm decision-makers with numbers but to present findings that will help him or her make better marketing decisions. Before preparing the written report, the researcher should think about the reader's perceptual style (quantitative? visual?), level of research sophistication, and role in the institution.[7] Most research reports would be better understood if authors gave greater attention to creating easy-to-grasp visual displays of their results.

The marketing research report should clearly describe the following:

1. The objective or principal question the research was designed to answer
2. The research questionnaire or experimental procedure
3. The characteristics of the sample
4. The qualitative and/or quantitative results
5. Clear statements of the research findings
6. The implications of the research findings
7. Recommendations for action

In addition to preparing a written report, the researcher should meet with the decision-makers who requested the study to go over the major findings of the research and to explain the recommendations. This meeting is an opportunity to make sure the results are clearly understood before any action plans are implemented.

The decision-maker is then responsible for charting a course of action that will help the organization to gain the most benefit from the research. Unfortunately, many research studies end up filed away and ignored because the decision-maker didn't understand the results, or the time for action passed while the research was in progress, or because there are inadequate resources to implement the recommendations.

On the other hand, much competently conducted research never gets used in decision-making because some decision-makers experience "analysis paralysis," fearful of making decisions without "complete" knowledge of "all" the facts. Some decision-makers keep gathering more information to make the "best" decision, when they should use the information already at hand to make better decisions with greater efficiency. At other times, when there is turnover in administrators or managers, the existence of these studies may be forgotten or overlooked.

Marketing research can help the institution to be more effective, but only if the process is purposeful and timely, and the results are put to good use.

Information gathered by the company's marketing intelligence and research systems often requires more analysis and sometimes managers may need more help to apply the information to their marketing problems and decisions. This help may include advanced statistical analysis to learn more about both the relationships within a set of data and their statistical reliability. Such analysis allows managers to go beyond means and standard deviations in the data and to answer questions about markets, marketing activities, and outcomes.

Information analysis might also involve a collection of mathematical models that will help marketers make better decisions. Each model represents some real system, process, or outcomes. These models can help answer the questions of *what if* and *which is best.*

CUSTOMER SATISFACTION RESEARCH

While customer satisfaction research employs both qualitative and quantitative techniques, we believe it is so important to the area of professional services marketing that it needs to be highlighted on its own. As we have discussed throughout the book and will develop in even more depth in Chapter 13, one of the most important steps a professional service firm can take is to develop relationships with its clients. Customer satisfaction research measures the strengths of those relationships.

Current interest in customer satisfaction research is largely an outgrowth of the rise of customer-driven quality. The term *customer satisfaction research*, however, is not easily defined. In one sense, all consumer and marketing research is customer satisfaction research. Frequently, the terms *customer satisfaction research* and *customer satisfaction measurement* are used interchangeably. For our purposes we will refer to customer satisfaction measurement as the "measure of the extent to which a service's perceived performance matches the buyer's expectations."

Five of the most common customer satisfaction measurement objectives are:

1. *To get closer to the customer.* The intent is to improve understanding of the customer's needs, preferences, and priorities.

2. *To measure continuous improvement from the customer's perspective.* The intent is to determine if the continuous improvement efforts by total quality management are resulting in improved perceptions by the customer.

3. *To solicit customer input as the driver for product and/or process improvement.* The intent is to use the customer as a source of innovation and as a partner in improvement efforts.

4. *To measure competitive strengths and weaknesses.* The intent is to guide strategy by providing external benchmark data that identify areas of distinctive competence or areas of strategic weakness.

5. *To link customer service measurement data to internal performance and reward system measures.* The intent is either to determine the relationship between customer satisfaction and employee satisfaction or financial performance, or to reward desired outcomes (an improved customer satisfaction level).[8]

Customer Satisfaction Measurement as a Closed Loop

The closed loop process of customer satisfaction measurement involves four steps that provide a basic model for measuring and managing customer satisfaction, retention, and security. Properly implemented, the process will ensure that customer input drives an organization's effort to improve and innovate and that the impact of these efforts can be accessed. See Figure 5-4.

Figure 5-4. Closed Loop Process.[9]

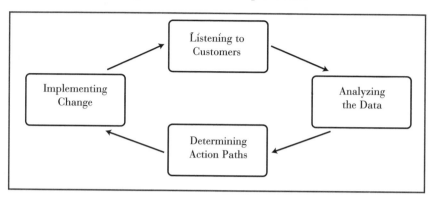

Step 1: Listening to customers

The first step in the process involves listening to customers. The data provided by customers furnishes the lifeblood of the process. It is important to realize that there are many different customers whose input should be considered. In addition to the immediate customer, in other words the client, there can be internal customers, such as other departments within the organization. In order for a client to be satisfied, departments within the firm must work to provide timely service to each other. Measuring the quality of service between departments as a group is therefore very important. Finally, there is the employee as a customer. Because services are inseparable from those delivering them, and employees have such a strong impact on the profit service chain, it is important to measure their level of satisfaction as well. An employee is likely to treat clients the way the employee perceives himself or herself to be treated and it's virtually impossible for an unhappy employee to treat clients in a consistently friendly manner.

A common characteristic of exemplary systems is the use of multiple customer and market "listening posts," or ways of listening to the customer. The use of multiple customer and marketing listening posts is critical, because no individual approach is without limitations. As Len Berry points out in **On Great Service**, "a combination of approaches enables a firm to tap the strengths of each and compensate for weaknesses."[10] A brief description of customer and market listening posts include:

- *Inbound customer comments and complaints.* Although most consumers don't bother to provide either positive or negative feedback (see Chapter 3), those who do should be paid attention to. They are typically individuals who are extremely satisfied or extremely dissatisfied with the service they received. In either case, the fact that they are providing the feedback, even if it's a complaint, demonstrates a predisposition on their part to maintain the relationship, because if they didn't, they would just move on to another service provider rather than make the effort to make their feelings known. All customers' comments, good or bad, should be captured and the customers should be thanked for their time and efforts.

- *Service business reviews.* This is a qualitative technique whereby on some fixed basis, typically once a year, someone from the firm—ideally the managing director or one of the partners—meets individually with the firm's best customers to interview them about their level of satisfaction with the firm during the past year. The interviewer should ask specific questions about what the firm did well and ways in which it can improve. This interview also provides the firm with the opportunity to learn valuable information about its clients' needs that it might be able to satisfy in the coming years. More than anything else, taking the time to have a high-level representative from the firm sit down one-on-one with customers shows that the firm truly cares about the relationship. Although it's impossible to conduct such interviews with all clients, it's important to do so with those who mean the most to the future of the organization.

- *Customer advisory panels.* It may be useful to organize a panel of clients to meet on a quarterly basis. This advisory panel should provide feedback about the firm as well as information regarding strategic moves competitors may be making, and to gain insight about changes in the marketplace. Members of customer advisory panels should be rotated on and off on a regular basis so as to keep a fresh perspective and avoid the problem of having panel members see themselves as part of the firm rather than as clients.

- *Focus groups and in-depth interviews.* Both of these have been discussed earlier in the chapter. They are both excellent techniques to identify the issues important to clients and uncover problems before they get too big.

- *Transaction surveys.* It is not a bad idea to send out a survey at the end of every project completed for a client. This survey will measure and identify strengths and weaknesses in the process the firm uses to deliver its services. For example, clients can be asked about the strength of communications, the timeliness of completion, as well as their overall satisfaction with the result. Such surveys can identify problems that otherwise may not be uncovered and can allow the firm to implement a service recovery program.

- *Comprehensive customer/market expectation survey.* One of the most important types of research an organization can do is a comprehensive survey taken at least once a year. Typically, this survey covers three important areas. First, it measures relative importance of different variables in the minds of clients. For example, clients can be asked such questions as: *How important is credentialing in choosing consultants? How important is price when making decisions about services? How important is a Web page as a form of communication?* Second, this type of survey identifies how well a firm is doing in delivering on expectations. Finally, the survey can be used to determine how well competitors are perceived to be delivering on the same performance issues. It is important to stress, again, that this survey should be conducted on a regular basis; hopefully, at least once a year. Some might wonder why this survey is necessary if the firm is using other types of listening posts, such as business reviews, advisory panels, or transaction surveys, but allow us to illustrate a point. Think of an annual occasion in an individual's personal life—a birthday or holiday, for example—when family pictures are typically taken. Putting these annual pictures side by side makes it possible for the observer to notice changes that may not be evident otherwise. For example, one member of the family may be taller, another grayer, another older, and another thinner. These are changes that one wouldn't observe in his or her day-to-day interactions with family members. The same is true within an organization where professionals may be so focused on day-to-day activities that they don't see the slow and gradual changes that may be occurring in the marketplace or among clients. Therefore, it is wise to take an annual snapshot of how well the firm is doing. (The strategic use of this survey will be further developed in Chapter 6.)

- *Problem-tracking surveys.* Comprehensive and transaction surveys many times uncover a problem that appears to be persistent within the organization. Whether it's responsiveness, timeliness, or communication issues, one is likely to implement some form of corrective action. At the same time, you do not wish to wait an entire year to find out if you have solved the problem. Therefore, you may do more focused and frequent pieces of research on that particular issue until you are satisfied that it has been corrected.

- *Former customer surveys.* One of the most important and most underused types of research is that of surveying former or lost customers. A professional service firm will have a very difficult time maintaining a high retention rate of clients if it doesn't know why clients leave the firm. Because this kind of research can be psychologically difficult to conduct, many firms choose to sidestep it. With this kind of survey, the client is being asked why he or she rejected the firm, and the firm must be ready to listen, objectively, to the answers.

Step 2: Analyzing the data

The second step in the customer satisfaction measurement process consists of analyzing the data. Data analysis centers on transforming and integrating customer data in order to define priorities and targets for improvement, innovation, and decision support. We have already discussed the basics of data analysis previously in the chapter. Below are some common questions for analysis of customer data:

- What is our current level of overall client satisfaction and loyalty?
- Which service features are most important to our clients?
- Which ones drive client satisfaction and loyalty?
- What are the key client problems or complaints?
- Which problems do the most damage?
- What is the financial bottom-line impact of customer satisfaction and/or dissatisfaction?
- Which areas should be targeted and given priority with regard to improvement, innovation, and resource allocation?

Step 3: Determining action paths

The third step in the customer satisfaction measurement process involves determining action paths for areas targeted for changes as a result of analyzing customer data. Failure to implement this step effectively is a leading cause of an ineffective customer satisfaction measurement process.

The process of determining action paths involves the following three steps.

1. Identifying the individuals responsible for each issue or area targeted for improvement and innovation.
2. Assessing those individuals' as well as the organization's readiness to take action for each area targeted for improvement. For example, if the firm determines that quality improvement initiatives must be implemented, the initiatives will fail if top management is not totally behind them.
3. Developing an action plan for areas targeted for changes.

Step 4: Implementing Change

The fourth step in the process involves actual implementation of improvement efforts, innovations, and/or organizational change. This may include such things as:

- Developing new products or services to further address clients' changing needs.

- Implementing training and developing initiatives so that all members of the firm understand the implications of their behavior and/or efforts with regard to maintaining clients.

- Making changes in internal and customer or market communication systems to improve the efficiency and effectiveness of one's communications.

- Revising reward and recognitions systems. If one wants customer satisfaction, one has to reward its employees to satisfy its clients. If the firm wishes to retain clients and develop long-term relationships, it needs to compensate for that, more than rewarding bringing in new clients.

Closing the Loop: Back to Listening to the Customers

The process comes full circle, when after developing and implementing improvements based on prioritization of customer inputs, an attempt is made to gauge the impact of such efforts by once again gathering data from customers and/or market listening posts.

In closing, we will identify the reasons most customer satisfaction measurement efforts fail. According to Randy Brandt, Senior Vice President for Burke Customer Satisfaction Associates in Cincinnati, Ohio, these reasons are:

1. Failure to involve the right persons in developing the customer satisfaction measurement process, such as customers and customer contact personnel and survey sponsors, owners, and users.

2. Failure to design customer and marketing listening posts capable of producing actionable data.

3. Failure to translate customer/market data through analysis into information that provides necessary answers or decision support.

4. Failure to link customer data and changes in customer dis/satisfaction metrics, to quality, operational, and financial or marketplace performance data.

5. Absence of a formal, closed-loop process for measuring and managing customer satisfaction and loyalty. In other words, the parties responsible for measuring customer expectations and satisfaction are disconnected from the parties who are responsible for managing customer expectations and satisfaction.[11]

SUMMARY

Every professional service firm must identify its marketing issues, then gather marketing information to clarify the nature of the problems and guide its marketing activities. The necessary work can be done within the firm by professional staff or with the help of outside consultants. Marketing research takes time and money; therefore, when setting the budget for marketing research, the decision-makers should consider the magnitude and the urgency of the issue and the likelihood of useful research results.

Four systems make up the marketing information system. The first is the internal records system, which consists of all the information the institution gathers in the regular course of its operation. It includes information on clients' service offerings and finances. Many research questions can be answered by analyzing the information in the internal records system. So far, however, few firms systematically gather and organize their records to make them useful for decision-making.

The second, the marketing intelligence system, describes the set of sources and procedures by which administrators obtain their everyday information about developments in the marketplace. An institution can improve the quality of its marketing intelligence by motivating its employees to scan the environment and report useful information and by hiring intelligence specialists to find and disseminate information within the firm.

The third, the marketing research system, consists of a systematic design, collection, analysis, and reporting of data, in findings relevant to specific marketing situations. The marketing research process consists of four steps: developing the research objectives and problem definition; exploratory research; formal survey and/or experimental research; and data analysis and report presentation. Each step involves a series of judgments about which questions must be answered and the most appropriate methods of obtaining needed information.

The fourth part of the marketing information system is the analytical marketing system, which consists of analyzing the relationships within a set of data and their statistical reliability in implementing quantitative models that help make better marketing decisions.

Customer satisfaction research is the lifeblood of developing and maintaining relationships with clients. It typically uses a closed-loop methodology that consists of listening to customers and clients through listening posts, analyzing the data received, developing actions paths based upon the analysis, and implementing changes.

NOTES

[1] Adapted from "Going After Law Firms as Clients," by Stuart Kahan. *The Practical Accountant* (February 1997), v30, p48.

[2] Fuld, Leonard, cited in "Competitive Intelligence: A New Grapevine," *The Wall Street Journal* (March 12, 1988), B2.

[3] "Introduction to Marketing Research," The Training & Development Center, Burke, Inc. (2000).

[4] "Researching Researchers," *Marketing Tools* (September 1996), p35-36.

[5] Kogan, Raymond F. "Straight from the Source," *Journal of Management in Engineering* (March/April 1995), p13-15.

[6] Leavitt, Theodore. *The Marketing Imagination*, New York: Free Press, 1983, p138.

[7] Ewell, Peter T., "Putting It All Together: Four Questions for Practitioners," *Enhancing Information Use in Decision Making, New Directions for Institutional Research*, No. 64, San Francisco: Jossey-Bass (Winter 1989), p85-90.

[8] Naumann, E. and Giel, K., *Customer Satisfaction Measurement and Management*, Thompson Executive Press, 1995, p12.

[9] This model is borrowed from Burke Customer Satisfaction Associates, a division of Burke, Inc., and used with permission.

[10] Berry, Leonard. *On Great Service*, New York: Free Press, 1995, p35.

[11] Brandt, D. R. "Build Actionability Into Your Customer Surveys," Institute for International Research, 6th Annual Conference on Measuring and Improving Customer Satisfaction, Las Vegas, June 12-14, 1995.

6 Strategic Planning and Organization

"Most people skate to where the puck is, I skate to where the puck is going to be."
WAYNE GRETSKY
Hockey hall of famer

THE STRATEGIC MARKETING PLANNING PROCESS

Strategic planning may be relatively new to most professional service firms. We define strategic planning as follows:

Strategic planning is the process of developing and maintaining a strategic fit between the organization's goals and capabilities and its changing marketing opportunities. It relies on developing a clear institutional mission, supporting goals and objectives, sound strategy, and appropriate implementation.

This definition suggests the appropriate steps a professional service firm can take to improve its effectiveness. This chapter presents an overview of the strategic planning process. (See Figure 6-1.) Just as "customer centeredness" is the right way of "thinking" about marketing, the strategic marketing planning process is the right way of "doing" marketing.

Strategic planning is organized in three stages. First, the professional service firm must carry out an analysis of the current and expected

At age seventy-two, Norman Lipshie, founding father of Weber, Lipshie and Company (once the 35th largest U.S. accounting firm), was handling consulting and bankruptcy work at a smaller company. He had intended to enjoy retirement, but he lost his entire savings in a rescue attempt of Weber Lipshie. Unfortunately, Norman's experience is not isolated. Since 1982 approximately one-half of the mid-sized accounting firms have either gone out of business or been acquired.

Public accounting firms are not the only victims. A large number of mid-sized consulting firms are also losing clients. Gemini Consulting went from being one of the fastest growing management consulting firms in 1992 to an industry laggard. In 1995, its domestic revenue fell 23 percent and 150 of its 850 U.S. consultants were released and research spending was reduced. Mid-sized firms such as Gemini Consulting were too big to develop profitable niches the way smaller firms do and too small to become sufficiently involved in the fast-growing information technology environment.

Competition in accounting has never been so intense and predictions indicate that competition will escalate further. Local and regional CPA firms are especially affected, being squeezed from above by large public firms and from below by non-CPA firms.

Big Five accounting firms, under profit pressures and potentially stagnating revenues, actively seek new clients. Corporate downsizing by large corporations and merger activity has effectively shrunk their client base. Consequently, large accounting firms, in need of new business, actively compete with mid-sized accounting firms for new business. Big Five firms are especially competitive due to their wide array of services and their ability to spend millions of dollars on new technology to develop new products. (And the Big Five just keep getting bigger. Worldwide revenues of all Big Five firms increased 20 percent to $59.5 billion for fiscal 1998 from $49.6 billion in 1997. This increase compares with growth of 14.5 percent in 1997, 11.6 percent in 1996, and 16.7 percent in 1995.)

Big Five accounting firms have ample capital to weather periods of poor financial results. Being international, Big Five firms can take a loss in one region and make it up in another region, something local and regional firms cannot duplicate. The Big Five's size and international reach also allow them to provide services for companies involved in geographical expansions. Local and regional firms may not be able to provide timely services for companies dispersed throughout the country or the world.

The loss of a mid-sized corporation's annual audit and advisory services fee can represent a significant portion of a local and regional firm's annual revenue. When Weber Lipshie's audit client Empire Brush Company was acquired by Rubbermaid Company, it switched to KPMG Peat Marwick, Rubbermaid's auditor. The loss of Empire's $500,000 annual fee proved fatal for Weber Lipshie.

Mid-sized accounting firms are also finding competition from non-CPA accounting firms. Fueled by American Express's legal success, permitting non-CPA firms to employ CPAs, non-CPA accounting firms are presenting increased competition, particularly for local and regional public accounting firms. These non-CPA accounting firms frequently have lower overhead and can underprice many local and regional firms. What they lack in an array of services can be made up by attractiveness of price. Their success is evidenced by the fact that four of the ten fastest-growing U.S. accounting firms are non-CPA firms. It may be just a matter of time before reviews and audits fall to non-CPA firms, as long as they pass the peer review process.

Certainly, public accounting firms, particularly local and regional firms, face significant obstacles in an increasingly hostile environment. Without proper strategies and goals, these firms could fail or be forced to merge with other firms to survive.[1]

Figure 6-1. Strategic Planning Process Model.

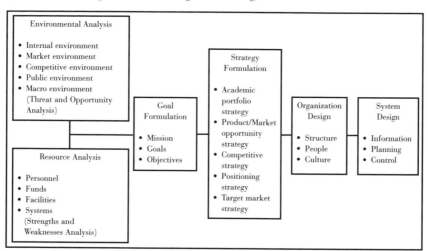

environment. Second, the firm must set its goals and objectives and strategy (choice of target markets and marketing mix). Third, the firm must set and carry out its implementation plan.

In this chapter we will discuss the analysis of the internal and external environments and an overview of strategy formulation. In the next two chapters we will consider strategy, targeting, and positioning (STP).

Performing an Internal and External Audit

The first step of strategic planning is to understand the firm's internal and external environment. The process of developing this understanding can be, especially the first time it is being done, a very long and arduous task. However, it is a very important task. Understanding the firm's internal and external environment is the bedrock on which all strategies should be formulated. The better one is at this step of the process, the more likely one will be able to develop strategies and tactics that will ultimately prove successful. The more one knows about his or her own capabilities and understands the environment in which they operate, the more he or she should be able to anticipate scenarios and outcomes with a higher probability. Pete Gillen, at the time of this writing, is head coach at the University of Virginia. He likes to tell a story that as a young assistant coach with Digger Phelps at Notre Dame, he was given the assignment of scouting Bobby Knight and the Indiana basketball team. He attended several games, took copious notes, and came back ready to answer any questions Coach Phelps might ask him. The first question he received, however, shocked him. Coach Phelps wanted to know what kind of basketball the Indiana team used, and Pete had to admit he didn't know the answer. Digger Phelps went on to explain that because they would be playing Indiana at Indiana, it was important to understand every idiosyncracy of their court. Coach Phelps felt that every brand of basketball had its own feel and it was important to practice with the ball they would be using in the game. A very successful coach in his time, Digger Phelps understood that a plan was only as good as the assumptions it was based upon.

Assessing the Firm's Internal Environment

A firm engaged in marketing planning needs to consider four resource issues associated with its internal environment.

- Its institutional environment and character;
- Its stage in the institutional life cycle;
- Its potential for adaptation; and
- Its tangible resources and market assets.

Institutional Environment and Character

Every firm has an environment, character, or culture. This culture has been shaped by such factors as its original mission, early history, the firm's geographical location, size, past success, and the match between the institution's offerings and its market. A firm's management and marketers can often learn a great deal by reviewing the firm's history. What were the economic, social, and other forces that inspired the founding of the firm and maintained the organization in the past? Have these forces changed? What is the organization's distinctive character? Has this changed?

The firm's culture can be a help or a hindrance to its survival and growth. For example, a physician group with an entrepreneurial culture can respond quickly to rapid changes occurring in the healthcare environment. On the other hand, a very conservative Midwest law firm may find that its style of management and decision-making does not transfer well when it opens a branch office in Los Angeles.

Institutional Life Cycle

Organizations, like everything else, have a beginning and end. Ideally, those two points are not too close together in time. Figure 6-2 shows the four main stages in the life cycle of a typical firm. The institution is founded at some point and grows slowly (the introduction stage). If successful, a period of growth follows (the growth stage). The growth eventually slows down and the institution enters maturity (the maturity stage). If it fails to adapt to new conditions or reestablish a sense of direction, it will enter a period of decline (the decline stage). The duration of a firm's life cycle may be relatively short or it may last for multiple decades.

Figure 6-2. Typical S-shaped Life-Cycle Curve.

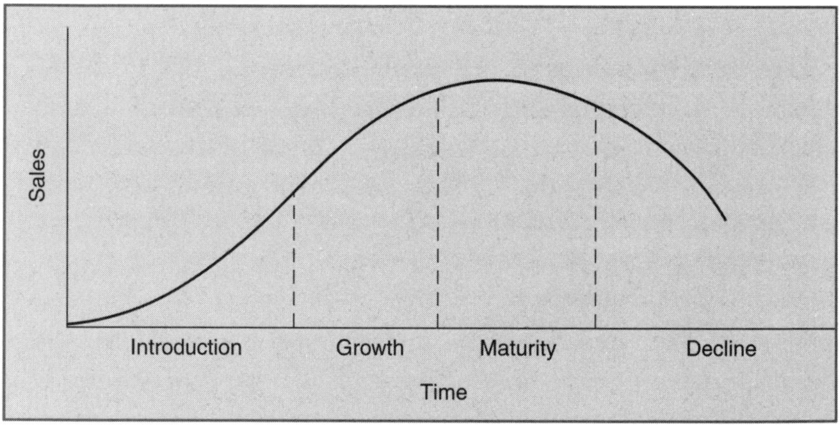

Organizations that pass through maturity and go into decline are usually those that failed to adapt to changing circumstances. One of the major contributions of a marketing analysis is to identify new opportunities by which an institution can return to a period of healthy growth or enjoy an extended maturity. An adaptive institution is ready to revise its mission, goals, strategies, organization, and systems when warranted by changing opportunities. In doing so, the adaptive institution extends its life cycle (see Figure 6-3). For example, if a law firm had anticipated the growth of the Internet, the firm would have likely positioned itself and developed the skills necessary to provide expert legal advice regarding intellectual property.

Figure 6-3. Extending the Firm's Life Cycle.

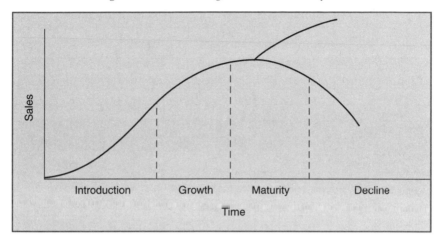

Preparing a Resource Analysis

A professional service firm should prepare a resource analysis to identify its strengths and weaknesses. It should pursue goals, opportunities, and strategies congruent with its strengths, and avoid those where its resources are too weak. Figure 6-4 shows a resource analysis checklist suitable for the professional service firm. The major resources listed are people, money, facilities, systems, and market assets. Management indicates whether its position with respect to each resource constitutes a strength (high, medium, low), is neutral, or constitutes a weakness (low, medium, high). Suppose that based on this analysis, a firm believes that it has adequate and skilled professionals who, unfortunately, are not very enthusiastic, loyal, or service-minded. As for money, the firm has several big corporate clients who are very loyal, because of old ties to certain partners, and who provide a base amount of revenues that the firm can rely upon to avoid financial problems—at least for the near future. The firm's physical facilities are somewhat lacking, with no spare office space to allow for firm growth, a poor library, antiquated filing and typing equipment (with only limited word-processing capabilities), and an inconvenient location for both staff members and clients. Its management systems for information, planning, and control are quite weak. Finally, the firm is in a relatively strong position with respect to clients, contacts, and general reputation.

Figure 6-4. Organization Resource Analysis.

(H = high; M = medium; L = low; N = neutral; checks are illustrative)

Resources	Strength			N	Weakness		
	H	M	L		L	M	H
People							
1. Adequate	✓						
2. Skilled	✓						
3. Enthusiastic							
4. Loyal							✓
5. Service-minded						✓	
Money							
1. Adequate		✓					
2. Flexible					✓		
Facilities							
1. Adequate							
2. Flexible							
3. Location quality						✓	
Systems							
1. Information system quality					✓		
2. Planning system quality							
3. Control system quality						✓	
Market assets							
1. Client base							
2. Contact base	✓						
3. General reputation		✓					

In considering opportunities, this organization should generally avoid those for which necessary resources are weak or inadequate. For example, if a law firm is considering making a bigger commitment to tax law, but has few staff members with good accounting backgrounds and/or tax experience, then the idea should be dropped. However, if the firm's other resources can support it, then an organization may be able to obtain experienced people and might proceed in this direction.

As a clue to its best opportunities, the organization should pay attention to its *distinctive competencies*, which are those *resources and abilities that the organization is especially strong in.* If a law firm happens to have two people who are well known and experienced in handling large negligence cases, then it might want to consider expanding its practice in this area. Organizations will find it easiest to work from their existing strengths rather than trying to build up a more balanced set of strengths.

At the same time, a distinctive competency may not be enough if the organization's major competitors possess the same distinctive competency. Thus, an organization should pay close attention to those strengths in which it possesses a *differential advantage*—that is, where it can outperform competitors on that dimension. For example, a law firm may not only have a distinctive competency in antitrust law, but by having a former commissioner of the Federal Trade Commission as a firm partner, it may have a differential advantage in pursuing clients who face FTC complaints. The differential advantage permits the firm to build a sustainable competitive position in the marketplace.

In evaluating its strengths and weaknesses, the professional service organization should not rely on its own perceptions, but should go out and do an *image study* of how it is perceived by its key publics. For example, an architectural firm may believe it designs beautiful modern office buildings, but an image study may reveal that facilities managers perceive the firm as designing sterile, unimaginative, expensive glass boxes. Image studies frequently yield surprising findings that challenge the managers.

One tool that is useful in identifying the organization's strengths and weaknesses is the Importance/Performance Matrix. The first step is to identify those attributes that are important to one's clients in the delivery of a given service. Consider a plastic surgery practice seeking to identify attributes that clients deem as important when choosing a plastic surgeon. A focus group might yield the following factors: cost, payment plans, board certification, location, years of experience, reputation, free consultation, and computer imaging. A quantitative study is then carried out where respondents are asked to rate the importance of each attribute and the practice's perceived performance on each attribute. It is also helpful to include the perceived performance of competitors on the same attributes. Figure 6-5 shows an example of an Importance/Performance grid for this fictitious plastic surgery practice prepared for potential male clients. (A separate Importance/Performance grid should be prepared for each market segment.) First, price is seen to be very important to this segment, and

Figure 6-5. Importance/Performance Matrix.

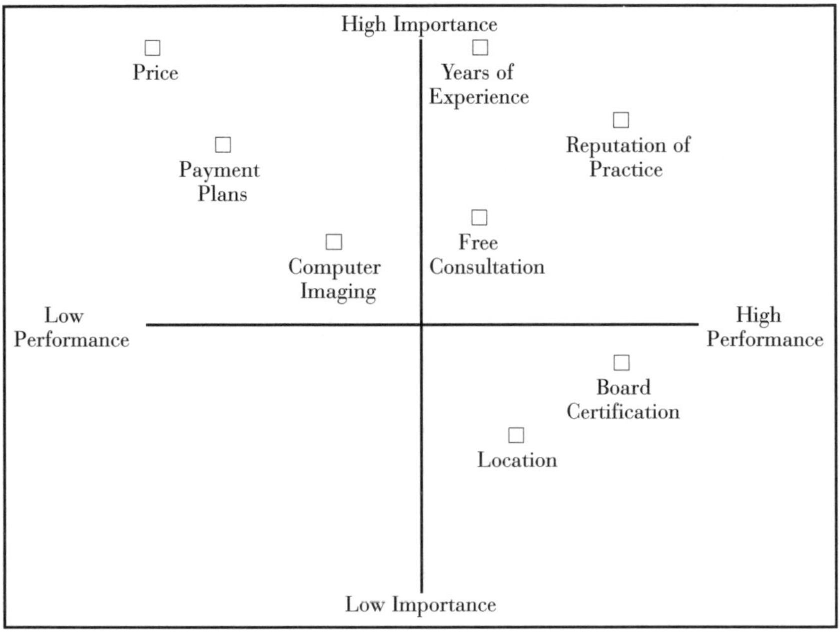

this particular firm appears to be on the expensive end. At the same time, the position of the payment plan on the grid indicates that this organization is also not developing methods that allow patients to conveniently pay for the services. It would behoove the practice in this situation to develop more convenient payment plans and thereby move that box into the right-hand top quadrant. Another potential strategy could be identified by the fact that board certification is not seen as that important. It appears that all the plastic surgeons in this particular group are board certified. One strategy would be to educate their public as to the importance of board certification, thereby positioning themselves in a stronger competitive light. Reputation is seen as something that is both important and that this firm possesses. This could be the differential advantage that the practice wants to use in its communications, providing that its competitors are not seen as having an even stronger reputation.

Assessing the Firm's External Environment

The marketer operates in a constantly changing environment with the following three components:

1. Public environment—consisting of publics that take an interest in the activities of the focal organization.

2. A competitive environment—consisting of groups and organizations that compete for attention and the loyalty of the audiences of the individual firm.

3. The macro environment—consisting of large-scale forces that shape opportunities and pose threats to the organization, specifically demographic, economic, technological, political, and social forces.

Publics

Every professional service organization has several publics and must manage responsive relationships with most or all of them. We define a public in the following way:

> A **public** is a distinct group of people and/or organizations that has an actual or potential interest in and/or impact on an organization.

It is fairly easy to identify the key publics that surround a particular organization. Not all publics are equally active or important to an organization. A mutually *welcome public* is a public that likes the organization and whose support the organization welcomes. A *sought public* is a public whose support the organization wants but that is indifferent or negative towards that organization. An *unwelcome public* is a public that is negatively disposed towards the organization and that tries to impose constraints, pressures, or controls on the organization.

Publics can also be classified by their functional relation to the organization. Figure 6-6 represents such a classification. An organization is viewed as a resource conversion machine in which certain input publics supply resources that are converted by internal publics into useful goods or services that are carried by intermediary publics to designated consuming publics.

Not all publics are equally active or important to an organization. Publics emerge because the organization's activities or policies may draw support or criticism from outside groups. Figure 6-6 presents a classification of the publics of a healthcare organization such as a hospital.

Figure 6-6. The Main Publics of an Organization.

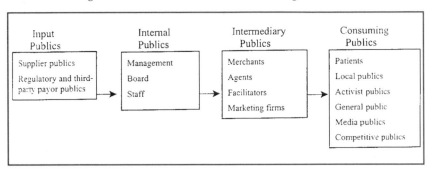

We can distinguish four types of publics. The first are input publics who mainly supply original resources and constraints to the organization, such as suppliers and regulatory publics. Suppliers are those organizations that sell needed goods and services to the focal organization, in this case, physician offices. Regulatory publics consist of those who impose rules of conduct on the organization, such as the federal government or the American Medical Association.

Second are the internal publics who refine and carry out the organization's strategy, such as the managers and staff.

Third are intermediary publics who assist in promoting and distributing services to final consumers. These can include other referring physicians or the hospital that provides the physician with discounted office space.

Fourth are the consuming publics such as the patients and their families and friends.

Let's look at the various publics more closely.

Input Publics

Input publics mainly supply original resources and constraints to the organization, and can consist of suppliers and regulatory and third-party payer publics.

Suppliers. Suppliers are those organizations that sell needed goods and services to the focal organization. A local university might "sell" customer service training to the staff of a physician's office or legal practice. A marketing research firm may sell its research expertise to a professional service firm in order to help that practice achieve its strategic goals.

Regulatory and third-party payor organizations. A second input public consists of regulatory publics. The regulatory publics of a medical practice include federal, state, and local government agencies, medical associations, and various board certification accreditation associations. The focal organization must monitor these organizations and be ready to argue against regulations that will harm its ability to create value for clients. Healthcare providers such as physicians who do not rely entirely on self-paying patients must also include third-party payors such as HMOs in this input public.

Internal Publics

The various inputs are managed by the professional service organization's internal publics to accomplish the organization's mission. The internal publics consist of at least three groups: management, a board of directors, and staff.

Management. Every organization has a management group that is responsible for running the organization, reporting to the top manager, a president, or chief administrator, or high-level managers who are organized by function, products, markets, and/or geographical area. For example, a law firm may have a number of partners reporting to a senior partner. These partners may be responsible for offices in different cities or be responsible for functional lines, such as the development and retention of clients in intellectual property, real estate law, or merger and acquisition.

Board of Directors. The president and management group may be responsible to a board of directors. Traditionally, the primary function of many boards of directors has been defined as overseeing the organization and assuring that it is operating efficiently to reach its objectives. Among a board's more important responsibilities may be:

1. selecting or approving the chief officer of the firm;
2. participating in setting or approving long-range strategy for the firm;
3. developing or approving policies for the conduct of organizational affairs;
4. developing or approving compensation levels and salaries of high management; and/or
5. considering major issues that have come before the firm.

Because of their important role, board members must be carefully selected. Organizations must make trade-offs between prestigious members (who may miss a number of meetings and not be able to do much work because of their other obligations) and working members. The management of some professional service firms may seek "window dressing boards" that do not interfere with the management's plans. These are boards in name only because they do not fulfill the primary responsibilities of a board as outlined above. Other firms prefer a more active and participatory board structure.

Staff. The staff consists of employees who generally work on a paid basis. It may include middle management, administrative support, maintenance and housekeeping crews, receptionists, information systems employees, as well as other types. Professional service marketers face the same challenge as managers of any other industry in building an effective staff: defining job positions and responsibilities, recruiting qualified people, training them, motivating them, compensating them, and evaluating them.

Intermediary Publics

The focal organization enlists other individuals and organizations called *marketing intermediaries* to assist in promoting and distributing its goods and services to the final consumers. There are four types of marketing intermediaries: merchants, facilitators, agents, and marketing firms. Because professional service firms produce services and not products, merchants and facilitators generally play a less important role than agents and marketing firms.

Merchants. Merchants are organizations such as wholesalers and retailers that buy, take title to, and resell the merchandise. For example, a franchisee might make an arrangement with a franchisor to buy, promote, and use its legal software in order to provide the franchisor's service to its own clients.

Facilitators. Facilitators are organizations such as transportation companies, communication firms, and real estate firms that assist in the distribution of products, services, or messages. They do not take title or negotiate purchases. An example would be a local physician, lawyer, or even certified public accountant working with the local welcome wagon in order to distribute promotional literature to new residents within a geographic area.

Agents. Agent middlemen are organizations or individuals who find and/or sell to buyers the organization's products or services without taking possession of the product or service. In a traditional product setting, manufacturers' representatives or brokers are agents. They are hired by the focal organization and paid for their services.

The term commonly used in professional service organizations for an agent's role is a *referral*. Referrals are one of the major forms of promotion in many professional service settings. A general practitioner who refers a patient to a specialist is certainly helping to promote that specialist's practice, but at the same time is neither hired nor paid by the specialist for their agent service.

Marketing firms. Marketing firms are organizations such as advertising agencies, marketing research firms, and marketing consulting firms that assist in identifying, developing, and promoting the service firm's products and services to the right markets. A legal practice may hire the services of these types of firm to identify attractive, new sites for its practice, to identify and help research new services to present to potential clients, and to create promotional strategies for the new centers and new services.

Consuming Publics

Various groups consume the output of the organizations: clients, local publics, activist publics, the general public, and media publics.

Clients. Clients represent an organization's primary public, its reason to be. Management expert Peter Drucker has long insisted that the only valid purpose of a business is to create a customer. He would propose that hospitals exist to service patients, while accounting, legal, and engineering firms exist to serve their respective clients.

Local publics. Every firm is physically located in one or more areas and comes in contact with local publics such as neighborhood residents and community organizations. These groups may take an active or passive interest in the activities of the organization.

Many service firms develop a community relations position. The role of the staff member in this position is to monitor the community, attend meetings, answer questions, and make contributions to worthwhile causes. Responsive organizations do not wait for local issues to erupt. They make investments in the community to help it run well and acquire a bank of goodwill.

Activist publics. Many professional service firms, such as lawyers, are increasingly being petitioned by consumer groups, business round-tables, and other public interest groups for certain concessions or support. Witness the recent calls for tort reform within the legal practice. Organizations would be foolish to attack or ignore the demands of activist publics; instead, responsive organizations can either train their management to include social criteria in their decision-making or assign a staff person to stay in touch with these groups and to communicate more effectively the organization's goals, activities, and intentions.

General public. Professional service firms must also be concerned with the attitude of the general public towards their activities and policies. Although the general public does not act in an organized way towards organizations as activist groups do, members of the general public do hold images of many organizations, images that affect patronage and legislative support.

Media publics. Media publics include media companies that carry news, features, and editorial opinion—specifically newspapers, magazines, radio, and television stations. Most professional service organizations are acutely sensitive to the role played by the press in affecting their capacity to achieve their marketing objectives. All service firms normally would like more and better press coverage than they get. Getting more and better coverage calls for understanding what the press is really interested in. The effective press relations manager knows most of the editors in the major media and systematically cultivates a mutually beneficial relationship for both of them. The manager offers interesting news items, informational materials, and quick access to top management; in return, the editors are likely to give the organization more and better coverage.

Competitive publics. Most, although not all, professional service organizations face competition. An organization must be sensitive to the competitive environment in which it operates. That competitive environment consists not only of similar organizations or services but also of more basic forces. For example, a consulting firm may face competition directly from firms similar to itself, but it may also experience competition from other types of professional service firms, such as accounting firms that provide consulting as an ancillary service. The consulting firm may also face competition from non-traditional sources such as a local university.

Competitive Environment

Many professional service firms fail to appreciate the extensive competition they face. First, they face other firms in the same line of work competing for the same customers or clients. Second, they face competitors from non-traditional sources. Management consultants are facing competition from major accounting firms; physicians are facing competition from holistic alternative medicine firms; and CPA firms are facing competition from non-CPA firms.

Professional service firms must have a thorough understanding of the strengths and weaknesses of the competitors they have identified. What type of resources do the competitors have? What are their advantages and expertise? What are their opportunities and constraints? Once again, the Importance/Performance Matrix might be helpful in identifying these issues.

The Macro Environment

It is crucial for the professional service firm to understand the broad forces creating the world in which they must operate. These broad forces can be divided into demographic, economic, technological, political/legal, and social/cultural categories. While these forces are uncontrollable, they must be monitored and their potential impact considered. For example, a downturn in the economy would adversely affect architects because construction activity would subside, but the same downturn may favor divorce attorneys by leading to a higher divorce rate. And changing demographics would have a considerable impact on physicians. For example, an aging population might lead more new physicians to focus on gerontology rather than pediatrics.

THE MARKETING AUDIT

A useful tool for assessing the internal and external environment of the firm is the marketing audit. We define the marketing audit as follows:

> A **marketing audit** is a *comprehensive, systematic, independent,* and *periodic* examination of an organization's marketing environment, objectives, strategies, and activities, with the view of determining problem areas and opportunities and recommending a plan of action to improve the organization's strategic marketing performance.

Its specific characteristics are:

1. *Comprehensive.* The marketing audit covers all the major marketing issues facing an organization, rather than only one or a few marketing trouble spots. The latter would be called a functional audit if it covered only advertising, pricing, or some other marketing activity.

2. *Systematic.* The marketing audit involves an orderly sequence of diagnostic steps covering the organization's marketing environment, internal marketing system, and specific marketing activities. The diagnosis is followed by a corrective action plan involving both short-run and long-run proposals to improve the organization's overall marketing effectiveness.

3. *Independent.* The marketing audit is normally conducted by an inside or outside party who has sufficient independence to attain top management's confidence and the needed objectivity.

4. *Periodic.* The marketing audit should normally be carried out periodically instead of only when there is a crisis. It promises benefits for the organization that is seemingly successful, as well as the one that is in deep trouble.

The person or team who carries out the marketing audit collects secondary data and also interviews managers, clients, intermediaries, and others who might throw light on the organization's marketing performance. A guide to the kinds of questions that the marketing auditor will raise is included in the Appendix at the end of this chapter. Not all the questions are important in every situation. The instrument will be modified depending on whether the professional service organization is a law firm, architectural firm, accounting firm, medical practice, or other.[2]

ANALYZING ORGANIZATIONAL MISSION, OBJECTIVES, AND GOALS

A major step in strategic planning consists of the organization determining its mission, goals, and objectives. These terms are defined as:

- **mission**—the basic purpose of an organization, that is, what it is trying to accomplish.

- **goal**—a major variable that the organization will pursue, such as market share, profitability, or reputation.

- **objective**—a goal of the organization that is made specific with respect to magnitude, time, and responsibility.

Mission

The mission statement defines the core purpose of the firm. It guides the firm's day-to-day business as well as the paths it takes in the future. In fact, it might be helpful to think of the mission of an organization as being similar to an individual's self-concept. For example, if a person thinks of himself as shy and timid, that's typically how he will act. If someone thinks of herself as a risk taker, she is likely to take risks. If an individual is put in a situation that is outside his psychological comfort zone, in other words, outside the realm of how the individual typically thinks of himself or herself, it will produce anxiety that will lead the individual to make every effort to move back within the confines with which he or she is comfortable. How an organization defines itself works in the same manner. It answers the question: *What business are we in?*

The mission statement is the strongest force in an organization for a number of reasons. Number one, it is the first criteria by which new products and services are evaluated. As an idea might arise to add a service to an organization, if it does not match the mission, it is not likely to be further pursued. Second, top management typically develops mission statements. In many cases it may be difficult for an individual who is lower in the organization to suggest a product or service that is not in line with the mission, or even more boldly, to suggest that the business the firm should be in is different from the one that is now stated.

A good mission statement typically has three components. It says *what the organization does, for whom, and in what context.* For example, a family practice physician might craft a mission statement as follows: *To provide healthcare to high-income families in the Greater Cincinnati area utilizing a holistic, nurturing approach.* This mission is specific in that the physician is in the business of providing healthcare; it clearly identifies the target market of high-income families in the Greater Cincinnati area; and it provides the framework by which the physician operates, that of holistic medicine. From a managerial prospective, the mission statement works because it is short and can be easily memorized. It is therefore useful in providing clear direction to staff members as well.

Goals

The organization's goals are the variables that it will emphasize. For example, in 1997 Medical Mutual of Ohio had the following goals.[3]

- "To position the company as the best healthcare insurer and processor in each market where it operates.
- Perform and be perceived as a leader in the service delivery of healthcare benefits administration.
- Become the healthcare benefits administrator of choice.
- Develop business opportunities outside the state of Ohio.
- Seek other revenue-generating and profit opportunities."

It is unlikely that Medical Mutual of Ohio can give equal emphasis to all these goals. In any given year it might choose to emphasize certain goals depending on management's perception of the major problems facing the organization at the time.

Objectives

The organization's goals should be stated in an operational and measurable form known as objectives. The goal of Medical Mutual of Ohio, for example, might be to increase enrollment in the next fiscal year by 15 percent. A good objective has the following characteristics: It is measurable; it is time bound; it is realistic; and it has organizational buy-in. If the objective is not measurable, one will never know if it was achieved. If it is not time bound, then management can claim that the goal will still be reached later. If it is not realistic, then the organization is destined to fail at this goal. If the staff does not accept the objective, it will not be achieved.

STRATEGY FORMULATION

The firm's mission, goals, and objectives define where the organization wants to go. The question then becomes how best to get there. The organization needs a "grand design" for achieving its goals. This is called *strategy*. Strategy involves choosing a basic plan. It is to be distinguished from tactics that amount to specific actions and assignments for carrying out the strategy.

In developing its strategy, the organization should proceed in two stages. First, it should develop a service portfolio strategy, defining its current major services. Second, it should develop a service/market expansion strategy, to indicate what new services and markets to add.

Service Portfolio Strategy

Most professional service organizations are multiservice operations. The different services offered will vary in their importance and contribution to the organization's mission. It is important for an organization to periodically evaluate its portfolio of services and make hard decisions about the future of services it offers.

The first step in portfolio analysis is to identify the key services of the organization. For example, a management consulting firm might provide government contract services, expert legal testimony, corporate strategy consulting, and new product feasibility studies. The firm then has to determine which services should be given increased support *(build)*, maintained at the present level *(hold)*, phased down *(harvest)*, and terminated *(divest)*. The idea is that the firm's resources should be allocated in accordance with the current and future "attractiveness" of each service rather than equally to all services. The task is to identify appropriate criteria for evaluating the attractiveness of various services. Different schemes have been proposed. We will examine one of them.

Boston Consulting Group Portfolio Approach. One of the most popular portfolio evaluation approaches was developed by the Boston Consulting Group (BCG). Its scheme called for rating all of the organization's products or services along two dimensions, namely *market growth* and *market share*. Market growth is the annual rate of growth of the relevant market in which the product or service is sold. Market share is the organization's revenues as a ratio to the leading firm's revenues. By dividing market growth into high growth and low growth, and market share into high share and low share, four types of services emerge (see Figure 6-7):

Figure 6-7. Boston Consulting Group Portfolio Approach.

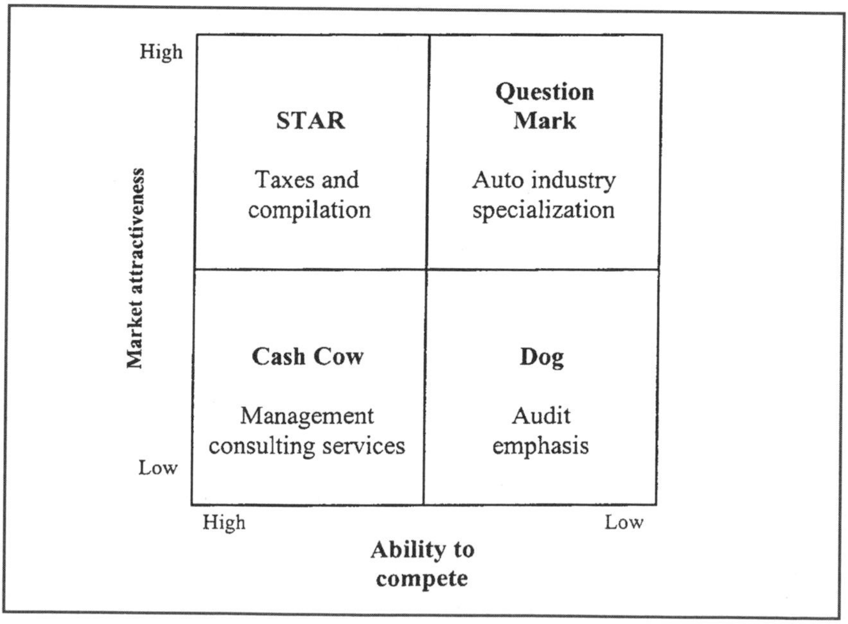

1. An organization's *stars* are those services for which the organization enjoys a high share in fast-growing markets. The organization will pour increasing resources into its stars in order to keep up with the market's growth and maintain its share leadership.

2. An organization's *cash cows* are those services for which the organization enjoys a high share in slow-growth markets. Cash cows typically yield strong cash flows to an organization and pay the bills for those other services that lose money. Without cash cows, an organization would need continuous subsidy.

3. An organization's *question marks* are those services for which the organization has only a small share in a fast-growing market. The organization faces the decision of whether to increase its investment in its question-mark services, hoping to make them stars, or to reduce or terminate its investment, on the grounds that the funds could find better use elsewhere in the business.

4. An organization's *dogs* are those services that have a small market share in slow-growth or declining markets. Dogs usually make little money or lose money for the organization. Organizations often consider shrinking or dropping dogs unless those services should be offered for other reasons.

Applying this scheme, a law firm might find that its negligence law practice was a star, its marital law practice was a cash cow, its tax law practice was a question mark, and its real estate law practice was a dog. The BCG evaluation is useful for organizations interested in tracing the cash implications of their portfolios. High revenues generate cash and high growth consumes cash.

While the Boston Consulting Group Matrix and other formal methods revolutionized strategic planning, such approaches still have limitations. They could be difficult, time consuming, and costly to implement. Management may find it difficult to define strategic business units and measure market share and growth. In addition, these approaches focus on classifying current business but provide little advice for future planning. Management must still rely on its own judgment to set the business objectives for each service line and determine what resources to allocate to each.

Service/Market Expansion Strategy

As a result of examining its current portfolio of services, a professional service organization might discover that it does not have enough stars or cash cows and that it must become more aggressive in searching for new services and markets. What the firm needs is a systematic approach to identifying growth opportunities that can supplement the opportunity analysis discussed earlier. A useful device for doing this is known as the service/market opportunity matrix. (See Figure 6-8.) Originally a 2-by-2 matrix proposed by Igor Ansoff,[4] here it is expanded into a 3-by-3 matrix. Markets are listed at the left and services along the top.

Each cell in Figure 6-8 has a name. Management should first consider cell 1, *market penetration.* This cell raises the question of whether the organization can maintain or expand its revenues by deepening its penetration into its existing markets with its existing services. Clients may not be utilizing the organization's services as frequently or in as large amounts as they could or should. For example, dental patients may be missing their regular checkups; or the clients of a CPA may be obtaining

Figure 6-8. Service/Market Opportunity Matrix.

	SERVICES		
	Existing	Modified	New
Existing	1. Market penetration	4. Service modification	7. Service innovation
Geographic	2. Geographic expansion	5. Modification for dispersed markets	8. Geographic innovation
New	3. New markets	6. Modification for new markets	9. Total innovation

only a portion of the consulting advice they need on financial-control procedures. Market penetration could also be called for when clients could provide more new referrals if asked.

Market penetration can generally be accomplished more efficiently and effectively than other expansion strategies. Reminder notices and telephone calls to existing clients, or simple requests of clients to let their friends know about the organization's services, can often accomplish much more at a lower cost than going after new markets and/or offering new services. But if penetration opportunities have clearly been exhausted, then the other cells in the matrix may provide useful guidance.

Cell 2 raises the question of whether the organization should try to expand by offering existing services to similar types of clients in new geographic markets. A *geographic expansion* strategy could involve opening branch offices in new localities or simply increasing the organization's travel and communication budgets. The biggest risk associated with this strategy is the threat to quality control presented by having services provided where they cannot be monitored as easily. Also, clients in different geographic locations may differ in subtle ways that could make existing services undesirable to new geographic markets.

A *new markets* strategy (cell 3) involves trying to expand by offering existing services to new types of clients. For example, a slump in construction has led architects to search for new markets and clients. Some firms have contracted with cities to redesign closed school buildings for alternative community uses; others are looking for clients interested in interior design or historic preservation; one firm is specializing in the redesign of crowded prisons. The major risk here is that existing services may not appeal to the new target markets.

Next, management can consider whether it should modify some of its current services to attract more of the existing market. A *service modification* strategy (cell 4) could involve making important changes in the actual services provided and/or giving a more appealing and descriptive label to those services. Service modification may help an organization attract a larger proportion of a certain category of clients or obtain larger fees from existing clients. The strategy can backfire if existing clients liked the old services just the way they were.

Cell 5 is named *modification for dispersed markets* and cell 6 is *modification for new markets*. The organization can try to modify and tailor its existing services to the tastes and desires of new geographic or target markets. Although these strategies are market oriented, they require dealing with new markets and assuming some risk.

Service innovation (cell 7) involves developing totally new services for existing clients. An engineering firm may add architectural services for its clients, hoping that they will find it more convenient to commission engineering and architectural services in one package. Similarly, a CPA firm may start to offer computer system consulting services for its audit clients. This is a sound strategy as long as the people who supply the new services are experienced in that particular area and can maintain high professional standards. The organization must also be careful not to dilute the quality of its existing established services in its enthusiasm for adding the new services.

Finally, *geographic innovation* (cell 8) and *total innovation* (cell 9) would have the organization offer totally new services to new geographic or other target markets. Needless to say, these are the riskiest strategies of all. They require acquisition of *both* substantial knowledge of the new markets and experienced professionals to provide the new service to those mar-

Figure 6-9. Sample Strategic Planning Matrix for a CPA Firm.[5]

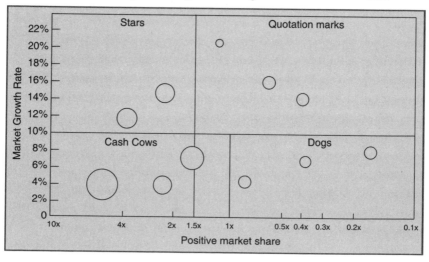

kets. An example might be a high-priced law firm developing a tax accounting preparation service for medium- to low-income families. It is not within their traditional line of work and is aimed at a different market.

The service/market opportunity matrix helps the organization imagine new opportunities in a systematic way. Once these opportunities are evaluated, the better ones can be pursued. The service/market analysis and the previous portfolio analysis allow the organization to formulate more focused and effective strategic marketing plans.

Another type of strategic planning matrix is shown in Figure 6-9. The vertical axis represents market attractiveness and the horizontal axis represents the ability to compete. Market attractiveness includes measures of community growth, size, and composition of local and regional markets, their profitability, availability of labor, and existing competitors. The ability to compete depends on the organization having distinctive competencies or lower costs of operations. Here it is illustrated for a CPA firm, and shows different potential businesses it might engage in.

FORMULATING MARKETING STRATEGIES

Once a basic organizational strategy has been formulated, marketing strategies are needed. The professional service organization must develop a marketing strategy for each service market it chooses to compete in. We define marketing strategy as follows:

> **Marketing strategy** is the selection of *target markets*, the choice of a *competitive position*, and the development of an effective *marketing mix* to reach and serve the chosen clients.

We shall examine the three basic components of marketing strategy in the following sections.

Target Market Strategy

The first step in preparing a marketing strategy is to understand the market thoroughly. We define a market in this way:

A **market** is the set of all people and organizations that have an actual or potential interest in a service and have the ability to pay for it.

When looked at closely, every market is heterogeneous—that is, it is made up of quite different types of buyers, or *market segments*. Therefore, marketers find it helpful to construct a market segmentation scheme that can reveal the major groups making up the market. Then they can decide whether to serve all of these segments (mass marketing) or concentrate on a few of the more promising ones (target marketing).

There are many ways to segment a market. (This will be covered in greater detail in Chapter 7.) Segmentation can be done based on the type of industry, size, location, service needs, or other characteristics of potential clients. The market analyst tries different segmentation approaches until a useful one is found. For example, an architectural firm might find the most useful way to segment the business firm market is by three service needs (e.g., corporate headquarters design, prison design, or college design) and by three locations (e.g., Sunbelt, Northeast, Midwest). Thus, the firm might identify a needs/market segmentation scheme containing nine different segments it could serve (three needs × three markets). The firm would then have to decide whether to pursue target marketing and, if so, what pattern of target marketing to choose.

There are five basic patterns of market coverage possible with a given needs/market segmentation scheme. They are shown in Figure 6-10 and are described below.

1. *Need/market concentration* consists of an organization concentrating on only one market segment, such as Sunbelt corporations seeking corporate headquarters designs.

2. *Needs specialization* consists of the organization deciding to serve a single need for all markets, such as the need for prison designs.

3. *Market specialization* consists of the organization deciding to serve all the needs of a single market, such as Northeast architectural services.

4. *Selective specialization* consists of the organization deciding to serve several market segments that have no relation to each other except that each constitutes an individual attractive opportunity.

Figure 6-10. Five Patterns of Market Coverage [6]

Need/market concentration

	M1	M2	M3
N1			
N2			
N3			

Need specialization

	M1	M2	M3
N1			
N2			
N3			

Market specialization

	M1	M2	M3
N1			
N2			
N3			

Selective specialization

	M1	M2	M3
N1			
N2			
N3			

Full coverage

	M1	M2	M3
N1			
N2			
N3			

(N = needs, M = market)

5. *Full coverage* consists of the organization deciding to serve all the market segments.

After choosing a desired coverage, *subsegmentation* can be done to evaluate whether the desired market coverage should be defined in narrower terms. Thus, if the firm decides to serve the corporate headquarters design needs of Sunbelt corporations, it may want to subsegment by project size and type of industry, perhaps eventually deciding to target high-technology companies with opportunities offering greater than $100,000 in fees.

Competitive Positioning Strategy

Once a target market has been selected, the next step must be to develop a competitive positioning strategy. We define competitive positioning as follows:

> **Competitive positioning** is the art of developing and communicating meaningful differences between one's services and those of competitors serving the same target market.

The key to competitive positioning is to identify the major attributes used by the target market to evaluate and choose among competitive organizations. Suppose research conducted with auditor selection committees and chief financial officers of large corporations revealed that the attributes considered most carefully in selecting a CPA firm are (1) the amount of extra advice and service provided during audit engagements and (2) the aggressiveness of the CPA firm in seeking new business. Further, suppose that the research revealed that this selection committee perceived four major CPA firms as having the competitive positions shown in Figure 6-11 (see page 158) on these attributes. In this case, firms A and B are competing head-on against one another for clients who prefer moderately aggressive firms providing much extra service. Firm C is positioned to obtain clients seeking unaggressive firms that, nevertheless, provide much extra service. Firm D is in the unenviable position of being perceived to be both unaggressive and weak on providing extra service. Management of Firm A should consider repositioning their firm to

The Challenge of Standing Apart from the Crowd: Differentiation Strategies of Professional Service Firms[7]

A recent study of four hundred twenty-two professional service firms across the United States and Canada sought to answer the question "What differentiation strategies and tactics are firms using to establish, maintain, or extend a competitive advantage?" The answers found in this comprehensive study are both interesting and very educational for the professional service practitioner.

Respondents to the survey expressed a "strong sense of discomfort" related to their competitiveness in a rapidly changing marketplace. As a result, the following were the most commonly cited reasons for embarking on differentiation plans.

- Respond to increased competition.
- Respond to commoditization of core services.
- Meet client needs for new services, or increased or changed client expectations.

As one might expect, respondents cited a spectrum of differentiation strategies they chose to remedy the above mentioned challenges. The ten most commonly used approaches were:

Differentiation Approaches	Percent of Respondents
Improved or evolved our current services.	68%
Reorganized practices or lines of business.	55%
Entered into joint ventures, alliances, or referral networks with firms that extend our services.	53%
Hired specialized individuals.	52%
Added new variables to our prices.	46%
Repackaged current services.	43%
Used new techniques and tools to "deliver" our services (i.e., printed reports now delivered via CD-ROM).	42%
Trained professionals to follow our proprietary methodologies.	40%
Developed a new positioning.	40%

The least commonly cited approaches were:

Differentiation Approaches	Percent of Respondents
Developed new risk sharing arrangement with clients.	15%
Developed new-to-the-world services.	13%
Acquired another firm.	12%
Merged with another firm.	5%
Decreased our prices.	4%
Sold parts of the firm.	3%

Each of the least commonly used strategies may have appeared too different or risky for the service firm to attempt regardless of the potential magnitude of establishing a real competitive advantage.

At the same time, the responding firms demonstrated shifting attitudes toward what differentiation strategies they planned to employ in the following year. The tables below identify those strategies participating firms reported that they would decrease or increase in usage in the year following the survey.

The Differentiation Approaches With the Greatest Expected DECREASE in Use in the Next Year

Differentiation Approaches	Prior Year	Next Year
Improve or evolve our current services.	68%	60%
Reorganize practices or lines of business.	55%	38%
Repackage current services.	43%	35%
Develop a new positioning.	40%	29%
Create a new visual identity (logo, letterhead, etc.).	36%	19%
Communicate our firm's positioning through a new motto or tag line.	34%	21%
Eliminate services.	15%	12%

The Differentiation Approaches With the Greatest Expected INCREASE in Use in the Next Year

Differentiation Approaches	Prior Year	Next Year
Use new techniques and tools to "deliver" our services (i.e., printed reports now delivered via CD-ROM).	42%	48%
Train professionals to follow our proprietary methodologies.	40%	51%
Implement a formal relationship management program to strengthen our bonds with current clients.	29%	40%
Embark on a public relations campaign.	29%	38%
Increase the speed of our service delivery.	27%	34%
Embark on an advertising campaign.	22%	31%
Develop new risk-sharing arrangement with clients.	15%	19%
Acquire another firm.	12%	19%
Merge with another firm.	5%	8%

The most used differentiation approaches were not necessarily found to be the most useful. The matrix below clearly demonstrates this.

Use and Success of Differentiation Approaches in the Last Year

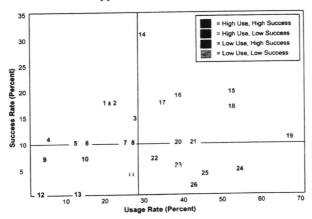

1. Embarked on an advertising campaign.
2. Added new-to-our-firm services that blend into the services of another industry.
3. Implemented a formal relationship management program to strengthen our bonds with current clients.
4. Merged with another firm.
5. Acquired another firm.
6. Developed new risk sharing arrangement with clients.
7. Created new divisions or subsidiary companies.
8. Increased the speed of our service delivery.
9. Decreased our prices.
10. Eliminated services.
11. Increased our prices.
12. Sold parts of the firm.
13. Developed new-to-the-world services.
14. Embarked on a public relations campaign.
15. Entered into joint ventures, alliances, or referral networks with firms that extend our services.
16. Added new-to-our-firm services that are within our industry.
17. Created a new visual identity.
18. Hired specialized individuals.
19. Improved or evolved our current services.
20. Developed a new positioning.
21. Repackaged current services.
22. Communicated our firm's positioning through a new motto or tag line.
23. Trained professionals to follow our proprietary methodologies.
24. Reorganized practices or lines of business.
25. Added new variables to our prices.
26. Used new techniques and tools to "deliver" our services.

An important finding of this research was that a firm's industry appeared to have little impact on the biggest challenges and subsequent success of implementing differentiation plans. As seen in the table below, the best strategies poorly planned or executed will face difficulties.

What was the single most difficult problem you encountered in implementing your differentiation plans within the past one year?[7]

Problem	A/E/C	Accounting	Consulting	General Contractors	All Industries
... took longer amd more effort to implement than we expected.	25%	24%	45%	30%	30%
... never got rully integrated throughout our organization.	25%	18%	10%	19%	21%
... was more difficult to communicate to our outside publics than we thought.	15%	9%	18%	19%	15%
... never had a defined process for implementation.	9%	9%	10$	0%	8%
... kept getting derailed during implementation.	12%	3%	3%	4%	6%
... never had clear objectives.	4%	15%	5%	4%	6%
...never got final approval from critical decision-makers.	4%	12%	3%	7%	5%
... cost more to implement than we thought.	3%	3%	5%	7%	5%
Other	2%	6%	3%	11%	4%

Colors signify ranking:

■ = 1

■ = 2

■ = 3

differentiate it from Firm B. They may see an opportunity "niche" for highly aggressive firms with much extra service. At the same time, Firm D will need to think seriously about repositioning itself.

Repositioning can be difficult because it involves trying to change people's long-standing images or impressions of an organization. Successful repositioning requires a well-formulated and executed marketing mix. This will be further discussed in Chapter 7.

Marketing Mix Strategy

The organization must now choose a marketing mix that will support and reinforce its chosen competitive position. An organization that wants to be perceived as aggressive and service-minded will have to hire aggressive, hungry professionals and train them extensively in how to communicate and offer the organization's services. It will also have to charge highly competitive fees and have a large-scale communication program to tell clients that their business is eagerly sought. Thus, the chosen competitive position dictates the elements of the marketing mix that the firm must emphasize.

SUSTAINABLE COMPETITIVE ADVANTAGES

The aim of target marketing, competitive positioning, and marketing mix is the development of a sustainable competitive advantage. The hope is to identify, develop, and take advantage of those areas in which a tangible and preservable business advantage can be achieved. Figure 6-12 (see page 159) illustrates four factors that are required for the creation of sustainable competitive advantage. The first is the way the firm competes (which could be its positioning strategy, distribution strategy, etc.). The strength of many professional service firms is their ability to be seen as experts in a given field. Stan Chelsey is widely perceived as the "King of Class Action Suits" based on his success in mobilizing large groups of individuals to argue for changes as a result of fires, product defects, or potentially dangerous products.

Figure 6-11. Perceived Positions of Four CPA Firms[8]

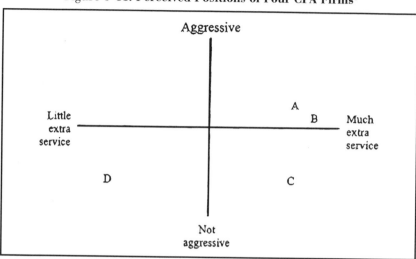

A second factor is the basis of competition. For example, positioning a service as one of high quality is usually easily imitated. But what is less easy to imitate is the actual delivery of high quality that can require specialized assets and skills. This will not succeed unless the right people and culture are in place.

A third factor that influences sustainable competitive advantage is where the firm competes. Some target markets may be easier to hold on to than others.

The final factor is whom the firm competes against. Sometimes an asset or skill will form a sustainable competitive advantage only given the right set of competitors who cannot match or neutralize the firm's strength.

Here are some additional factors that influence sustainable competitive advantage:

1. Having a large initial advantage, because having only a small edge on the competition may not provide a long-term sustainable advantage.

2. Having an advantage in the face of environmental changes and competitive actions. Some information technological innova-

Figure 6-12. The Sustainable Competitive Advantage

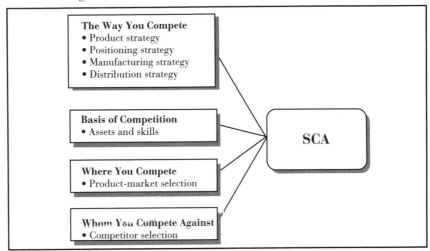

tions, such as Merrill Lynch's Cash Management Counsel, can be replicated by followers and were not so much of an advantage they were first thought to be.

3. Sustainable competitive advantage should be leveraged into visible business characteristics that will influence customers. Service reliability is not something that the customer can typically see; however, one can support reliability through a strong communications plan that makes the claim believable.

Sustainable Competitive Advantages Are Varied

Managers of 248 businesses in the service and hi-tech industries were studied and asked to name the strategic competitive advantage of their business. Figure 6-13 indicates that a wide variety of strategic competitive advantages were mentioned, each representing distinctive competitive approaches. Most of these represent assets or skills such as customer-based quality reputation or good management. It is interesting to note that the study found that the average number of strategic competitive advantages per business was close to five, suggesting that it is usually not sufficient to base a strategy on a single competitive advantage.

Figure 6-13. Sustainable Competitive Advantages of 248 Businesses.[9]

	High-Tech	Service	Other	Total
1. Reputation for quality	26	50	29	105
2 Customer service/product support	23	40	15	78
3. Name recognition/high profile	8	42	21	7
4. Retain good management and engineering staff	17	43	5	65
5. Low-cost production	17	15	21	
6. Financial resources	11	26	14	51
7. Customer orientation/feedback/market research	13	26	9	48
8. Product-line breadth	11	23	13	47
9. Technical superiority	30		9	46
10. Installed base of satisfied customers	19	22	4	45
11. Segmentation/focus	7	22	16	45
12. Product characteristics/differentiation	12	15	10	37
13. Continuing product innovation	12	17	6	35
14. Market share	12	14	9	35
15. Size/location of distribution	10	11	.13	34
16. Low price/high-value offering	6	20	6	32
17. Knowledge of business	2	25	4	31
18. Pioneer/early entrant in industry	11	11	6	28
19. Efficient, flexible production/operations adaptable to customers	4	17	4	26
20. Effective sales force	10	9	4	26
21. Overall marketing skills	7	9	7	23
22. Shared vision/culture	5	13	4	22
23. Strategic goals	6	7	9	22
24. Powerful well-known parent	7	7	6	20
25. Location	0	10	10	20
26. Effective advertising/image	5	6	6	17
27. Enterprising/entrepreneurial	3	2	5	11
28. Good coordination	2	2	5	10
29. Engineering research and development	8	2	10	10
30. Short-term planning	2	1		8
31. Good distributor relations	2	4	1	7
32. Other	6	20	5	31
Total	315	539	281	1136
Number of businesses	68	113	67	248
Average number of SCAs	4.63	4.77	4.19	4.58

Strategic Thrusts

Most sustainable competitive advantages are a result of one or a combination of five strategic thrusts or underlying generic strategies. Harvard University business strategy expert Michael Porter first identified three of these thrusts. They were low cost, differentiation, and focus. Two others are a preemptive strategy and a synergistic strategy.

Low-cost strategies typically represent a no-frills service. Examples would include a franchise law firm that offers $100 wills and $250 divorces, or organizations that have advantages due to economies of scale or efficient operations that reduce their overall costs. A differentiation strategy means that there is an element of uniqueness about a strategy that provides value to the customer. For example, firms might differentiate their offerings by enhancing performance, quality, reliability, prestige, or convenience. A focus strategy typically means that a firm is concentrating on either a particular service, a segment of the population, or a geographic region. A preemptive strategy is one that employs first-mover advantages to inhibit or prevent competitors from duplicating or countering. And finally, synergistic strategies rely on a synergy between a business and other businesses in the same firm. For example, an orthopedic surgeon who also offers physical rehabilitation services will have an advantage over surgeons who don't. The patient, in essence, can experience one-stop shopping in one potentially convenient location.

The particular strategic thrust a professional service firm employs will be the result of careful analysis of internal and external environments, and the firm's missions, goals, and objectives. The firm's leaders must choose the path that is right for the organization.

In 1997 there was a study of the "best-managed" architectural firms in the United States. One of the objectives of this study was to identify the innovative marketing strategies that successful firms have used to set themselves apart. Some of the strategies used were:[10]

1. Establishing strategic alliances with giant foreign design-build companies to pursue international work.

2. Developing data bases of more than 1,500 prospects and tracking them on an ongoing basis.

3. Creating strategic alliances with other architectural and engineering firms.

4. Hiring experts in their specialized area of architecture, such as healthcare and laboratories, to bring customers' perspective into the firm.

5. A principal from the firm wrote a book and held a national symposium on innovative architecture in the firm's particular area of expertise in order to establish the firm as an expert.

A Final Note about Sustainable Competitive Advantages

Some business strategy experts warn that there is no such thing as strategic thrusts. Chief among these individuals is Richard D'Aveni who has coined the term "hypercompetition." D'Aveni contends that due to the fierceness of competition and the speed in which competition reacts, sustainable competitive advantages go through a much shorter life cycle than at any point of time in history. In short, he is saying that sustainable competitive advantages are really temporary competitive advantages. Some of the tenets of his perspective about the way in which external conditions change so rapidly suggest that an organization would be better off finding and building temporary advantages through market disruption rather than expecting a sustainable advantage over a long period of time. He suggests that there are a number of ways of achieving temporary advantages.[11]

1. Through strong research that keeps an eye on what's happening in the marketplace.

2. Through positioning and designing the organization for speed—and the faster one can move, the better.

3. By positioning the organization for the unexpected. In other words, real strengths may come by going where competitors don't expect the organization to go.

4. By continually shifting the rules of the game. This might mean developing a new process in which to deliver service that gives the organization a competitive advantage.

5. By signaling strategic intent. This implies that the organization may use announcements and publicized shifts into new markets to emphasize its strategic intent and aggressiveness.

6. Through simultaneous and sequential strategic thrusts. In other words, the organization needs to be moving in several directions at once.

7. Through stakeholder satisfaction that defines the customer as the most important focus of the organization.

D'Aveni uses the following analogy to try to illustrate what happens to an organization that stays with the same strength too long. If one regularly plays tennis with a certain friend and knows that friend cannot hit a backhand, this gives the individual a competitive advantage—one that he will probably capitalize on by continually hitting to his opponent's backhand. In a world that does not change, this player would likely continue to win the matches over time because of this strength and the corresponding weakness of his opponent. However, the opponent—being a competitor—is likely to improve. The opponent may improve simply because of the practice of being fed a steady stream of backhands or he may decide that he is tired of losing and seek help or lessons to improve the backhand. What will eventually happen is that the competitor, in addition to his previous strengths, can now neutralize the one strength that the first player had. Just as with tennis, D'Aveni suggests, in order to continue winning, an organization must continually shift the point and type of attack to keep its competitors off guard.

Strategy Never Stops

Regardless of the strategic thrust a firm employs or the strategic competitive advantages that result from them, or even how hypercompetitive a firm's particular market is, one thing is certain: Strategy formulation is an ongoing process. Strategy must be consistently reviewed, revised, and reformulated and, if done properly, is a process that will never be finished. In formulating a firm's strategy, it is important to have a clear set of goals and objectives, know the assumptions on which the strategy is being built, understand the firm's customers, know the firm's competitors, leverage your firm's strengths and minimize its weaknesses, emphasize those things the firm is best at in relation to its competitors, and make the strategy clear, concise, and attainable. Most important, when designing a strategy, it is important that while Plan A is being developed, Plans B, C, D, and E are also being prepared in order to build in flexibility based on multiple scenarios.

ORGANIZATIONAL STRUCTURE AND SYSTEMS

The purpose of strategy formulation is to develop strategies that will help the organization achieve its goals. But the existing organization must be capable of carrying out these strategies. It must have the *structure, people*, and *culture* to implement the strategy successfully. A responsive organization should be in place, with the chosen strategy providing guidance concerning the finer points of the organization design.

Most organization theorists believe that "structure should follow strategy," rather than the other way around. Thus, a strategy that places emphasis on a large public relations effort would require the hiring of staff and, perhaps, the establishment of a new department to handle this effort. Similarly, a strategy that calls for the organization to provide highly specialized services to clients or patients would require a modification of an old organizational "culture" that encouraged all professionals to be generalists.

Successful Strategic Implementation

In order for a strategic plan to be successfully implemented, the organization's state of "readiness" must be evaluated. This involves assessing the existence of a strong organizational vision, the necessary skills of employees, incentives to act, the resources necessary to accomplish the task, and a clear action plan outlining the tactics needed to accomplish the strategy. If all these are in place, success is more likely to be achieved (assuming there are no changes in the environment and competition). Without a clear vision, confusion over where and why the strategy is important may result. Without the skills, employees may feel anxious

Figure 6-14. Successful Strategic Implementation.[12]

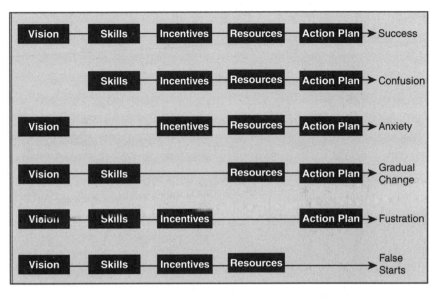

about their ability to accomplish the task. Without incentives to act, at best, gradual change may occur. Without the resources necessary to implement the strategy, frustration may occur. Finally, without a solid action plan that provides a clear direction for the firm and its many departments, there are likely to be many false starts. Departments will have difficulty coordinating their efforts, overcoming role conflicts, and maintaining a focused effort. (See Figure 6-14.)

SUMMARY

Strategic planning is the major tool for adapting to a changing environment, and it consists of several steps. The first step is environmental analysis, in which the organization researches its five environments: internal environment, market environment, public environment, competitive environment, and macro environment. Each environment component should then be subdivided into factors, the major trends for each factor should be identified, followed by the identification of the implied opportunities and threats. The organization must then prepare plans for its most important opportunities and threats, and monitor those that might have some eventual significance.

Following the environment analysis, the organization is to identify its major strengths and weaknesses in personnel, funds, facilities, systems, and market assets. It will favor those opportunities where it has distinctive competencies and differential advantages in relation to competitors.

The environmental and resources analyses are followed by goal formulation, in which the organization establishes what it wants to achieve. The firm's basic mission, its major objectives (qualitative variables to pursue), and its specific goals (quantified objectives with respect to magnitude, time, and who is responsible for achieving them) must all be formulated.

Strategy formulation is the organization's effort to figure out its broad strategy for achieving its goals. First, the organization analyzes its current service portfolio to determine which businesses it should build, maintain, harvest, and terminate. Second, it seeks ideas for new or modified services and markets by using a service/market expansion matrix.

Following the choice of particular service/market targets, the organization proceeds to develop marketing strategies for each service market. Marketing strategy is the selection of a target market segment(s), the choice of a competitive position, and the development of an effective marketing mix to reach and serve the chosen customers. Marketing mix consists of the particular blend of product, price, place, and promotion that the organization uses to achieve its objectives in the target market.

The driving force behind marketing strategies is to create sustainable competitive advantages that set the firm apart from others in its field. These sustainable competitive advantages are characterized by how the firm competes, where it compete, and against whom it competes. They are sustainable, competitive, and leveraged. Most successful firms have multiple sustainable competitive advantages. At the base of these sustainable competitive advantages is typically at least one of the following five strategic thrusts: differentiation, low cost, focus, preemption, and synergy. According to some strategic planning experts, however, there is no such thing as a sustainable competitive advantage, and in order to survive in the future the firm must move rapidly from one temporary advantage to another and reinvent its marketing before it is reinvented by others or by external factors.

The organization's strategy is likely to call for changes in the organization's structure, people, and culture. Organizational structure should not dictate strategy, but an organization's strategy should shape its structure.

Implementation of organizational strategy requires a level of "readiness" within the firm. This readiness involves ensuring that the proper vision, skills, incentives, resources, and action plan are all in place.

Appendix

....

Part I. Marketing Environment Audit

Macro Environment

A. Demographic
1. What major demographic developments and trends pose opportunities or threats for this organization?
2. What actions has the organization taken in response to these developments?

B. Economic
1. What major developments and trends in income, prices, savings, and credit have an impact on the organization?
2. What actions has the organization taken in response to these developments and trends?

C. Ecological
1. What is the outlook for the cost and availability of natural resources and energy needed by the organization?
2. What concerns have been expressed about the organization's role in conservation and what steps has the organization taken?

D. Technological
1. What major changes are occurring in relevant product, service, and process technology? What is the organization's position in these technologies?
2. What major generic substitutes might replace this product or service?

E. Political
1. What new legislation could affect this organization? What federal, state, and local agency actions should be watched?
2. What actions has the organization taken in response to these developments?

F. Cultural
   1. What changes are occurring in consumer lifestyles and values that might affect this organization?
   2. What actions has the organization taken in response to these developments?

Task Environment

A. Markets
   1. What is happening to market size, growth, and geographical distribution?
   2. What are the major market segments? What are their expected rates of growth? Which are high-opportunity and low-opportunity segments?
B. Customers
   1. How do current customers and prospects rate the organization and its competitors, particularly with respect to reputation, product quality, services, sales force, and price?
   2. How do different classes of customers make their buying decisions?
   3. What are the evolving needs and satisfactions being sought by consumers in this market?
C. Competitors
   1. Who are the major competitors? What are the objectives and strategy of each major competitor? What are their strengths and weaknesses? What are the sizes and trends in market shares?
   2. What trends can be foreseen in future competition and substitutes for this product?
D. Distribution and Dealers
   1. What are the main distribution channels bringing products to customers?
   2. What are the efficiency levels and growth potentials for the different distribution channels?
E. Suppliers
   1. What is the outlook for the availability of different key resources used in production?
   2. What trends are occurring among suppliers in their pattern of selling?

F. Facilitators and Marketing Firms
1. What is the outlook for the cost and availability of transportation services?
2. What is the outlook for the cost and availability of warehousing facilities?
3. What is the outlook for the cost and availability of financial resources?
4. How effectively is the advertising agency performing?
G. Publics
1. What publics (financial, media, government, citizen, local, general, and internal) represent particular opportunities or problems for the organization?
2. What steps has the organization taken to deal effectively with its key publics?

Part II. Marketing Objectives and Strategy Audit

A. Organization's Objectives
1. Is the mission of the organization clearly stated in market-oriented terms? Is the mission feasible in terms of the organization's opportunities and resources?
2. Are the organization's various objectives clearly stated so that they lead logically to the marketing objectives?
3. Are the marketing objectives appropriate, given the organization's competitive position, resources, and opportunities?
B. Marketing Strategy
1. What is the core marketing strategy for achieving the objectives? Is it a sound marketing strategy?
2. Are enough resources (or too many resources) budgeted to accomplish the marketing objectives?
3. Are the marketing resources allocated optimally to prime market segments, territories, and products of the organization?
4. Are the marketing resources allocated optimally to the major elements of the marketing mix, that is, offer quality, service, sales force, advertising, promotion, and distribution?

Part III. Marketing Organization Audit

A. Formal Structure
   1. Is there a high-level marketing officer with adequate authority and responsibility over those organizational activities that affect the customer's satisfaction?
   2. Are the marketing responsibilities optimally structured along functional, product, end user, and territorial lines?
B. Functional Efficiency
   1. Are there good communication and working relations between marketing and sales?
   2. Is the product management system working effectively? Are the product managers able to plan profits or only sales volume?
   3. Are there any groups in marketing that need more training, motivation, supervision, or evaluation?
C. Interface Efficiency
   1. Are there any problems between marketing and operations that need attention?
   2. What about marketing and R&D?
   3. What about marketing and financial management?
   4. What about marketing and purchasing?

Part IV. Marketing Systems Audit

A. Marketing Information System
   1. Is the marketing information system producing accurate, sufficient, and timely information about developments in the marketplace?
   2. Is marketing research being adequately used by managers?
B. Marketing Planning System
   1. Is the marketing planning system well conceived and effective?
   2. Is sales forecasting and market potential measurement soundly carried out?
   3. Are sales quotas set on a proper basis?
C. Marketing Control System
   1. Are the control procedures (monthly, quarterly, etc.) adequate to ensure that the annual plan objectives are being achieved?

2. Is provision made to analyze periodically the profitability of different products, markets, territories, and channels of distribution?
3. Is provision made to periodically examine and validate various marketing costs?

D. New Product Development System
1. Is the organization well organized to gather, generate, and screen new product ideas?
2. Does the organization do adequate concept research and business analysis before investing heavily in a new idea?
3. Does the organization carry out adequate product and market testing before launching a new product?

Part V. Marketing Productivity Audit

A. Profitability Analysis
1. What is the profitability of the organization's different products, customer markets, territories, and channels of distribution?
2. Should the organization enter, expand, contract, or withdraw from any market segments, and what would be the short- and long-run profit consequences?

B. Cost-Effectiveness Analysis
1. Do any marketing activities seem to have excessive costs? Are these costs valid? Can cost-reducing steps be taken?

Part VI. Marketing Function Audits

A. Products
1. What are the product line objectives? Are these objectives sound? Is the current product line meeting these objectives?
2. Are there particular products that should be phased out?
3. Are there new products that are worth adding?
4. Are any products able to benefit from quality, feature, or style improvements?

B. Price
1. What are the pricing objectives, policies, strategies, and procedures? To what extent are prices set on sound cost, demand, and competitive criteria?

2. Do the customers see the organization's prices as being in line or out of line with the perceived value of its offer?

3. Does the organization use promotional pricing effectively?

C. Distribution

1. What are the distribution objectives and strategies?

2. Is there adequate market coverage and service?

3. Should the organization consider changing its degree of reliance on distributors, sales reps, and direct selling?

D. Advertising, Sales Promotion, and Public Relations

1. What are the organization's advertising objectives? Are they sound?

2. Is the right amount being spent on advertising? How is the budget determined?

3. Are the ad themes and copy effective? What do customers and the public think about the advertising?

4. Are the advertising media well chosen?

5. Is sales promotion used effectively?

6. Is there a well-conceived public relations program?

E. Sales Force

1. What are the organization's sales force objectives?

2. Is the sales force large enough to accomplish the organization's objectives?

3. Is the sales force organized along the proper principle(s) of specialization (territory, market, product)?

4. Does the sales force show high morale, ability, and effort? Are they sufficiently trained and encouraged?

5. Are the procedures adequate for setting quotas and evaluating performances?

6. How is the organization's sales force perceived in relation to competitors' sales forces?

NOTES

[1] Adapted from "Positioning Your Public Accounting Firm for Success," by Jay G. Kreuze and Gale E. Newell. *The National Public Accountant* (1997), v42, n7, p8.

2 Kotler, Philip; Gregor, William; and Rodgers, William. "The Marketing Audit Comes of Age," *Sloan Management Review* (Winter 1977), p25-43.

3 Gibson, Susan. "Out of the Blues and Into the Black," *Business and Management Practices* (1998), v8, n10, p26-30.

4 Ansoff, A. Igor. "Strategies for Diversification," *Harvard Business Review* (July 17, 1978), p92.

5 Reprinted with permission from *Long-Range Planning*, February 1977, B. Hedley, "Strategy and the Business Portfolio," p. 12, copyright 1977, Pergamon Press, Ltd.

6 Adapted from Derek F. Abell, *Defining the Business: The Starting Point of Strategic Planning* (Englewood Cliffs, N.J.: Prentice-Hall, © 1980), Chapter 8.

7 Adapted from *Expertise Marketing's Survey on Differentiation Strategies*, 2000 and used with permission.

8 David A. Aaker, *Developing Business Strategies*. John Wiley & Sons, 1995.

9 Ibid.

10 Linn, Charles and Pearson, Clifford. "Lessons from America's Best-Managed Firms," *Architectural Record* (January 1997), p106.

11 D'Aveni, Richard. *Hypercompetition*. New York: The Free Press, 1994.

12 *Source:* American Productivity and Quality.

7 | Segmenting, Selecting, and Appealing to Markets

....

*"I don't know the key to success, but the key to
failure is to try to please everyone."*
BILL COSBY
Comedian, Actor

Organizations that offer their services to consumer and business markets recognize that they cannot appeal to all buyers in those markets—at least not to all buyers in the same way. Buyers are too numerous, too widely scattered, and too varied in their needs and buying practices. Different service organizations vary widely in their ability to serve different segments of the market. Rather than trying to compete in an entire market, sometimes against superior competitors, each firm must identify the parts of the market it can best serve.

There are basically five ways of appealing to the marketplace. These are:

One-Size-Fits-All (Mass) Marketing. A management consulting firm could develop one consulting approach in an attempt to attract every eligible client to it. This is an example of mass marketing. The mass marketer pays little or no attention to potential differences in consumers' preferences, but assumes they are all alike. This approach might work well in a monopolistic situation, but in a competitive world it is akin to organizational suicide.

Program Differentiated Marketing. A management consulting firm could also develop two or more consulting programs or specialities

The consulting firm of Anderson Zurnuehlen and Company in Helena, Montana, developed a standardized approach to technology consulting and, as a result, was able to implement a huge price increase for its services. Between 1994 to 1997, the firm's net income from a full-time technology engagement for installing a client's server and SQL Accounting Software Systems jumped from an average of $9,000 to $50,000. Sam M. Allred, partner in charge of technology consulting, explained that the increase was directly attributable to the firm adopting a standardized approach to technology consulting.

The process involved spending a significant amount of time refining the marketing message and approach to be used as well as determining the market and type of client to be sold. This was a two-step process. The first step was to develop a list of procedures, check-lists, and other work papers designed to standardize service delivery, and successfully execute them. To accomplish the first phase of the process, Anderson Zurnuehlen and Company had to do up-front research into the prospective clients' needs and business goals; implement planning that identified the major component of the process; conduct environmental preparation, which involved a systematic review of the client's hardware, software, and operating system; provide information and training to the clients which involves the successful implementation of the system along with the delivery procedure and training manuals and exercises; and conduct an exit interview to ensure that all steps were successfully completed and the customer was satisfied.

The second step, client selection, is a key component in Anderson Zurnuehlen's success as well. The firm established clear guidelines as to the type of clients it would serve. Allred said, "The firm will not accept a new client unless it has met virtually all of the following attributes: (1) the ability to attract and retain quality people, (2) an attitude of teamwork and commitment, (3) a strong upper management team, (4) high commitment to technology, (5) a belief in a thorough planning process for change, (6) recognition and payment for quality service, (7) reasonable expectations, (8) willingness to take advice, (9) an investment versus expenses approach to technology, and (10) good profitability and a strong industry position." As a result of their efforts, Anderson Zurnuehlen and Company enjoyed financial success with "25 percent to 30 percent of gross revenue finding its way to the bottom line after sizeable bonuses to all consulting staff."[1]

and, like a cafeteria, invite clients to select what they want. The service offerings might differ in levels of intensity, content, or other features. The management consulting firm with such differentiated offerings hopes that each potential client will find something suitable among its varied offerings. Many of the largest consulting firms have a mandate to meet a broad range of clients' needs and interests and are committed to this approach.

Focused (Target) Marketing. A more tailored approach to satisfying a market comes from focusing the firm's efforts on identifying and serving a *particular target market*. The firm distinguishes among the different segments that make up the market, chooses one of these segments to focus on, and develops market offers specifically to meet the needs of the selected target market. The previous example of Anderson Zurnuehlen fits this scenario.

Target marketing can provide at least three benefits:

1. The firm can spot market opportunities better when it is aware of different segments and their needs, because by monitoring those segments the firm can note potential clients whose needs are not being fully met by existing competitors.

2. The firm can make finer adjustments of its program to match the desires of the market. It can interview members of its target market to determine their specific needs and desires and how the existing programs should be adapted.

3. The firm can make finer adjustments of its marketing mix. Instead of trying to reach all potential clients with a single approach, the institution can create separate marketing programs aimed at each distinct target market.

Niche Marketing. Normally, market segments are large identifiable groups within a given market. A niche is a more narrowly defined group whose needs are not being well served. Niches are usually identified by dividing a market segment into smaller subsegments or by identifying a group of individuals who may require a distinct set of benefits.

As smaller segments of the market, niches attract less competition. Because larger, more mature organizations may find it unwieldy or cost prohibitive to attempt to satisfy smaller markets, niches attract smaller or newer professional service firms. The firm serving niche markets succeeds through specialization, developing economies of scale, and an ability to charge premium prices for a service others do not provide. At the same time, niche marketers are in a precarious situation because they rely on a limited market and risk losing their customer base if something happens to change the demands of the niche.

Micro Marketing. Micro marketing is the practice of tailoring products and marketing programs to suit the tastes of specific clients. This is sometimes called one-to-one-marketing or mass customization. In many ways, micro marketing is the hallmark of the professional service firm. Lawyers, management consultants, and doctors all would be expected to tailor their individual services to the needs of each client. In recent years the ability to tailor one's services to specific clients has been enhanced by advances in technology that allow the firm to store, retrieve, and analyze more minute information about its clients and tailor communication in a personal manner. For example, Mercury Asset Management, a division of Merrill Lynch, sends a bi-annual newsletters to all of its clients. However, based upon captured client profiles outlining purchase behavior and needs, this company customizes each newsletter to individual clients, and every bi-annual mailing consists of a total of 7,000 combinations.[2]

BASES FOR SEGMENTING CONSUMER MARKETS

There is no single best way to segment a market. A marketer has to try different segmentation variables and combinations to find the best way to view a market structure; however, a segmentation base is best if it yields segments possessing the following characteristics:

1. MEASURABILITY: The degree to which the size, purchasing power, and profile of segments can be readily measured. Not all segments are easy to measure. For example, a psychiatrist wishing to tailor his or her services to upper income women with a shopping addiction would find it hard to estimate the size of this market.

2. REACHABILITY: The degree to which the resulting segments can be effectively reached and served through the firm's normal processes of doing business. It would be hard, for example, for a psychiatrist to develop the proper avenues to locate and communicate with female shopping addicts.

3. SUBSTANTIALITY: The degree to which the resulting segments are large or profitable enough to warrant special effort.

4. MUTUAL EXCLUSIVITY: Each segment should be different from the other segments. For example, classifying clients into present customers and former customers would be confusing for a client who is both a present and a former customer; instead, it would be more useful to classify customers according to their income level or the state in which they live or work.

5. EXHAUSTIVENESS: Every potential target member should be included in some segment.

6. DIFFERENTIAL RESPONSIVENESS: A segmentation plan may meet all the above criteria, but several segments may respond exactly alike to different types of strategy. For example, a plastic surgeon may find that women in their twenties as well as in their fifties may respond identically to advertisements focusing on rhinoplasty even though in everything else they are dissimilar. In such cases, it is not necessary to separate the segments.

The net result of segmentation would ideally be a situation where the professional service firm would be able to identify segments that would be most responsive to identified strategies and could easily be reached. Sometimes the cost and time involved in achieving ideal segmentation is such that marketers settle for approximations. For example, segmentation is often based on demographics, and the good professional service marketers assume that demographic characteristics will be related to likely responsiveness and reachability. A law firm that sponsors a radio program on National Public Radio, for example, is relying on demographics to access what its marketers perceive to be higher educated, high-income, potential clients.

A single firm may focus on multiple segments at the same time. A corporate practice law firm might decide that the potential target market for its corporate services will be the chief executive officers of all manufacturing companies located in a given state with annual sales in excess of $2 million. The commercial real estate practice group of the same law firm may decide that the target market for the firm's real estate services consists of the senior partners of all real estate developers in a major city in that state. The trust and estates partner with the firm may decide his target market consists of all residents of certain affluent suburbs within which that partner has personal and professional connections.

The target market for each service will differ from that of the other services. And each partner in the firm may provide additional legal services, the target markets of which will also have to be defined.[3]

Because the same clients can fall within various segments of this firm's practice, it is important for the different practice groups within the firm to communicate and coordinate their target market objectives; otherwise, multiple partners may call on the same clients and create the perception that the firm is poorly run and disorganized.

THE FOUR SEGMENTATION VARIABLES

The four major variables that are typically used in segmenting consumer markets are: geographic, demographic, psychographic, and behavioral variables. (See Table 7-1.)

Geographic Segmentation

In geographic segmentation, the market is divided into geographical entities such as nations, states, regions, counties, cities, ZIP Code areas, or neighborhoods, based on the notion that consumer needs or responses vary geographically. The professional service firm must decide on whether to (1) operate in one or a few geographic areas, or (2) operate in all, but pay attention to variations in geographic needs and preferences. Thus, some law firms restrict their practices to a particular state while other firms develop practices in multiple states, taking into account the unique needs created by the laws of each state.

Table 7-1. Major Segmentation Variables for Consumer Markets.

GEOGRAPHIC

World region or country	North America, Western Europe, Middle East, Pacific Rim, China, India, Canada, Mexico
Country region	Pacific Mountain, West North Central, West South Central, East North Central, East South Central, South Atlantic, Middle Atlantic, New England
City or metro size	Under 5,000; 5,000-20,000; 20,000-50,000; 50,000-100,000; 100,000-250,000; 250,000-500,000; 500,000-1,000,000; 1,000,000-4,000,000; 4,000,000-over.
Density	Urban, suburban, rural
Climate	Northern, southern

DEMOGRAPHIC

Age	Under 6, 6-11, 12-19, 20-34, 35-49, 50-64, 65+
Gender	Male, female
Family size	1-2, 3-4, 5+
Family life cycle	Young, single; young, married, no children; young, married with children; older, married with children; older, married, no children under 18; older, single; other
Income	Under $10,000; $10,000-$20,000; $20,000-$30,000; $30,000-$50,000; $50,000-$100,000; $100,000 and over
Occupation	Professional and technical; managers, officials, and proprietors; clerical sales; craftspeople; foremen; operatives; farmers; retired; students; homemakers; unemployed
Education	Grade school or less; some high school; high school graduate; some college; college graduate
Religion	Catholic, Protestant, Jewish, Muslim, Hindu, other
Race	Asian, Hispanic, black, white
Nationality	North American, South American, British, French, German, Italian, Japanese

PSYCHOGRAPHIC

Social class	Lower lowers, upper lowers, working class, middle class, upper middles, lower uppers, upper uppers
Lifestyle	Achievers, strivers, strugglers
Personality	Compulsive, gregarious, authoritarian, ambitious

Table 7-1. Major Segmentation Variables for Consumer Markets (*cont.*).

BEHAVIORAL	
Occasions	Regular occasion, special occasion
Benefits	Quality, service, economy, convenience, speed
User status	Non-user, ex-user, potential user, first-time user, regular user
Usage rate	Light user, medium user, heavy user
Loyalty status	None, medium, strong, absolute
Readiness stage	Unaware, aware, informed, interested, desirous, intending to buy
Attitude toward product	Enthusiastic, positive, indifferent, negative, hostile

A small practical unit of a geographic segmentation is the nine-digit postal ZIP Code that is used to define targets for direct-mail campaigns. The marketing research firm Claritas uses the U.S. census data and market data from commercial data services to divide U.S. households into 62 clusters.[4] These clusters are assigned distinctive, descriptive names, such as "money and brains," "shotguns and pickups," and "over the goal posts." Claritas then identifies the representation of these segments in each postal ZIP Code in the country so that marketers can select the most promising areas in which to send direct-mail promotions. This type of information would be particularly useful to lawyers and certain types of physicians.

Demographic Segmentation

Demographic segmentation involves dividing the market into groups based on demographic variables such as age, sex, family size, family life cycle, income, occupation, education completed, religion, ethnicity, and nationality. Demographic variables are the most popular basis for distinguishing buying groups. This is true for three reasons: First, customer wants, preferences, and usage rates are often highly associated with demographic variables. Second, demographic variables are easier to define and measure than most other segmentation variables. And, third, even when the target market is described in non-demographic terms, for example, lifestyle, the link back to demographics is necessary to know the size of the target market and how to reach it efficiently.

Here are a number of illustrations of segmentation based on demographic variables:

Age and Life-Cycle-Stage Segmentation. Consumer wants and capacities change with age and circumstances. Thus, how old individuals are, if they are married, if they have children, and the ages of those children can all have an impact on need states. For example, each characteristic would suggest different healthcare and/or legal requirements. A family with small children will require pediatric services, while an elderly individual living alone will typically need geriatric care. At the same time, a lawyer may focus on families with teenagers in order to practice juvenile criminal law, and another lawyer may focus on an elder population to practice estate law.

Gender Segmentation. Males and females differ in their needs for professional services and in their approach to buying these services. Men and women have different healthcare problems, and may often have different financial and legal problems, and there are organizations and firms such as colleges, hospitals, and banks that have aligned themselves with particular sexes because of these segments' unique needs. Consequently, many lawyers, doctors, consultants, and other professionals have also formed practices that emphasize service to one sex. Other professionals have used sex as a segmentation variable without choosing to service only a single sex, but to create different promotional messages.

Ethnicity Segmentation. In the United States, the Hispanic market is becoming more important because of its rapidly increasing size. This market has its own particular characteristics and resulting needs. Perhaps the most obvious is the high incidence of Spanish as the primary language within the household. Some professional service firms view the Hispanic population as an attractive market opportunity. The Delta Medical Center in Memphis, Tennessee, is such an organization. Dr. Bart Thrasher, a family practice physician and medical director of Delta's emergency department, noticed that he was seeing more and more Spanish-speaking patients in the emergency room. He spearheaded an effort to reach out to the hospital's Hispanic patients. As a result, three of the other emergency department physicians learned medical terminology in Spanish so as to better communicate with the patient base (Dr. Thrasher already spoke Spanish), the hospital posted Spanish billboards in the community, and hospital forms and directions were made available in Spanish. Dr. Thrasher and Delta's goal was to show the Spanish-speaking population of Memphis that Delta was sensitive to their needs. They hoped that this segmentation approach would increase physician referrals and use of the hospital's emergency services.[5]

Income or Wealth Segmentation. It is common for professional service firms to attempt to serve only individuals or companies within certain size or income brackets. Carriage-trade lawyers, tax-shelter accountants, investment counselors, legal aid clinics, and bankruptcy lawyers all aim to serve segments with well-defined levels of financial resources.

Multi-Variable Segmentation. Organizations frequently segment a market by combining two or more variables. For example, age and income might be combined with location in order for a physician to identify the ideal place to open a practice. A dermatologist, for example, might find that middle-income and higher neighborhoods with lots of families with teenagers might be best suited to grow his or her business.

Psychographic Segmentation

People with similar demographic characteristics might exhibit very different psychographic profiles. In psychographic segmentation, prospects are divided into groups on the basis of their social class, lifestyle, or personality characteristics.

Social Class. Social classes are relatively homogeneous and enduring divisions in a society. They are hierarchically ordered and their members share similar values, interests, and behaviors. Social scientists have distinguished six social classes: (1) upper uppers (less than 1 percent); (2) lower uppers (about 2 percent); (3) upper middles (12 percent); (4) lower middles (30 percent); (5) upper lowers (35 percent); and (6) lower lowers (20 percent), using variables such as income, occupation, education, and type of residence.[6] Social classes tend to show distinct consumption preferences. For example, most upper-class people would not want to be seen walking into an H & R Block office for tax advice. At the same time, most lower-class people will shy away from professionals with fancy offices in high-rent locations.

Lifestyle. Different consumer lifestyles are found within and even between social classes. Researchers have found that they can identify lifestyle segments by clustering people into groups sharing common activities, interests, and opinions. Lifestyle segmentation is built on the notion that "we do what we do because it fits into the kind of life we are living or want to live." Lifestyle is often a much better explanatory variable than any of the traditional social characteristics, such as income and education, when explaining the market for such services as financial planning or elected plastic surgery.

Personality. Personality variables can also be used to segment markets. An organization can try to match its organizational personality (or image) to the individual personalities (or self-images) of the clients it wishes to serve. Thus, a CPA firm might want to portray itself in promotional materials and personal communications as aggressive and competitive in order to appeal to clients who see themselves as aggressive and competitive.

Behavioral Segmentation

Sometimes professional service marketers are particularly interested in how clients respond to a service rather than in the clients' lifestyle or personality. Many marketers believe that behavioristic variables are the best starting point for constructing useful market segments because behavior has direct implications for what firms and services consumer segments may choose. Some variables in behavioral segmentation include:

Purchase Occasion. Clients can be distinguished according to occasions when they purchase a service. For example, individuals may buy preventive or emergency healthcare services. Different sets of resources are required to serve preventive versus emergency clients. Serving the emergency segment requires an ability to provide help very quickly and a larger professional staff will probably be needed to insure that someone is always "on call." For this group of clients, the ability to respond quickly would be stressed in promotional materials.

Benefits Sought. Consumers can be segmented according to the particular benefits they are seeking from a service. Many markets are made up of three core benefit segments: *quality buyers, value buyers,* and *economy buyers.* Quality buyers seek out professionals with the best reputations and credentials and have little concern for cost. They will go after big-name firms and talent. Value buyers look for the best value for the money and expect the service to match the fee or price. They are content with less prestigious professionals, but insist on getting considerable attention and satisfactory performance for what they can afford to pay. Economy buyers are primarily interested in minimizing their cost and favor the least expensive market offer. They are willing to go to paraprofessionals and unlicensed or uncertified practitioners to obtain the lowest-cost services.

In addition to general benefits, each service should be evaluated for the specific benefits that different clients might seek. Some clients of CPA audit services may seek "management letters" with much "free" consulting advice in them, while other clients will not even think about this. Some clients of architectural services may seek unusual, high-style designs, while others may seek only functional designs. A separate marketing strategy can be worked out for each segment, based on the unique benefits sought and the associated characteristics of the segment members. Benefit segmentation works best when people's preferences are correlated with demographic and media characteristics, making it easier to identify them efficiently.

User Status. Many markets can be segmented into non-users, ex-users, potential users, first-time users, and regular users of a service. Many of the new clinic-type professional service practices have been designed to attract non-users and turn them into first-time or regular users. More traditional professional service organizations target their efforts exclusively toward regular users. An overlooked segment is often the ex-users (of, for example, consulting or engineering services), who may really be potential users but who need to be contacted occasionally to determine their interest in becoming a user again (perhaps to take advantage of a new service).

Usage Rate. Markets can also be segmented into light-, medium-, and heavy-user groups of a service (called volume segmentation). Heavy users are often a small percentage of the market but account for a high percentage of total consumption. For example, the federal government is only one of many buyers in several markets, but it consumes an extremely large amount of consulting, engineering, accounting, and other professional services. Targeting the heavy users of certain services is a strategy many professional service organizations pursue. Needless to say, the competition for the heavy users in most markets is intense, because obtaining just a few heavy users as clients can keep an organization profitable.

Loyalty Status. A market can also be segmented by client loyalty patterns. An organization should research its own and its competitors' clients to determine their degree of loyalty. Four groups can generally be distinguished: (1) *hard-core loyals,* who are exclusively devoted to one organization; (2) *soft-core loyals,* who are devoted to two or three organizations; (3) *shifting loyals,* who are gradually moving from favoring one organization to favoring another organization; and (4) *switchers,* who show no loyalty to any organization. If most of an organization's clients are hard-core loyals, or even soft-core loyals, the organization is basically healthy. It might study its loyals to find out the basic satisfactions they derive from their affiliation, and then attempt to attract the shifting loyals of competing organizations who are seeking the same satisfactions.

Buying Structure. Organizations and family units vary greatly in the formal procedures and structures they use in buying. Governments, for example, typically have extremely rigorous procedures involving numerous committees, competitive bidding, and much red tape. Some families are reasonably formal about large purchases, having family meetings to determine budgets and spending plans. At the other end of the spectrum are organizations and families with no formal procedures whatsoever.

Professional service organizations frequently use segmentation by buying structure. Many firms choose not to go after business from clients who have certain types of buying structures. Thus, there are architectural firms that refuse to enter design competitions; CPA firms that avoid competitive bidding situations; law firms that do not seek work from clients who request written proposals from prospective attorneys; and consulting firms that avoid government work unless available on a "sole-source" basis.

Primary Referral Agent. Segmentation by primary referral agent involves recognizing that clients vary in the types of people they rely on for advice and for professional services. Some clients, because of a desire for privacy or fear of being misunderstood, make buying decisions by themselves, but most clients rely heavily on others for guidance. Depending on the service to be bought and their unique circumstances, clients may turn to trusted sources such as lawyers, bankers, doctors, local college faculty, competitors, club and association acquaintances, and so forth for referrals. Professional service organizations that segment by referral agent include CPA and law firms that target the clients of certain banks, professionals of all types who target those who receive advice from certain college professors, or specialized physicians who target the patients of certain general practitioners. Of course, when such segments are targeted, the professional service provider must devote considerable effort toward maintaining excellent relationships with the chosen referral agents.

Attitude. The clients in a market can be classified by their degree of enthusiasm for a professional service. Five attitude classes can be distinguished: enthusiastic, positive, indifferent, negative, and hostile. In most cases, professional service organizations will want to target the enthusiastic and positive clients, recognizing that the other three segments can be difficult and expensive to attract. But some professional service organizations may find their best opportunities for growth lying within segments that are indifferent, negative, or even hostile. An ability to turn lawyer-haters, dentist-haters, doctor-haters, and other negative individuals—who may seriously need professional services—into satisfied clients can prove to be very profitable for some firms.

Marketing Factors. Markets can also be segmented into groups who respond differently to such marketing factors as personal selling, advertising, and price. For example, there are clients who are turned off by advertising of professional services; and there are clients who see such advertising as legitimate and useful. Knowing the marketing factor sensitivities of different segments can be very helpful in allocating marketing resources.

BASES FOR SEGMENTING ORGANIZATIONAL MARKETS

Professional services are marketed to organizations as well as to individual consumers. Public accounting firms, legal and management consulting firms, and advertising agencies all may wish to identify appropriate organizations that may need their services.

Here are several bases for segmenting organizational markets.

1. **Organizational size and resources:** Large organizations can afford more expensive services, but typically have more complex purchasing processes. Medium and small organizations may have less to spend, but often can be the focus for niched strategies.

2. **Interest profile:** Organizations differ in their goals, treatment of their staffs, and their time horizons. A physician practice, for example, may target law firm partners as potential clients in an executive health-screening program. Because partners are of extreme importance to the profitability of the firm, these individuals may clearly see the benefits of health maintenance measures.

3. **Buying criteria:** Some organizations are concerned about cost effectiveness; others about accruing prestige. For example, using a well-known law firm as an organization's legal team may communicate power and signal the willingness to use it.

4. **Buying process:** Some organizations require a good deal of paperwork and a long time period before making a commitment; others may act in a few days on the basis of a verbal promise and a handshake. Some use committees to make decisions; others may be dominated by a strong leader. A professional service firm must have procedures to match a number of purchase processes.

5. **Degree of local autonomy:** Major national or international organizations differ in the degree of autonomy they allow local representatives in purchasing outside services. When dealing with a corporate headquarters of a large organization, a professional firm will need more extensive documentation and longer time periods to process information and/or proposals.

MARKET TARGETING

Market segmentation reveals the market segment opportunities facing the organization. Then the institution has to decide how best to target these segments. The three broad strategies (shown in Figure 7-1) are:

1. *Undifferentiated Marketing.* The organization goes after the whole market with one offer and marketing mix, trying to attract as many consumers as possible (this is another name for mass marketing).

2. *Differentiated Marketing.* The organization goes after several market segments, developing an effective offer and marketing mix for each.

3. *Concentrated Marketing.* The organization goes after one market segment and develops the ideal offer and marketing mix.

Figure 7-1. Three Alternative Market-Coverage Strategies.

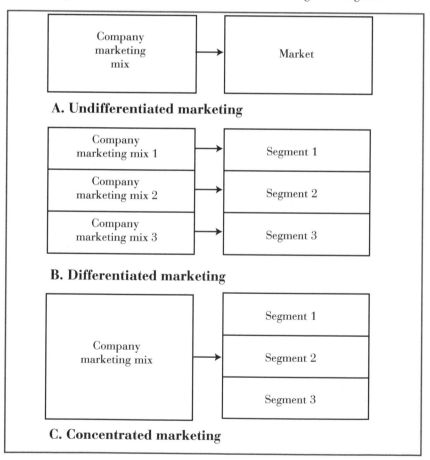

Let's take a look at the logic and merits of each of these strategies.

Undifferentiated Marketing

In undifferentiated marketing, the organization chooses not to recognize the different market segments making up the market. It treats the market as an aggregate, focusing on what is common in the needs of clients rather than on what is different. The organization tries to design services and a marketing program that appeal to the broadest number of clients. This type of marketing would be exemplified by the consulting firm that offers the same computer software to everyone or the law firm that offers the same uncontested divorce settlement to everyone.

Undifferentiated marketing is typically defended on the grounds of cost economies. Many legal clinics use this technique for "simple wills" or "uncontested divorces." Service costs, research costs, promotion costs, and training costs are all kept low by offering a limited line of services. The lower cost, however, is usually accompanied by reduced client satisfaction through failure of the organization to meet individually varying needs. Competitors have an incentive to reach and serve the neglected segments, and become strongly entrenched in these segments.

Differentiated Marketing

Under differentiated marketing, an organization decides to operate in two or more market segments but designs separate services and/or marketing programs for each. By offering service and marketing variations, it hopes to attain higher sales and a deeper position within each market segment. It hopes that a deep position in several segments will strengthen the clients' overall identification of the organization with its professional field. Furthermore, it hopes for greater loyalty and repeat purchasing, because the organization's services have been bent to the desires of clients rather than the other way around.

The net effect of differentiated marketing is to create more total revenues for the organization than undifferentiated marketing. However, it also tends to create higher cost of doing business because the organization has to spend more in service design, marketing research, communication materials, and training. Because differentiated marketing leads to higher sales and higher costs, the optimality of this strategy can't be determined until it is used. However, some professional service organizations push differentiated marketing too far in that they run more segmented programs than are economically feasible. Other organizations probably err in not pushing differentiated marketing far enough in light of the varying needs of their clients.

Concentrated Marketing

Concentrated marketing occurs when an organization decides to divide the market into meaningful segments and devote its major marketing effort to one segment. Instead of spreading itself thin in many parts of the market, it concentrates on serving a particular market segment well. Through concentrated marketing, the organization usually achieves a strong following and standing in a particular market segment. It enjoys greater knowledge of the market segment's needs and behavior and it also achieves operating economies through specialization in service provision and promotion. This type of marketing is done, for example, by law firms that specialize in handling particular types of litigation or by consultants who specialize in the management problems of a single industry. Other examples include interior designers who specialize in certain types of offices such as banks, CPAs who specialize in formulating tax shelters, or surgeons who specialize in certain types of surgery. Consider the following examples of successful concentrated marketing:

> In Port Washington, New York, Security Resolution Advisors, a law firm, helps investors who believe that they have been victimized by fraudulent practices such as unauthorized trading, churning, misrepresentation of financial statements, or unstable investment recommendations. The firm chose to focus on this segment because its management felt that fraud was increasing in the financial industry, but fewer people were trying to recoup their losses. The firm believed that clients rarely sued because they would have to put a lawyer on retainer, paying as they go. As a result, Security Resolution Advisors is willing to work on a contingency basis, claiming a fee only if they win. The company doesn't use any type of asset cut-off. It takes cases of all financial sizes and its clients range from individual investors who felt cheated to a suit in which they represented 538 individuals in a $7.1-million claim.[7]

Similarly, the accounting firm of Porter, Keadle, Macer (PKM) in Atlanta found that representing clients before the Securities and Exchange Commission can set them apart from competitors. "It is akin to lawyers going before the Supreme Court," according to Tim Keadle, a partner in PKM. It can also be profitable. This speculation represents 34 percent of the firm's fees.[8]

Concentrated marketing does involve higher-than-normal risk in that the market may suddenly decline or disappear. Becoming dependent on only one segment also holds the risk of being bad for an organization's reputation, as clients and competitors may begin to question the independence and integrity of a firm that appears beholden to a specific set of clients. This last problem developed in the following situation:

A two-person Minneapolis law partnership was doing extremely well specializing in handling liability suits filed against A. H. Robins Co., the manufacturers of the ill-fated Dalkon shield intrauterine birth-control device. After handling more than 900 cases, the firm found itself the target of considerable adverse publicity and several investigations about the way it was handling the Dalkon cases. It was charged that a "cozy" relationship between the law firm and an insurance adjuster allowed the firm to obtain rapid, but allegedly inferior, cash settlements in its cases. The firm became so bogged down with handling all the charges against it that it was forced to withdraw from 104 Dalkon cases at a time when the charges against the firm had not really been substantiated.[9]

There is a second danger in using a concentrated approach. Sometimes niche players exist because larger firms allow them to exist. A law firm that specializes in handling a particular type of litigation may do so because it is a market so specialized and perhaps so small that it would be difficult for a larger organization to devote resources and time to this particular segment. In this case, the smaller law firm should consider expanding to avoid depending on one niche; however, when the smaller firm expands, it is no longer considered harmless by the larger firm. Now it is considered a threat and the larger organization may direct its resources to attack the new market provider.

CHOOSING A MARKET
COVERAGE STRATEGY

The actual choice of a marketing strategy depends on specific factors facing the organization. If the organization has *limited resources*, it will probably choose concentrated marketing because it will not have enough resources to relate to the whole market and/or tailor special services for each segment. If the market is fairly *homogeneous* in its needs and desires, the organization will probably choose undifferentiated marketing because little would be gained by differentiated offerings. If the organization aspires to be a leader in several segments of the market, it will choose differentiated marketing. If *competitors* have already established dominance in all but a few market segments, an organization might try to concentrate its marketing in one of the remaining segments. Many organizations start out with a strategy of undifferentiated or concentrated marketing and, if they are successful, evolve into a strategy of differentiated marketing.

Whether a firm elects a concentrated or differentiated marketing strategy, it must identify the best segments to serve. A market segment is worth further consideration when it satisfies the following two criteria:

(1) The segment is attractive in its own right. Several factors contribute to making a market segment attractive. The following are the major features:[10]

- *Market size.* Large markets are more attractive than small markets.

- *Market growth rate.* Markets with high growth rates are more attractive than markets with low growth rates.

- *Ability to pay.* Markets with a large ability to pay are more attractive.

- *Competitive intensity.* Markets that are served by few competitors or substitute services are more attractive than markets that are served by many and/or strong competitors.

- *Variability.* Markets that fluctuate in size are less attractive than those that are stable or growing.

- *Scale economies.* Markets that can be served at lower unit cost as size increases are more attractive than constant-cost markets.

- *Learning curve.* Markets are more attractive when the firms serving them experience lower unit costs as they gain more experience serving their needs than where no learning curve exists.

(2) The firm possesses the factors required to succeed in that segment. Strength factors include:

- *Relative market share.* The higher the firm's relative share of its market, the greater the firm's strength.
- *Price competitiveness.* The lower the firm's costs relative to competitors, the greater its strength.
- *Program quality.* The higher the quality of the firm's offerings relative to competitors, the greater its strength
- *Knowledge of consumer/market.* The deeper the firm's knowledge of consumers and their needs and wants, the greater its strength.
- *Marketing effectiveness.* The greater the firm's relevant marketing effectiveness, the greater its strength.
- *Geography.* The greater the firm's geographical presence and advantages in the market, the greater its strength.
- *Profitability.* The greater the level of profitability relative to its competitors, the greater the strength.

When a firm evaluates possible market segments, it must carefully weigh both market segment characteristics and institutional success requirements. The considered segments must also be a good match with the firm's mission and values. A good example of a firm that segmented the market based upon company values is the architectural firm of Miller/Hull of Seattle. In keeping with the firm's environmental values, Miller/Hull created a program called "Design for Environment" that focuses on "green" buildings to implement its values.[11]

POSITIONING FOR
COMPETITIVE ADVANTAGE

Once a professional service firm decides on its target market, it must "position" its service offering. A service's position is the way the service is to be defined by target consumers—the place the service is to occupy in the consumers' minds relative to competing services.

Consumers are overloaded with information about products and services. To simplify the buying process, clients organize services in categories or position services and companies in their minds. The service's position is the complex set of perceptions, impressions, and feelings that the consumers hold for the service compared with those of its competitors. Consumers position services with or without the help of marketers, but marketers do not want to leave their service positions to chance. They must plan positions that will give their services the greatest advantage in the selected target markets and they must design marketing mixes to create these planned positions. The organization has to undertake a competitive analysis to identify the positions of existing competitors as a prelude to deciding what should be done about its positioning.

Using the techniques for measuring beliefs or images introduced in Chapter 5, the organization should be able to develop a *perceptual space map* that indicates where clients in a segment perceive the different competitors to be positioned along specific attributes. An example of a perceptual space map is presented in Figure 7-2. This example represents how the clients in a targeted segment tend to see a group of competing law firms on the attributes of prestige and friendliness. Firm A is seen as highly prestigious and very unfriendly, Firm B as moderately prestigious and moderately friendly, and so forth.

Formulating a positioning strategy for a firm like B would next involve researching what clients in the target segment view as the most desirable configuration of attributes for a law firm to have. Clients could be asked to indicate "ideal" levels of attributes on rating scales. It might be discovered that most clients in the segment prefer to retain highly prestigious and moderately friendly firms (those near point 1), with a substantial minority preferring moderately prestigious and very friendly firms (those near point 2). Management of Firm B would then have to choose among the following positioning approaches.

1. Seeking to improve the firm's prestige to position itself near point 1. This might be done by hiring a well-known political figure or by taking on a highly publicized *pro bono* case.

Figure 7-2. Product Space Map for Four Law Firms.

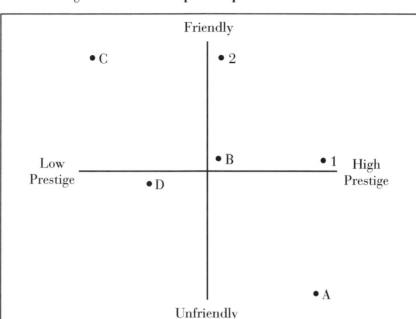

2. Seeking to improve the firm's friendliness to position itself closer to point 2. This might be done by staff training or by a revision of hiring and promotion policies.

3. Some combination of the above in order to try to position itself to be attractive to all clients in the segment.

Choosing a positioning strategy essentially becomes a market targeting task, as a decision must be made on which *subsegment*—using "benefits sought" as the subsegmentation variable—to target: those who prefer prestige or those who prefer friendliness. As was just discussed, market targeting (and therefore positioning) should be based on the attractiveness of the segments and on the strengths of the organization.

Choosing and Implementing a Positioning Strategy

Some firms find it easy to choose their positioning strategy. For example, a firm well known for its quality in certain segments will go for this position in new segments if there are buyers seeking quality. In many cases, two or more firms will go for the same position, then each will have to find a way to set itself apart, by offering high quality or lower cost, or high quality with more technical service, for example. Each firm must differentiate its offering by building a unique bundle of competitive advantages that appeal to a substantial group within the segment.

The positioning task consists of three steps: (1) identifying a set of possible competitive advantages in which to build position; (2) selecting the right competitive advantages; and (3) effectively communicating and delivering the chosen position in the marketplace.

Identifying possible competitive advantages. Consumers typically choose services that give them the greatest value. The key to winning and keeping customers is to understand their needs and buying processes better than competitors and deliver more value. The competitive advantage is typically gained through providing greater benefits and/or reducing overall costs *better* than the competitors.

To find points of differentiation, marketers must think through the customers' entire experience with such organizations. A service firm can differentiate itself by following the service itself, its people, or its image.

Consider the following examples of differentiating the service offer:

Finstein, Simpson, Gilbert, and Morowitz, LLC is considered Atlantic City's premier accounting and consulting firm, representing more than 900 individual and business clients. It has a particular expertise in the gaming industry. While the firm traditionally provided services to casino executives, such as tax planning and financial planning, in 1992 the firm made a strategic decision to provide consulting services to the gaming industry itself. The firm's staff was trained, outside resources were brought in, and systems were redesigned to provide process improvement for back office operations of casinos, such as human resources and the credit area. What particularly differentiated the firm were their industry reports that set them apart and made them experts in the field.[12]

Another service firm that created an interesting differentiation strategy was Bennett Gold, an accounting firm in North York,

Ontario. This firm was the first in Canada to obtain the WebTrust Seal, which is a Web site audit that examines how companies conduct themselves on-line and ensures that they meet certain standards. The result was that it successfully positioned itself in the developing e-commerce wave of business.[13]

Companies can also gain a strong competitive advantage by hiring and training better people than their competitors do. Management consulting firms McKinery & Co. and Accenture are constantly battling for the top MBAs in the country. Because services are inseparable from people, this is particularly important in professional service firms.

Still other companies work on differentiating their image. Richard Tackett, a lawyer with New York's Golenbock, Eiseman, Assor, and Bell, created a trade association in the textile industry specifically designed to help combat international design piracy in a cost-efficient manner. The association, known as the Textile Producers and Suppliers Association, not only has twelve dozen members but also includes the producers themselves and suppliers such as 3M and Dupont, as well as design houses. Mr. Tackett hopes to draw people's attention to the issues addressed by the organization as well as to the fact of his expertise. By developing this trade association, he has positioned his firm and himself as the leader in the area of international trade design piracy. Only his firm has him, which is a very strong competitive advantage. Even when competing services look the same, buyers may perceive a difference based on company or brand image.

Selecting the right competitive advantages. Suppose a company is fortunate enough to discover several potential competitive advantages. It must now decide on how many differences to promote and which ones. Many marketers think that companies should aggressively promote only one benefit to a target market. Ad man Rosser Reeves, for example, said that companies should develop a unique selling proposition (USP) for each brand and stick to it. Each brand should pick an attribute and promote itself as number one on that attribute. The logic is that buyers tend to remember number one better in an over-marketed society. Other marketers think that a company should position on more than one factor. This may be necessary if two or more firms are claiming to be best on the same attribute.

A company needs to avoid at least three major positioning errors. The first is underpositioning, or failing to position the company at all. Some firms may discover that buyers have only a vague idea of the company and what it does, or that they do not really know anything special about it. The second error is overpositioning—giving buyers too narrow a picture of the company. Organizations using a niched strategy need to be especially careful to avoid overpositioning. Finally, companies must avoid confused positioning—leaving clients with a confused image of the company. This normally occurs when an organization's communications stress different strengths without tying them to a core attribute or strategy.

Not all brand differences are meaningful or worthwhile, and each difference has the potential to create costs as well as benefits for an organization. Therefore, the organization must carefully select the ways in which it will distinguish itself from competitors.

A professional service firm can differentiate itself in many ways, including:

- Location
- Quality
- Special features
- Performance quality
- Technologies used or available
- Price charged
- Personable manner of the employees

On which specific features should a professional service firm differentiate itself? Some differences will be more valued by clients, some will be easier for the firm to implement successfully. The features the firm selects should meet the following criteria:

- *Important*: The difference delivers a highly valued benefit to target buyers.
- *Distinctive*: Competitors do not offer the difference, or the company can offer it in a more distinctive way.
- *Superior*: The difference is superior to other ways that customers might obtain the same benefit.

- *Communicable*: The difference is communicable and visible to buyers.

- *Preemptive*: Competitors cannot easily copy the difference.

- *Affordable*: Buyers can afford to pay for the difference.

- *Profitable*: The company can introduce the difference profitably.

Choosing competitive advantages on which to position a professional service can be difficult, yet such choices may be crucial to a firm's success.

Some competitive advantages may be quickly ruled out because they are too slight, too costly to develop, or too inconsistent with the company's profile. Suppose that a company is designing its positioning strategy and has narrowed its list of possible competitive advantages to four. The company needs a framework for selecting the one advantage that makes the most sense to develop. Table 7-2 shows a systematic way to evaluate several potential competitive advantages and choose the right one.

In Table 7-2, the company compares its standing on four attributes—technology, cost, quality, and service—to the standing of its major competitor. Let's assume that both companies stand at 8 on technology (1 = low score; 10 = high score), which means they both have good technology. The company questions whether it can gain much by improving its technology further, especially given the high cost of new technology. The competitor has a better standing on cost (8 instead of 6), and this can hurt the company if the market gets more price sensitive. The company offers higher quality than its competitor (8 instead of 6). Finally, both companies offer below-average service (4 and 3).

At first glance, it appears that the company should go after cost or service to improve its market appeal relative to the competitor. However, the firm must consider other factors. First, how important to the target customers are improvements in each of these attributes? The fourth column shows that both cost and service improvements would be highly important to customers. Next, can the company afford to make the improvements? If so, how fast can it complete them? The fifth column shows that the competitor's ability to improve service is low, perhaps because the competitor doesn't believe in service or is strapped for funds.

Table 7-2. Finding Competitive Advantage.

Competitive Advantage	Company Standing (1-10)	Competitor Standing (1-10)	Importance of Improving Standing (H-M-L)	Affordability and Speed (H-M-L)	Competitor's Ability to Improve Standing (H-M-L)	Recommended Action
Technology	8	8	L	L	M	Hold
Cost	6	8	H	M	M	Watch
Quality	8	6	L	L	H	Watch
Service	4	3	H	H	L	Invest

The final column then shows the appropriate actions to take on each attribute. It makes the most sense for the company to invest in improving its service. Service is important to customers; the company can afford to improve its service and can do it fast, and the competitor probably will not be able to catch up.

Communicating and delivering the chosen position. Once it has chosen a position, the company must take strong steps to deliver and communicate the desired position to target consumers. All the company's marketing mix efforts must support the positioning strategy. Positioning the company calls for concrete action, not just talk. If the company decides to build a position on better quality and service, it must first *deliver* that position. Designing the marketing mix essentially involves working out the tactical details of the positioning strategy.

Companies often find it easier to come up with a good positioning strategy than to implement it. Establishing a position or changing one usually takes a long time. In contrast, positions that have taken the firm years to build can quickly be lost. Once a company has built the desired position, it must take care to maintain the position through consistent performance and communication. It must closely monitor and adapt the position over time to match changes in consumer needs and competitors' strategies. However, the company should avoid abrupt changes that might confuse consumers. Instead, a product's or service's position should evolve gradually as it adapts to the ever-changing marketing environment.

SUMMARY

Target marketing involves distinguishing the different groups that make up a market and developing appropriate services and marketing mixes for each target market. The key steps in target marketing are market segmentation, market targeting, and market positioning. Market segmentation is the act of dividing a market into distinct groups of clients who might merit separate services and/or marketing mixes. The organization tries different variables to see which reveal the best segmentation opportunities. Segmentation variables can be classified as geographic, demographic, psychographic, and behaviorial. The effectiveness of the segmentation analysis depends upon arriving at segments that are measurable, accessible, substantial, and actionable.

Next, the organization has to select the best market segment(s). The first decision is how many segments the firm will cover. The organization can ignore segment differences (undifferentiated marketing), develop different market offers for several segments (differentiated marketing), or go after one or a few market segments (concentrated marketing). The attractiveness of each segment must be weighed against the organization's strengths in targeting the segment. Finally, market targeting involves defining the organization's competitors and positioning possibilities. The organization should research the competitors' positions and decide whether to take a position similar to some competitor or go after an unoccupied position. The organization can then build an entire marketing program around the position or image that it has chosen.

NOTES

[1] Adapted from "Standardizing Engagements: One Firm's Keys to Success," *Practical Accountant* (December 1998), v31, n12, p14.

[2] Peppers and Rogers@1 to 1, Cyberworld Meets Real World, e-newsletter (July 29, 1999), v20, n50.

[3] Whitfield, Robert. "How to Define Target Market for Your Legal Services," *Illinois Legal Times* (April 1994).

[4] Weiss, Michael J. *The Clustering of America*. New York: Harper & Row, 1988.

[5] Larson, Jennifer. "Delta Medical Marketing Emerging Services to Area's Growing Hispanic Community," *Memphis Business Journal* (April 24, 1998), v19, n52, p8.

[6] Coleman, Richard P. "The Continuing Significance of Social Class to Marketing," *Journal of Consumer Research* (December 1983), p265-280 and Richard P. Coleman and Lee P. Rainwater, *Social Standing in America: New Dimensions of Class*. New York: Basic Books, 1978.

[7] "New Law Firm Fights Investment Fraud," *Bank Investment Marketing* (September 1998), v6, n9, p10.

8   Kahan, Stuart. "Performing at the Highest Level," *Practical Accountant*, August 1999.

9   Bluestein, Paul. "How 2 Young Lawyers Got Rich by Settling IUD Labeling Claims," *The Wall Street Journal* (February 24, 1982), p1.

10 These criteria for market attractiveness and institutional success factors are based on the General Electric Strategic Business Planning grid.

11 "Designers Establish Programs to Meet Clients Needs," *Building Design and Construction* (September 1996), v37, n9, p16.

12 Kahan, Stuart. "Rolling the Dice and Coming Up a Winner," *Practical Accountant* (November 1997), v30, n11, p80.

13 Middlemiss, Jim. "State Your Claim," *CA Magazine* (May 1999), v132, n4, p18-23.

8 | Understanding the Individual Client

·······································

*"Everyone is kneaded out of the same dough, but
not baked in the same oven."*
YIDDISH PROVERB

The marketing manager of a professional service firm must understand consumer behavior because the firm's success depends on it.
There are four broad classes of marketing decisions for which an understanding of consumers are especially crucial. These are:

1. *How to aggregate consumers into similar groupings for purposes
   of marketing planning.* This is the issue of segmentation, which
   was covered in Chapter 7.

2. *How to market to each chosen segment.* The marketer must
   decide what to offer in benefits and costs (service and pricing
   decisions), how to communicate these (promotion decisions), and
   how to make them available (access decisions).

3. *How much to market to each segment.* These strategic allocation
   decisions involve questions about how many dollars in investment and operating budget to put into a particular market, how
   much personnel to use, and how much time to spend.

4. *When to apply the marketing efforts to the segments.* These timing decisions are also critical strategic choices. They involve the

Choosing a Consultant: What Should Clients Look For?[1]

Choosing the proper consultant may mean the success or failure of a client's current project—even the client's job security may depend upon it. If the client makes the right decision, she may get a raise; if the client slips up, she may end up turning in her company ID to the Human Resources Manager. All this can make a client anxious, concerned, and perhaps even a little overwhelmed. How does one know which consultant is right? Here are nine factors that may influence a client's decision-making process in choosing a consultant.

1. **Client's needs.** Does the client need a consultant for technical or subject expertise? For example, a consultant with subject expertise may understand how a Web presence may help market a firm, but he or she may not know how to create the Web site.

2. **Buzzword barrier.** Can the consultant translate technical material into information that the client's staff can easily understand? Clearly, two-way communication is the foundation of project success.

3. **Walk-away clause.** Is the consultant willing to negotiate a walk-away clause in the contract? Such a clause may give the client the opportunity to walk-away from the contract without penalty if the consultant's work is not satisfactory.

4. **Billing.** Can the client pay the consultant and terminate the contract upon completion of predetermined project milestones or does the consultant require a payment after all deliverables are achieved? In some cases, the client may wait for a deliverable that cannot or never will be achieved.

5. **Current industry knowledge.** Does the consultant have knowledge of current business issues or industry drivers?

6. **Resources.** Does the consultant have access to appropriate business and technical resources? Such resources allow the consultant to reach beyond his or her own knowledge base.

7. **Appropriate costs.** Does the client have to sell his or her first-born to get value and good deliverable? The client does not necessarily have to pay "major firm consulting costs" for relatively simple and small projects.

8. **Proven industry track record.** The client may want a list of references. Is the consultant willing to disclose past engagements?

9. **Cultural fit.** Does the consultant answer questions honestly and openly? Will the client's staff feel comfortable working with the consultant?

allocation of resources over time as well as sequencing decisions for various tactics within a given strategy.

There are four levels at which a marketing manager may wish to understand consumer behavior in order to make better decisions:

1. **Descriptive understanding.** At the simplest level, the manager may wish to profile the characteristics of the market at a given point in time. How many buyers of what age, sex, and occupational status are in market A, creating how many exchanges of type B, in month Y, costing X marketing dollars, and so on? At a more sophisticated level, the manager may wish to categorize consumers in terms of complex indexes such as their social class, family life cycle, or psychographic profile. The marketing manager of a plastic surgery practice may wish to look at the trends involving the number of face-lifts done in each of the months for the last several years. He or she may wish to see how many men versus women had the surgery performed and how they made their payment.

2. **Understanding of the associations.** At this level, the manager may desire to know what behaviors or characteristics in the profile are associated with what other behaviors or characteristics. The marketing manager of a plastic surgery practice may wish to know which procedures are associated with age, or perhaps, personal income.

3. **Understanding of causation.** If a curvilinear association is found between electing to have a procedure like a face-lift and one's increasing age and income, a manager may wish to know whether this is truly causal. This level of understanding moves beyond association to show determinacy. Such information is even more valuable if "the cause" can be influenced by managers.

4. **Ability to explain causation.** Ideally, a marketer would like to move beyond knowing that "A" causes "B" to know why this is so. That is, the marketer may know that age and income have a curvilinear association with certain procedures. But the manager may only have hypotheses as to why this is so. These two factors may simply create the ability to have the surgery and the greater potential need for the surgery. However, the real cause might be some other variable such as the individual's need for acceptance.

Developing a sophisticated understanding of various consumer markets is not easy. It comes with time and experience and the careful use of the research approaches discussed in Chapter 5. Personal observation and formal research are both likely to be more effective if they are based on an awareness of what we already know about consumers and on sound conceptualization.

In this chapter, we will cover the subjects of organizational buyer behavior and individual buyer behavior in separate sections. In addition, we offer a few suggestions on research methods to use in studying behavior. The major questions we recommend investigating are the following:

1. What buying decisions do buyers make?
2. Who participates in the buying process?
3. What are the major influences on the buying process?
4. What are the main steps and features of the decision process of buyers?

ORGANIZATIONAL BUYER BEHAVIOR

The organizations that professional service organizations seek as clients are extremely varied. Big businesses, small businesses, government agencies, trade associations, hospitals, educational institutions, charities, and other potential organizational clients exhibit different ways of buying professional services; therefore, there is no general, comprehensive description of how organizations buy professional services. Nevertheless, we can offer a framework for studying organizational buying of professional services that can be used in the analysis of different types of buyers. The framework is described below.

Types of Decisions

The first issue to examine in understanding organizational buyer behavior is the type of buying decisions being investigated. The *marketer* must recognize that some decisions are more complex, risky, or important than others, and that the number of people involved with a decision and the steps taken to make a decision will vary depending on the characteristics of that decision. The traditional way of categorizing organizational buying decisions was originally suggested by Robinson et al.[2] They distinguished among the following three types of buying situations called *buyclasses*.

1. **Straight rebuy.** This occurs when the organization reorders something without any modifications. It is usually handled on a routine basis by the purchasing department. Based on past buying satisfaction, the buyer simply chooses from the various suppliers on a list. Decisions on who should conduct a business firm's financial audits or who should perform a land developer's land survey are typically straight rebuy situations. These decisions do not usually require the involvement of many individuals nor do they require an extensive decision process characterized by much information gathering. Those service firms that enjoy the straight rebuy status typically focus on retention and service quality issues. They may even propose a retainer system so the purchasing agent will save decision

time. Those firms that are on the outside of the straight rebuy window will typically try to offer something new or exploit dissatisfactions with the present supplier so the buyer will consider them. They try to get their foot in the door with a smaller-scale service and enlarge the purchase share over time.

2. Modified rebuy. Here the buyer wants to modify service specifications, prices, terms, or, perhaps, even suppliers. The modified rebuy usually involves more decision participants than the straight rebuy. A business firm's decision to consider changing its CPA firm for an audit plus some specialized tax work could fit this description. Modified rebuys represent a more complex decision process requiring more information gathering. This type of buying decision may be seen by the incumbent service firm as an opportunity to increase its business or it may be seen as a threat signaling its clients' dissatisfaction with some aspect of its service.

3. New task. In this situation the buyer is purchasing unfamiliar services from unfamiliar professionals. In such cases, the greater the cost or risk and the larger the number of decision participants, the greater their efforts to collect information will be. A large corporation needing a product liability attorney for the first time would be in this situation, and so would a physician requiring the services of a market research firm to do his/her first customer satisfaction survey.

The marketer will want to identify the types of decisions being made by potential clients within the firm's target markets. Existing clients in straight-rebuy situations should be studied to see how their past behavior can be reinforced so that they will automatically reorder services and refrain from considering other suppliers. These clients could also be studied to uncover ways to shift them tactfully to modified-rebuy or new-task situations where they will buy more from the firm. The risk in this, of course, is that buyers shifted to these situations may expand their set of considered suppliers. The marketing manager would want to evaluate whether reminder notices, follow-up visits, training seminars, and other forms of communications could help in accomplishing these objectives at minimal risk.

For clients in a firm's target markets who are in straight-rebuy situations, but who buy from competitors, the marketing manager will want to evaluate the probabilities of getting them to switch. These probabilities might be estimated with the help of knowledgeable informants such as the professionals from other fields who service those clients. The firm should concentrate on non-clients with high switching probabilities.

The marketer should conduct intensive study of organizations in target markets that are in modified-rebuy or new-task situations. These organizations represent "live leads" and they should be investigated thoroughly to identify the participants in their buying decisions, the influences on their decisions, and the nature of their decision processes. (See Figure 8-1.)

Figure 8-1. Major Influences on Business Buying Behavior.

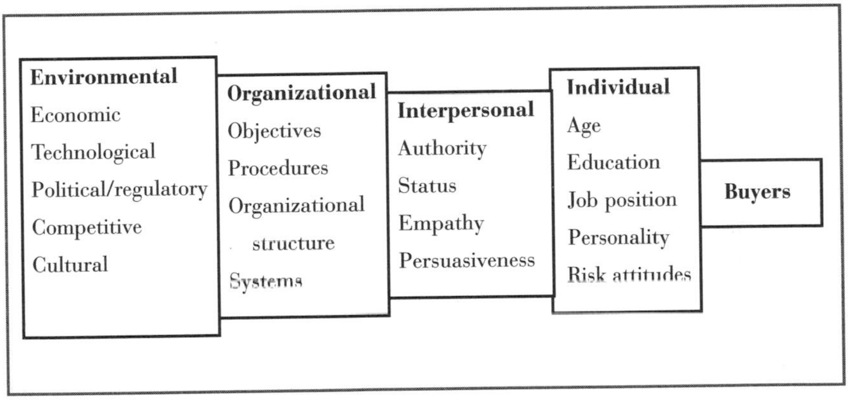

Participants in Oganizational Buying Process

The marketing manager must attempt to identify the people in the target clients' organizations who are likely to get involved in the buying process. This decision-making unit of a buying organization is called its *buying center* and comprises all the individuals and units who participate in the particular buying decision-making process. The members of the buying center can play any of five roles in the purchase decision process.

1. USERS. Users are members of the organization who will use the service. In many cases, the users initiate the buying proposal and help to define service specifications.

2. INFLUENCERS. Influencers often help define specifications and also provide information for evaluating alternatives. Expert personnel or outside advisors are particularly important as influencers as are many technical personnel.

3. BUYERS. Buyers have formal authority to select the supplier and arrange the terms of purchase. Buyers may help shape product service specifications, but their major role is in selecting vendors and negotiating. In more complex purchases, buyers might include high-level officers participating in the negotiations.

4. DECIDERS. Deciders have formal or informal power to select to approve the final suppliers. In routine buying, the buyers are often the deciders. In more complex buying, the officers of the buying organizations are often the deciders.

5. GATEKEEPERS. Gatekeepers control the flow of information to others. For example, certain individuals within an organization, like personal assistants, often have the authority to prevent salespersons from seeing users or deciders.

Whether it is an auditor selection committee, a facilities planning committee, or some other complex entity, the buying center and the power relationships among its members deserve close attention. The great uncertainty associated with buying professional services tends to allow certain individuals with special knowledge, information, or expertise—who can reduce buying uncertainty—to dominate the decision process within many buying centers. The marketing manager's task is to identify the members of the buying center and try to figure out (1) in what decisions they exercise influence, (2) their relative degree of influence, and (3) the evaluation criteria each decision participant uses.

Major Influences on Organizational Buyers

Organizational buyers are subject to many influences when they make their buying decisions. Some marketers assume that the major influences are purely economic. They believe buyers will favor the supplier who offers the lowest price or the best service; therefore, they concentrate on offering strong economic benefits to buyers. However, organizational buyers actually respond to economic *and* personal factors. Far from being cold, calculating, and impersonal, organizational buyers are human and social as well. They react to both reason and emotion.

When suppliers' offers are very similar, organizational buyers have little basis for a strictly rational choice, and because they can meet organizational goals with any supplier, buyers can allow personal factors to play a larger role in their decisions. However, when competing services differ greatly, organizational buyers are more accountable for their choice and tend to pay more attention to organizational factors. There are also at least two other influences on the organizational buyers' decision process. These are environmental and interpersonal. All four will be briefly examined here.[3]

Environmental Factors

Organizational buyers are influenced heavily by factors in the current and expected economic environment, such as the level of primary demand, economic outlook, and the cost of money. As economic uncertainty rises, organizational buyers cut back on new investment and may attempt to reduce overhead. Organizational buyers are also affected by technological, political, and competitive developments in the environment. Culture and customs can also strongly influence organizational buyer reactions to the marketer's behavior and strategies. This is especially true in international marketing environments. For example, in the United States a management consultant may have the ability to acquire a new client by responding to a request for a proposal and then providing a presentation at the client's offices. In the Pacific Rim, however, the management consulting firm will find that it needs to spend considerably more time developing a relationship and trust between the consultants and the prospective client before any contract will be signed. The marketing manager must watch all these factors, determine how they will affect the buyer, and try to turn these challenges into opportunities.

Organizational Factors

Each buying organization has its own objectives, policies, procedures, structure, and system. The marketing manager must know these organizational factors as thoroughly as possible. Questions such as these must be addressed: How many people are involved in the buying decision? Who are they? What are the evaluative criteria? What are the company's policies and limits on its buyers?

The marketing manager must be sure that his or her service is positioned in line with the potential client's objectives. It is also important to understand who plays what roles within the potential client's organization, as to make sure that the firm's communications and sales efforts are not being directed at the wrong individual.

Interpersonal Factors

The buying center usually includes many participants who influence each other. The marketing manager often finds it difficult to determine what kinds of interpersonal factors and group dynamics enter into the buying process. As someone once noted, "Managers do not wear tags that say 'Decision-Maker' or 'Unimportant Person.' The powerful ones are often invisible, at least to vendor representatives."

Individual Factors

Each participant in the business buying-decision process brings in personal motives, perceptions, and preferences. Personal characteristics such as age, income, education, professional identification, personality, and attitudes towards risk affect these factors. Further, buyers have many different buying styles. Some may be more precise and comprehensive in their approach, making in-depth analyses of competitive proposals before choosing a supplier. Others may be intuitive negotiators who are adept at pitting the sellers against one another. In marketing to a potential client, the marketer must assess his or her own interpersonal style as well as those of the prospective client's decision-makers in order to adapt behavior to the needs of the situation.

The Organizational Buying Process

Table 8-1 lists eight stages of the business buying process.[4] The steps taken by an organization in buying professional services will vary depending on the type of decision, the decision participants, the type of services, and several other factors. The decision process can consist of

**Table 8-1. Major Stages of the Business Buying Process
in Relation to Major Buying Situations.**

	Buying Situations		
Stages of the Buying Process	New Task	Modified Rebuy	Straight Rebuy
1. Problem recognition	Yes	Maybe	No
2. General need description	Yes	Maybe	No
3. Service specification	Yes	Yes	Yes
4. Supplier search	Yes	Maybe	No
5. Proposal solicitation	Yes	Maybe	No
6. Supplier selection	Yes	Maybe	No
7. Order routine specification	Yes	Maybe	No
8. Performance review	Yes	Yes	Yes

only a step or two or numerous steps and sub-steps. Buyers who face a new-task buying situation usually go through all stages of the buying process; buyers making modified- or straight-rebuy situations may skip some of the stages. We will examine each of these steps for the typical new-task buying situation.

Problem Recognition. The buying process begins when someone in an organization recognizes a problem or need that can be met by acquiring the services of outside professionals. Problem recognition can result from either internal or external stimuli. Internally, the organization may be deciding on developing new services or products themselves that require the help of outside management consultants, legal work, or accounting services. Sometimes, professionals within the organization hear about internal professional services that are available, and ask specifically for help. Externally, the buyer in an organization may get an idea from something seen, read, or heard. Other times, external forces, such as legal or regulatory developments or natural disasters, literally force organizations to obtain professional help.

Knowing how an organizational buyer identifies needs will help the professional service firm position itself to satisfy those needs. If a buying organization identifies its needs as a result of recommendations, marketing toward opinion leaders, networking, and testimonials may put the firm in front of the organizational buyer. If buyers recognize needs as a result of reading or listening, then an intensified public relations effort, containing speeches or news releases, might be effective.

General Need Description. Once an organization has identified a need for professional help, it may then develop criteria to use in determining a set of professionals who will receive some consideration. Determining the criteria used by organizations to identify candidate professionals is an essential task for the marketing manager. Some organizations will consider only using firms they have used in the past. This is especially true in moderate to large projects where the risk of choosing the wrong professional is greater. Other organizations may consider only using the biggest, the oldest, the closest, or the cheapest professionals available. Professional service firms need to know the minimal attributes required to put themselves in the running for targeted opportunities.

Service Specification. While the general need description outlines the general characteristics that are required from a potential professional firm, the specific requirements relate to the details that the professional service firm candidates may have to address. Many times these service specifications are identified in the request for a proposal of the organizational buyer; other times this information must be identified through discussions with the organizational buyers' decision-makers and/or purchasers.

Supplier Search. The organizational buyer now conducts a search for professional service firms that can best solve their particular problems. (See Exhibit 8-1.) The buyer can compile a list of qualified firms by reviewing trade directories, doing computer searches, or working from the recommendations of colleagues. The professional service firm must make sure it is in the appropriate directories.

Proposal Solicitation. In the proposal solicitation stage of the organizational buying process, the buyer invites qualified professional service suppliers to submit proposals. To increase a firm's chances of being successful in having its proposal accepted, professional service marketers must be skilled in researching, writing, and presenting proposals in response to the buyer solicitations. Proposals should be marketing docu-

Exhibit 8-1. Comparing Advice on Choosing an Architect, Accountant, and a Lawyer. Is It All That Different?

Choosing a service professional can be a difficult decision. The fact that services themselves are intangible and don't lend themselves easily to comparison is bad enough. However, the outcome of choosing an architect, accountant, or lawyer may be extremely important, thereby increasing one's level of anxiety as well. Below are suggested checklists we found for choosing each one of these professionals. The similarities are readily apparent.

Choosing a Lawyer[5]

1. Look for fields of expertise and check their credentials. *The Martindale-Hubbell Law Directory* is the definitive source. You can find all 27 volumes in most public libraries. Based on confidential interviews with other lawyers, it notes attorney's legal abilities from "A" for "very high to pre-eminent" to "C" for "fair to high."

2. Is the lawyer's experience in line with your needs?

3. Check for the lawyer's level of commitment to your business. Are there potential conflicts of interest?

4. Check who will be doing your work. (Will it be a partner or a junior colleague?)

5. How does the lawyer conduct him/herself? (Is he or she assertive without being belligerent?)

6. Is the lawyer a good value for the dollar? An experienced lawyer may get the same results in three hours at $175 an hour that a less expensive attorney can produce in six hours at $110 per hour.

7. Does the lawyer seem straightforward with his or her opinion? You want to hire a professional, not someone who will give you the answer you may want to hear.

8. Check references.

Choosing an Architect[6]

1. Check for the architect's level of expertise and experience in the project type at hand. The American Institute of Architects provides project-specific lists. (This means if you are building a museum, the architect should have experience with museums.)

2. Evaluate the architect's experience with the size of your project. (Can the firm provide a wide range of experience?)

3. Invite the architect to provide a sales presentation. (Is he or she able to develop and ask the right questions?)

4. Does the architect have strong interpersonal skills? (People buy a person, not a firm.)

Exhibit 8-1. Comparing Advice on Choosing an Architect, Accountant, and a Lawyer. Is It All That Different? (*cont.*)

---

5. Is the architect committed to your business?

6. Is he or she a good value for the dollar?

Choosing an Accountant[7]

1. Does the accountant have the proper experience with your type of problem?

2. Does the firm have the resources that can provide a range of services if needed? (Can it provide one-stop shopping?)

3. Does the accountant have knowledge of the environment and community in which you work? (Does he or she know the territory?)

4. What is the accountant's interpersonal style?

5. Is the accountant a good value for the money?

6. What is the turnover of associates in the firm? (Can you count on your accountant to be there in the future?)

It is apparent that clients will be looking for information and behavior that establish the credibility of a firm, the interpersonal style of its staff, the firm's commitment to a long-term relationship, and value for the dollar. Can you assure your prospective clients of these capabilities with your firm?

---

ments and must inspire confidence in the buyer so that the professional service firm can stand out from competitors.

Supplier Selection. The buyer now reviews the proposals and selects a supplier or suppliers. During supplier selection, the buyer often will draw a list of the desired supplier attributes and their relative importance, such as geographic location, performance history, and reputation. The buyer will rate suppliers against these attributes and identify the best suppliers.

As part of the selection process, a buyer may prefer a larger supplier base. In other words, the buyer may wish to employ several professional service firms each handling a specific section of one's business. This tactic may help the firm gain price concessions from professional suppliers.

Many companies, however, may prefer to select a professional service firm that is capable of handling all of its needs, such as a law firm that can cover real estate law, intellectual property, and civil law. This is known as "single sourcing." The advantage to this tactic is the ability to develop deeper relationships and more personal service. The downside is the possibility of losing a broader view of the options and opportunities that multiple suppliers might bring.

Order Routine Specification. Once a professional service firm is chosen, a final order is developed that outlines what services are needed, expected time of delivery, and any other points that have been negotiated.

Performance Review. In this stage, the buying organization reviews the performance of the professional service firm with which it has contracted. In some cases, the buyer may contact users within the organization to ask them to rate their satisfaction with such areas as service quality, timeliness, and other attributes important to the buying organization. The performance review may lead the buyer to continue, modify, or drop the arrangements with the professional service firm. The seller's job is to monitor the same factors used by the buyer, to make sure the seller is providing expected levels of satisfaction.

INDIVIDUAL BUYER BEHAVIOR

In the remainder of this chapter, we will present a framework for studying how individual clients buy professional services. We address the same basic questions that we did for organizational buyer behavior.

Types of Decisions

The manner in which a person buys a professional service varies with the type of decision being made. Some buying decisions are more important, more complex, and more risky, and consequently, tend to involve more buying participants and more deliberation. One way of categorizing individual buying decisions has been suggested by Howard and Sheth:[8]

1. **Routinized response behavior.** The simplest type of buying behavior occurs in the purchase of relatively low-cost, frequently purchased goods and services. The buyer typically is well acquainted with the available offerings and has definite preferences among them. The buying of routine health checkups, treatment for

minor health problems, and other regularly bought professional services can often fit in this category. Individuals do not give much thought, search, or time to these purchases but merely go to the professionals they always use for these services (for example, the "family" doctor).

2. Limited problem solving. Buying is more complex when buyers are purchasing familiar offerings but have little familiarity with the available sellers of those offerings. This situation occurs when a person moves to a new locality and must select dentists, doctors, accountants, or lawyers. It can also occur when a person decides to discontinue buying from his or her current professional. People in this situation generally undergo much search and deliberation.

3. Extensive problem solving. Buying reaches its greatest complexity when buyers are purchasing unfamiliar offerings from unfamiliar sellers. The unhappily married person seeking a divorce lawyer is probably in this situation (unless the person has experienced a previous divorce). Likewise, a person seeking professional guidance to deal with serious financial or health problems would be in this situation. A lack of understanding of even the criteria to use to evaluate alternatives will lead these buyers to engage in considerable search and deliberation.

The marketing manager will want to evaluate the people within each target market to identify the buying situations in which they tend to fall. Existing clients exhibiting routinized response behavior should be studied to see how their loyalty can be reinforced and how they might be convinced to purchase more services. The effectiveness of various types of reminder notices and other printed communications could be evaluated. On the other hand, people who exhibit routinized response behavior, but who buy from competitors, should probably receive minimal attention from the marketing manager. Nevertheless, the marketing manager might want to devote some effort toward discovering what makes or could make these people switch professionals.

In addition, limited and extensive problem solvers deserve careful examination by the marketing manager. Learning more about how these people eventually select certain professionals can be quite useful for developing strategies to improve referral networks, communications, and fee structures. A portion of the necessary information can be obtained by having people fill out questionnaires on this subject during one of the first times they receive services. These questionnaires should ask more than "Who referred you?" They should seek data on who was consulted during the person's search, the criteria that were employed in making the decision, and other factors that may have been influential.

Decision Participants

In an effort to reduce the great uncertainty experienced in buying professional services, people tend to seek large amounts of information from others before making a decision. Family members, friends, co-workers, and other trusted sources will often become involved with a person's decision. The marketing manager must therefore attempt to identify the kinds of people who might be playing each of the following roles in the decision-making of the individuals in the firm's target markets:

1. **Initiator.** The initiator is the person who first suggests or thinks of the idea of buying the particular service.
2. **Influencer.** An influencer is a person whose views or advice carries some weight in making the final decision.
3. **Decider.** The decider is a person who ultimately determines any part of or the entire buying decision: whether to buy, what to buy, how to buy, or where to buy.
4. **Buyer.** The buyer is the person who makes the actual purchase.
5. **User.** The user is the person(s) who receive(s) the services.

Discovering who plays these roles can guide the design of services, the creation of promotional messages, and the allocation of promotional budgets. If it is discovered, for example, that wives tend to be the deciders on where their husbands go for dental work, then a dental clinic will want to direct most of its advertising toward wives instead of husbands. Knowing the main participants and the roles they play helps an organization fine-tune its marketing program.

Influences on Decisions

Clients' purchases are influenced strongly by cultural, social, personal, and psychological characteristics. (See Figure 8-2.) For the most part, the marketing manager of the professional service firm cannot control such factors, but he or she can take them into account. The marketing manager will want to identify the most important factors and judge their relative impact upon decision-making. We will briefly examine each of the major characteristics.

Cultural characteristics are the broadest influence on the buyer. The *buyer's culture, subculture,* and *social class* can have extremely important yet subtle effects on decision-making. Cultural influences have been learned and ingrained in the individual since childhood. The primary forces of these influences are one's family, school, and, later on, place of employment.

The impact of culture can have especially strong influences on professional service marketers' success in two particular areas. The first is when expanding one's services internationally; the second is when deal-

Figure 8-2. Detailed Model of Influential Buyer Characteristics.

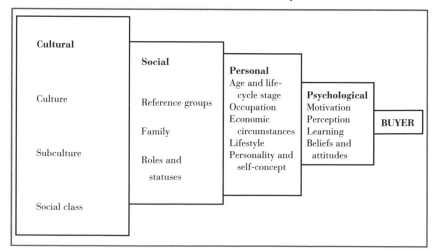

ing with first-generation immigrants. A professional service firm that is expanding its operations internationally must be aware of cultural differences and how they might affect how the firm sells and communicates its product to potential buyers. Issues regarding time, norms of behavior, negotiation, and many others will be affected by cultural norms. In many instances, dealing with first-generation immigrants will also have its cultural challenges. A woman physician may find that males from certain cultures would be too uncomfortable dealing with a woman in personal matters. At the same time, cultural norms or traditions may serve as a cue to a physician to problems that their patients are experiencing. For example, physicians treating Cambodian refugees have reported that it is customary for a Cambodian to scratch his or her stomach with a nickel to "cure" a stomachache. While the physician may not be able to speak to the patient due to language differences, the scratch marks will serve as a clue to the patient's ailment. Each culture contains smaller subcultures or groups of people who share value systems based upon common life experiences and situations. Subcultures can include nationalities, religions, racial groups, or geographic regions. Each group will have certain characteristics or habits that the marketer must take into consideration.

Finally, social classes within each culture can also have an impact on professional service firms. For example, people of upper-class backgrounds may be uncomfortable entering a dentist's or lawyer's office located in a strip mall; while people of lower-class background may feel uncomfortable entering an office in an imposing office building. Also social class may be correlated with the use of certain professional services. For example, upper social classes may more frequently seek psychotherapy or estate planning services than lower social-class counterparts.

Social characteristics. A person's buying behavior can also be influenced by social factors such as the client's family, the groups he or she belongs to, social roles, and status. A desire to please, impress, or upstage family members, friends, co-workers, or others can lead to the selection of certain types of professionals over others. For example, some purchasers of professional services may feel obliged to use the services of a family member or friend, while others may select a professional service firm to show independence or superiority.

Personal characteristics. A buyer's decisions are also influenced by personal characteristics such as the buyer's age and life-cycle stage, occupation, economic situation, lifestyle, and personality or self-concept. For example, wealthier individuals may require more sophisticated levels of legal advice and may use a tax accountant to prepare their income tax filings. Similarly, older people will require different services from health-care professionals than younger people, thus the buyer's age is a critical factor for the marketer to consider.

Psychological characteristics. A person's buying choices are further influenced by four major psychological factors: *motivation, perception, learning,* and *beliefs and attitudes.* The marketing manager will want to examine these characteristics. A physician running a smoking-cessation program is certainly aware of the impact that motivation has on the possibility of an ultimately successful outcome. However, motivation in itself may not be enough. A motivated person is ready to act, but how the person acts is influenced by his or her perception of the situation. An individual seeking legal help may perceive a lawyer as intelligent and professional, while the next individual may perceive him as untrustworthy and insensitive.

People learn from their past actions. As a result of an experience with a professional service firm, an individual may be positively or negatively reinforced as far as deciding to use the firm the next time. If the experience was positive, the person will be more likely to use the same firm again.

Through doing and learning, people acquire beliefs and attitudes that also influence their future behavior. Beliefs and attitudes put people in a frame of mind of liking or disliking things, of moving toward or away from them. A client who has had consistently positive outcomes with a tax accountant in the past and has a firm belief that the government takes too much of his or her money through taxes, is certainly more likely to see the tax accountant as a professional service ally.

The Consumer Decision Process

To market services effectively, marketing managers need to understand the thought process used by consumers during their decision process. We will examine a five-step decision process, shown in Figure 8-3.

Figure 8-3. Model of the Individual Buying Decision Process.

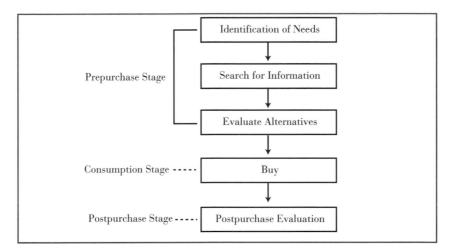

Of course, marketing managers should use this as an initial framework, making modifications of this model that describe with greater accuracy the buying behavior toward particular professional services and their individual clients.

Step 1. Identification of needs. The buying process begins with the buyer recognizing a need or a problem. This need can be triggered by internal cues, social cues, or commercial cues. An internal cue consists of the person beginning to feel the need for or readiness to do something. The cue may take on a physiological stimulus, such as illness or injury, requiring the need for a physician, or psychological stimulus, such as loneliness or anxiety, requiring a social worker. Social cues are obtained from the individual's peer group or significant others. A person may discover the need for a will based upon the prompting of the spouse. Or a person may seek the aid of a tax accountant based upon the advice of a friend. Commercial cues are the result of promotional efforts. As examples, a prospective client may be exposed to a commercial from a law firm or hear a physician's speech on hypnosis as a technique for weight loss.

The marketing manager must be aware of the types of cues that trigger interest in the relevant professional service. He or she will want to know not only where the cue originates but also the strength of its intensity. This information will come from experience as well as data drawn from research such as focus groups, in-depth interviews, and surveys.

Step 2. Search for information. Once a need has been identified, an individual may or may not search for information about ways to satisfy the need. If the consumer does conduct a search, it may take a limited form called *heightened attention* or a more extensive form called *active information search.*

Heightened attention means that a person is especially receptive to messages relevant to his or her need. Active information search involves purposeful data gathering. Yet consumers seldom consider all feasible alternatives that turn up; instead, they consider a limited number of alternatives on the basis of past experiences, convenience, and knowledge. The considered alternatives are called the *evoked set.* In services, evoked sets are typically smaller than in physical goods.

One source for gathering data is referred to as an *internal search.* An internal search accesses the consumer's own memory about possible alternative service firms that may be able to solve the problem. An internal search is a passive approach to gathering information. The internal search may be followed by an external search, which would involve the collection of new information from additional sources such as personal (family, friends, or neighbors), commercial (advertising, salespersons, professional societies, professionals in related fields), public (mass media), and experiential (where the customer tries a little bit of the service). The extent of a person's search depends on the intensity of the need, the amount of information available to start out, and the costs and the benefits he or she perceives to be associated with searching.

Marketing managers can clearly benefit from studying how and where individual buyers search for information. This information can help the professional service firm design and place more effective communications.

Step 3. Evaluation of alternatives. The search for information will usually allow the individual buyer to narrow available professionals down to a *choice set.* The next step therefore involves an evaluation of the members in the evoked set. The marketing manager will find it useful to obtain information on the following:

1. The **attributes** buyers consider in looking at alternative providers of the professional service. This information could be obtained from personal interviews with buyers.

2. The **relative importance** buyers assign to the considered attributes. Which attributes have the greatest importance in forming an overall judgment of a provider, and which attributes have lesser importance? Buyers could be asked to fill out rating scales to indicate the importance or weight given to different attributes in their decision-making.

3. The **beliefs** buyers have about how much of each important attribute the alternative providers have. Measures could be obtained of where buyers see providers' ranking on the attributes. The set of beliefs a person has about a provider make up the person's image of that provider.

4. The **ideal levels** for each attribute. Marketers can measure what levels of each attribute are considered most desirable or ideal to buyers.

5. The **evaluation procedures** may consist of either nonsystematic evaluation of alternatives, such as the use of intuition, simply choosing an alternative by relying on a gut feeling, or it may involve a systematic evaluation technique, such as a multi-attribute model. Marketing theorists have made extensive use of multi-attribute models to simulate the process of evaluating products. Typically, consumers employ a number of attributes when evaluating a service. For example, clients may compare law firms based on reputation, familiarity with the firm's partners, location and number of offices, fee structure, and experience with one's industry or specialization. Clients then combine the weighted scores of the different attributes to arrive at a preference.

Table 8-2 shows a matrix involving the choice of a law firm. Across the top of the table are two types of variables. The first is the evoked set of the firms to be evaluated. The second type of variable is the importance rating the client assigned to the various attributes. For example, in Table 8-2 the client rates the firm's reputation as the most important attribute followed by familiarity with the lawyers, and so on. To complete the table, the client rates each firm on each attribute based on his or her expectations of that attribute. This particular client gives legal firm A top marks

Table 8-2. A Multi-attribute Choice Matrix.

	Evoked Set of Firms				Importance Weighed
	Firm A	Firm B	Firm C	Firm D	
Reputation of firm	10	10	10	9	10
Familiarity with partners	10	10	9	9	9
Location and Number of Offices	10	10	10	10	8
Fee structure	8	9	9	8	7
Experience with clients' industry/ specialization	10	8	8	7	6

for reputation, familiarity with the firm, and location and numbers of offices. At the same time, the client perceives the firm as not being so strong in areas such as fee structure.

Given this table, various choice processes might be employed. The *linear compensatory approach* proposes that the client create a global score for each firm by multiplying the firm's rating on each attribute by its importance and adding the scores together. Firm A would score 10×10 on reputation, plus 10×9 on familiarity with partners, plus 10×8 on location and numbers of offices, and so on. The client would then choose the firm with the highest score, Firm A in this example.

Another type of multi-attribute approach used is the *lexicographic approach*. This technique describes a decision process whereby decision-makers take a short-cut. They look at each attribute in turn, starting with the most important, in trying to make a decision. The client, whose preferences are shown in Table 8-2, would first look at reputation and rule out Firm D. Next, familiarity with partners would rule out Firm C. At this stage, the choice is reduced to Firms A and B, but location and numbers of offices produce a tie in scoring. Finally, the choice would be made in favor of Firm B based upon the next attribute, fee structure. Thus, a different decision rule results in a different choice: Firm B under the lexicographic model and Firm A under the linear compensatory model.

Multi-attribute models are quite popular in their use of the description and explanation of clients' service-decision processes. The strengths of these models lie in their simplicity and explicitness. The attributes identified cover a wide range of concerns related to the service experience and they are easily understood by the service manager.

But multi-attribute models also have limitations. The primary one is that such models adopt a static perspective on an experience that is really a series of dynamic interactions. A problem in one area of the service encounter may adversely affect the customer's perceptions on a wide array of attributes, and thus, there is no way to track or identify the real source of the problem. For example, a crowded doctor's office may not only give its patients a perception of a poor service environment, but might also affect the relationship between the staff and the clients. The patients may feel that the office staff is unfriendly and unhelpful, when actually they are trying to speed up the work pace to cope with the large crowd of patients. On the other hand, the staff may feel that the patients are too demanding of the nurses when they are working under pressure. In this case, it may not be the best strategy for the office manager or physician to focus solely on training and behavior of its staff; instead, the focus should be on the real source of the trouble, the crowded waiting room.

Obtaining consumer information can pay great dividends when formulating an effective marketing program. A firm can find out where it is currently positioned in the minds of target buyers by looking at beliefs information; it can identify new potential positions by examining the most important attributes and the ideal levels of those attributes; the firm can even evaluate whether it is capable of providing services that are perceived to have the ideal levels of the most important attributes. If this is too difficult to accomplish, the firm may attempt through its communications to alter what clients see as important or ideal and persuade them to prefer providers with attributes that the firm can provide.

Finally, the firm may consider whether it is possible to persuade buyers to change their evaluation procedures to an approach that favors the firm. For example, a small firm that would stand to lose if buyers merely selected the biggest or oldest provider might try to convince buyers that they should weigh several attributes when making a decision.

Step 4. Buy. The evaluation of alternatives leads to the identification of a favored provider. But this provider may not necessarily be the one from whom a purchase is made. The *attitude of others*, such as respected family members or friends, or *unanticipated situational factors*, such as the loss of a job or a sudden illness, may discourage or prevent purchase from the favored provider. Buying could also be delayed or prevented if the buyer sees high *perceived risk* associated with the purchase. People cope with high perceived risk in many different ways, including the gathering of more information or the complete avoidance of making a decision.

Knowing the kinds of obstacles that can prevent favored services from actually being bought can be helpful to the marketing effort. Arguments can be prepared to offset any last-minute anxiety that arises. And people can be assigned to "hand-hold" or communicate frequently with buyers to remind them of how much their business is desired.

Step 5. Postpurchase evaluation. After buying and using a particular service, the buyer will revise beliefs about the service providers and form some overall judgment about satisfaction or dissatisfaction. Obtaining information about the satisfaction levels of individual buyers can be extremely helpful in planning service improvements and communications programs. For example, if a firm finds that past clients have been highly satisfied with the services they have received, then this information can be featured in promotional materials and presentations.

SUMMARY

Understanding consumer behavior is the cornerstone of a successful marketing program. Understanding the needs, wants, and buying behavior of target organizations and clients allows more effective marketing programs to be formulated.

Organizational buyers vary in their buying behavior, depending on whether they are making a straight-rebuy, modified-rebuy, or new-task decision. In many organizations, a buying center will influence the purchase of professional services, with several people becoming involved filling roles as users, influencers, buyers, deciders, and gatekeepers. Their decisions tend to be influenced by organizational, individual, interpersonal, and environmental factors. A complex decision process—containing steps in which needs are identified, information is sought, criteria are set, alternatives are evaluated, suppliers are selected, and satisfaction is determined—often takes place.

Individual buyers proceed differently, depending on whether they are engaged in routinized response behavior, limited problem solving, or extensive problem solving. An individual will often draw others into the buying of professional services and allow them to serve as influencers or even deciders of needed decisions. Numerous cultural, social, personal, and psychological characteristics can influence a person's buying of professional services. An individual's decision process can often be complicated, involving identification of needs, search for information, evaluation of alternatives, buying, and postpurchase evaluation.

NOTES

[1] Adapted from *Nine Consultant Selection Tips from I/S Professionals*, Damon Braly, Health Management Technology, November 1995.

[2] Robinson, Patrick J.; Faris, Charles W.; and Wind, Yoram. *Industrial Buying Behavior and Creative Marketing*, Boston: Allyn & Bacon, 1967.

[3] Ibid.

[4] Adapted from *Industrial Buying Behavior and Creative Marketing*, p14.

[5] Macedonio, Rosemary A. "Consider 5 Factors in Choosing a Lawyer," *The Plain Dealer* (October 23, 1994) p21.

[6] Trivers, Andres. "Do It Right: Selecting the Right Architect and Negotiating the Right Relationship," *Fund Raising Management* (April 1999).

[7] McLean, Bea. "Choosing an Accounting Firm," *Financial Manager's Statement* (September/October 1991).

[8] Howard, John A. and Sheth, Jagdish N. *The Theory of Buyer Behavior*, New York: John Wiley & Sons, 1969.

9 | The Service Mix

....

"When your work speaks for itself,
don't interrupt."
HENRY KAISER

The most basic marketing decision organizations must make is what products/service offerings to provide their target markets. The professional service firm must carefully define a service mix or offering strategy for its targeted clients. Professional service organizations face a large number of decisions in developing a sound service strategy. In this chapter, we will examine the following questions:

1. What are the characteristics of a service, especially a professional service?

2. How can the organization configure and improve its overall service mix?

3. How can the organization configure and improve individual services in its mix?

4. How can the organization manage and improve its services over its life cycle?

5. How can the organization best modify its service strategy?

A Consulting Firm by Any Other Name . . .[1]

In 1998, as part of its separation from Arthur Andersen, Andersen Consulting launched a new branding strategy in conjunction with the development of a new logo. The revamp was the firm's first "change of identity" since its establishment in 1989. Having been planned for two years, Andersen Consulting's managing director, James Murphy, of Global Marketing, stated that the new identity would differentiate Andersen Consulting from its competitors and allow it to break away from the pack.

The logo was the focal point of the branding revamp and was designed by San Francisco-based Landor Associates, the strategy design arm of Young and Rubicam. The initials of the firm are now represented as "A^C." "A" as the first letter of the alphabet was designed to convey primacy while the superscript "C," which stands for consulting, represented the exponential change. Along with the logo, Andersen Consulting developed a musical signature whose purpose was to develop an aural representation of the firm's brand. As a further means of launching its new branding strategy, Andersen Consulting also rebuilt its Web site and increased its advertising and event sponsorship.

On January 1, 2001, Andersen Consulting changed again. This time it changed its name as well as its logo. The impetus for the new name change within two years of the much publicized A^C launch was the result of an arbitration ruling that allowed it to separate from Andersen Worldwide. Independence cost $1 billion, far less than the $14 billion Arthur Andersen had sought, but the name Andersen stayed with the parent company.

The new name, Accenture, is a coined name that (they hope) puts an accent or emphasis on the future. CEO Joe Forehand stated in a release that "Accenture expresses what we have become as an organization, as well as what we hope to be, a business that transcends the bounds of traditional consulting. . . ."

> Accenture executives maintain that replacing the Andersen name in the minds of the market would not be difficult. James E. Murphy of Accenture states, "Twelve years ago, it (Andersen Consulting) did not have any meaning. Now it's the biggest in the business."
>
> While this is a very positive spin on the situation, we believe twelve years is a long time and represents a great deal of investment in the establishment of the brand. We are sure Accenture would have kept Andersen Consulting as a name if they had the chance.

THE NATURE OF SERVICES

One of the major developments in the United States over the last ten years has been the phenomenal growth of the service industries. Service businesses represent 76 percent of our gross domestic product and more than 73 percent of payroll jobs. As a result, there is a growing interest in the special characteristics of service marketing and how to improve service productivity.

We define a service as follows:

> A **service** is a deed, a performance, or an act that is essentially intangible and does not necessarily result in the ownership of anything. Its creation may or may not be tied to a physical product.

Services range from renting a hotel room, to depositing money in a bank, to traveling on an airplane, to visiting a psychiatrist, to having a haircut, to seeing a movie, to getting advice from a lawyer. Services can be pure, in the sense that there are virtually no physical components, such as with management consulting, or services that have very much of a physical component, as with fast food.

The Nature of Professional Services

In Chapter 1 we examined the unique characteristics of marketing services. These included: intangibility, inseparability, variability, perishability, and the customer being involved in the process. Our discussion of the nature and characteristics of services applied to all services. One of the earliest experts in professional services model, Evert Gummesson cites the following criteria for identifying professional services:

- The service should be provided by qualified personnel, be advisory, and focus on problem solving.

- The professional should have an identity, be known in the market for his or her specialties, and have a specific name such as "architect" or "management consultant."

- The service should be an assignment given from the buyer to the seller.

- The professional should be independent of suppliers of other services or goods.[2]

Gummesson goes on to indicate that professionals have specialist know-how, a standard methodology of carrying out assignments, and an interest in finding solutions and seeing them implemented.

Improving Service Productivity

As competition increases and costs rise, professional service firms are under great pressure to increase productivity. There are five approaches to improving service productivity. The first is to have service providers *work harder or smarter* for the same pay. Working harder is not a likely solution, but working smarter can occur through better selection and training procedures. The second is to *increase the quantity of service* by surrendering some quality. Psychotherapists, for example, could give less time to each patient. The third is to *add equipment* to increase service capabilities. A personal computer can provide the technological means to expand professional services. The fourth is to *reduce or make obsolete the need for a service* by inventing a product solution. Thus, the invention of penicillin reduced the need for tuberculosis consulting. The fifth is to *design a more effective service*. Nonsmoking clinics and jogging may reduce the need for expensive medical services later on. Hiring paralegal workers reduces the need for expensive legal professionals.

SERVICE-MIX DECISIONS

Most professional service organizations are multi-service firms. They have a "service mix" consisting of *the set of all service lines and individual services that they make available to clients*. A "service line" can be viewed as a *group of services within a service mix that are closely related, either because they serve similar needs, are made available to the same clients, or are marketed through the same types of channels*. For example, CPA firms generally have a service mix with three basic service lines: auditing, tax advisory, and management consulting. Similarly, law firms typically offer multiple service lines in areas such as personal injury law, real estate law, family law, antitrust law, and so on.

We can describe an organization's service mix in terms of its *length*, *width*, and *depth*. These concepts are illustrated in Figure 9-1 for the service mix of a hypothetical law firm. We see that the service mix, in terms of its length, consists of three service lines: personal injury, real estate,

Figure 9-1. Length, Width, and Depth of a Law Firm's Service Mix.

	Personal Injury	Real Estate	Family
	← ————— Service Mix Length ————— →		
Service Line Width ↑ ↓	Product liability (5)*	Commercial (3)	Divorce (2)
	Automobile accidents (3)	Residential (4)	Adoptions (1)
	Medical malpractice (2)		

*The numbers in parentheses indicate the number of professionals assigned primarily to provide the corresponding service.

and family law. Each line has a certain width; thus, the personal injury line includes product liability, automobile accidents, and medical malpractice. Finally, each individual service has a certain depth: The firm has five attorneys who work primarily on product liability litigation.

Suppose the firm is thinking of expanding its service mix. This could be accomplished in any of three ways. The firm could lengthen its service mix by adding, say, some attorneys with expertise in tax law. Or the firm could add another personal injury area, say airline crashes, extending the width of one line. Or the firm could add a sixth attorney who does product liability litigation, deepening its service mix in this area.

Suppose, on the other hand, that the firm is considering contracting its service mix either to bring down its costs or to attain a more specialized position in the marketplace. The firm could drop real estate and even family law, concentrating exclusively on personal injury. It could, alternatively, eliminate certain personal injury areas or decide to reduce the staff in certain areas.

In considering the service mix, we should recognize that the various services differ in their relative contribution to the organization. Some services constitute the *essential* services of that organization and others are *ancillary* services. Thus, auditing is the essential service of most CPA firms and management consulting is an ancillary service. Furthermore, certain *flagship* services provided by certain *superstar professionals* may play a major role in drawing clients to the organization. An organization can showcase these services and professionals in its literature and promotion. The high cost of acquiring a superstar may be well repaid by the public relations value it produces.

A professional service organization should periodically reassess its service mix. Its service mix establishes its position vis-à-vis competitors (i.e., it differentiates it) in the minds of buyers. But its service mix is also the source of its costs. The organization must be constantly alert to services whose costs have begun to exceed their benefits, and whose elimination would release funds for bringing new, more worthwhile services into its service mix.

INDIVIDUAL SERVICE DECISIONS

In developing an individual service to offer to a market, the marketing strategist has to distinguish three levels of service: the core, perceptible, and augmented levels.

Core Service

At the most fundamental level stands the core service, which answers the questions: What is the client really seeking? What need is the service really satisfying? A business firm that retains a tax attorney is really buying savings on its tax bill and not just tax advice. A corporate president arranging for an architect to design a corporate headquarters may be seeking a "monument" to his leadership and not just a functional building. With many professional services, clients may be really buying a "sense of security" or "peace of mind." The marketing person's job is to uncover the essential needs hiding under every professional service so that service benefits, not just service features, can be described in the firm's communications. The core service stands at the center of the total service, as illustrated in Figure 9-2.

Figure 9-2. Three Levels of Service.

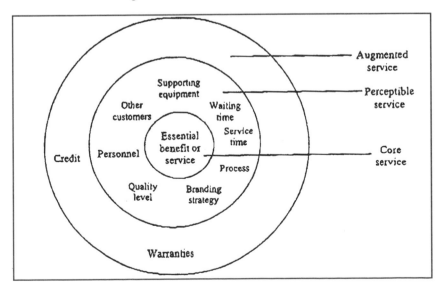

Perceptible Service

The core service is always made available to the client in some perceptible form. Professional service marketers can attempt to configure the following eight basic attributes of a service.

1. *Personnel.* The people who perform the service.

2. *Quality level.* The level of professional confidence with which the service is performed.

3. *Branding strategy.* The name and associate descriptions given to the service or to the set of services.

4. *Process.* The sequence of activities necessary to deliver the service.

5. *Service time.* The amount of professionals' time required to perform the service (i.e., billable time).

6. *Waiting time.* The amount of time the client has to wait before the service is completed satisfactorily.

7. *Supporting equipment.* The machinery, instruments, and other facilities the professional uses to help deliver the service.

8. *Other customers.* Other customers that the client may be exposed to or interact with during the service.

While fee level or price could be considered another basic attribute of a professional service, we prefer to discuss this attribute separately in the next chapter. The eight attributes listed above are treated in more detail below.

Personnel. The people who provide a professional service are the key attribute of that service. Professional services are inseparable from those who deliver them. Furthermore, clients often buy "people" rather than services and it is crucial for the professional service marketer to pay close attention to how professionals are perceived by clients. The experience levels, education levels, personalities, communication skills, and other characteristics of the professionals have to be pleasing to the clients. In particular, many clients focus intensely on experience levels, because they prefer not to take the risk of being one of the first clients to use a professional. The selection of highly experienced professionals can provide an organization protection from criticism if something goes wrong.

Because services are inseparable from the people who deliver them, hiring and development of the right personnel becomes imperative for an organization. Individual excellence is of extreme importance and may require a new mindset in the hiring and training process. An organization should think of this process as product development. Because the service professionals are the product, this area demands a great deal of top management focus and attention.

Developing a strong "people" attribute requires a number of steps. First, the organization must make a strong commitment to recruiting talented personnel. This process begins with focusing on the internal service environment that creates an atmosphere where professionals can grow, both professionally and personally. Second, the organization must work hard to seek recruits who are not only professionally competent, but also exhibit a service disposition. It cannot be emphasized enough that this is a hiring issue and not a training issue. In other words, it's much easier to hire friendly people than to train unfriendly people to be friendly. Hiring individuals with a service disposition will require the professional service firm to actively seek out individuals with this characteristic and compete for them.

Beyond effective hiring practices, it is also imperative that the professional service organization implement the proper training that introduces new service professionals to the importance of service quality and the role of marketing within the organization. Many young professionals are likely to have incorrect ideas about marketing and limited understanding of its potential benefits. So as to positively reinforce the performances of employees who are in line with service quality goals, the firm should also focus on measuring and rewarding those service behaviors that it values and that have been taught in training.

Any training sessions dealing with marketing and quality should first be presented to top management, because their understanding, support, and commitment to the concepts are absolutely essential if marketing is to take hold in the organization. Once top management has been trained, further training can be provided to operations, financial, and others within the organization to ensure team work and cooperation.

Finally, decisions must be made as to which personnel should provide which services. This is often difficult for the professional service organization. It is only natural for clients to want the most experienced, knowledgeable, and friendly professionals working on their particular projects or cases. However, allowing senior partners or principals to do most of the work for every client is impossible for several reasons. First, using only senior people on a job makes the job much more expensive, and this would necessitate a level of pricing that clients would find unacceptable. Having less experienced professionals working on a job allows the organization to charge more competitive fees and, in turn, allows the organization to earn greater profit. Second, using only senior personnel prevents the newer and junior professionals from obtaining the necessary experience that might help them obtain work on their own and contribute to the firm's growth. Finally, using most senior people to perform services makes it more difficult to find time for these people to make their very much needed contribution to marketing the organization's services.

Quality level. Maintaining a high quality level for a professional firm is no easy task. Keeping track of how professionals perform services, without destroying autonomy, can be a difficult task, and making sure that clients follow professional advice can also be difficult. Furthermore, trying to measure the actual quality level of a professional service can be problematical because the ideas of different professionals and of buyers on what constitutes quality may vary widely.

In spite of these difficulties, professional service organizations must continually monitor their quality levels to keep them high and must resist pressures to lower quality levels because of a need to match the lower fees of competitors. A lessening of quality can severely damage a firm's reputation and leave it open to malpractice or liability suits. Careful recruiting and training can help to maintain high quality levels, as can a strong effort to educate buyers about the benefits of following professional advice. Supervisor reviews, peer reviews, and self-regulation programs can also be helpful. Finally, customer satisfaction research can tell an organization much about how the quality levels are perceived.

Branding strategy. Technically, branding means the use of a name, term, symbol, or design or a combination of these to identify a product or a service. It includes the use of brand names, trademarks, and practically all other means of product identification. More important, branding strategy is dedicated to instilling those distinctions that give the brand substance, validity, and acceptance. A strong brand strategy can offer a number of benefits to the service organization.

- A strong brand presents a promise of value. It promises a solution to a client's problems and/or the reduction of certain costs.

- A strong brand conjures up a personality. Because of branding strategy, a management consulting firm might be perceived as creative and innovative; a law firm as aggressive and detail-oriented; an architectural firm as avant garde or traditional.

- A strong brand conjures up a process. A process may be built around technology, individual attention, customization, or complex decision processes.

- A strong brand is one that conjures up a sense of reliability and consistency. Reliability is the most important measure of quality in services. It is the basis of trust and client peace of mind.

- An extremely strong brand often creates an aura of brand repute. In the legal profession, the firm of Fish and Neave is equated with excellence in intellectual property, while Kirkland and Ellis is well known for its litigation expertise.

An organization must earn brand awareness and acceptance with a strong service offering and effective communication. How well an organization's target market services are known is referred to as the *brand familiarity*. The degree of brand familiarity affects the planning for the rest of the marketing mix. Five levels of brand familiarity can be distinguished: (1) rejection, (2) non-recognition, (3) recognition, (4) preference, and (5) insistence.

A service firm with a poor brand image may result in *brand rejection*. Rejection may be the result of experience, negative publicity/communication, or both. Overcoming such a negative image is difficult and can be very expensive. It typically necessitates a substantial improvement in the service quality or at least a shift to a target market that has a neutral or better perception of the firm.

Brand rejection is a big concern for professional service organizations because of the difficulty of controlling the quality of service. A patient who has a negative experience with one physician in a hospital may very well generalize his or her perception of care for the rest of the hospital. Yet no hospital can ensure that every physician will provide a high level of quality medical care every time. Thus, every hospital must strive to make sure that every physician provides the highest overall medical care possible.

Some services are seen as basically the same. *Brand non-recognition* means that the target markets don't recognize a brand at all. This may be especially true in areas that exhibit high levels of competition and high numbers of service professionals, such as lawyers and management consultants.

Brand recognition means that the clients or patients remember the brand. This can be a big advantage if there are a large amount of competitors that suffer from brand non-recognition. Even if the clients can't recall the brand or the firm's name without help, they may be reminded when they see it in a professional directory or even the Yellow Pages.

Most firms would like to win *brand preference*, which means that their target customers would choose their brand over other brands. Perhaps this could be because of habit or favorable past experience. Although brand preference is clearly desirable, the ultimate objective of any professional service organization is *brand insistence*, which means that customers insist on the firm and are willing to search for it.

Because of the importance of brand recognition and brand insistence, a professional service firm should work to build and establish what is known as *brand equity*—the value of a brand's overall strength in the marketplace. Brand equity affects the ability of a firm to retain its current customers as well as its ability to attract new customers. It is made up of three core elements: the image of the organization, the loyalty of clients toward the organization, and the price-value relationship perceived to be associated with the firm. These three characteristics of a brand are so tightly interrelated that we refer to this system as the *brand equity molecule*.[3] (See Figure 9-3.)

The arrows in Figure 9-3 indicate how each area affects the others and how all three are tightly bound together. A strong image reinforces the hold on loyal buyers. Loyal customers help build a strong image through word-of-mouth. Image helps the firm charge a premium. A premium price, if supported by a strong value perception, helps build a strong image. One professional service segment that has long understood the value of brand equity in building brand identities has been accounting. In 1998 the Big Five accounting firms spent an estimated $41 million on advertising alone, and then easily eclipsed that in 1999.

Figure 9-3. Brand Equity Molecule.

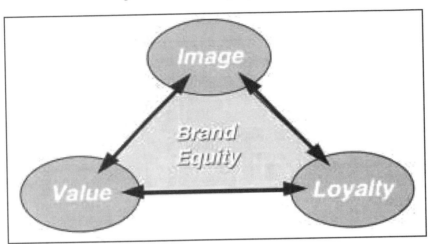

Because it is costly to build brand recognition, some professional service organizations may prefer to acquire established "brands" rather than to build their own. An example would be a hospital that recruits a strong cardiology practice. The cardiology practice is the established brand that provides instant credibility and strength to the hospital.

It's unfortunate that traditional financial statements do not show brand equity or the future profit potential of having a loyal customer base, because having this information could aid in getting more financially based managers to view marketing efforts as an investment rather than as an expense.

Process. The process by which a service is delivered conveys important messages regarding the level of attentiveness, the degree of customization, the role of technology, and the desired role of customers as service co-producers. By observing and participating in the process, the client receives important information regarding this professional service offering. How a management consultant works with a client, or a physician interacts with a patient, heavily influences the client's perception. For example, Cancer Care Centers of America differentiates itself by the way it treats cancer patients. In addition to traditional care and treatment, Cancer Care Centers also include many non-traditional treatments, including such psychological techniques as positive imagery, among others.

The law firm of Womble, Carlyle, Sandridge & Rice has built a print campaign around a bulldog to enhance their brand image and retention. They hope to send the message that the firm is a tenacious, though approachable, advocate.[4]

LarsonAllen undertook a detailed and carefully studied program to develop a brandmark that "reflected the philosophy and approach of the entire firm . . . a concept that captured the way the firm interacted with its clients, symbolizing its work ethic and firm culture." The image of the sun is used to signal energy, leadership, and progressive growth toward business, and their slogan is the firm's promise to apply its talent and resources to bring about the results the client wants.[5]

Service time. The amount of time it takes to perform a service can have a big influence on how clients evaluate that service. Professional service organizations should educate their clients about appropriate service times. At the same time, the professional marketer should use marketing research to understand the clients' perspectives of an acceptable range of service time.

Professionals should also be discouraged from any time-wasting activities when charging hourly rates. On the other hand, they should be encouraged to spend time in less formal discussions with clients when in a fixed-fee situation. Author Norman Cousins once said, "Doctors who spend more time with their patients may have to spend less money on malpractice insurance policies."[6]

Waiting time. The shorter the time clients have to wait to begin receiving a professional service and to have that service performed satisfactorily, the more they like it. Further, by managing their clients' expectations with regard to waiting time, the professional service provider will avoid creating unnecessary client dissatisfaction. For example, a patient in a doctor's waiting room should be informed of the approximate time in which he or she can anticipate seeing the physician. If the approximate wait time is ten minutes, the patient should be informed that the wait should be no longer than fifteen minutes. This accomplishes two tasks. First, if seen by the physician within ten minutes, the patient has had his or her expectations exceeded. At the same time, if it takes longer than the expected ten minutes, the service provider has an additional five minutes before the patient is likely to become restless.

People dislike waiting in offices, waiting on the phone, waiting for proposals, or waiting for reports. The professional service organization that has enough staff to respond rapidly to client demands and that does careful scheduling of its work will be viewed more favorably by clients. Although many clients like to use professionals who are very "busy"— seeing this as an indicator that a professional is highly competent—most clients like it when a professional can "make time for them."

Supporting equipment. Clients also evaluate the supporting equipment used to deliver the service. Thus, clients will often be favorably impressed by CPAs carrying the most modern portable laptops, lawyers having access to the most modern computer search facilities, land surveyors possessing the most modern photogrammetry equipment, and dentists using the most modern drilling and x-ray machines. Where research indicates that clients in the target markets are highly sensitive to the type of supporting equipment, efforts must be made to obtain the favored equipment.

A dentist we know has taken this concept a step further. Dr. Skip Gay, a dentist in Cincinnati, Ohio, long ago understood that a patient needs to be physically present but not mentally present to have his or her dental work performed. When the Sony Walkmans were first invented, he used these in the doctor's office so patients could listen to their choice of music during the dental procedures. These were later replaced by Discman; the Discman was later replaced by virtual-reality goggles. Now, as a patient is having a crown put on, he or she has the choice of watching one of many videos that Dr. Gay has in his library. This system works so well, that one of Dr. Gay's patients who watched a Gloria Estefan concert during a procedure remarked afterwards that she was hoping the procedure would not end before the concert concluded.

Other customers. Finally, other clients and customers also influence a client's perception. A young teenager may feel very uncomfortable visiting a pediatrician with a waiting room full of younger children or babies. On the other hand, a list of present clients may provide credibility to clients of a management consulting firm.

Augmented Service

The professional service marketer can offer to the target markets additional services and benefits that go beyond the perceptible service, thus making up an augmented service. For example, a plastic surgeon can provide patients with an easy payment plan, offer a guarantee of satisfaction with all work done, and offer free educational materials on the benefits, risks, and procedures used in plastic surgery. Organizations augment their perceptible services to meet additional clients' wants and/or differentiate their services from competition. Competing in terms of the "extras" is becoming more and more necessary in many professions as competition escalates.

In sum, a professional service is not a simple thing, but a complex offer consisting of a core need-satisfying service, a set of perceptible characteristics, and a set of augmented benefits. The organization should deeply examine each service and design it in a way that will distinguish it from competitors' offers. The more the service can be taken out of the commodity class and moved toward a branded or specialized class, the more control the organization will have over the level, timing, and composition of demand for its service.

SERVICE LIFE CYCLE

It is not possible for a professional service's attributes and marketing approach to remain optimal over time. Broad changes in the macro environment (population, politics, technology, and culture) as well as specific changes in the market environment (buyers, competitors, referral sources) will call for major service and marketing adjustments at key points in the service's history. The nature of the appropriate adjustments can be conveyed through the concept of the *service life cycle*.

Many services can be viewed as having something analogous to a "biological" life cycle. They received high acceptance at one time and then moved into a period of decline later. One only has to think of the ups and downs of management consulting ideas or services such as "zero-based budgeting" or "management by objectives" to recognize that life cycles exist. The life of a typical service exhibits an S-shaped revenues curve marked by the following four stages (see Figure 9-4):

1. *Introduction* is a period of slow billings growth as the service is introduced in the market.
2. *Growth* is a period of rapid market acceptance.
3. *Maturity* is a period of leveling off in billings growth because the service has achieved acceptance by most of the potential clients.
4. *Decline* is the period when billings show a strong downward drift.

The service life-cycle (SLC) concept can be defined according to whether it describes a service class (mental health service), a service form (psychoanalysis), or a brand (Menninger Clinic). The SLC concept has a different applicability in each case. *Service classes* have the longest life cycles. The billings of many service classes can be expected to continue in the mature stage for an indefinite duration. Thus, "mental health services" began centuries ago with organized religion and can be expected to persist indefinitely. *Service forms*, on the other hand, tend to exhibit more standard SLC histories than service classes. Thus, mental health services are dispensed in such forms as psychoanalysis, bioenergetics, group ther-

Figure 9-4. Typical S-shaped Life Cycle Curve.

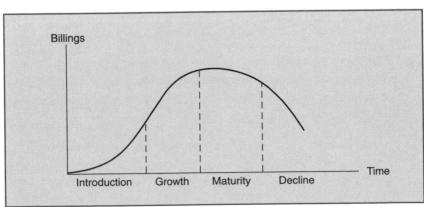

apy, and so on, some of which are beginning to show signs of maturity. As for *brands*, they are the most likely to show finite histories. Thus, the Menninger Clinic is a well-known psychoanalytically oriented clinic that had a period of rapid growth and is now mature. It will pass out of existence eventually, as is the fate of most brands and institutions unless they take proactive steps to extend the life cycle of their services.

It is important to note that not all services exhibit an S-shaped life cycle. Three other common patterns are:

1. *Scalloped pattern* (Figure 9-5A). In this case, service billings during the mature stage suddenly break into a new life cycle. The service's new life is triggered by service modifications, new uses, new users, changing tastes, or other factors. For example, the market for psychotherapy reached maturity at one point and then the emergence of group therapy gave it a whole new market.

Figure 9-5. Three Anomalous Service Life-Cycle Patterns.

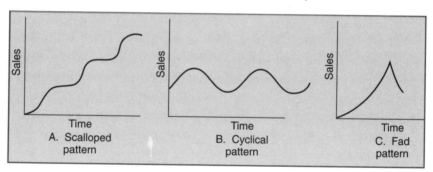

2. *Cyclical pattern* (Figure 9-5B). The billings of some services show a cyclical pattern. For example, architectural services go through alternating periods of high billings and low billings, reflecting changes in demand and supply in the construction market. The decline stage is not a time to eliminate a service but to maintain as much of it as possible, waiting for the next boom.

3. *Fad pattern* (Figure 9-5C). Here a new service comes on the market, attracts quick attention, is adopted with great zeal, peaks early, and declines rapidly. The acceptance cycle is short and the service tends to attract only a limited following of people who are looking

for excitement or diversion. Some tax-shelter deals and therapy forms exhibit the pattern of a fad.

We will now return to the S-shaped SLC and examine the characteristics and appropriate marketing strategies at each stage.

Introduction Stage

The introduction stage takes place when the professional service (class, form, or brand) is first made available for purchase in the marketplace. The introduction into one or more markets takes time, and billings growth is apt to be slow. Slow growth could occur because firms often have difficulty (1) staffing up to provide a new service, (2) working out the details of the service, (3) finding ways to distribute the service, and (4) getting clients to accept the service. These situations have faced consulting firms offering new computer software packages, law firms offering prepaid legal services, CPA firms offering less expensive "reviews" instead of full-scale audits, and architectural firms offering computer-assisted design services.

In the introductory stage, costs are high because of the low adoption and the need for heavier promotion expenses. People have to be informed about the new unknown service and induced to try it. The organization should direct its selling effort to those clients who are the readiest to buy, namely, early-adopter types. Studies of early adopters of a variety of products and services have shown them to generally be younger, more educated, more cosmopolitan, and more exposed to mass media.[7]

Growth Stage

If the new professional service satisfies the market, billings will start climbing substantially. The early adopters will continue their purchasing and other clients will follow their lead, especially if there is favorable word-of-mouth. New competitors will enter the market, attracted by the opportunity. They will introduce feature, brand, and packaging variations, and this will expand the market. During this stage the organization tries to sustain rapid growth as long as possible. This is accomplished in several ways:

1. The organization undertakes to improve service quality and add new service features and packages.

2. It vigorously searches out new market segments to enter.

3. It keeps its eyes open for new physical locations to gain additional service exposure.

4. It shifts its communications from building service awareness to trying to bring about service conviction and purchase.

The major challenge facing professional service firms during a period of rapid growth is to maintain a high level of service quality. There is usually a shortage of experienced personnel and they are strained to work long hours to meet the demand. The firm hires new personnel as rapidly as possible but there is a "breaking-in" time. The firm should resist the temptation to take on more business than it can service at a high-quality level. Otherwise, it will damage its reputation and this will hurt it when demand levels off.

Maturity Stage

At some point a professional service's rate of billings growth will slow down, and the service will enter a stage of relative maturity. This stage normally lasts much longer than the previous stages, and it poses some of the most formidable challenges to people with marketing responsibilities. *Most professional services are in the maturity stage of the life cycle, and therefore most of the marketing of professional services deals with mature services.*

The beginning of a slowdown in the rate of billings growth has the effect of producing overcapacity in a professional service area, which leads to intensified competition. Competitors engage more frequently in fee or price cutting, and there is a strong increase in promotional budgets. Other organizations increase their research and development budgets to find better versions of the service. Still others resort to modifying their client mix or service mix. These steps result in higher costs. Some of the weaker competitors start dropping out. The area eventually consists of a set of well-entrenched competitors whose basic orientation is toward gaining competitive advantage.

Decline Stage

Many professional services eventually enter a stage of billings decline. This happens for a number of reasons. Technical advances may give birth to new service classes, forms, and brands, which become effective substitutes. Thus, the demand for "family" doctors declined and gave way to demand for internal medicine practitioners and pediatricians. In addition, changes in politics, fashion, or tastes may lead to client erosion. Developments such as these have the effect of intensifying overcapacity and competition.

As billings of a service decline, firms should give thought to withdrawing or reducing the service in order to invest their resources in more attractive markets. Unless strong retention reasons exist, carrying a weak service is very costly to the organization. The cost of maintaining a weak service is not just the amount of uncovered cost. No financial accounting can adequately convey all the hidden costs. The weak service tends to consume a disproportionate amount of management's time; it often requires frequent fee adjustments; it requires both advertising and selling attention that might better be diverted to making the "healthy" services more profitable; its very unfitness can cause client misgivings and cast a shadow on the organization's image. The biggest cost imposed by carrying weak services may lie in the future. By not being eliminated at the proper time, these services delay the aggressive search for replacement services; they create a lopsided service mix, long on "yesterday's breadwinners" and short on "tomorrow's breadwinners"; they depress current cash and weaken the organization's foothold on the future.

It should be noted that in the face of declining interest, some organizations will abandon markets earlier than others. Those that remain may often enjoy a temporary increase in clients, as they pick up those from withdrawing institutions. For example, in the legal profession fewer and fewer firms are actively practicing tax law. This is due to the fact that many of the tax loopholes and shelters have been abolished, thereby reducing the need for lawyers or firms that specialize in this particular area. As law firms withdraw from the area, each institution must face the issue of whether it should be the one to stay in the market until the end.

If it stays in the market, the firm faces further strategic choices. It could adopt a *continuation* strategy, in which case it continues its past marketing strategy: same market segments, channels, pricing, and promotion. In this case, the number of consumers will likely shrink. Or it could follow a *concentration* strategy, concentrating its resources in its strongest markets while phasing out its efforts elsewhere. Finally, it could follow a *harvesting* strategy, in which case it sharply reduces its expenses to increase its positive (or decrease its negative) cash flow, knowing that these cuts will accelerate the rate of decline and the ultimate demise of the specialty.

During the period of decline, the firm needs to adopt some temporizing measures while it searches for new pastures. It may have to let go some of its professionals, lower its fees, close some offices, or possibly relocate its headquarters.

A PROCESS FOR DEVELOPING NEW SERVICES

New services should not be left to whim or chance. The professional service organization that wishes to be entrepreneurial must set up systems to develop and launch successful new services. There is an effective methodology for introducing new offerings/services that, while not guaranteeing success, at least usually raises the probability of success. Figure 9-6 shows the overall steps involved in new service development. These steps are described in the following sections.

Figure 9-6. Steps of New Service Development.

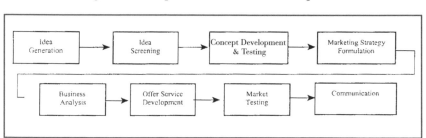

Idea Generation. Organizations differ in their need for new ideas. Some professional service firms can be quite busy carrying out their current activities and do not need to look for new things to do. On the other hand, the changing environment may necessitate the search for new services for the firm to offer.

The idea-generation stage is most relevant to firms that need one or more ideas to maintain or expand their service base. Given the high failure rate of many new ideas, the more ideas an organization generates and the more diverse they are, the greater the chance of finding successful ideas. Ideas can come spontaneously without a formal procedure from "natural sources" such as:

- Personal inspiration of one or more members of the organization.

- Random stimuli from the environment—for example, learning of a competitor's new idea.

- Client requests for new offerings or modifications of existing offerings.

Such sources have two major shortcomings. First, relying on them requires a chance combination of an idea appearing and management alertness in recognizing it. Second, the type of ideas that are typically generated from such sources are more often minor variations on a theme or simple extensions of existing services.

If an organization is to be both systematic and creative in its idea generation, four steps must be taken: (1) A commitment must be made to seek new ideas routinely and formally; (2) responsibility for this task must be specifically assigned to an individual or a group; (3) a procedure must be put in place for systematically seeking new ideas; and (4) the procedure must include a creative component if truly new ideas are sought. Table 9-1 shows additional sources of new ideas.

Information-gathering techniques should be employed on a routine and formalized basis. Further, a formal reporting and assessment mechanism should be developed to insure that each idea will be formally considered. Finally, the system should be designed so that threatened managers should not be able to label ideas as inappropriate or unworkable.

Table 9-1. Sources of New Ideas.

1. Similar organizations
   a. Structured roundtables or jointly funded clearinghouses could be established to share new ideas.
2. Competitors
   a. By paying close attention to competitors' movements, their literature, and their Web sites, one should be able to detect new ideas.
   b. By observing the hiring practices of competitors, one can anticipate where they might be heading.
3. Journals, newspapers, magazines
   a. The firm should identify potential published sources of ideas, acquire subscriptions, and assign someone or several people to peruse these sources routinely.
   b. The firm should subscribe to a clipping service.
   c. The firm can hire a librarian to handle these tasks.
   d. The firm can subscribe to a computer-based information retrieval system.
4. Conferences, travel shows, lectures
   a. People should be routinely assigned to attend important gatherings to collect ideas and useful literature.
5. Customers
   a. The organization should solicit its clients or patients for their ideas rather than wait for them to appear spontaneously.
   b. Many firms obtain some of their best new ideas by soliciting or actively listening to customers.
6. Employees and staff
   a. The organization should solicit employees for suggestions and reward them monetarily or in some other way when these ideas are fruitful.

Idea Screening. Once the idea-generating system has accumulated a significant array of ideas, some of which are sure to be patently outrageous, some attempt must be made to identify the most promising ideas. There is some chance that screening might result in an excellent idea being prematurely dropped. What might be worse, however, is accepting a bad idea for further development as a result of poor screening. Each idea that is developed takes substantial management time and money. The purpose of screening is, therefore, to eliminate all but the most promising ideas.

Several steps should typically be taken to insure effective idea screening for the organization. (1) A formal screening committee should be established to evaluate new ideas. The committee should include representatives of each key functional area within the firm who have expertise that bears on one or more of the proposed undertakings. (2) Regular meetings should be scheduled to evaluate new ideas. (3) Criteria should be developed against which ideas are evaluated. The criteria should be consistently applied over many evaluation sessions. Examples of some of the more common criteria include the following: (a) the organizational mission statement; (b) the size of the potential target audience; (c) the size of financial investment necessary; (d) the organization's present levels of expertise; (e) the probable demand on management's time and energy; (f) the newness of the idea to the target audience; (g) the consequences of the idea on the organization's public image; (h) the extent of probable competition; (i) the downside consequences if the idea fails. (4) Weights for each criteria should be developed. (5) Each idea should be evaluated based on the criteria, along with how confident the evaluator is of the rating on each criterion. (6) A weighed value rating for each new idea is computed along with a weighed certainty rating. These scores are compared to a pre-determined cut-off point. For example, a hospital may look at many options for market development and weed out those that require a great deal of investment (Cancer Care Center, for example) or those where they have little expertise (Neonatal ward, for example). They may focus on a wellness center that is an "extension" of their cardio unit.

Concept Development and Testing. Those ideas that survive screening must undergo further development into full concepts. This stage is very important because an idea that is attractive to the organization is not necessarily attractive to the target audience. A professional service firm must be able to describe its proposed program or idea to potential clients to learn their level of interest. Each concept should be prepared in a written form in enough detail to allow clients to understand it and express their reactions.

Market Strategy Formulation. Once a concept has been chosen, the firm should develop a preliminary outline of the marketing strategy for introducing this new service to the target audience. This is necessary so that the full revenue and cost implications of a new service can be evaluated in the next stage of the business analysis.

The core marketing strategy should be spelled out in a statement consisting of three parts. The first part describes the size, structure, and behavior of the target market, the intended positioning of the new offering in this market, and the volume and impact goals for the first few years. For a hypothetical plastic surgeon this might be as follows:

> The target market is adults over the age of 40 living in the greater metropolitan area who have the financial means and motivation to seek plastic surgery procedures that have the goal of providing a more fit and sleeker physical appearance. The program will be differentiated from others by offering computer simulation and imaging of the potential before and after results. The practice will seek an average of five procedures a day with the aim of achieving net income of at least $250,000.

The second part of the marketing strategy statement outlines the offering's intended price, access strategy, and marketing budget for the first year. The third part of the marketing strategy statement describes the intended long-run goals and marketing-mix strategy over time.

Business Analysis. As soon as a satisfactory service concept and marketing strategy have been developed, the organization is in position to do a formalized business analysis of the attractiveness of the proposal. It must estimate such financial figures as its anticipated return on investments and break-even analysis.

Offer Service Development. If the firm is satisfied that this concept is financially viable, it can begin developing the program into a more concrete form. The person in charge of the concept can develop brochures, schedules, ads, or other materials to implement the service. Each of these materials should be consumer tested before being printed and issued. A sample of potential clients might be asked to respond to mock-ups of these materials. This usually yields valuable suggestions leading to better materials.

Market Testing. When the organization is satisfied with the initial materials and schedules, it can set up a market test to see if the concept is really going to be successful. Market testing is the stage at which the offer and marketing program are introduced to an authentic client setting to learn how many clients are really interested in the program. One way of testing the new service would be to implement it in one or more of the organization's branch offices. This gives the concept the ability to compete and be evaluated in a real environment against real competition. If the new service proves successful in one or all of these test markets, it can then be launched throughout the rest of the organization where appropriate.

Commercialization. Commercialization is the set of activities undertaken following positive test-market results. The first step is to make four crucial decisions about the launch.

1. *When to launch.* Factors to be considered are: (a) whether there is a need to first phase out an old service; (b) whether there is a seasonal peak time for introducing the service; (c) whether further work on the offer could be profitably carried out; or (d) whether there is any risk that important rivals will reach the market first.

2. *Where to launch.* If the service is to be marketed in a wide geographic area, the organization must decide whether to tackle the whole market at once or to start slowly, rolling out the service on a market-by-market basis. The "whole market approach" has the advantages of preempting competitors' possible scale economies and achieving significant promotional impact. It does, however, assume that the program has been finalized and its chances of ultimate success are excellent. The advantages of a roll-out introduction that can compensate for its slower speed and greater total cost are that (a) one can learn as one goes; and (b) if optimistic projections are not realized, the project can be aborted or sent back to the drawing boards at a lower economic cost and less embarrassment to the firm.

3. *To whom to aim the launch.* Even in a local roll-out, the program manager must decide whether to aim at all eventual clients or to focus first on (a) those most likely to respond to the offer; (b) those most likely to have important leadership roles for others; or (c) both of these groups.

4. *How to launch.* Tactical decisions must be made about how to achieve the maximum impact at launch date and thereafter. Included are decisions about teaser ads, degree of secrecy, amount and type of media coverage, and so on.

It is imperative in a product launch that a formal scheduling procedure is established to ensure that all the needed tasks are (1) done in the right order, (2) done on schedule, and (3) done at the least possible cost.

EVALUATING AND MODIFYING SERVICE PROCESSES

An important question every organization must address is whether its existing processes and services can be improved or enhanced in any way. This question can be based on the desire to increase customer satisfaction, to lower cost or improve profits, or to respond to client complaints. An important tool in addressing any of these circumstances is the *service blueprint.*[8]

The service blueprint is a picture or map that portrays the service situation so that the different people involved in providing it can understand and deal with it objectively, regardless of their roles or individual points of view. A service blueprint visually displays the service by simultaneously depicting the process of service delivery, the roles of employees and customers, and the visible elements of the service.

A complete blueprint will show each of the actions on a flowchart. The blueprint will show a line of visibility that demarcates the actions observable to the customer from those that are invisible to the customer. The blueprint shows the facilitating goods that are necessary to perform the service, the approximate time each activity takes to perform, and the possible places where problems could surface. Figure 9-7 shows a simplified blueprint for a general practitioner service. Such blueprints clearly show the interrelationship of several different functions that must be coordinated to achieve the organization's and the customers' objectives.

Devising a service blueprint may sometimes be complicated, particularly if the service performance comprises many components. The process requires those in charge to become very familiar with the operational aspects of the service. It is often necessary to bring together employees from different departments or positions within the organization to develop an accurate blueprint of the total service. This step is nec-

Figure 9-7. Simplified Blueprint.

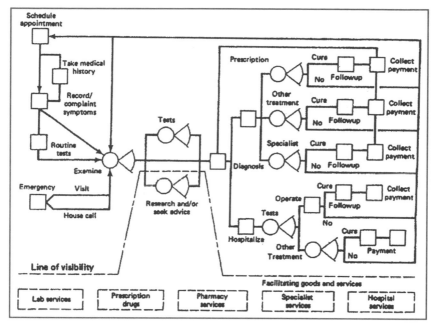

essary because no individual has a complete understanding of the many dimensions of the organizational service.

A blueprint allows an individual to ascertain the service's level of complexity and divergence. *Complexity* refers to the number and intricacies of steps involved in the service performance; *divergence* refers to the amount of flexibility or variability involved in any particular step of the service performance. Some services are very low in divergence and low in complexity. For example, if a patient hurts his wrist and needs it x-rayed, the x-ray technician is only going to take three shots of the wrist—flat, at a 90-degree angle, and at a 45-degree angle. At the same time, the technician is not allowed to be creative in taking x-rays of the wrist, because physicians and other medical practitioners have been trained to look for differences in established shots. On the other hand, caring for other types of illnesses might involve high levels of complexity as well as divergence. Physicians, based upon their backgrounds, experience, and beliefs, as well as bedside manner, might approach patients differently. Accordingly, the tests and procedures a patient requires might also vary in complexity based upon the physician's diagnosis.

Once developed, a service blueprint gives employees a clear picture of the overall service, and in doing so, may help to define the importance of their roles in the service performance. Further, a blueprint may help an organization improve its service by directing its attention to steps that could be altered, added, or deleted. Service blueprints are, therefore, indispensable tools for planning an organization's service performance.

SUMMARY

Most professional service organizations are multi-service firms. They make decisions on the service mix, on each individual service, and on marketing-mix strategies for each service at each stage of its life cycle.

Services have to be defined. Services are a deed, performance, or act that are essentially intangible and do not necessarily result in the ownership of anything.

An organization's service mix can be described in terms of its length, width, and depth. Some of the organization's services constitute its core services and, others, its ancillary services. Organizations like to develop a flagship service or superstar professional to help publicize the organization. Rising costs and increasing competition are forcing professional service firms to search for ways to increase their productivity.

Three levels of concept of a service can be distinguished. The core service answers the question: What need is the service really meeting? The perceptible service is the form in which the service is seen. It includes the following service attributes: personnel, quality level, branding strategies, process, service time, waiting time, supporting equipment, and other customers. The augmented service consists of the perceptible service and the additional services and benefits such as warranties or credit. As competition increases, organizations augment their service offering to compete more effectively.

Services pass through a life cycle consisting of four stages: introduction, growth, maturity, and decline. The S-shaped life cycle is the most common. The other patterns include the scallop pattern, cyclical pattern, and fad pattern. Each stage of the product of the life cycle presents new marketing challenges and requires adjustments in the target market and marketing mix.

As certain programs become irrelevant or new needs emerge, the firm must consider launching new services. To be successful in developing new services, the organization must be both creative and systematic. The professional service firm generally develops new services through the following steps: idea generation, idea screening, concept development and testing, marketing strategy formulation, business analysis, service development, market testing, and commercialization.

The institution may also need to modify existing services and programs. Continuous improvements in service design and performance contribute to customer satisfaction and reduced costs. Service blueprinting can identify better ways to implement new services or to improve the functioning of existing ones.

NOTES

[1] Adapted from "Change of Identity for A^C," *International Accounting Bulletin* (230) p2, June 30, 1998, Laferty Publications, Ltd; "Andersen Consulting Puts Accent on a New Name," www.Standard.com, October 26, 2000; Clark, Philip. "Divorced Andersen Readies a New Name," B to B, October 9, 2000.

[2] Gummesson, Evert. "The Marketing of Professional Services—25 Propositions," in *Marketing of Services*, James H. Donnelly, and William R. George, editors (Chicago: American Marketing Assoc., 1981*)*.

[3] Goldstein, Matt. "Branding Comes to the Bar: Marketing Savvy Outsiders Drive Local Law Firms to Sell Themselves," *Crain's New York Business* (May 3, 1999), p3.

[4] Schmitt, Richard B. "Lawyers Try In-Your-Face Pitches," *The Wall Street Journal* (January 12, 2001).

[5] Von Brachel, John. "Make Your Brand a Household Name," *Journal of Accountancy* (May 1999).

[6] Norman Cousins, as quoted in *Time* (June 21, 1982, p3) in a report on his graduation address before the Tulane School of Medicine in New Orleans.

7   Rogers, Everett M. *Diffusion of Innovations*. New York: Free Press, 1962.

8   Shostack, Lynn G. "A Framework for Service Marketing," in *Marketing Theory, Distinguished Contributions*, Stephen W. Brown and Raymond P. Fisk, eds., New York: John Wiley & Sons, 1984, p250. Also see "Designing Services that Deliver," *Harvard Business Review* (1984), p133-139.

10 | Pricing Professional Services

....

*"If you give something worth paying for,
they'll pay."*
TOM PETERS

Times have certainly changed with respect to fee setting in most of the professions. Clients are no longer willing to accept whatever fee a professional chooses to charge. Government actions and other developments, such as competition and strong third-party influences, have helped to create a climate where clients are much more informed than ever before about the fees being charged by rival professional service firms. They are using this increased amount of information to guide them in demanding fees that are seen as fair and equitable. Increased price competition, something that was alien to most of the professions, has been the result.

Increased client sensitivity to fees and resulting price or fee competition has elevated the importance of carefully developing the price or fee component of the marketing mix. Careful attention to fee setting can bring substantial returns to the firm, helping it attract clients away from competing firms and obtain clients who previously may have avoided a particular professional service because of the fear that it would cost too much. An incorrect price misstates the value of a service and leads to diminished fee generation.

The fee-setting process involves multiple considerations. We shall address the following issues in this chapter:

The Thomas Group, Inc., a management consulting firm from Irving, Texas, has successfully used a performance-based model of pricing. The payment is contingent on results and the consulting firm agrees to base fees on a percentage of savings or earnings generated for a client as a result of its recommendations. Calling its team of consultants "Resultants," Thomas Group focuses on business processes including product and service development, engineering, manufacturing, infrastructure, and sales. The firm aims to increase revenues and reduce costs for its clients.

James E. Dykes, executive vice president for corporate development, says that in some cases up to fifty percent of Thomas Group's fees are based on quantifiable results. Such results may include various cycle-time reductions, inventory reduction, margin enhancements, profit improvements, or revenue increases.

Thomas Group's strategy is to first understand what the client is trying to improve. The next steps include an initial analysis to evaluate how the client's business is performing and an estimate of what levels of performance the business should be reaching if it implements the suggested process improvements. "Many times the people don't believe the numbers are possible," says Dykes. "One of the reasons for the incentives is that we believe we can achieve those numbers. We'll risk our profit. It passes the credibility test."

In situations in which Thomas Group and its clients are equal partners, both management teams have the same incentive to achieve the desired results in focusing on a win-win situation.[1]

1. How do consumers perceive prices in a service industry?
2. What should be the objective of fee setting?
3. What basic strategies are available in fee setting?
4. What tactics are available for implementing fee strategies?
5. How should fees be changed?
6. How can fees be negotiated, billed, collected, and allocated most effectively?

PRICING SERVICES

Pricing of professional services can be very different from the pricing of consumer package goods. In particular, there are three key differences between customer evaluation of pricing for services and pricing for goods. They are: (1) Customers often have inaccurate or limited reference prices for services, (2) monetary price is not the only relevant price to service customers, and (3) in the United States, price is a key signal to quality in services. We will develop each of these further.

Customer Knowledge of Service Prices

Ask someone who does not normally use a lawyer, an accountant, or a management consultant how much any of these services costs and you are likely to find that they are relatively clueless. Ask the same individuals how much they might pay for a certain brand of automobile, a color television set, or a laptop computer and they may be more likely to answer the question. Many consumers of professional services have no reference prices for these services. A reference price is a point in memory for a good or service and can consist of the price last paid, the price most frequently paid, or the average of all prices customers have paid for similar offerings.[2] Most people are not as accurate in their reference prices for professional services as they are for household goods and are likely to feel more uncertain about the reference prices they hold.

This may be true for four reasons. First, with professional services, providers may be unable or unwilling to estimate a price in advance. Consider management consulting or legal services. In both cases, these professionals are rarely willing, or even able, to estimate a price in advance. The primary reason is not that they are being difficult, but they are unlikely to know what the services will involve until they have fully examined the patient's or the client's situation.

A second reason is that because services are intangible and created upon demand, service firms have greater flexibility in the configurations and combinations of services they offer. A professional service firm can conceivably offer a veritable "Chinese menu" of pricing options, combinations, and variations, leading to a complex and complicated pricing structure. Depending on what options the client is interested in and how complex each option becomes, this will have a major impact upon the cost of the final service.

A third reason is that individual customer needs vary. These needs may vary based upon the complications in their situation or even because of the role the client is willing to play. Consider two individuals who are in business and seeking a CPA to prepare their business-based tax returns. The first individual has a relatively simple business enterprise, a handful of large clients, works exclusively with a small number of subcontractors, and keeps very good records and receipts. The second individual has many clients, works with a multitude of subcontractors, is not nearly as organized, and brings his records to the CPA in shoe boxes. Although both individuals may do the same amount of business in dollars, serving the second businessperson will cost more.

Finally, clients may find it burdensome to research professional service fees. One would have to contact several service providers, sit down with each, explain circumstances, and answer questions in order to get a reasonable estimate of the cost of the service. The fact that services are intangible makes this process even more overwhelming, because there is no true way to ascertain the level of quality that accompanies these services until after the services have been performed.

The Role of Non-Monetary Costs

The monetary price is not the only cost to a consumer in purchasing a professional service. Non-monetary costs, such as time, convenience, and social costs, also enter into the evaluation of whether to buy or rebuy a service and may, at times, be an even more important concern than the money itself.

Price as an Indicator of Service Quality

Traditionally, the less one knows about the service he or she is purchasing, the more likely price will become an important indicator of the quality of that service. When a customer is fully informed about a purchase decision and what goes into the make up of a product or the creation of a service, price is likely to be less influential in the decision process. For example, when purchasing a stereo, someone trained in engineering can easily read the output specifications of different options of stereo equipment and will know exactly what these products are capable of. In this circumstance, he or she is not likely to be swayed by the pricing that accompanies the product. At the same time, a chemist who is contracting for a lawn-care service would easily be able to identify the differences between competitors' offerings with regard to the treatment of his or her lawn. However, someone who doesn't have the proper background in either of these situations may find it very difficult to compare the product or service and would therefore look towards pricing, typically accompanied by brand name, as an indication of quality. The same function holds true in the pricing of professional services. The average purchaser of professional services does not have the knowledge base to understand what goes into creating a quality service. In these circumstances, the client may believe that price is the best indicator of quality. Another factor that increases the dependence on price as a quality indicator is the risk associated with the service purchase. In high-risk situations, many of which involve a great deal of trust such as medical treatment or management consulting, customers are much more likely to look to price as an indicator of quality.

DETERMINING OBJECTIVES
FOR FEE-SETTING

One of the first considerations in setting fees is determining what the firm wants to accomplish with its fee strategy. A firm that seeks to maximize profits will charge different fees from one that seeks to earn merely satisfactory profits. In general, the clearer a firm is about its objectives, the easier it is to set price. In this section we will review several alternative fee-setting objectives and discuss their implications for fee-setting strategy.

Current Profit Maximization

Some firms seek to attain the highest possible current profit levels. Each year, they attempt to set fees and other marketing variables at levels that will maximize profits. They make forecasts about how clients, competitors, intermediaries, suppliers, regulators, and others will respond to the marketing mixes and they choose the mix (and fee) that appears likely to bring the largest profits.

In theory, the profit-maximizing firm should set fees or prices using the price-setting approach of economics. The normal assumption is that higher fees will be accompanied by lower demand. The firm would set the price so that the difference between the resulting revenue and cost would be maximized. Essentially, the firm should set fees so that the marginal (additional) revenue brought in for the last hour of work billed just equals the marginal cost of doing that last hour of work. In this way, the firm should be in a situation where each hour of work produces more additional revenues than additional costs. However, this approach requires oversimplifying the pricing problem. In addition, the firm must make rigid assumptions about the manner in which competitors, clients, suppliers, regulators, intermediaries, and the firm's own staff will react to different fee levels.

Nevertheless, assessing carefully how much revenues and costs will result from various fee levels is worth close consideration. Even firms that have objectives other than profit maximization will generally find it valuable to consider these factors carefully.

Market Penetration

Many professional service firms set the objective of achieving high penetration of the target market. A firm with a market-penetration objective will be inclined to focus on its competition when setting fees. This will typically lead the firm to charge fees that are lower than its competition.

Low fees may be particularly advisable if: (1) The market appears to be highly sensitive to fee levels, and therefore a low fee will stimulate more rapid market growth; (2) a low fee would discourage actual and potential competition; (3) a low fee would not be viewed by clients as an indicator of poor quality work; and (4) the more experience the firm obtains, the lower its costs of attracting and servicing clients. If none of these four conditions hold, then a firm may want to avoid fee-cutting as a means of penetrating a market and turn to other marketing objectives.

Market Skimming

Some firms seek to make a large amount of profit from a small number of clients. They charge high fees and only a limited number of clients are attracted. They could make more short-run profits by charging lower fees and seeking a larger market, but they prefer to "skim" the market.

This objective will be appealing to firms in situations where: (1) High fees may actually be viewed by targeted clients as an indicator of better quality, (2) high fees will not attract new competitors, (3) the costs of attracting and servicing clients do not decline appreciably as more experience is obtained, (4) a shortage of well-qualified professional staff makes it difficult to service more than a few select, high-paying clients, and (5) high fees will not attract the scrutiny of government regulatory officials or the wrath of third-party payors like insurance companies or the government.

Satisfaction Bases

Many professional service firms do not emphasize profitability—either in the short or long run—in the way they conduct their affairs. The world is filled with professionals who just "get by" but continue to practice because of love for their profession. These professionals tend to have objectives of earning a satisfactory level of profits; enough to allow them to cover their expenses, live comfortably, and earn reputations for being fair and competent. Fee setting for these people therefore focuses on trying to cover expenses with fees that are viewed as fair and equitable.

STRATEGIC OPTIONS IN FEE-SETTING

A professional service firm's fee-setting objectives provide guidance for the development of the two key elements of a fee or pricing strategy: (1) the *average fee level* and (2) the *fee presentation approach.* The firm needs to decide how low or high it wants its fees, on average, to be, and how it wants to present or package fees for clients (for example, time and expenses, retainer, etc.). We now discuss the strategic options in both of these areas.

Selecting an Average Fee Level

A professional service firm needs to decide where it wants to position itself on a cost or expense dimension. Does the firm want to be seen by targeted clients as cheap, expensive, or somewhere in between? Of course, the selection of a penetration objective will generally dictate the use of a low fee level; while the selection of a skimming objective will generally dictate the use of a high fee level. Most firms use one of three basic calculation methods to help them select a specific average fee level: (1) *cost-oriented methods*, (2) *competition-oriented methods*, and (3) *demand-oriented methods.* Cost-oriented methods tend to be used by firms with satisfaction-based objectives; while demand-oriented and competition-oriented methods tend to be used by firms with skimming and penetration objectives, respectively. Profit-maximizing firms typically use aspects of all three methods. We will now illustrate how a management consulting firm might use each method.

Cost-oriented methods. Setting fees in a cost-oriented way would have a management consulting firm calculating what it costs to provide a given amount of service to a client and then setting a fee to insure that costs are covered and a specified level of profits is earned. Typically, the firm would develop a "multiple" or markup that it could automatically multiply times the hourly/daily salaries of professional staff members to arrive at an hourly/daily fee for their services. Such a multiple would be designed to be large enough to allow the total fees received to cover both overhead expenses and a targeted level of profits.

A management consulting firm might calculate its multiple in the following way.[3] First, it would estimate the total cost per year of maintaining its professional staff (C). It would do this by multiplying the number of hours per year it expects each professional to work (H) times the number of professionals on its staff (N) times the average salary (and benefits) paid to professionals per hour (S). For example, the firm might make the following calculations:

$$C = H \times N \times S$$
$$C = 2{,}000 \times 50 \times \$35$$
$$C = \$3{,}500{,}000$$

Next, the firm would determine its total yearly overhead costs (F) by examining its expected expenses for secretarial and clerical staff, marketing staff, office rentals, professional dues, insurance, and so forth. For this example, let us assume that the total comes to $2,000,000.

The firm would then assume that total revenues are equal to total professional costs times the yet unspecified multiple (M) times a "productivity rate" (P) which reflects the proportion of hours worked by the average professional staff member that are billable hours. In other words, for the present example it would be assumed that:

$$R = C \times M \times P$$
$$R = \$3{,}500{,}000 \times M \times 0.7$$
$$R = \$2{,}450{,}000(M)$$

If profits (Z) are equal to

$$Z = R - C - F$$
$$Z = \$2{,}450{,}000(M) - \$3{,}500{,}000 - \$2{,}000{,}000$$

then the remaining task becomes to figure a value for M that would allow Z to reach a targeted level, say $625,000. This could be done as follows:

$$\$625{,}000 = \$2{,}450{,}000(M) - \$5{,}500{,}000$$
$$M = 6{,}125{,}000 \: / \: 2{,}450{,}000$$
$$M = 2.5$$

Another way to arrive at this multiple would be to solve the profit formula for M and then plug in the example values (as follows):

$$Z = R - C - F$$
$$Z = HNSMP - HNS - F$$
$$HNSMP = Z + HNS + F$$
$$M = Z / HNSP + HNS / HNSP + F / HNSP$$
$$M = (1/P) \left[\frac{(Z + F)}{C} + 1 \right] \qquad (10\text{-}1)$$
$$M = (1/.7) \; [(625{,}000 + 2{,}000{,}000)/3{,}500{,}000] + (1/.7)$$
$$M = 2.5$$

Equation 10-1 could be used to formulate a multiple to assist many different types of firms in their fee setting. The formula suggests that higher targeted profit levels and larger overhead tend to make multiples higher, while higher productivity rates and higher professional staff costs tend to lower the multiples needed to achieve given profit levels.

The major positive feature of cost-oriented methods is their relative simplicity. All one usually needs to set the billing rate for a professional is to multiply the person's hourly/daily salary times the calculated multiple. Since these methods have great popularity in the professions, they tend to lead to similar fees by competitors. And clients become familiar and comfortable with the resulting fees, helping to improve communication between clients and professionals.

But these methods have a serious weakness. To calculate a multiple using formula 10-1 amounts to assuming that average productivity rates (or percent billable time) will stay at some fixed level regardless of what multiple is finally selected. This assumes that the amount of work professionals obtain in a given year is not influenced by what fees they are charging. This is a difficult assumption to accept. To avoid problems that might occur from making this assumption, a firm may want to give simultaneous consideration both to possible multiples and to possible productivity rates. The multiple finally selected should be one that could be confidently predicted to provide a productivity rate that would allow the firm to achieve its targeted profit levels.

There are other problems with the cost-oriented approach to pricing. First of all, cost may be more difficult to trace in professional service businesses that provide multiple services to their clients. Additionally, because a major component of cost is employee time, the value of people's time is not easy to calculate.

Fee for service. The most common cost-oriented approach used in professional service is that of fee for service. Management consultants, accountants, lawyers, psychologists, and other professional service providers charge for their services on an hourly basis. Before the 1970s, lawyers were far more likely to bill clients a certain fee for services rendered regardless of the amount of time they spent delivering them. Then law firms began to bill on an hourly rate. This method offered accountability to clients and an internal budgeting system for the firm. Today, lawyers and accountants must keep track of the time they spend for a given client, down to ten-minute increments. This technique has been the subject of criticism because it does not promote efficiency and sometimes ignores the expertise of lawyers. An experienced lawyer may be able to accomplish a great deal more than a novice in the same period of time. Despite these concerns, the hourly bill still dominates the industry with 77 percent of revenues being billed this way.[4]

Competition-oriented methods. When a firm sets its prices chiefly on the basis of what its competitors are charging, its pricing policy can be described as competition-oriented. It may charge the same as its competition, a higher price, or a lower price. A distinguishing characteristic is that the firm does not seek to maintain a rigid relationship between its price and its costs or its demand. Its own costs and demand may change, but the firm maintains its price because competitors maintain their price. Conversely, the same firm will change its prices when competitors change theirs, even if its own costs or demands have not been altered. The most common type of competition-oriented pricing occurs when a firm tries to keep its price at the average price charged by others in the industry. Called *going rate* or *imitative pricing*, this method is popular for several reasons. Where costs are difficult to measure, it is believed that the going price represents the collective wisdom of the industry concerning the price that would yield a fair return. It is also felt that conforming to a going price would be least disruptive of industry harmony. The difficulty of knowing how buyers and competitors would react to price differentials is another reason for this pricing.

Sometimes competition-oriented methods are also called *ballpark pricing* because, as the name implies, service providers are trying to set their price somewhere in the same ballpark as competitors. Another reason for this practice is that it shifts competition to an area other than price. If prices among competitors are basically the same, potential customers are likely to look to other factors for a point of differentiation, such as the firm's image, reputation, additional services, or even level of responsiveness or access.

Competition-oriented fee setting can be successful for a firm if (1) it has accurate information about competitors' fees, and (2) clients are aware of fee differentials between competitors and react to those differentials. Competition-based pricing is not without its problems, however. Small firms may charge too little to be viable. Given that they may not have the same economies of scale as large firms, they may not make margins high enough to remain in business. Second, many services are by nature heterogeneous, making a competition-oriented pricing method difficult to use. Different service firms may employ different processes and range of services, making their services difficult to compare. The result is that prices cannot be standardized.

Professional service firms confronted with competitive bidding situations must employ a form of competition-oriented fee setting. Even if the client is not committed to going with the lowest bid and it is possible to outbid competitors by showing well on attributes other than fees, it is wise to think in a competition-oriented way about the fee portion of a competitive bid. The problem of competitive bidding has received considerable attention from management scientists and other researchers. Exhibits 10-1 and 10-2 demonstrate two different philosophies to making competitive bids.[5]

Demand-oriented methods. Cost-oriented and competition-oriented approaches to pricing are based on the company and its competitors rather than customers. Neither approach takes into consideration that customers may lack reference prices, may be sensitive to non-monetary prices, and may judge quality on the basis of price; however, a company's pricing decision should account for all of these factors The third major approach, demand-oriented pricing, involves setting prices consistent with customers' perceptions of values. In other words, prices are based on what customers will pay for the services provided.

Exhibit 10-1. Effect of Different Bids on Expected Profits.

In a competitive bidding situation, a firm bases its price on how it thinks competitors will price, rather than on its own costs or demand. The firm wants to win a contract and winning the contract requires pricing lower than other firms.

Yet the firm cannot set its price below a certain level. It cannot price below cost without harming its position. In contrast, the higher the company sets its price above its costs, the lower the chance of getting the contract.

The net effect of the two opposite poles can be described in terms of the expected profit of that particular bid.

Table: Effect of Different Bids on Expected Profit

COMPANY'S BID	COMPANY'S PROFIT (1)	PROBABILITY OF WINNING WITH THIS BID (ASSUMED) (2)	EXPECTED PROFIT [(1) X (2)]
$ 9,500	$ 100	0.81	$ 81
10,000	600	0.36	216
10,500	1,100	0.09	99
11,000	1,600	0.01	16

Suppose the firm bids $9,500. It estimates that it would have an 81% probability of winning the contract, and it would realize a low profit of $100. The expected profit with this bid would be $81.00. If the firm bid $11,000, its profit would be $1,600 but its chance of getting the contract might be reduced to 0.01; the expected profit would only be $16.00. The company should bid the price that would maximize the expected profit. In our example, our best bid would be $10,000 for which the expected profit would be $216.

Using expected profit as a basis for setting prices makes sense for the large firm that makes many bids; it is playing the odds and the firm will make maximum profits in the long run. But a firm that bids only occasionally or needs a particular contract badly will not find the expected profit approach useful. The approach, for example, does not distinguish between $100,000 profit with a 0.10 probability and a $12,000 profit with an 0.80 probability, yet the firm that wants to keep production going would prefer the second contract to the first.

Exhibit 10-2. Winning Bidding.[6]

Bidding can be a boom or bust proposition. Many companies use competitive bidding to drive suppliers' prices down. Others have to get a number of bids even when they know who they want as supplier. The professional service marketer who doesn't find out why a company wants to bid can be at a disadvantage. Bids that get business reflect standard good-selling practices. Below are ten tips for winning competitive bids.

1. **Find out what it's all about.** Familiarize yourself with common practices and procedures to enter the bidding arena with greater confidence.

2. **Choose carefully.** Before you spend your time and energy, consider your long-term return on investment and make sure you and your buyer are a good match.

3. **Show them the value.** Your bid should give buyers the most for the money—make sure they understand what they're getting and what it's worth.

4. **Serve now, serve later.** Even before you bid, be at your buyer's service. Offer advice, help analyze needs, do whatever you can to assist at bid selection time.

5. **Know what buyers value.** To make your bid uniquely irresistible, uncover your buyer's hot buttons and design your bid according to their preferences.

6. **Scan the marketplace.** You can't be sure your bid is competitive until you know how your offer stacks up to everyone else's. Keep up with competitor products, services, and rates, and find out who won the contract you bid on last and how.

7. **Know your decision makers.** Titles may be meaningless, so find out who really has the power and who will have the most influence on the decision-making process.

8. **Build relationships.** Make sure as many people as possible at the buying company are on your side. Also, relationships with secretaries may serve you as well as ties to top execs.

9. **Get the facts.** Complement your knowledge of buying-company personnel with a thorough understanding of their products, services, business challenges, and goals.

10. **Do the legwork.** Changing vendors may create hassles for your buyer. Offer to do anything your buyers need done in order to make you their new supplier.

The basis of establishing the price-value relationship in the client's mind is expressed in the following formula:

Value = Benefits – Costs

While this formula is simple in its expression, it is very powerful in its result. The professional service firm that offers the greatest value to its clients is the one that provides the greatest difference or ratio of benefits to costs.

A benefit is a solution to a client's problem. Problems in turn can be as varied as clients. One client's problem may be to successfully merge two businesses to create a stronger position in the marketplace. Another's may be to survive an IRS audit. The professional services firm's task is to make its clients' or patients' problems go away as much as possible and as soon as possible.

Sometimes the easiest way to increase perceived value on behalf of the clients is through reducing the clients' costs. When most people think of costs, what comes to mind first is financial cost; however, there are at least seven other costs that the professional service firm may try to reduce. In many instances, by reducing these other costs a firm can charge a premium price for its services. Here are the different kinds of costs.

1. **Sensory costs.** When visiting a dentist, patients may worry more about the resulting pain than the financial cost. A cost of plastic surgery beyond the fee would be the resulting discomfort while the patient's body heals. A professional service provider should take steps to reduce the sensory costs to a client or patient by making the service experience as pleasant as possible.

2. **Time/convenience.** Benjamin Franklin once said, "Do not waste time because it is the stuff that life is made of." In many instances, a client buying professional services is actually buying time. A popular advertising campaign by H & R Block during the year 2000 tax season portrayed a series of humorous vignettes where an individual was spending days preparing his or her tax return and then communicating that H & R Block could accomplish this task in a matter of hours. According to a study by the American Medical Association, the average amount of time that

patients will be willing to wait in a doctor's office is 20.6 minutes.[7] If a patient has to wait longer than this period of time on
a regular basis, he or she might decide to switch physicians.
Professionals should strive to save clients time.

3. **Hassle.** Another potential cost to clients is the hassle one experiences in trying to purchase the service. This hassle could be the
result of an overly complex service process requiring the client to
go through a number of steps to obtain the service. This could be
especially true if the steps need to be repeated upon every visit.

4. **Opportunity.** Each choice of a professional service firm means
giving up the others. This is called an opportunity cost, and
occurs, for example, when the client subsequently realizes that
the other professional service firm would have done a better job.

5. **Psychological costs.** Any time an individual makes a decision,
he or she is likely to experience "cognitive dissonance," that is,
some anxiety. The greater the perceived risk in a decision, the
greater the level of anxiety. The prospective client may be ner-
vous and very ambivalent in his or her decision process. Clients
will try to second-guess themselves and look for confirming
information that will support their decision.

The professional service firm that understands this can find ways
to reduce that anxiety. The firm can provide timely reinforcement to a consumer's decision, provide a guarantee, or manage
clients' expectations by a clear explanation of the process and
likely outcomes.

6. **Social costs.** In cases where individuals are given the responsibility of hiring a professional service firm, they will be concerned
about how their choice will reflect on them within their own firm.
If the professional service firm the individual hires is difficult to
work with or performs poorly, the person who hired it is likely to
be criticized. His or her decision-making capabilities may be
called into question. As a result, buyers of professional services
tend to make "safe" decisions. The professional service firm must
strive to reduce any potential social costs within the minds of

those making the decision. As one management consultant said, "(My) job is to make those hiring us look good."

7. **Physical costs.** Finally, another potential cost to a client could be a physical cost. This is especially true in the medical fields. The decision to use or not use a certain doctor or to have or avoid having a certain procedure performed may be directly related to the perceived possibility of other physical costs that the patient may experience. The real or perceived physical costs require the medical service provider to take the necessary time to address patients' fears and concerns. For example, in the late 1990s news stories about deaths that occurred as a result of what was believed to be a simple liposuction procedure required plastic surgeons to spend more time addressing and alleviating this potential fear in the minds of their patients.

Increasing value in the minds of customers. Given the formula for value, where value equals benefits minus costs, there are three ways to increase a client's perceived value of a service. The first is to increase benefits and hold costs constant. The second is to hold benefits constant and decrease costs. The third is to increase benefits and simultaneously reduce costs. All of these approaches will result in a net increase in perceived value.

Problems with demand-oriented pricing. There are two difficulties in implementing demand-oriented pricing. First, it is often difficult to learn what target customers would pay for a given product or service. This is especially true for new service offerings. For example, a physician offering acupuncture in a new community would find it hard to estimate how demand would respond to different prices. Another difficulty with demand-oriented pricing is an ethical one. Many services may have high value to target audiences. For example, pills to reduce hypertension would have high value to persons who have lost relatives to high blood pressure. It would be possible to charge very high prices for the pills based on their high perceived value; however, a firm would typically charge a lower price than what the traffic will bear because of the firm's broader ethical responsibilities.

Selecting a Fee-Presentation Approach

In addition to setting the fee level, the firm must decide on the presentation approach to use with fees. There are nine presentation approaches: (1) time and expenses, (2) fixed sum, (3) percentage, (4) contingency, (5) performance based, (6) value based, (7) retainer, (8) equity based, and (9) hybrid. Each approach is described and evaluated below.

Time and expenses. With this approach, fees are set by multiplying the number of hours/days of professional service by an hourly/daily billing rate and then adding the amount (or some multiple of the amount) of out-of-pocket expenses incurred for materials, travel, computer time, and other expenses.

The major advantage of the time-and-expenses approach is that it allows the firm to be sure of covering all its costs. Extra time spent in wrapping up a project can be billed to a client and does not have to reduce the project's profitability. This approach is often seen as "fair" by clients. This approach also makes staff members more conscious of the need to spend most of their time in billable rather than non-billable activities.

The major disadvantage of the time-and-expenses approach is the uncertainty and consequent dissatisfaction it might create in clients. Clients like to know what something is going to cost them before they make the buying decision. Yet all they can get is an estimate which might be far off the mark after the engagement is over. Clients will worry about projects or litigation taking longer than they should, and this can put a strain on the relationship between professionals and their clients.

Fixed sum. With this approach, fees are set at some fixed amount prior to providing services and are not changed regardless of how much time or expenses are required to provide the services. This approach can alleviate client uncertainty about fees and make them much more comfortable with their relationship with professionals. It can also be used to "hide" high hourly/daily rates that clients may have a difficult time accepting. But this approach transfers much of the uncertainty and risk over to the professional service firm. Unforseen events or a lack of client cooperation can be disastrous for the professional who bills on a fixed-sum basis. The pressures created by sticking to a fixed sum can even lead firms to compromise their standards and not implement quality work as vigorously as they would if each hour were being billed.

Percentage. In some professions, the fees are set as a percentage of some "placement" value. Advertising agencies often receive a commission of 15 percent on the media space they purchase for their clients. Travel agents frequently receive a 10-percent commission on the value of the travel they arrange. Executive recruiting firms receive a percentage of the first-year salary of clients they place in a new job.

The percentage approach has the advantage of being straightforward and easy for clients to understand. To the extent that higher placement values yield higher real values for clients, clients should not mind the higher fee. The professional's problem arises when a traditional percentage (such as 10 or 15 percent) is no longer adequate to cover the rising expenses and yield an adequate rate of return. For example, from time to time, advertising agencies try to convince the media to pay high commissions or these agencies resort to charging clients for certain services in addition to the media commissions they receive.

Contingency. With this approach, fees are determined by taking a percentage of figures such as the amount of a legal judgment or settlement, the cost of constructing a building, the amount of cost savings accomplished by instituting a recommended change, or some other figure that reflects how much a professional has accomplished.

The contingency approach has the advantage of being relatively simple for clients to understand. It also projects an image of being "fair" to these people. It is hard for people to feel cheated, for example, by a lawyer who takes a reasonable percentage of a personal injury award or an architect who takes a reasonable percentage of the cost of constructing a building. However, this approach can create incentives for professionals to act against their clients' best interests. It can encourage lawyers to do only a little bit of work and accept a small (but sure) settlement instead of doing much litigation to obtain a large (but unsure) award. Or it can encourage an architect to add design features to a building that a client does not really need in order to increase total construction costs.

Performance based. Similar to contingency fees are performance-based fees like those discussed in our opening vignette with the Thomas Group Inc. In performance-based fee structures, at least part of a firm's fees are tied to measurable results, as in cycle time reductions, margin enhancements, profit improvements, and so forth. Another management consulting group, called The George Group, Inc. of Dallas, has been linking its fees to results since 1994.[8] The George Group focuses on improving the value of a company by improving operating income and reducing working capital. From 1987 when the company was founded until 1992, the company offered a money-back guarantee for its work. However, in 1994 they expanded that approach to fees directly tied to results. Now the George Group takes one half of its fees in fixed payments while the other half is contingent on getting the results the firm promises. Performance-based fees have advantages in that both parties share incentives to achieving desired results and both share accountability. However, results-based arrangements also carry potential pitfalls. One concern is that a consultant might be inclined to go the short-term route and the client may be wondering if the consultant is making recommendations based upon getting higher fees or on what makes the most sense for his or her company. In fact, as part of its professional code of conduct, the New York-based American Institute of Certified Public Accountants (AICPA) says that its members shall not "perform for a contingent fee any professional services for, or receive such a fee from, a client from whom the member or the member's firm performs." AICPA defines a contingent fee as "a fee established for the performance of any service pursuant to an arrangement to which no fee will be charged unless a specified finding or result is attained or in which the amount of the fee is dependent on the finding or result of the service."[9]

Value based. Value-based pricing is typified when a consultant asks a client how much the solution to a problem is worth and, in terms of that, how much the client would be willing to pay to get the job done right. Lewis Walker, in an *Accounting Today* article titled "Holistic Planners," said that in the 21st century, planners will be paid "for value-added consulting services and for the trust they inspire, not transactions." He went on to focus on personal reputation and independence as being paramount in developing value-based approaches.[10] In order for value-based approaches to truly work, clients have to be willing to tell the professional service provider how important projects are to them. A typical list of questions to ask clients in order to arrive at a reliable answer would be the following:

1. What keeps you awake at night?

2. What is your worst professional nightmare?

3. How does it unfold?

4. What does it cost the firm financially?

5. What does it cost you personally?

Once a client answers these and similar questions, it should be possible to develop a value equation that focuses on the specific benefits or solutions to problems that the client is seeking and the costs that the client is most interested in reducing. Of course, these could include psychological and social costs as much as financial.

Value-based pricing does have some limitations, including clients' and professionals' difficulty in budgeting for this pricing. In addition, the marketplace may not be used to this type of pricing arrangement.

Retainer. With this approach, fees are set prior to a "covered" time period during which clients will receive up to a predetermined level of services without paying any extra fees. For some prepaid health and legal service firms, the retainer or prepaid fee entitles clients to unlimited services.

This approach has the major advantage of providing some certainty for both professionals and their clients. Both sides are able to predict the financial consequences of their relationship. However, the firm that uses a retainer approach must be skilled at forecasting how frequently its services will be utilized in the covered time period, just like an insurance company must skillfully estimate how many claims it will receive. If usage is underestimated when determining the fee, then the firm could incur serious losses.

Equity based. Another payment option is equity-based fees, or working for stock or options instead of cash. This approach might be used in situations where emerging firms do not have enough cash to spend on consulting fees.

Parthenon Group, a Boston consulting firm, has worked for stocks or options instead of cash and specializes in strategy consulting. Chris Jenny, managing director of the firm, says one-third of Parthenon's clients pay in equity. In 1997, 15 percent of the firm's revenue was in equity rather than cash and was credited with the consulting firm's revenue growth of 20-35 percent annually for four years straight.[11]

Equity-based pricing has some limitations. It is somewhat risky for the professional firm because there is always the possibility that the stocks or options could ultimately be of little value. It may also require a high price to be paid by the client. For example, in a hypothetical work for stock, where a consultant's fee is $50,000, the consultant might get $25,000 in cash and $150,000 in options. The advantage of this fee approach is that unlike performance or contingency pricing, there is less concern about a conflict of interest. The consultant would be more inclined to be working for long-term benefits of a smaller firm due to the potential for a greater payout.

Hybrid. For many professional service firms, the best fee-setting approach will amount to a hybrid or combination approach. A certain law firm may find it best to use a prepaid or retainer approach combined with a time-and-expenses approach for any hours worked beyond a specified level per year. The best approach will depend on a host of factors, including the firm's objectives, the nature of its target markets, and its competitive situation. For instance, a firm seeking to penetrate a very fee-sensitive market with many competitors will most likely be forced to use a fixed-sum approach and charge very low fees. On the other hand, a firm seeking to skim a fee-insensitive market with little competition will most likely turn to a time-and-expenses approach and charge whatever the market will bear.

TACTICS FOR FEE-SETTING

A variety of tactical moves are available to a professional service firm to help make its fee-setting strategy more effective. Fees can be structured and presented to certain clients in ways that will produce added revenues for a firm. Instead of always staying very close to the selected average fee level and always using the same presentation approach, a firm can use fee tactics that introduce variation around a basic fee strategy. Thus, a firm can offer "discounts," require "premiums," or utilize other fee tactics while still basically pursuing a strategy that, for example, stresses very high fees and time-and-expenses presentation approaches.

The offering of discounts is a common fee tactic in the professions. Firms will often offer to lower a normal hourly/daily rate or other type of fee for clients who:

1. Buy a very large volume of services,

2. Require services in a "slow" time period or season,

3. Need the services to support a socially beneficial venture, or

4. Pay directly to the service provider and/or make cash payments.

Receiving a discount can make a client feel special and can mean the difference between obtaining or missing a new client or keeping or losing an old client. In healthcare, more and more physicians facing the loss of professional autonomy and perceived reductions in financial compensations attributed to managed care are offering deep discounts in their pricing strategies. They are seeking a niche among patients who lack adequate coverage or are dissatisfied with their existing health plans. Some estimates put the cost of paperwork and administrative costs of health maintenance firms at 30 to 40 percent of the total cost of healthcare. Many physicians are, therefore, willing and even eager to accept lower payments directly from patients in order to avoid this paperwork and at the same time increase their professional autonomy with regard to what they perceive is best for patients.

Requiring a "premium" is another fee tactic. A request for a higher-than-normal fee may be a profitable tactic when:

1. Clients want work completed in an especially short period of time.

2. Particularly unique and specialized services are required.

3. Clients want work done that presents certain risks to the reputation of the professional service firm (e.g., defending a legal client in a highly publicized court case).

A client who does not understand the need to pay a premium in these situations may not be worth going after. Doing time-pressured, difficult, or risky work at normal fee rates can, over the long run, prove to be unprofitable.

Some professional service firms also vary their rates based on the "type of encounter" professionals have with clients. For example, some management consultants charge different rates for having luncheon meetings, doing training or teaching, conducting interviews, writing reports, or talking on the phone. Similarly, doctors often vary their rates for normal office visits, emergency office visits, and hospital visits. A firm using this tactic must carefully establish a fee structure that encourages desired types of encounters and discourages undesirable encounters—without discouraging all types of encounters. A consultant, for instance, does not want to set a high fee for luncheon meetings if that will tend to discourage too many desirable clients from exploring possibilities further.

Another fee-setting tactic commonly used in the professions is the "high estimate." This is where the professional service firm gives a client an overly conservative estimate of how long it will take to provide a service or of how much the service will probably cost. The firm's best guess of what the fees will actually be is significantly lower than what it states in the estimate. Assuming that this high estimate does not lead too many potential clients to use competitors—which is a definite risk of using this tactic—the firm will have the advantage of being able to deliver a "pleasant surprise" to many of its clients when they finally receive their bills. By presenting them with total fees that are less than what they expected, the firm can often create more highly satisfied clients who are willing to pass on good word-of-mouth about the firm.

INITIATING CHANGES IN FEES

No matter what fee strategy a professional service firm chooses to use, fees must be changed as cost, demand, and competitive factors evolve. When a firm must change its fees, decisions must be made about the direction and the extent of the change. Should the firm implement a general change in fees covering all offerings or should it only make a selective change? When changing fees, it is essential to guage the reactions of key groups, including competitors (will they undercut your cuts? will they follow your hikes?), staff members (will they demand higher salaries if fees are increased?), and regulatory officials. However, the reactions of clients are probably the most important to consider when initiating fee changes.

But trying to predict how clients will react to fee changes can be quite difficult. The great uncertainty that many people experience when buying professional services tends to make their behavior with respect to fees difficult to understand. This behavior becomes even more difficult to understand in situations where either buying decisions are made under great time pressure (e.g., selecting emergency medical care, retaining a criminal lawyer) or services are paid for in some significant part by insurance.

Valerie Zeithaml, a service quality expert, examined the issue of how *individuals* react to the fees charged by professionals.[12] Drawing from the considerable amount of research that has been done on how consumers react to prices of various *products* when faced with great uncertainty, limited information and time pressure, she developed several hypotheses about how people react to the fees of professionals. Some of her notions include:

1. People tend to ignore or avoid information about fees prior to purchase, paying most attention to this information after services have been received.

2. People depend upon fees to indicate quality in services high in credence attributes (i.e., those services that they have difficulty evaluating even after they have received them).

3. People may prefer professionals with high fees over those with low fees in situations where high risk is perceived to exist.

4. People will tolerate higher fees for professionals with strongly positive reputations or images.

5. People experienced with a professional service are more likely to use fees as an indicator of quality than people with no experience.

6. Fees may be more important in the decision to return to a professional than they are in the initial decision.

7. When the need for a professional service arises urgently or unpredictably, people do not consider fees in making buying decisions.

8. When insurance covers professional care, fees are not a pivotal factor in the purchase decision.

What Zeithaml suggests, among other things, is that for many professional service firms, raising fees may be highly effective. However, for certain market segments that are well informed about fees and have an ability to judge quality work on their own—or for those segments that refrain from using needed professional services because they perceive fees as being unaffordable—raising fees would be a reckless move.

FEE COMMUNICATION AND ADMINISTRATION

Fee-setting involves dealing with several other problems that deserve some discussion. First, in many situations, final fees cannot be determined until after negotiations have been conducted between the professional service firm and its clients. Once fees have finally been determined, the firm must develop an approach to billing clients. In addition, an approach to collecting delinquent accounts must also be formulated. Finally, some firms need to reach decisions with regard to whether fee-splitting should be done with referral sources. We will briefly discuss how these tasks might be performed in a way that supports and does not detract from a firm's marketing effort.

Negotiations

Some professional service firms have a policy of never negotiating over fees. Once they determine what they want to charge, they essentially tell their clients or patients, in a nonthreatening way, to "take it or leave it." They refuse to haggle over fees. Assuming that the fees offered have been carefully formulated to take account of cost, demand, and competitive conditions, such a policy can be highly effective—particularly for the firm with considerable experience and a strong service reputation. By avoiding negotiations, the firm does not risk possible damage to its reputation that could arise if it is perceived as being too ready to compromise its fees.

But for firms that find a "take it or leave it" approach unacceptable—either because certain business is attractive no matter how it is obtained or because targeted clients seem to *enjoy* negotiating before buying—negotiations should be approached in a systematic manner. Research should be conducted to obtain a full understanding of the financial situation and attitudes of the potential client. How much can they afford to pay? How much would it cost them not to use the service? What services or expenses do they particularly dislike paying large amounts for? This information can be obtained by questioning potential clients directly or by talking to others who may be familiar with their situations.

Once this information has been acquired, the firm should attempt to formulate an offer that will be perceived by the other party as a "win." This type of offer would contain concessions that are designed to give the other party a lower hourly fee, the use of less expensive supporting equipment, or other changes from previous fee requests that they desire most. If this offer is not accepted, other concessions should be considered and offered if deemed appropriate. At all times, discussions should remain friendly and nonthreatening, with a focus on the benefits of using the service rather than on the costs.

Billing and Collecting

The major idea to keep in mind when designing billing and collecting systems is to *avoid negative surprises.* Clients should be informed about fees or changes in fees long before they actually receive bills. They should also receive regular monthly statements (if appropriate). It is also usually better to send people several small bills rather than a single very large bill to cover a big project. Whether bills should be itemized or contain merely a lump-sum figure is a matter of some debate. The disadvantage of itemizing is that it might stimulate clients to question specific charges, either in terms of the cost or whether the activity was even necessary. The advantages of itemizing include what it can contribute to educating clients and building a sense of trust. The approach should probably be dictated by the preferences of the client.

A professional service firm should give priority attention to getting people to pay bills on time. There is no magic solution to getting people to pay on time. Making the task easier for them by doing things like filling out insurance forms, accepting credit cards, or (for firms) helping them find needed credit can help. So can the sending of appreciation notes to clients who are prompt bill payers. But perhaps the best approach is the use of regular communication to remind them of their obligation. Threatening notes and collection agencies should be used only when clients have delayed payment over an unreasonable time period.

Fee-Splitting

Any professional services marketing program must rely heavily on referral sources for obtaining leads and providing testimonials and recommendations. And one way to insure that referral sources keep working for your firm is to compensate them in some way, perhaps by giving them a small percentage of the fees brought in as a result of their referrals. But fee-splitting is a very controversial topic in most of the professions, and it is even banned or considered unethical in some fields and in some locations.

The argument against fee-splitting is that it could lead professionals to refer clients to other professionals because they are being paid to do so and not because they think those professionals can best serve the client's interests. For most professional service firms, the decision on whether to split fees must be made with extreme caution and with a full understanding of the legal and ethical ramifications of taking this action.

An alternative to fee-splitting is the keeping of a "scorecard" on referrals. The frequency and dollar amounts of referrals could be recorded for all referral sources and receivers. Periodically, meetings could be held with each member of a firm's referral network to review the scorecard and see who is sending more referrals to whom. If referrals are out of balance, then special efforts could be made to rectify the situation. If a firm finds that it is giving many more referrals than it receives from another firm for an extended period of time, then an adjustment in referral practices may be in order. At the very least, the receiving firm must periodically express its gratitude to the referring firms and offer tangible or intangible tokens of appreciation (for example, tickets to sporting events or Broadway shows, small gifts, etc.).

SUMMARY

Fee-setting has become a much more challenging task for professional service firms in recent years. Increased buyer sophistication about fees has created pressures to do fee-setting in a more careful, thoughtful manner.

Customers evaluate pricing for services differently from goods. Three characteristics of how clients evaluate pricing of professional services are: (1) They often have inaccurate or limited reference prices for services; (2) monetary price is not the only relevant price to service customers; and (3) price is the key signal to quality in services.

The first consideration in setting fees is the firm's objectives. Different strategies toward fee-setting will be dictated depending on whether the firm seeks to maximize profits, penetrate a market, skim a market, or merely satisfy.

Fee-setting strategy is defined by the average fee level and the fee-presentation approach adopted by the firm. Levels can be determined using cost-oriented, demand-oriented, or competition-oriented methods. Possible fee-presentation approaches include time and expenses, fixed sum, percentage, contingency, performance based, value based, retainer, equity based, and hybrid. The best strategy will depend on the firm's objectives and on the competitive situation it faces. Several fee tactics, such as the use of "high estimates," can make fee strategies more effective.

A firm must initiate fee changes with caution because the reactions of other parties to fee changes are difficult to predict. In particular, it is hard to forecast how clients will react to fee changes, as many may even see higher fees as indicating that better quality services are being provided. The firm must conduct sound research on potential client reactions prior to any fee changes.

Fee-setting can also involve negotiations over fees, the development of billing and collection systems, and the determination of a policy with regard to fee-splitting. All of these tasks should be carried out with an eye toward supporting and not hindering the firm's marketing program.

NOTES

[1] Hasek, Glen. "Sharing the Risk: Consulting Firms Shake Traditional Fee Models," *Industry Week* (May 4, 1998), v 247, n9, p50 (3).

[2] Monroe, Kent. "The Pricing of Services," *Handbook of Services Marketing*, Carole A. Congram and Margaret L. Friedman, eds. New York: AMACOM, 1989, p20-31.

[3] Stevens, Amy. "Firms Try More Lucrative Ways of Charging for Legal Services," *The Wall Street Journal* (November 25, 1994), pB11.

[4] Chase, Marilyn. "Whose Time is Worth More: Yours or the Doctor's," *The Wall Street Journal* (October 24, 1999), pB1.

[5] See Hasek, Glen.

[6] Adapted from "Winning Bidding," by Richard Ilsley, *Selling Power*, June 1999, pp. 22-25.

[7] Walker, Lewis, "Holistic Planners," *Accounting Today* (July 22-23, 1998).

[8] See Hasek, Glen.

[9] Hasek, Glen.

[10] Zeithaml, Valerie A. "The Acquisition, Meaning and Use of Price Information by Consumers of Professional Services," *Working Paper*, Texas A&M University, 1982.

[11] See Monroe, Kent.

[12] See Zeithaml, Valerie A.

11 | Making Services Accessible

....

"Location, Location, Location."
WILLIAM DILLARD

Professional service organizations are learning that they can no longer count on clients being willing to come to their offices at any time or in any place. While the days of "house calls" seem to be over, most professionals must give increased attention to whether their services are available to target markets in a timely and accessible manner. People prefer to use professionals who are nearby, easy to reach, and easy to see when they need to see them. When a person perceives difficulty in gaining access to a particular professional, they may choose a more accessible professional.

The need to be readily accessible to clients has long been recognized by big national CPA and consulting firms. They have typically set up well-staffed offices within a reasonable distance of any large concentration of clients.

But, the need to have accessible branch offices has increasingly been recognized by a large number of law, architectural, medical, and engineering firms. They recognize that being physically close can give them an advantage in a targeted area over competing nonlocal firms that may be perceived as "outsiders" possessing little commitment to the area. Thus, many Chicago and New York law firms have established offices in

297

If you have ever lived in an area of the country that experiences winter snowfalls, you are probably aware of the phenomenon known as "Plan B." In the morning after a heavy snowfall, radio stations broadcast the local school and business closings and announce those schools and businesses that are on Plan B. Plan B typically refers to an hour or two-hour delay before the beginning of school. The purpose of Plan B is to allow parents to get their children to school in a more relaxed manner, cutting down the chances of having some type of automobile accident due to rushing to school in slippery conditions. An orthopedic surgeon in Cincinnati, Ohio, has his own version of Plan B. Rather than a delay in opening his practice, this particular doctor has a delay in closing. On heavy snow days, his office will typically go on Plan B. Instead of closing at 5 P.M., the office may stay open an additional three hours. The physician knows that in snowy conditions, people are more likely to be injured. Many accidents are likely to happen when people are leaving or heading to their homes after work, or when children are playing after school. What he wishes to avoid is that his or a potential patient may slip and fall, go to the local emergency room, and as a result be referred to a physician other than himself. By being on Plan B the physician is ensuring that he is there when his patients need him.

Washington, D.C., while many architectural and engineering firms have set up new offices in growing Sun Belt cities. Where they find it impossible to establish branch offices, many firms are increasingly turning to joint-venture and subcontract arrangements with established firms in targeted areas.

In effect, branch offices and collaborating out-of-town firms are becoming the *channels of distribution* for many professional service organizations. They provide a channel or conduit through which a professional service firm can become more accessible to targeted clients. They are serving functions similar to that of wholesalers and retailers of tangible products.

Clearly no single channel of distribution is right for all professional service organizations. But no matter what channel arrangement an organization uses, the channel should provide:

1. Locations for delivering services that are convenient and attractive to large numbers of targeted clients.
2. Offices that will work cooperatively to provide a coordinated marketing program.

In this chapter, we will focus on how the desired channel features can be obtained by a professional service organization, how points of access can facilitate the attraction of clients and the service process, and finally, how physical evidence plays a role in the service experience.

SELECTING LOCATION

Decisions concerning the locations of offices can be divided into two basic tasks. First, an organization must decide whether each targeted geographic segment deserves being served by its own office. Second, an organization must decide upon the best physical site for locating each office. We will discuss each task separately, although they should be addressed in an interrelated fashion.

Does an Area Need an Office?

As a professional service firm grows from a small local practice to perhaps a regional, national, or even international firm, management must make decisions on how many branch offices to open and where they should be located. It needs to make a careful analysis of the market potential of that area. Consideration should be given to the difference in billings that could occur as a result of establishing an office in the area as compared to either providing service from out of town or collaborating with existing firms. Also, the firm's management must determine whether a new office will add billings to the firm that it would not obtain otherwise, or merely lead to the spreading around of the existing level of billings. The last thing an organization wants to do is cannibalize its present efforts. The idea of opening additional offices is to attract new clients by successfully competing against firms, not merely dividing your client base between two or more locations.

In addition to estimating how revenues will be affected, the impact of such a move on costs must also be examined. Both the new costs and the cost savings of establishing a branch office must be considered.

Table 11-1 lists possible ways that setting up a branch office might affect the financial situation of a professional service organization. Forecasts of the market potential of the targeted area should be combined with assessments of the financial consequences and probability of occurrence of the effects listed in the table. Eventually, an overall judgment can be made of the benefits and costs of opening a branch. For some professionals, the best solution may involve the establishment of a temporary branch office designed to serve a particular client for the duration of a project or contract. The use of temporary offices is reasonably common in architectural and engineering professions. Many times the professional service firm may locate its employees within the corporate offices of its clients. The employees may have an office and support staff "in-house" in order to provide the best possible service and to enhance communications between the service provider and the client.

Selecting an Office Site

When an organization decides it needs to establish an office in a new geographic area—or it needs a second office in its present area—numerous factors must be considered. Foremost among these factors are the *attitudes and behavior* patterns of targeted clients. If the targeted clients feel comfortable with shopping-mall offices rather than offices in high-rise buildings, then various shopping malls should be evaluated as possible sites.

If targeted clients prefer to go to high-rent districts to obtain services, then sites in these districts should be considered. In addition, the mode of transportation typically used by targeted clients should be examined. If people typically come by automobile, then a site with good access roads and easy, inexpensive parking is essential. Consideration should also be given to whether available sites can have interior decorating that clients find appealing.

Table 11-1. Possible Effects of Opening a Branch Office.

Could increase revenues by:

1. Allowing prospective clients to phone or visit with less expense and difficulty.

2. Allowing the firm to respond faster to inquiries and requests from prospective and existing clients with phone calls,

3. Increasing the visibility of a firm, making it more likely to be considered by prospects.

4. Suggesting to clients that a firm is more "personal" and has a strong commitment to serving its local geographic area.

5. Motivating staff members to work harder at marketing the services of "their" office.

Could reduce costs by:

1. Cutting the time and expenses needed for travel and phone calls to have discussions with clients.

2. Allowing more efficient office management systems (e.g., word processing) to be used without having to replace old systems.

Could reduce revenues by:

1. Creating an uncoordinated marketing effort.

2. Making it more difficult to maintain quality control.

3. Taking talented personnel away from the "home" office where they might be able to attract more work through already established contacts and networks.

4. Inviting competing firms to

Could increase costs by:

1. Creating an uncoordinated marketing effort containing wasted time and expenses.

2. Requiring much travel time and expenses for having high-level people work at attaining coordination and control.

3. Requiring the firm to move existing staff or hire new staff.

4. Adding real estate, leasing, utility, security, and other expenses for running the office.

5. Stimulating competitive reactions increase their efforts in the area. that make it necessary to use more expensive forms of promotion.

Here are some considerations:

1. *Competitors' locations.* In some professions, having sites closer to targeted clients than the competitors' sites can make a difference.

2. *Proximity to frequently used facilities.* Locating near hospitals, courthouses, universities, and libraries can be very helpful, as long as the site is still attractive to clients.

3. *Proximity to "facilitating intermediaries."* Locating near bankers, consultants, lawyers, accountants, laboratories, insurance companies, or others who supply supplemental services to clients (for example, financing, consulting, tests) can be convenient and it can also increase the frequency of referrals provided by these intermediaries, who may say: "Why don't you go see the _____ next door?"

4. *Proximity to restaurants and clubs.* Having convenient places to entertain clients can be helpful, particularly because it may help to overcome the resistance of staff members to spend time entertaining and "selling" prospective or previous clients.

5. *The costs of mortgages, leases, utilities, security, parking, and maintenance.* Cost is a major factor in choosing a location. Firms typically face a choice between a high-cost location in the central business district near clients and referral sources and a low-cost location that will involve more travel time. Many hospitals have developed medical office buildings immediately adjoining their central hospital location. The medical office building provides very inexpensive office space to physicians who are affiliated with that hospital. By making it financially attractive to physicians to set up their office location on campus, the hospital also increases the likelihood that physicians will refer patients to that particular hospital. This not only provides the physician lower facility costs, but also increases his or her convenience when making patient rounds or performing some type of medical procedure in the hospital.

6. *Anticipated trends in population, real estate prices, shopping patterns, and other features of an area.* An office needs to be well situated in future years as well as in the present. Phoenix-based Baptist Hospitals and Health Systems, Inc., includes three hospi-

tals, long-term care apartments, and a home health agency. However, to stand out in a crowded Arizona market, it also runs the Wellness Connection at two local shopping malls. The organization offers nutrition counseling and blood pressure checks, as well as screening for cholesterol, respiratory, heart, and prostate problems, and makes referrals to network doctors. Coupons are also given out to mall shoppers for the tests. Baptist Hospitals and Health Systems, Inc., believes in being where its customers are.[1]

7. *The flexibility of the arrangement for the site.* Can the office space be rearranged or expanded if necessary? Can the site be abandoned without overwhelming costs if it is later deemed inappropriate? When building in a new location, it is often wise to build with future expansion in mind. This may mean being able to add pipes, air conditioning and heating ducts, and potential wiring systems to a blank wall.

8. *Non-overlapping trading areas.* A trading area is defined as the natural boundary from which one's business comes. The natural boundaries can be determined by road systems, neighborhoods, or even physical impediments like rivers, oceans, or mountain ranges. By literally mapping out the home or work addresses of its clients, the firm can identify the primary, secondary, and tertiary markets of its client base. The primary market base typically consists of 80 percent of a firm's customers; the secondary expands this to 90 percent; the tertiary expands this base further to include the remaining percentage. Because a firm must avoid cannibalizing its own business, it is necessary to make sure that its primary and secondary trading areas don't overlap. (See Figure 11-1.)

There is no magic formula for combining all these factors into a decision about a site. However, some organizations formulate point systems in which each site is given a total score determined by calculating a weighted sum of scores given to each factor. Weights are assigned to each factor based on how important the factor is to an organization. Exhibit 11-1 represents an example of how a point system might be applied by a particular law firm choosing between two sites. In this case, the greater expense of site one is compensated for by its greater client favorability

Figure 11-1. Trading Area Analysis.

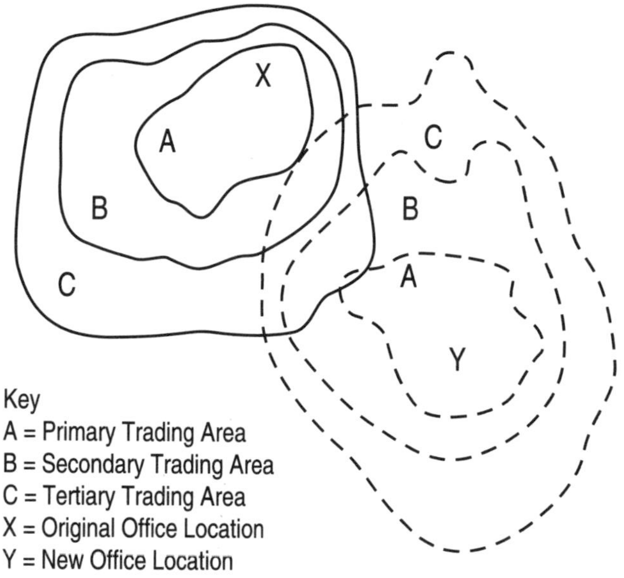

Key
A = Primary Trading Area
B = Secondary Trading Area
C = Tertiary Trading Area
X = Original Office Location
Y = New Office Location

Exhibit 11-1. Example of a Site-Selection Point System.

Selection Factor	Importance Weight for Factor (5 = very imp., 1 = not imp.)	Scoring for Site 1*	Scoring for Site 2*
Client favorability	5	5	3
Absence of competitors	1	1	2
Proximity to facilities	2	5	4
Proximity to intermediaries	3	4	3
Proximity to entertainment	2	4	3
Low costs	4	2	4
Favorability of future trends	4	3	3
Flexibility	3	3	4
Total weighted score		85	80

*5 = Has very much of factor.
 1 = Has very little of factor.

and closer proximity to everything. Such a point system can help firms choose better sites as can the use of certain mathematical models that have been employed extensively by retail chains. Ultimately, however, no matter which approach a firm uses, research on each prospective site must form the basis for decision-making.

COORDINATING AND CONTROLLING CHANNEL MEMBERS

The professional service firm can choose between three basic organization structures to achieve coordination and control with a set of branch offices (and/or collaborating firms): a *macropyramid* structure, an *umbrella* structure, and a *conglomerate* structure.[2] The macropyramid structure includes *all* planning and strategic decision-making being done at a central office, with branch offices being left to implement strategies and carry out operations under a strict set of guidelines or procedures. The umbrella structure gives more autonomy to each branch and allows them to develop their own plans and strategies, as long as they remain consistent with the overall mission and strategic direction of the firm. The conglomerate structure gives even more autonomy to the branches, even allowing them to develop their own missions and strategic directions. What ties the branches together under this structure is only a dependence on a common financial resource base, such as a group of founding partners or investors. Figure 11-2 depicts the basic differences among these three structures.

The macropyramid structure obviously provides the most coordination and control, but the other two structures, by allowing offices to adapt to local conditions, can occasionally be more profitable. Even if an umbrella or conglomerate structure is adopted, an emphasis on coordinating and controlling branch-office activities still should be present. Among other things, coordination and control are needed to make a marketing program function smoothly, with no offices working at cross-purposes to one another. Moreover, coordination and control are needed to keep work quality high so as not to damage the firm's national (or regional) reputation.

Figure 11-2. Three Alternative Organizational Factors for Attaining Coordination and Control of Channel Members.

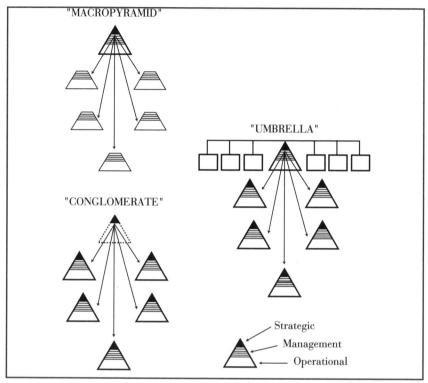

Regardless of which organizational structure is employed, three basic approaches are available for improving coordination and control with branch offices or collaborating firms. First, the home office can offer *information and expertise* that channel members need, making them more willing to cooperate with home-office programs and procedures. Second, the home office can offer *financial incentives* that encourage cooperation and support. Finally, the home office can create *legal agreements* that essentially force channel members to comply.

The "information and expertise" approach can be highly effective and is unlikely to cause some of the conflicts that the other approaches can produce. This approach can be used when channel members have a need for data, guidance, specialized personnel, or other resources in order to serve their constituencies most effectively. The home office can offer needed information and expertise in exchange for cooperation. For example, when Big Five CPA firms provide branch offices with elaborate manuals, training sessions, and easy-to-complete planning forms to guide their marketing effort, they do so with the hope that the branch offices will find it so easy to use the supplied materials that all recommended policies and procedures will be automatically followed. In a similar vein, home offices make certain that highly skilled professionals or support personnel (for example, proposal writers, marketing researchers) are readily available to branch offices in the hope that these "loaned" experts will help shape some consistency in the overall marketing program.

The offering of financial incentives, in addition to the offering of information and expertise, is a somewhat riskier but potentially more effective way of gaining coordination and control with channel members. Commissions, bonuses, and other incentives can be offered to top management and individual professionals of branch organizations if they contribute to the achievement of marketing goals established by the home office. These people might receive financial rewards if they identify a certain number of "live" leads in targeted segments during a year or if they win a given percentage of the competitive bidding situations they enter during the year. Such incentives can serve as a potent motivator of desired behaviors. However, the risk of using incentives is that it may lead branch personnel to focus too much on obtaining the rewards instead of managing with a broader perspective designed to help the entire organization carry out its basic mission. Conflicts and jealousies can also erupt over the way rewards are allocated.

The approach of setting up legal agreements—essentially to force coordination and control—may be necessary when the channels of distribution are made up of other organizations or legal entities. Having a carefully drawn joint-venture or subcontracting agreement can help to insure that certain marketing functions are performed by all parties. The danger with legal agreements is that conflicts can arise during the process of drawing them up, and even more serious and bitter conflicts (and lawsuits) can develop if an agreement is broken.

One form of legal agreement that can be used to achieve coordination and control with channel members is the *franchise* agreement.

Franchising

Historically, franchising has been an extremely popular way to distribute all types of commercial products and services. Cars, gasoline, fast food, hotel accommodations, and countless other products and services have been distributed effectively in this way.

A *franchise system* can be defined as follows:

> The licensing of an *entire* business format where one firm (the franchisor) licenses one or more outlets (franchisees) to market a product or service and engage in a business developed by the franchisor using the franchisor's trade names, trademarks, service marks, know-how, and methods of doing business.

Thus, a professional service organization serving as a franchisor might provide the organizations that are its franchisees a name (for example, Jacoby and Myers Legal Clinic), know-how about how to run an automated office, national advertising support, advice on fee-setting, and so forth. In exchange, the franchisees (which would be under separate ownership) might provide the franchisor with an opening franchise fee, additional fees based on a percentage of billings per year, the performance of certain marketing functions, the maintenance of a certain required appearance and quality standards, and so forth.

Franchising can provide numerous benefits to both parties. The franchisor can obtain a less costly way of expanding to reach new markets, because the franchisees bear much of the expenses of expansion. In addition, the franchise agreement provides the franchisor with a means of coordinating and controlling the activities of its distribution channels (the franchisees).

For the franchisee, the benefits include the following:

a. Easier entry to markets

b. Financial aid for getting started

c. Less risk

d. Expertise in marketing, management, finances, purchasing, and site selection

e. Name recognition

Nevertheless, franchising has several drawbacks for both franchisors and franchisees. Franchisors can find themselves in situations where they have less control and are earning less money than they would if they owned and staffed all facilities and offices themselves. On the other hand, franchisees may find themselves mistreated by franchisors and have no recourse but to mount expensive lawsuits to obtain fair treatment. Most important, both franchisors and franchisees can find themselves somewhat limited in terms of the market segments they can attract. Just like many people prefer to avoid fast-food outlets, many clients prefer to obtain professional services from sole-standing organizations.

POINTS OF ACCESS

The old adage of site success, "location, location, location," doesn't tell the whole story anymore. Due to increasingly stronger competition, the commonly repeated mantra for professional service firms' success is to provide one's service to the client "immediately, perfectly, and free." Because of increased competition and the instant availability of many service, via the Internet, consumer expectations are on the rise and it is up to professional firms to make their services as accessible as possible. This may mean providing access on a 24-hours-a day, 7-days-a-week (24/7) basis. It is not uncommon for physicians and other healthcare providers to be on call 24 hours a day on a rotating basis, nor is it unheard of in the legal profession. Professional service firms must consider expanding their points and ease of access through the Internet, increased telephone services, more hours of operation, and non-traditional points of access (such as vending machines).

Internet. The development of a "virtual office" via the Internet is an excellent example of a point of access that is both accessible and convenient for clients. The law firm of McCutchen, Doyle, Brown, and Enersen has private locations for their clients to visit on the Internet. The sites, known as "extranets," provide secure access and 24-hour, instant interactivity. With extranets, documents can be simultaneously shared, altered, stored, and printed by all parties. Best of all, clients can access this information at any point in time, day or night, depending on their schedule and personal desires. Along with increasing client satisfaction, this process benefits the firm by dramatically reducing its costs for FedEx, telephone time, copying, and faxing and by allowing multiple parties to work on the same version of a document at the same time, minimizing confusion and duplication. (Chapter 13 provides more extensive coverage on the Internet.)[3]

Telephone. Telephones and recent telephone technologies make access to professional service organizations increasingly easier and more efficient. This is done through relatively simple and inexpensive techniques such as toll-free inbound telephone access to a firm, which reduces financial costs for clients, to more sophisticated telephony technology that identifies the telephone number and identity of the person calling, routes the phone call to the appropriate person or dedicated team within the service organization, and brings up on a screen the client profile before the telephone call is even answered. These systems allow for the delivery of a more personal, reliable, and efficient service. Telephone systems can also be used to address frequently asked questions. While this technique is slowly being replaced by Internet-based options, services such as "Ask-a-Nurse" are still common among healthcare institutions. These systems allow clients to make confidential calls to designated numbers on a 24-hour basis, and obtain answers to medical questions. Such service can potentially encourage further medical treatment or, when provided by insurance companies, can reduce costs by eliminating the need for a visit to a healthcare provider.

Increased hours of operation. Professional service providers must be available when their clients need or want them. This may mean extended hours either in the mornings or evenings, or extended weekend hours. It is imperative for the service firm to research its market and develop hours of operation that meet its clients' standards and not the firm's.

Non-traditional points of access. Points of access are only limited to the service provider's imagination and existing technology. One example of a non-traditional point of access might be the use of vending machines. Today, depending on the location and the culture, one can buy anything from insurance to boxer shorts to beer from a vending machine. In the United States there are approximately 4.5 million vending machines offering 24-hour convenience. Even medicine can be dispensed through a vending machine.

ADDS, Inc., in North Billerica, Massachusetts, has developed a medicine vending machine. ADDS's "telepharmacy" incorporates a computer, bar-code reader, printer, and dispensing cabinet. A doctor, say at a rural clinic, faxes a prescription to an off-site pharmacy, where the pharmacist then transmits the drug order via modem to the clinic's remote-controlled dispenser. The machine dispenses a pre-packaged vial and, to ensure that the right medicine comes out, a clinic worker scans the vial's bar code for prescription information and expiration date. The dispensers typically stock 30 to 60 types of commonly prescribed drugs. Because of their lower costs, a clinic need only order 25 prescriptions a day for the vending machines to be economical, compared with some 150 prescriptions for an in-house pharmacy. The devices are already in use in Utah, Wisconsin, and Michigan.[4]

THE ROLE OF PHYSICAL EVIDENCE

So far we have covered the importance of making the service operation physically and conveniently accessible. One cannot, however, underestimate the impact that the appearance of the firm's physical or Web site location may have on clients' ability to perceive the service firm as being accessible. Can clients, based upon the impressions they receive from the service firm's location, "see" the service firm as being capable of providing the desired service at the desired level of quality?

In her seminal work, Mary Jo Bittner identified the role physical evidence plays in both strategy and influencing the behavior of customers and/or employees.[5]

Physical Evidence as Strategy

Because services are intangible, consumers find it difficult to objectively evaluate service quality. This often forces clients to rely on tangible evidence surrounding the service. Physical evidence can fall into three broad categories: (1) facility exterior, (2) facility interior, and (3) other tangibles. The facility exterior includes exterior design, signage, parking, land-scaping, and the surrounding environment. For example, a professional service firm may have extravagant offices designed by a "brand-name" architect, or be located in a low-rent strip mall on the outskirts of town. The facility interior includes elements such as interior design, equipment, signage, air quality, and temperatures. Other tangibles that make up the firm's physical evidence include such items as business cards, stationery, reports, employee appearance, and uniforms.

The use of physical evidence may vary according to the type of professional service firm. Pediatric physicians or orthopedic surgeons who focus on athletes may use physical evidence rather extensively, whereas a lawyer dealing in corporate circles can only make limited use of it. Regardless of the variation of usage, all service firms need to understand the importance of managing their physical evidence in its role in (1) packaging service, (2) facilitating flow in the service delivery process, (3) socializing customers and employees with regard to their respective roles, behaviors, and relationships, and (4) differentiating the firm from its competitors.[6]

Packaging. Although services are, in themselves, intangible, and do not require a package in the traditional sense, the firm's exterior, interior elements, and other tangibles create the package that surrounds the service. The firm's physical facility serves as a client's initial impression concerning the type and quality of the service provided. Clients will have one impression if upon visiting a professional service firm's office they are surrounded by Persian rugs, expensive wood furniture, and etched glass, and an entirely different impression if they enter an office furnished with plastic chairs, chrome and glass tables, and the last three years' subscriptions to popular celebrity magazines.

Facilitating the service process. The firm's physical evidence can also facilitate the flow of activities that produce the service. This could include signage and specific room layouts that aid in the delivery of the service. For example, many psychiatrists and psychologists not only have a waiting room but they also have a separate room where clients can take time to psychologically or emotionally regroup before departing as well as bypass patients in the waiting room so neither clients' privacy will be compromised.

Socializing employees and customers. Socialization is defined as *the process by which an individual adapts to and comes to appreciate the values and norms and required behavior patterns of an organization.* The firm's physical evidence plays an important role in facilitating the socialization process. Requiring staff to dress in professional business attire will create a different impression than would an office where everyone is dressed in "casual Friday" outfits. Each dress code sends a distinct message to clients about the way the organization does business.

A means of differentiation. Physical evidence can also serve to differentiate the firm from its competitors. Differentiation can be achieved in the uniforms staff members wear or in the facilities themselves, both interior and exterior. Some service firms apply the concept of "show management"—whereby architectural design and theatrical elements are coordinated to create a particular unique experience for clients—as a means of differentiation. An example of this type of physical evidence would include a restaurant with a rain-forest theme, such as *Hotel Discovery* or the *Rain Forest.*

Show management is managing the coordination between architectural design and theatrical elements to make a client's experience come to life. It is used to create a themed environment through technology and show elements such as lighting, audio and video production, props, and special effects. Imagine visiting a dental office and as you enter the room you are immediately greeted by a receptionist who is dressed in the uniform of a Star Fleet Federation officer—straight out of the "Star Trek" television series or is it "Star Trek: The Next Generation"? As you look around the room, you notice the entire office gives off the appearance of a Star Fleet spaceship complete with simulated teleporter beam to beam clients mentally out of what could be an anxious situation. Everywhere you look are cardboard cut-out figures of Star Trek characters from all the various Star Trek television shows and movies. Star Trek paraphernalia adorns the walls, including toys and figurines. If you're in such an office, you are probably in the office of Dr. Dennis Bourgvignon, DMD, who practices family dentistry in Orlando, Florida. Dr. Bourgvignon and his wife, who is also his assistant, came upon the idea of such a themed dentist office while visiting a science fiction show several years ago. Both he and his wife also dress in complete Star Trek regalia as part of the service delivery system.[7]

Physical Evidence and the Behavior of Clients and Employees

According to Bittner, there are three basic dimensions of physical evidence that can be manipulated: First, the ambient conditions such as temperature, lighting, and noise level (the more time people spend in a facility, the more important these elements become); second, the spatial layout and functionality of the environment, which affects the ease and efficiency with which employees and customers can accomplish their tasks; and third, signs, which instruct and guide service participants, sometimes using symbols and artifacts to communicate.

These dimensions, in turn, affect customers and employees in three ways. First, there is a cognitive response as people interpret the cues. Clients may develop an impression about the quality of the firm and the service being offered or develop an impression about the importance of the individual with whom they are dealing. (For example, a top floor corner office with a view is likely to create the impression that the occupant of that office is very powerful and important.) Second, there is an emotional response to the surroundings that can greatly influence a person's satisfaction level. For example, a dental office decorated in a Star Trek theme may create a favorable reaction in some patients, while others may see such an environment as lacking in professionalism. Finally, there is a physiological response such as discomfort created by hard seating or an uncomfortable temperature or, as in some cases of medical procedures, outright pain inadvertently created in the delivery of the service, such as pain suffered by a patient because of a physician who is less than gentle in setting a broken leg. Negative responses to physical evidence can affect both the client enjoyment and the ability of the service provider to do quality work.

Recognizing the importance of physical evidence, Northwestern Memorial Hospital in Chicago redesigned its physical space, calling the new design "Patients First." The design focused on the visitor's initial impression of the facility, and incorporated features such as a hotel-style lobby, a three-story atrium, and large windows throughout the hospital. Project executive John Westcott states, "The idea is to include in the design a welcoming, caring environment for the patient, the visitor, and the neighborhood." This change is in line with what Mo Stein, former president of the American Institute of Architect's Academy of Architecture for Health, says is a shift in changing the perception of hospitals as "warehouses for the sick" to "places of healing and support for wellness."[8]

Variables to Consider

Variables that affect the client cognitively, emotionally, and physiologically include the size and space within a facility, arrangement of objects within the environment, materials used, the shapes and lines, lighting and shadows, colors, temperature, noise, and other amenities. We will take a look at each.

Size and space. The size of a professional firm's waiting room, facility, and office and the amount of space given to clients can have an impact on their perceptions of the firm as well as their basic feelings of comfort. This is especially true in physicians' offices where patients may need to get around on wheelchairs or on crutches. Jeff Denning, a practice management consultant from Long Beach, California, has provided a relatively simple formula for computing the amount of space a professional service firm may need: Take the number of patients or clients seen during the firm's busiest hour, subtract the number of examining/other rooms, then multiply that by three to arrive at the number of chairs necessary. Multiply the number of chairs by 20 square feet to determine the total space requirements.[9]

Arrangements of objects within the environment. Chairs, end tables, and lamps can be arranged in any number of ways. Lining chairs along the walls of a waiting room or foyer may give the impression of a sterile and unfriendly environment. A more desirable arrangement would be to set chairs in clusters to give a more home-like atmosphere.

Materials used. The texture and shape of materials used in an office also communicate a message to clients. Carpeting provides a much softer texture and perhaps a more professional look than tile; however, it must be maintained and cleaned because it may not hold up as well and may create an impression of sloppiness. Extravagant flooring such as marble might be used to create a highly successful image, but it may have the effect of scaring away potential clients who will see it as an indicator of extravagant fees.

Shapes and lines. The type of furniture and its corresponding shapes and lines can create an impression of the firm.

Lighting. In general, when lights are bright, communication between or among clients and/or between clients and professionals tends to be louder and more informal. Conversely, a dimly lit room tends to have a calming effect. Clients are more likely to talk softly when lights are low and the service environment is perceived as more formal.

Color. The color of a firm's physical evidence—such as a brochure, a business card, or the exterior or interior of the facility—often makes the firm's first impression on clients. Different colors tend to evoke different meanings. Lighter colors may make a room look larger, while darker colors may make a large empty space look smaller. Adults tend to favor softer tones, while children appear to favor brighter colors. It's important to understand clients and their objectives when choosing colors. In some cases, the wrong colors can be outright dangerous. For example, intense colors in a neurologist's waiting room could trigger seizures in certain patients.

Temperature. The temperature in a facility can affect the comfort and alertness of both clients and employees. Too warm an environment will make individuals more sluggish and less responsive, while too cold an environment makes it more difficult to concentrate. Further, the needs of clients who will be served by the firm must also take into account when determining the ideal temperature. For example, a physician dealing with geriatric patients may need to keep the office a bit warmer than would be needed for a younger clientele.

Noise. Noise can affect the clients of a professional service organization either positively or negatively. Using soft music as background noise might enhance clients' overall comfort and service experience, while undesirable sounds such as loud conversations of employees or customers or noisy heating and air-conditioning systems are likely to leave a negative impression on clients.

Amenities. Amenities can have a significant impact on clients' perception of the service firm. For example, offering clients fresh coffee and cookies may create a warm, inviting environment. Some physicians' offices have included telephones in each waiting room to allow patients to make free local phone calls to inform friends or family of their schedule. At Celebration Health, a new hospital in Florida that is part of the Walt Disney system, patients are given pagers so that they can be elsewhere until they get beeped for their appointments. Similarly, the magazines kept in the waiting room should be chosen with the interests of the target clientele in mind and should be kept up to date. Finally, one must be careful of the types of magazines in the waiting room.

SUMMARY

Professional service organizations are paying more attention to how accessible their services are to clients. When attempting to provide clients with services in a timely and convenient fashion, it's important to consider the service distribution channels.

One important decision that must be made about distribution is where to establish branch offices. Should a targeted geographic area have an office? If so, what site should be selected? Among the many factors that must be considered is how clients will react to having an office in various locations.

Coordination and control of the activities of channel members is essential for a smoothly functioning marketing program, regardless of whether a macropyramid, umbrella, or conglomerate organizational structure is developed. Coordination and control can be achieved by providing needed information and expertise, by offering financial incentives, and setting up legal agreements. The franchise agreement is a type of legal agreement that can be used within professional service firms.

Professional service firms must also realize that their physical location is not the final consideration when determining client access. Clients are increasingly demanding services based on their needs and time schedules. Professional service firms may provide greater access to their organization through the use of the Internet, telephone systems, expanding the hours of their operation, and the use of non-traditional points of access.

Finally, professional service firms must understand the impact that physical evidence may have on clients' abilities to access an organization cognitively and emotionally. Components of one's exterior and interior facilities along with other tangibles, will create impressions in clients' minds about the quality of the offered service. At the same time, the ambiance of physical evidence, the spatial layout, and the signs and symbols within a facility may produce cognitive, emotional, and physiological responses in clients. In particular, the manipulation of variables such as the size and space within a facility, arrangement of objects within the environment, materials used, shapes, lighting, color, temperature, and noise, as well as other amenities, all have an impact on clients and employees.

NOTES

[1] "See the Doctor, Get a Toaster," *Business Week* (December 8, 1997), no. 356, p86.

[2] These figures have been adapted from those suggested in Simon Majaro's *International Marketing*. London: Allen and Unwin, 1977. Reprinted with permission.

[3] Kohn, Lawrence M. and Ellis, Lia. "Market the Megabytes: Turn Technology into Competitive Advantage," *Legal Management* (March /April 1999) v18, p2.

[4] "The Prosac Machine Ate My Money," *Business Week* (June 9, 1997), no 3530, p83.

[5] Bittner, Mary Jo. "Servicescapes: The Impact of Physical Surroundings on Customers and Employees," *Journal of Marketing*, 56 (1997), p57-71.

[6] Hair, Lisa Paulsen. "Satisfaction by Design," *Marketing Health Services* (Fall 1998), p5.

[7] *Trekkies*, Documentary, Paramount Pictures, 1999.

[8] "Is Your Waiting Room a Practice-Builder—or Holding Pen," *Medical Economics* (July 13, 1998), v75, p132-145.

[9] Ibid.

12 | Integrated Marketing Communications

"The meek shall inherit the world, but they will
never increase market share."
WILLIAM G. McGOWAN
FOUNDER AND CHAIRMAN OF MCI

No news releases, no calls to reporters, no expensive and time-consuming media plans, no waiting for the victory in the big case, just high-profile, positive results quoting partners as experts in some of North America's major media—and all of this is accomplished as a result of tracking electronic news services and newspapers. Jaffe Associates used technology as an important part of shifting promotional activities from an order-taking mode where they tried to have stories run in key media, to a business-development-partner mode. (See page 320.)

Professional service firms need effective communications with their markets and publics. The three preceding chapters have explained marketing aspects of program development, pricing, and access decisions. But developing good programs and services, pricing them attractively, and making them readily available to target consumers is not enough. The firm must also inform consumers and others about its goals, activities, and offerings, and motivate them to take an interest in its professional services.

Communications take many forms. Many professionals typically think of communications in terms of brochures and newsletters describing their organization and its programs. But professional service firms

Working smarter and thinking strategically has been the hallmark of Jaffe Associates, a Washington, DC-based marketing communications firm specializing in law firm business development. As media consultants to law firms, Jaffe Associates' job is to help clients gain recognition as experts in the legal field. One tool that allows them to do this is the tracking of electronic news services and newspapers. Consider the following actual scenario:

Sunday, 1:40 P.M.: A quick scan of the Sunday *Wall Street Journal* on-line from a home computer indicates that Boeing and MacDonald-Douglas will announce a merger at a Sunday afternoon press conference. It will be the lead story for the paper edition of the Monday *Wall Street Journal*.

*1:55 P.M.: Knowing what the *Wall Street Journal* will run on Monday as its lead gives Jaffe Associates a head start on providing journalists with legal experts for their analyses stories (known as second-day stories), which will run over the next several days in newspapers, magazines, radio, and television around the country. Voice mail and e-mail messages are sent out to partners at Jaffe's client law firms who are experts in antitrust and merger and acquisition issues, specifically, including those who are third parties (attorneys with expertise but not involved in this merger), asking them if they will want to comment on these second-day stories.

*2:08 P.M.: Expecting that some of these partners will call Jaffe Associates first thing Monday morning requesting to be interviewed, staff members write a brief six-sentence news advisory that experts are available to comment on the merger. It is put into the organization's legal news service, subscribed to by several thousand reporters via e-mail, and scheduled to run the next morning.

*Monday, 10:00 A.M.: By this time, attorneys who want to comment have spoken to representatives at Jaffe Associates. With the touch of a button, the legal news service is distributed by e-mail with two other unrelated brief news stories to thousands of media subscribers. .

*10:18 A.M.: *Business Week*, NPR's *All Things Considered*, Dow Jones' News Service, American City Business journals (which publishes business journals in most of the major cities nationwide), and the *Toronto Globe and Mail*, among others, call for interviews.[1]

need to understand that everything they say and do communicates. The real task is to make sure that all their activities communicate the same thing.

Professional service firms must start with a clear picture of the communication tasks facing them. The following are typical:

- Maintaining or enhancing the image of the firm
- Gaining client loyalty and support
- Attracting new clients
- Providing information about the organization's offerings
- Attracting prospective employees to join the firm
- Correcting inaccurate or incomplete information about the firm
- Meeting the information needs of their employees and the public

Individuals who communicate on behalf of the professional service firm must consider the institution's purpose for preparing its communication and the target audience of that message. Only then can the form, content, and delivery of messages be planned to match the audience and achieve the intended purpose. Yet today clients are being exposed to a greater variety of marketing communications from a broad array of sources. However, clients do not always distinguish between message sources. In the clients' minds, the messages from different media such as magazines, on-line sources, and personal selling blur into one. They all become part of the same message about the organization. Conflicting messages from these different sources can result in a confused corporate image and brand position.

Advertising legend David Olgivy, in his book *On Advertising*, wrote that the members of an organization must determine what they want to say, and then everything they do should say it.

All too often organizations fail to integrate their various communication channels. The result is a hodgepodge of communications to consumers. A firm's advertisements may say one thing, while its client literature says something altogether different, its pricing sends yet another message, and its Web site only adds to the confusion by being out of synch with everything else. To communicate effectively, the professional service organization must ensure that it carefully integrates and coordinates its many communication channels—its advertising, personal selling, sales promotions, public relations, and direct marketing—to deliver a clear, consistent, and compelling message about the organization and its products. This is known as *integrated marketing communications* (IMC).

This chapter will develop the steps necessary to successfully implement an integrative marketing communication strategy. It will cover the steps for the planning of effective communication, reviewing the principles that apply to every form of promotion and communication, and explain the various components of the communication mix. These include personal selling, advertising, public relations, sales promotion, and direct marketing. Finally, some of the obstacles and special problems of implementing an integrated communications system will be addressed, along with the obstacles unique to the promotion of professional services.

THE COMMUNICATIONS PROCESS

Many times, marketing communications focus on creating immediate awareness, image, or preference within a target market. This approach, unfortunately, has its limitations. It is typically too short term and too costly and most of these messages fall on deaf ears. Today, marketers are moving toward viewing communications as the management of the customer buying process over time. Communications can reach clients in different stages of the buying process, which include pre-selling, selling, consuming, and the post-consumption stages. Because clients differ, communication programs need to be developed for specific client segments, niches, and even individuals. And given today's interactive communication technologies, companies must not only ask "How can we reach our clients?" but also "How can our clients reach us?"

The communication process should start with an audit of all the potential exposures, encounters, and interactions target clients may have with the service firm. For example, someone in search of an architectural firm to design and build a new office space may talk to others who have worked with such a firm, read articles, or examine a potential firm's brochure. The marketer needs to assess the influence each exposure will have at different stages of the buying process. This understanding will help marketers allocate their communications dollars more efficiently and effectively.

To communicate effectively, professionals need to understand how communication works. Communication involves the nine elements shown in Figure 12-1. Two of these elements—the *sender* and the *receiver*—are the major parties in a communication. Another two—the *message* and the *media*—are the major communication tools. Four more are major communication functions: *encoding*, *decoding*, *response*, and *feedback*. The last element is *noise* in the system. These nine elements are described for an Accenture (AC) ad.

1. *Sender*: the party sending the message to another party. Here, AC.

2. *Encoding*: the process of putting thoughts into symbolic form. AC's ad agency assembles words and illustrations into advertisements that will convey the intended message.

3. *Message*: the set of symbols that the sender transmits. The actual AC ad.

4. *Media*: the communication channels through which the message moves from sender to receiver. In this case, the specific television stations and programs where the ads appear.

5. *Decoding*: the process by which the receiver assigns meaning to the symbols encoded by the sender—in other words, a client reads the AC ad and interprets the words and illustrations it contains.

Figure 12-1. Elements in the Communication Process.

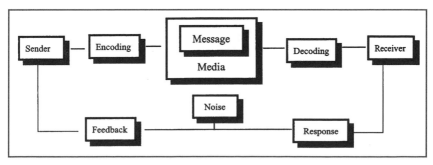

6. *Receiver*: the party receiving the message sent by another party—for example, the business traveler seeing the AC ad in an airport or on television.

7. *Response*: the reactions of the receiver after being exposed to the message. Any of hundreds of possible responses, such as a consumer being more aware of the attributes of AC, actually contacting AC, or doing nothing.

8. *Feedback*: the part of the receiver's response communicated back to the sender. AC research shows that clients are struck by and remember the ad, or clients write or call praising or criticizing the ad for AC's services.

9. *Noise*: the unplanned static or distortion during the communication process, which results in the receiver getting a different message from the one the sender sent. Noise may take the form of distraction on the part of the receiver as he or she rushes through an airport, or the receiver engages in other conversation while the ad is on television.

For a message to be effective, the sender's encoding process must mesh with the receiver's decoding process. Thus, the best message consists of words and other symbols that are familiar to the receiver. The more the sender's field of experience overlaps with that of the receiver, the more effective the message is likely to be; however, marketing communicators may not always share their consumer's field of experience. For example, an advertising copywriter developing an ad for a legal firm may not understand the mindset of another stratum, say blue-collar workers or wealthy business owners. But to communicate effectively, the marketing communicator must understand the consumer's field of experience.

This model points out several key factors in good communications. Senders need to know what audiences they wish to reach and what responses they want. They must be good at encoding messages that take into account how the target audience decodes them. They must send messages through media that reach members of the target audience and they must develop feedback channels so they can assess the audience's response to their message.

STEPS IN DEVELOPING EFFECTIVE COMMUNICATION

We will now examine the steps in developing an effective integrated communications program. The communications planning flow should begin with considering the target audience and working backwards to the communicator. The marketing communicator must do the following: identify the target audience, determine the communication objectives, design a message, choose the media through which to send the message, select the message source, and collect feedback.

Identifying the Target Audience

The marketing communicator starts with a clear target audience in mind. He or she will then speak directly to the concerns of that person or group. The audience may be potential buyers or current users, those who make the buying decision or those who influence it. The target audience will heavily affect the communicator's decisions regarding *what* will be said, *how* it will be said, *when* it will be said, *where* it will be said, and *who* will say it.

Determining the Communication Objectives

A good communication plan is designed to obtain a response from the receiver. The response may be a change in awareness of the firm and its offerings or a change in attitude. Or the firm may be seeking a behavioral response, such as a request for additional information, and ultimately, a purchase. But purchase is the result of a long process of consumer decision-making. The professional marketing communicator needs to know where the target audience now stands and to what stage it needs to be moved. The target audience may be in any of six buyer-readiness stages, the stages consumers normally pass through on their way to making a purchase. These stages include awareness, knowledge, liking, preference, conviction, and purchase. (See Figure 12-2.)

Figure 12-2. Buyer-Readiness Stages.

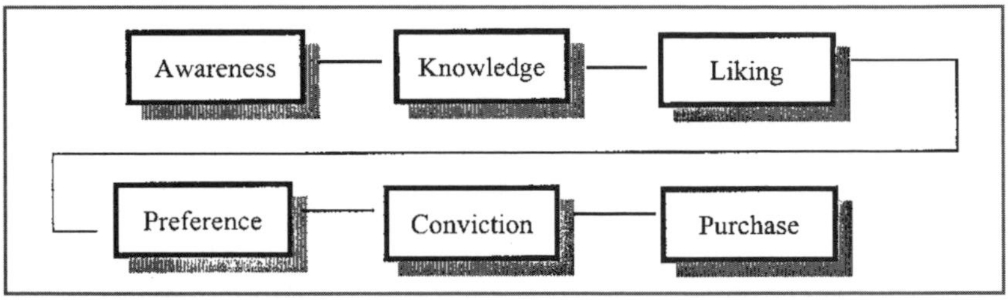

If a target market is totally unaware of the product, knows only its name, or knows only one or a few things about it, the communicator must first build awareness and knowledge. Assuming one's audience knows the product, the question is: *How do they feel about it?* Here communication objectives typically work and focus on liking and preference. Finally, some members of the target audience might be convinced about the service but not quite get around to making the purchase. The professional service firm must lead the clients to taking the final steps. This may involve actions as simple as asking for the business (closing the sale). The implication is that the consumer cannot be expected to reach the purchase stage unless he or she has gone through the preceding five stages. The marketer may need different messages for different stages. (In plastic surgery, this process can take up to eighteen months!)

Of course, marketing communications alone cannot create positive feelings and purchases of professional service. The service itself must provide superior value for the clients. As the old saying goes, "You can sell anything once." After the first sale, clients will quickly understand any gaps between rhetoric and reality.

Designing a Message

Having defined the desired audience response, one must then develop an effective message. Ideally, the message should get *attention*, hold *interest*, arouse *desire*, and obtain *action* (known as the AIDA model). In practice, few messages take the consumer all the way from awareness to purchase, but the AIDA framework suggests the desirable qualities of a good message. For example, a prospective patient for a plastic surgery procedure may notice an advertisement in the newspaper. The model in the ad along with the headline and copy maintains the individual's interest in what the ad has to say. Based upon a desire to learn more, the prospective patient calls the physician's office for an appointment and consultation.

A message has both *content* and *format.* Preparing the content requires understanding the target audience and what will motivate them to respond. In turn, the format must attract attention, arouse interest, and present the message clearly.

Choosing the Media

The communicator must now select efficient media or channels of communication. There are two broad types of communication channels: personal and non-personal.

Personal communications. In personal communication channels, two or more people communicate directly with each other. They may communicate face-to-face, over the telephone, or through e-mail. These channels are effective because they allow for personal addressing and feedback.

Some personal communication channels are controlled directly by the firm. For example, a senior partner may speak directly with a potential client. On the other hand, some forms of personal communications may reach target audiences through channels not controlled by the company. These might include independent experts in the field, business associates, neighbors, friends, or even family members of the target buyer. This channel, known as *word-of-mouth influence,* has considerable impact in many service areas.

Personal influence carries a great weight for professional service. This is true because they are typically more expensive, high in psychological and social risks, as well as highly visible. Furthermore, potential clients of professional service marketers are also more likely to initially trust a friend or a colleague more than a firm's ads.

Firms can stimulate personal influence channels to work on their behalf. They can (1) identify individuals and groups who are influential and devote extra time to them; (2) find and focus on opinion leaders by supplying them with information and asking them to help the firm; (3) work with community influentials, such as club presidents, elected officials, and others; (4) feature influential people in press releases and advertisements; and (5) develop communications that are high in "conversational value."

Table 12-1. Strengths and Weakneses of Alternative Media.[2]

Strengths	Weaknesses
TELEVISION	
High impact	High production costs
Audience selectivity	Uneven delivery by market
Schedule when needed	Upfront commitments required
Fast awareness	
Sponsorship availabilities	
Merchandising possible	
RADIO	
Low cost per contact	Nonintrusive medium
Audience selectivity	Audience per spot small
Schedule when needed	No visual impact
Length can vary	High total cost for good reach
Personalities available	Clutter within spot markets
Tailor weight to market	
MAGAZINES	
Audience selectivity	Long lead time needed
Editorial association	Readership accumulates slowly
Long life	Uneven delivery by market
Large audience per insert	Cost premiums for regional or
Excellent color	demographic editions
Minimal waste	
Merchandising possible	
NEWSPAPERS	
Large audience	Difficult to target narrowly
Immediate reach	Highest waste
Short lead time	High cost for national use
Market flexibility	Minimum positioning control
Good upscale coverage	Cluttered
POSTERS, BILLBOARDS	
High reach	No depth of message
High frequency of exposure	High cost for national use
Minimal waste	Best positions already taken
Can localize	No audience selectivity
Immediate registration	Poor coverage in some areas
Flexible scheduling	Minimum one-month purchase

Non-personal communication. Non-personal communication channels are media that carry messages without personal contact or feedback. These include: newspapers, magazines, radio, television, billboards, events (such as press conferences or exhibits), the Internet, and most direct mail. (See page 328.)

Communication through non-personal channels can encourage and reinforce personal communications. After seeing a news story on the design of a new building, a prospective client may call the architectural firm that designed it. After speaking with a management consultant about his or her service, a prospective client may then read brochures from the organization with increased interest. Therefore, professional service firms should strive to communicate and combine personal and non-personal channels of communications according to their relative strengths.

Selecting the Message Source

A message's impact on the target audience is also affected by how the audience views the communicator. Messages delivered by highly credible sources are more persuasive. Three factors affect source credibility: expertise, trustworthiness, and likeablility.[3] *Expertise* is the degree to which the communicator is perceived to possess the necessary authority for what he or she is claiming. Board certification for physicians and credentialing for other service professionals helps establish their expertise. *Trustworthiness* is related to how objective and honest the source is perceived to be. Audiences tend to put more trust in friends and others like themselves than in ads or strangers. Trustworthiness is also established by delivering the service in a reliable manner. *Likeability* is related to how attractive the source is to the audience. Qualities such as humor, candor, and naturalness make a source more likeable. The most highly credible source, then, would be a person who scores high in all three areas.

Collecting Feedback

The communicator should test the communication before using it and after sending it to determine its effect on the target audience. This may involve asking target audience members whether they remember the message, how many times they saw it, what points they recall, how they felt about the message, and their past and present attitudes towards the service and the firm. The communicator should also measure behavior resulting from the message—for example, how many people sought out the service or talked to others about it.

Feedback on marketing communications may suggest changes in the communications program or in the service itself. An organization should be satisfied if many people remember the ad and its points and ultimately contact the firm.

GENERAL GUIDELINES FOR DEVELOPING SERVICE COMMUNICATIONS

Based on the inherent characteristics of service (intangibility, inseparability, perishability, etc., as discussed in Chapter 1), as well as the unique indicators of quality for services (reliability, assurance, tangibles, etc.), certain guidelines exist for developing service communications.

Promise what is possible. Service firms will be judged by their reliability. If a professional service firm overpromises on its capabilities, two problems may occur. First, the client will lose trust in the service provider. Second, the firm's employees who have to deal with angry clients will be disheartened, and given the link between employee satisfaction and customer satisfaction, creating expectations that cannot be met can have devastating long-term effects.

Making the intangible tangible. Clients may have a difficult time conceptualizing a service due to its intangibility. They will, therefore, look for other types of clues that may indicate service quality. Orthopedic surgeons will typically use models of various body parts to educate a patient about an upcoming surgery. Architects can use computers to illustrate what a proposed building will look like.

Reduce client fears about variability. The variability of services may lead to a certain level of customer anxiety before and even after the service. The service communicator must provide information that alleviates this anxiety. This may be done by providing the firm's performance record or by communicating the number of times the service professional has successfully handled situations just like the one the client is facing.

Understand that the customer is in the factory. Given that a client's perception of service quality is related to his or her perceptions of quality at each step, each client exposure to the firm creates an impression about the firm. By being aware of this, the professional service communicator may have the opportunity to communicate how a firm works from the customer's perspective and also identify and highlight the firm's particular strengths in each area.

ELEMENTS OF THE COMMUNICATION MIX

A firm's communication mix, also called the promotional mix, consists of the following tools:

Personal selling: personal presentation by the firm's representative for the purpose of making sales and building customer relationships. In professional services marketing, this is traditionally the most important and most often-used tool within the promotional mix.

Advertising: any paid form of non-personal presentation and promotion of ideas, goods, and services by an identified sponsor. Television, radio, magazines, and the Internet are among the media used.

Public relations: building good relations with the firm's various publics by obtaining favorable publicity, building a good corporate image, and handling or heading off unfavorable rumors, stories, and events. Along with personal selling, this tool has also been a favorite of professional service firms.

Sales promotion: short-term incentives to encourage the purchase and/or sale of a product or service. Sales promotions can include anything from discounts to offers of extra services or gifts.

Direct marketing: direct communications with carefully targeted individual clients to obtain immediate response. Mail, telephone, fax, and e-mail are among the tools used.

In addition to these tools, the firm must remember that all the marketing-mix tools communicate, including the firm's price, physical setting, means of access, employees, and even other clientele. We will examine each of these elements in greater detail.

Personal Selling

Selling through personal contact is probably the most important of all the tools available to professional service firms, because the risks that most clients perceive in selecting a professional make it necessary to be able to reassure and persuade them through direct personal contact. Personal selling is also the most effective tool at certain stages of the consumer decision process, particularly in building a preference, conviction, and action on the part of buyers. This is because personal selling has three distinctive qualities in comparison to advertising:

1. *Personal confrontation*. Personal selling involves a living, immediate, and interactive relationship between two or more persons. Each party is able to observe the other's needs and characteristics at close hand and make immediate adjustments.

2. *Cultivation*. Personal selling permits all kinds of relationships to spring up, ranging from a matter-of-fact selling relationship to a deep personal friendship. In most cases, the professional artfully woos the target audience to gain their confidence.

3. *Response*. Personal selling makes the target audience member feel under some obligation for having listened to the talk or for taking up the professional's time.

We will now examine some of the major decisions in building and managing an effective personal selling effort within a professional service firm.

Organizing for selling. The entire staff of the professional service firm is doing part-time marketing in one form or another, from the way staff members answer the telephone to the way they look and act in their offices. The various messages sent by the staff should present the firm as friendly, conscientious, professional, and competent. But the bulk of the firm's personal selling will typically be done by a limited number of people.

A firm has a number of options regarding who should be doing the selling. First, a firm can rely on pure marketing and selling personnel who do not provide the actual service. This has the advantage of taking much of the demands of selling off overly busy professionals and helping to make sure that all selling functions get completed properly. The disadvantage of this approach is that clients may not like to be contacted initially by salespeople; they prefer to meet and deal with the professional who will service them.

A second option is to require junior professionals to budget some time for lead generation and cultivation. This has the advantage of imprinting the importance of client acquisition in new staff members. On the other hand, clients may prefer to be served by more senior members of the firm.

A third approach would be to require the senior professionals to develop new business. Some of them will be natural "rainmakers" and enjoy it. Others will resent this burden as interfering with the time needed to service their existing clients well. More professional firms are promoting juniors to partners only after they have shown that they are also capable of generating new business; thus, personal selling is an integral part at both professional levels.

The best approach for any given firm will depend on several factors. Consideration must be given to the desires and preferences of clients, capabilities and interests of staff members, and the selling approaches of competitors. When organizing the selling effort, someone in the organization must be assigned the responsibility of coordinating the sales effort toward each target market and perhaps toward each target client. Marketing managers, client officers, client managers, account executives—or individuals with similar titles—must be assigned the task of making sure that all necessary information about targeted clients is gathered and that the necessary selling functions are performed for those clients. In addition, individuals must also be responsible for selling or cultivating referral sources. The top marketing official of the firm will have to make sure that the various staff members are performing their selling tasks properly.

Sole practitioners and small firms must consider their alliances and referral partners as their sales team. For such professional firms, if they have a group of businesspeople or other professionals with whom they network, they should review referrals they've sent and received, and openly discuss their business strategy with these individuals so they know precisely the types of prospects they should send to the firm and vice versa.[4]

Allocating time and effort to selling. The need to have busy professionals devote some time to selling creates problems for many organizations. Other organizations have the opposite problem, where certain key people spend too much time in selling when they should be turning in more billable hours or spending more time building closer relationships with their present clients.

Striking a balance requires careful analysis, planning, and control. The top marketing official should work hard to make selling more convenient. "Tickler" lists should be sent to the relevant professionals on a regular basis, indicating which prospective clients need to be called, which existing clients need to be contacted or entertained, and which referral sources need to be cultivated during the coming time period. The marketing official could also provide professionals with recommended scripts or statements that could be used in discussions with clients.

Many opportunities for selling additional services emerge while services are actually being provided. Clients can be told about other services offered by the organization or be asked to recommend the organization to others. One clearly effective way to sell is simply to do good work in a friendly, industrious, honest, and patient manner. Clients who receive this type of service feel that they have been treated in a valued and respected manner and are more likely to do business with the firm in the future as well as to recommend the firm to others.

Firms may use marketing research occasions as times to also do subtle selling. Professionals can conduct telephone or personal interviews with existing or prospective clients to learn about their anticipated service needs, their decision-making procedures, and the attributes they seek in professionals. This may impress respondents and leave them with a positive impression of the professionalism and competence of the firm.

Using entertainment is another way to get some selling done. Professionals can be given a budget to take prospects or clients to favored restaurants, country clubs, or performances where they can enjoy the occasion and exchange information and concerns.

Finally, a firm can encourage professionals to spend more time selling by offering them monetary and status incentives. Bonuses, high salaries, commissions, or prizes can be offered to professionals for achieving a variety of different goals. Rewards can be based on the number of new client billings a professional brings in, the number of live or qualified leads in a targeted market a person identifies, or some other performance indicator. The indicator and rewards must be selected carefully so as not to misdirect or overly stimulate selling activity to the detriment of retention strategies. Rewards should be developed not only to encourage attracting new clients but also for keeping them.

Advertising

Acceptance of advertising professional service organizations has come a long way since the famous *Bates* decision of the Supreme Court (1976). However, some professional service firms resist the idea of paid advertising, feeling that it demeans their firm. On the other hand, some professional service marketers may expect too much from advertising or try to accomplish large objectives with inadequate skills and resources and may thus be disappointed. In fact, if used appropriately, advertising can play a positive role in a firm's communications program and can enhance, rather than demean, the firm.

The decision regarding whether or not to advertise should be made after considering a variety of factors, including the effectiveness of personal contact and public relations efforts. If an extensive personal contact and PR program is not attracting a sufficient number of targeted clients, then advertising may be needed to increase the number of clients. Advertising can reach more people cheaper (per exposure) and faster than personal contact efforts, and it can help make those efforts more effective. Clients may be more receptive to personal selling initiatives after exposure to an advertisement. Or salespersons may find it useful to refer to advertisements during presentations. A good advertising campaign can also serve to motivate individuals to put forth a more intense selling effort.

Other factors to consider in reaching a decision about whether to advertise include the types of services being offered, the types of markets being targeted, and the advertising policies of competitors. Naturally, an organization that offers highly specialized services that cannot be described appropriately in a short advertisement would be less inclined to advertise. But for organizations selling relatively uncomplicated services to markets accustomed to seeing the advertising of competitors—such as personal injury law—advertising may be a necessity.

If a professional service organization chooses to advertise, using the services of an advertising agency to develop an advertising program is a worthwhile expense. An agency's valuable help in writing copy, creating artistic effects, and selecting cost-effective media can often be acquired at a nominal charge. Agencies typically charge a client a fee for developing and placing advertisements that approximates what it would cost the client if it chose to place the advertisement in the media on its own. Agencies normally receive a 15-percent discount from the media when they place ads, and they use this 15 percent to cover their expenses (for developing copy, selecting media, etc.) and their profit.

Let us now briefly review the five major decisions that a professional service organization (and its advertising agency) must make to mount an advertising program. (See Figure 12-3.)

Figure 12-3. Major Decisions in Advertising Management.

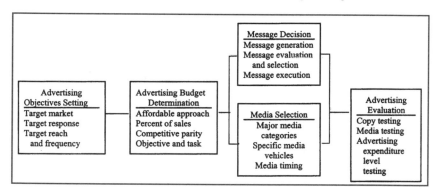

Setting advertising objectives. The first step of an advertising process is to establish the advertising objectives. The objectives must flow from prior decisions regarding the target market, positioning, and the overall marketing mix. Developing advertising objectives calls for defining the target market, target response, and target reach and frequency.

A marketing communicator must start with a clear target audience in mind. The audience may be potential buyers of the firm's services, current users, deciders, or influencers. The audience may consist of individuals, groups, particular publics, or the general public. The target audience will critically influence the communicator's decisions on *what* is to be said, *how* it is to be said, *when* it is to be said, *where* it is to be said, and *who* is to say it.

The marketing communicator must next define the target response that is sought. The ultimate response, of course, is purchase behavior. But purchase behavior is the end result of a long process of client decision-making. The marketing communicator needs to know in which state the target audience stands at the present time and to which state it should be moved.

Finally, the marketing communicator must determine the optimal target reach and frequency of the advertising. Funds for advertising are rarely so abundant that everyone in the target audience can be reached, and reached with sufficient frequency. Marketing communicators must decide what percentage of the audience to reach with what exposure frequency per period. For example, a small accounting firm might decide it would like to use direct mail advertising and buy 1,000 advertising exposures. This leaves many choices as to target reach and frequency. It could send one letter to 1,000 different executives or it could send two different letters a month apart to 500 executives, and so on. The issue is how many exposures are needed to create the desired response, given the market's state of readiness. One exposure could be enough to convert executives from being unaware to being aware. It would not be enough to convert executives from awareness all the way to preference.

Determining advertising budgets. The second step in developing an advertising program is determining the advertising budget. Advertising budgets can be determined in several ways. Four possible methods include:

1. *The affordable method.* Advertising budgets are set at the highest level that can be afforded.

2. *The percentage-of-revenues method.* A given percentage of current or anticipated revenues is budgeted for advertising.

3. *The competitive-based method.* A given proportion of what a competitor or group of competitors spends on advertising is budgeted for advertising.

4. *The objective-and-task method.* The amount budgeted for advertising equals what it is expected to cost to perform the tasks that will allow the achievement of specific advertising objectives.

We prefer the last method because it is important to consider the potential effects of different levels of advertising when determining the budget, and the first three methods do not do this particularly well. The affordable and percentage-of-revenues methods, for example, fail to account for the possibility that certain high levels of advertising might generate enough new business to allow a firm either to afford *more* or spend a *lower* percentage of revenues. These two methods tend to treat advertising as a residual or a "throwaway" instead of something that should be allocated according to what it can do for an organization. In addition, the competitive-based approach takes a rather simplistic view of what different advertising levels will accomplish, essentially assuming that the effectiveness of different levels will depend only on how those levels compare to the spending levels of competitors (and not on a host of factors).

We should emphasize that the appropriate amount to budget for advertising will vary across professions, organizations, and target markets. There are no minimum amounts or recommended ranges that we can suggest for advertising budgets for particular types of firms. In practice, advertising budgets are allocated to segments of demand according to their respective populations or sales levels or in accordance with some other indicator of market potential. It is common to spend twice as much advertising money in segment B as in segment A, if segment B has twice the level of some indicator of market potential. In principle, the budget should be allocated to different segments according to their expected marginal response to advertising. A budget is well allocated when it is not possible to shift dollars from one segment to another and increase total market response.

Formulating the message. The third step in developing effective advertising is to develop a creative message. The ideal message is one that would get attention, hold interest, arouse desire, and obtain action. This typically involves three steps. The first is the development of alternative messages (appeals, themes, motives, ideas) that will hopefully elicit the desired response from the target market. The second step is the selection of the best message out of a large number of possibilities based upon solid evaluative criteria. The message must say something interesting or desirable about the professional services being offered. It must say something exclusive or distinctive that does not apply to other rival organizations, and it should be believable or provable. Finally, the impact of a message depends not only on what is said but also how it is said, in other words, the message execution. The message has to be given a style, words, order, and format that will win the target audience's attention and interest. This involves using pictures, spokespersons, music, and art in a varied format to create different looks and sounds for an advertisement. It includes using words that are memorable and attention-getting, that will make headlines and slogans stand out and be read. It means ordering the ideas in such a way that they come across persuasively and it means formatting the ad so that it has maximum visual or auditory impact.

Advertising evaluation. The final step in the effective use of advertising is the evaluation of advertising itself. The most important components are copy testing, media testing, and expenditure level testing. Copy testing can occur both before an ad is put into actual media and after it has been printed or broadcast. Pre-testing is used to make improvements on the ad, while post-testing assesses whether the desired effect was achieved and what its possible weaknesses were. Media testing seeks to determine whether a given media vehicle is cost effective in reaching and influencing the target audience. Finally, expenditure level testing involves experiments in which the advertising expenditures are varied over similar markets to see a variation in response.

Public Relations

In carrying out its activities, a professional service firm needs to consider not only the interests of its clients but also the interests of other publics who may be affected by its activities. We define a *public* as follows:

A **public** is any group that has an actual or potential interest or impact on an organization's ability to achieve its objectives.

Figure 12-4 shows the key publics that a professional service firm needs to consider in serving its current and potential clients. Employees represent an internal public and the other groups represent external publics.

Figure 12-4. A Professional Service Firm's Publics.

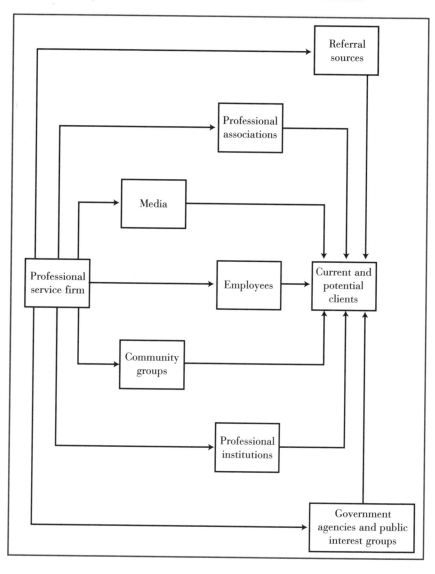

Although organizations must put their primary energy toward managing their clientele effectively, their success will be affected by how various publics view their activity. Organizations are wise to spend some time monitoring key publics, anticipating their moves, and dealing with them in constructive ways.

Most organizations use public relations professionals to plan programs for their various publics. Public relations people monitor the attitudes of the firm's publics and disseminate information and communications to build goodwill. When negative publicity breaks out, they act as troubleshooters. They also counsel management to eliminate questionable practices so that negative publicity does not arise in the first place.

Public relations is often confused with one of its subfunctions, such as press agentry, company publications, lobbying, fire fighting, and so forth. Yet it is a more inclusive concept. The most frequently quoted definition of PR is the following:

> **Public relations** is the management function that evaluates public attitudes, identifies the policies and procedures of an individual or an organization with the public interest, and executes a program of action to earn public understanding and acceptance.[5]

Sometimes a short definition is given, which says that PR stands for *performance* (P) plus *recognition* (R).

When marketing has been proposed as a useful function to install in organizations that already are receiving PR help, the existing public relations people have reacted in different ways. Some PR people feel that they are doing the organization's marketing work and that there is no need to hire a marketing person. Other PR people feel that they could learn quickly whatever is involved in marketing and that there is no need to add a marketer. Still other PR people see marketing and PR as separate but equal functions and do not feel threatened. Finally, some PR people see marketing as the dominant function to which they will one day have to report.

For our purpose, we will view public relations as primarily a set of communication tools to advance the firm's marketing objectives. We see three important differences between public relations and marketing:

1. Public relations is primarily a communications tool, whereas marketing also includes need assessment, service development, fee-setting, and distribution.

2. Public relations seeks to influence attitudes, whereas marketing tries to elicit specific behaviors, such as buying and providing referrals.

3. Public relations does not define the goals of the organization, whereas marketing is intimately involved in defining the organization's mission, target markets, and services.

Thus, public relations should essentially be used to maintain and enhance an organization's image. While many PR activities will stimulate inquiries or even buying by clients, the main purpose of these activities is to form, maintain, or change attitudes.

Figure 12-5 presents a five-stage process that should be carried out to implement a successful PR program. First, the organization's relevant publics must be identified. An active program to communicate to everyone is impossible, so those publics that are of greatest interest to the organization must be identified.

Next, the firm needs to find out how each public thinks and feels about the firm. Personal or small-group interviews might be conducted or small surveys might be used. Data obtained can then be used to take the

Figure 12-5. The Public Relations Process.

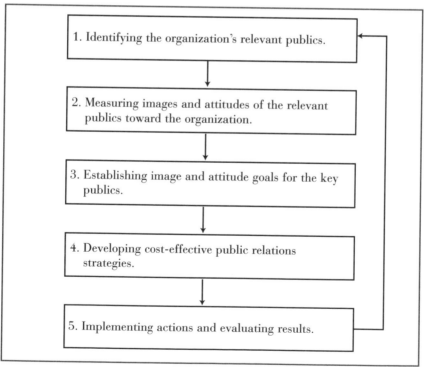

next step of establishing image and attitude goals for key publics. The organization should set up specific, realistic, and measurable goals reflecting how it wants to be seen and thought about by its relevant publics within a given period of time.

The next step involves the development of cost-effective PR strategies to attain the stated goals. Various PR tools must be evaluated to see whether they can be used at a reasonable cost to reach targeted publics and achieve desired perceptual and attitude changes.

Finally, the strategies selected must be implemented and evaluated. The persons responsible for performing various tasks must be monitored and the results they achieve must be assessed.

We would now like to examine the major public relations media and tools, which include: (1) written material, (2) audio-visual material and software, (3) institutional-identity media, (4) news, (5) events, (6) speeches, and (7) telephone information services.

Written material. Professional service organizations rely extensively on written material such as reports, brochures, and newsletters to communicate with their target publics. In preparing these publications, the public relations office must consider their purpose, aesthetics, and costs. For example, a brochure's purpose may be to establish the firm as an expert in a certain field. George W. Smith and Company, a two-million-dollar-a-year accounting firm in Southfield, Michigan, has been very successful in publishing brochures that summarize tax law changes.[6] Generally, a brochure targeted toward present clients should consist mostly of selling services those clients don't use yet or describing the breadth of the firm's offerings. A brochure to an audience that doesn't know the firm should aim to develop knowledge and an understanding of the firm's business. Aesthetics are also important, thus written material should also be readable, interesting, and professional. Cost acts as a constraint in that the organization will allocate a limited amount of money to each publication. Public relations personnel will have to reconcile considerations of function, aesthetics, and cost in developing each publication.

Audio-visual material and software. Emerging technologies have created cost-effective ways to produce and distribute audio cassettes, video tapes, CD-ROMS, and informational software. CD-ROMS in particular can not only carry volumes of information such as past speeches or articles written by partners in the firm, but can also allow interaction on behalf of the viewer. This heightens interest and promotes better comprehension of the firm's message.

Institutional-identity media. Organizations must strive to create a visual identity that the public immediately recognizes; otherwise, each of the organization's separate materials takes on its own look, which not only creates confusion, but misses an opportunity to create and reinforce an organizational identity. The firm should try to create a visual identity that the target public immediately recognizes. This visual identity is carried through the firm's media such as logos, stationery, brochures, business cards, buildings, and so on.

News. The public relations office should find or create favorable news about the firm that is interesting and made available to the appropriate media. The appeal of publicity is that it is "free advertising." As someone said, "Publicity is sent to a media and prayed for, while advertising is sent to a media and paid for." However, publicity is far from free because special skills are required to write good publicity and to reach the press. Good publicity costs money. See Exhibit 12-1 for tips on working with the media.

Publicity has three qualities that make it a worthwhile investment. First, it may have higher editability than advertising because it appears as normal news, not sponsored information. Second, it tends to catch people off-guard who might otherwise avoid sponsored messages. Third, it has high potential for dramatization because a newsworthy event arouses attention.

A good public relations director understands that the media seeks interesting stories and that professional service firms must compete for attention with all the other events of the day. The director will make a point of knowing as many news editors and reporters as possible and will provide them with press releases. He or she should also respond to media requests to interview partners. Examples of stories that would interest the media include the story of or an interview with a physician active in Doctors Without Borders or that of an architectural firm that lands a prominent and important building contract.

Events. A firm can increase its newsworthiness by creating events that attract favorable attention from target markets. Thus, a management consulting firm seeking more public attention might host a national conference with well-known speakers. Each well-run event impresses the

Exhibit 12.-1. Tips for Working with the Media.[7]

When working with media, keep these tips in mind:

1. Return any media call promptly. Journalists are even more deadline-driven than architects.

2. Don't be surprised if you speak to a journalist but are not included in the story. There can be many reasons for this, including cuts made by the editor or the possibility that you didn't have anything interesting to say.

3. You're in a service profession. If you can provide good service to a journalist—like calling back immediately with requested information—you'll win a friend or at least a higher position on the call list.

4. Bland is boring. If you want to become a frequent media source, speak your mind and let your natural personality show.

5. Don't ask to review the story before it's published. If you're discussing a complex or technical matter that you suspect may be beyond the reporter's knowledge, talk it through until you're satisfied, and then offer to be available for follow-up.

6. "Off the record," meaning that what you say will not appear in print, and "not for attribution," meaning the reporter can use the information as long as you are not identified as its source, are legitimate interview devices. Just be sure that the reporter agrees before you start talking.

7. Don't assume that placing an advertisement in publication will earn you special editorial treatment. The firewall between a publication's advertising and editorial functions is a journalistic tradition meant to preserve editorial integrity.

8. Don't send unsolicited slides or photos and then expect that someone will spend the time and money to return them to you. Color laser printouts or photocopies are adequate for many initial submissions; you can always send slides or prints later. If you do submit unrequested material that you want back, enclose a self-addressed, stamped envelope.

9. Label photos! Include the firm's name and address, the name of the project, and the photographer's name.

10. Does your receptionist know how to handle a journalist's call? Make sure he or she does.

11. Be succinct in all submissions.

12. There are no guarantees in journalism. Stories are often killed at the last minute for a variety of reasons, so don't get angry if you open up a magazine or newspaper to find your project missing.

immediate participants and provides the basis for several stories directed to relevant media vehicles and audiences.

Speeches. The public relations director will look for effective spokespersons for the firm and will try to arrange speaking engagements. If a law firm's senior partner is articulate and attractive, the public relations director can work to line up appearances on national and local television and radio talk shows and at major conventions. The director can also set up a speakers bureau for delivering appropriate talks to community organizations.

Telephone information services. Many firms have telephone information lines with toll-free service. Such telephone services are ways for the firm to show it cares about its publics, is easily accessible, and ready to serve them.

Good PR does not come cheap. Having outside public relations consultants can cost $5,000 to $8,000 per month, with a minimum one-year commitment. Some firms may choose to add PR to the job description of the marketing staff. A real concern is that if no one is given primary responsibility for PR, it may not get done.[8]

Sales Promotions

Sales promotion comprises a wide variety of tactical promotional tools, of a short-term incentive nature, designed to stimulate strong or early responses. These can be directed towards final clients (money refund offers, gifts, contests), intermediaries (cooperative advertising, referral bonuses), and towards one's own employees (bonuses, contests, or sales rallies).

No single purpose can be given to sales-promotion tools, because they are so varied. Overall, sales-promotion tools make three contributions: (1) communication—they gain attention and usually provide information that will, hopefully, lead to trying the service; (2) incentive—they incorporate some concessions, inducements, or contributions that represent value to the receiver; and (3) invitation—they include a distinct invitation to engage in the service now.

The decision by a firm to use incentives as part of its promotional plan calls for six distinct steps.

The first step is to specify the incentive's objective. The following three objectives can be distinguished: (1) to create an immediate behavioral response because the organization has excess capacity (such as during a slow season, as for an architect during the winter); (2) to promote trial of the service by groups that normally would not try it (for example, a small accounting firm may give away an incentive to try its tax-preparation service); (3) to win goodwill toward the organization (such as when the firm offers to match its employees' contributions to particular charities).

The second step is to specify the recipient of the incentive, such as prospective clients, intermediaries, or employees. For example, a tax-accountant might provide incentives to potential new clients to try the service, to current clients who refer new customers, or to employees who identify prospects.

The third step is to determine the inclusiveness of the incentive, whether it will be offered to individuals or to the groups. Most incentives are offered to individuals for their direct benefit. An example of offering an incentive to a group may be the same tax accountant offering reduced income-tax preparation to all the employees of a given organization.

The fourth step is to determine the form of the incentive, that is, whether it will consist of money or items of non-monetary value. The form of the incentive must be carefully researched because of its nuances and ability to offend the target groups. For example, although cash is a very tangible incentive, it may be viewed as corrupt or inappropriate, except in such situations as when it is presented as bonuses to employees.

The fifth step is to determine the amount of the incentive; too small an incentive is ineffective and an overly large one is wasteful. Finally, the sixth step is the timing of the payments of the incentives. Most incentives are paid immediately upon adoption of the target behavior.

Sales promotions are an important means of building business, but they must be carefully researched and planned.

Direct Marketing

Direct marketing consists of direct communications with individual clients or prospects to obtain an immediate response or cultivate lasting relationships. Using detailed data bases, direct marketers tailor their marketing offers and communications to the needs of narrowly defined segments or even individual buyers. Beyond brand or image building, they typically seek a direct, immediate, and measurable consumer response.

Early direct marketers, catalog companies, direct mailers, and telemarketers gathered customer names and sold goods through the mail and by telephone. Today, fired by rapid advances in data-base technology and new marketing media, especially the Internet, direct marketing has undergone a dramatic transformation.

BENEFITS AND GROWTH OF DIRECT MARKETING

Whether employed as a complete business model or a supplement to a broader integrated marketing mix, direct marketing brings many benefits to both buyers and sellers.

Benefits to buyers. Direct marketing benefits buyers in many ways. First, it is convenient. Customers don't have to battle traffic or find parking spaces to find information about the services they desire. They can do comparative shopping by browsing through brochures or surfing Web sites. Direct marketers may be reachable on a 24-hour basis, seven days a week. Buying is also easy and private. Customers encounter fewer buying hassles and can learn about services without waiting for or tying up time with salespeople. Direct marketing also provides shoppers with greater product information and selection.

Benefits to sellers. Direct marketing yields many benefits to sellers. First, direct marketing is a powerful tool for customer relationship building. Direct marketers build or buy data bases containing detailed information about potentially profitable clients. With today's technology, a direct marketer can select small groups or even individual consumers, personalize offers to their special needs and wants, and promote these offers through individualized communications. Direct marketing can also be timed to reach prospects at the right moment. As a result, direct marketing materials receive higher readership and response than blanket mailing. Direct marketing also permits easy testing of alternative media and messages. For example, a firm can spend $25,000 on a direct-mail campaign that contains a dedicated telephone number that serves as a code enabling the firm to know which mail piece buyers are responding to. The firm can then choose the most successful mail piece for future mailings. Direct marketing also gives the firm the ability to evaluate the cost effectiveness of its marketing effort. For example, if the direct mailing results in 100 inquiries and ultimately 25 of the inquiries are converted into clients, then the cost per inquiry is $250.00 ($25,000/100) and the cost per new client is $1,000 ($25,000/25). By computing these costs, a firm has the ability to compare different direct-marketing vehicles. Finally, direct marketing via the Internet offers sellers the advantages of reducing costs, increasing speed and efficiency, as well as greater flexibility as they can change the direct-mail piece overnight if necessary.

FORMS OF DIRECT MARKETING

The major forms of direct marketing include face-to-face selling, telemarketing, direct-mail marketing, catalog marketing, direct-response television marketing, kiosk marketing, and on-line marketing. (See Figure 12-6.)

Face-to-face selling. The original and oldest form of direct marketing is the sales call. Today most professional service marketers rely heavily on sales systems when the firm desires to locate prospects, develop them into customers, build long relationships, and grow the business.

Telemarketing. Telemarketing, the use of the telephone to sell or respond to clients, has become a major direct-marketing tool. Telemarketing expenditures now account for more than 38 percent of all direct-marketing media expenditures.[9] Marketers use outbound telephone marketing to sell directly to consumers and businesses and to find prospects and qualify them. Telemarketing through inbound toll-free 800 numbers can be used as a follow-up from television or radio ads, direct mail, or brochures.

Direct-mail marketing. Direct-mail marketing involves sending an offer, announcement, reminder, or other item to a person at a partic-

Figure 12-6. Forms of Direct Marketing.

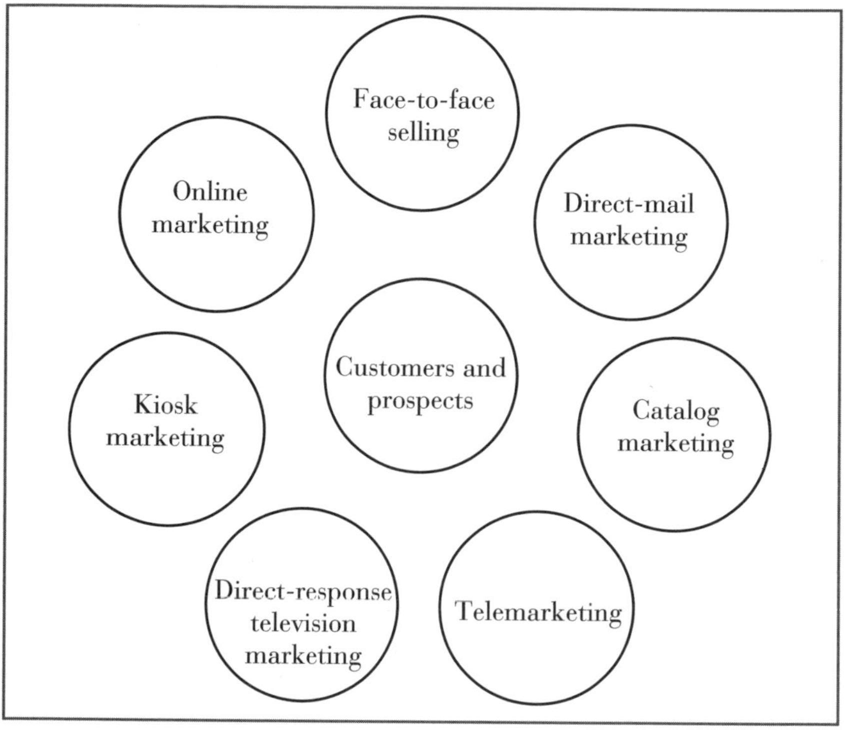

ular address. Using highly selective mailing lists, direct marketers can send out letters, ads, samples, and fold-outs. Direct mail accounts for more than 24 percent of all direct-marketing media expenditures. Telemarketing and direct-mail marketing together account for more than 60 percent of direct marketing expenditures and 66 percent of direct marketing sales.[10] Direct mail now includes fax mail, e-mail, and voice mail. Each of these new forms delivers direct mail at incredible speeds compared to post offices' "snail mail" pace.

A professional service firm that has used direct mail successfully is Frederiksen and Company in Mill Valley, California, a relatively small accounting firm. It mails to local new homeowners who have moved within the past two years with the hope of attracting new arrivals who may be looking for an accountant. The first letter focuses on welcoming the new arrivals to the neighborhood and inviting them to visit its offices. The second piece of mail is sent immediately after Thanksgiving. It promotes year-end tax planning and offers an hour's free consultation. The third is sent in early January. It includes an organizer checklist. This strategy has helped Frederiksen beef up its bottom line and customer base.[11]

Catalog marketing. Catalog marketing involves direct marketing through print, video, or electronic catalogs that are mailed to select customers, made available in stores and in one's offices, or presented on-line.

Direct-response television marketing. This technique takes one of two major forms. The first is direct-response advertising, sometimes known as infomercials. The other form is exemplified through the home shopping channels. Neither of these forms are typically used in professional services marketing.

Kiosk marketing. Some companies place information and ordering machines called *kiosks* in areas where their customers or clients are most likely to be found. Professional service marketers might envision using kiosks at trade shows to collect sales leads and to provide information on their organizations' services. Larger management consulting firms or accounting firms might use kiosks where business travelers are most likely to be found, such as in airports.

On-line marketing and electronic commerce. On-line marketing is conducted through interactive on-line computer systems that link clients to sellers electronically. These forms of direct marketing will be developed in Chapter 13.

THE INTEGRATED MARKETING COMMUNICATIONS CHALLENGE

We began the chapter by discussing the challenge of carefully integrating and coordinating the professional service firm's many communication channels—which include personal selling, advertising, public relations, sales promotions, and direct marketing—to deliver a clear, consistent, and compelling message about the firm and its services. To accomplish this task successfully the professional service marketing firm will have to take a number of steps. First, the company must work out the roles that the various promotional tools will play and the extent to which each will be used. Second, the firm must carefully coordinate the promotional activities and the timing of major campaigns. Third, it must keep track of its promotional expenditure by service, promotional tool, service life-cycle stage, and observed effect in order to improve future use of the promotional-mix tools. Finally, to help implement its integrated marketing strategy, the company must appoint a marketing communications director who has overall responsibility for the company's communication efforts. To integrate external communications effectively, the company must first integrate its internal communication activities.

SUMMARY

Everything a company says, is, and does communicates. The challenge of integrated marketing communications is to make sure they all communicate the same thing. An integrated marketing communications strategy focuses on integrating and coordinating an organization's many communication channels, which include personal selling, advertising, public relations, sales promotion, and direct marketing, to deliver a clear, consistent, and compelling message about the firm and its services. For these strategies to be effective, however, they must be grounded in a clear understanding of influence processes.

Influence typically involves persuasion. This requires the preparation and transmittal of specific messages. Messages must be encoded by the marketer, communicated through media, and decoded by the receiver. At each stage, considerable noise can be introduced into the communication process, such that the accumulated effect of the received message is very different from what is intended.

Planning effective communication involves: (1) identifying the target audience; (2) clarifying the objectives; (3) developing a message; (4) choosing the media; (5) selecting the message source; and (6) collecting feedback.

Personal selling, which involves personal presentation by the firm's sales force for the purpose of making sales and building customer relationships, is the most important communication technique used by professional service organizations. Organizing for personal selling involves determining who should do the selling and how the people should be assigned to selling functions and targeted clients. Most organizations find it desirable to have significant portions of their selling done by the professionals who provide services. Clients generally prefer to buy professional services from the people who are performing work for them rather than from sales or marketing personnel who never provide services.

Getting professionals to spend an appropriate amount of time at selling can be difficult. Support and encouragement from marketing personnel can help. Adequate amounts of time for selling can sometimes be obtained by having professionals mix selling with either doing marketing research or entertainment. In all cases, professionals should be rewarded for selling as well as retaining clients.

Advertising has produced some notable success stories in the professions since it began to be used after the Supreme Court's *Bates* decision in 1977. Advertising has also had failures. Deciding whether a professional service organization should use advertising requires careful analysis. Advertising should be looked at in terms of what it can contribute to the overall communications program.

The following five major decisions must be made if an advertising program is to be employed: (1) Advertising objectives must be set—these include determining a target market, target response, and target reach and frequency; (2) an advertising budget must be set, preferably using the objective and task method; (3) the message must be formulated; (4) the media channels and vehicles must be selected; and (5) the advertising program must be evaluated for its effectiveness.

The task of public relations is to form, maintain, or change public attitudes toward the firm. The process of public relations consists of five steps: (1) identifying the firm's relevant publics; (2) measuring the images and attitudes held by these publics; (3) establishing image and attitude goals for the key publics; (4) developing cost-effective public-relations strategies; and (5) implementing actions and evaluating results. Public-relations practitioners must be skilled communicators, adept at developing written material, institutional-identity media, news releases, events, speeches, and telephone information services.

Sales promotion involves a wide range of incentives designed to have short-term effects on specific segments of consumers, intermediaries, or employees. Sales-promotion incentives can motivate immediate action, but there must be careful planning of objectives, recipients, inclusiveness, and form, amount, and time of payment.

Direct-marketing techniques have allowed professional marketing communicators to focus more directly on targeted individual consumers to both obtain an immediate response and to cultivate lasting relationships. The benefits of direct marketing to buyers are its convenience, its ease, and privacy, as well as service access and selection. Its benefits to sellers focus on building customer relationships, higher readership and responses, easy testing of alternative media and messages, reduced costs, increased speed and efficiency, and flexibility. The most common types of direct marketing involve face-to-face selling, telemarketing, direct-mail marketing, catalog marketing, direct-response television marketing, kiosk marketing, and on-line marketing.

In order for integrated marketing communications to work, the firm must first integrate its internal communication activities. The professional service firm should appoint a marketing communications manager who has responsibility for the overall communication efforts and will be able to coordinate the use, timing, expenditures, and effectiveness of the communications mix.

NOTES

[1] Adapted from "Know Your Marketing: Using On-Line Newspapers Effectively" by Richard S. Levick in *Marketing for Lawyers*, March 1997, p1.

[2] Source: *A Program Manager's Guide to Media Planning* (Washington, D.C.: SOMARC, The Futures Group, no date). Reproduced with permission.

[3] Kolman, Herbert C. and Heuland, Carl I. "Reinstatement of the Communicator in Delayed Measurement of Opinion Change," *Journal of Abnormal and Social Psychology*, 48 (1953), p327-335.

4 Filip, Christine S. "Everyone Wants Clients, So, What's Your Plan?" *New Jersey Lawyer* (July 6, 1998), p7.

5 *Public Relations News* (October 27, 1947).

6 Stimpson, Jeff. "Marketing Gets Bolder," *Practical Accountant* (June 1998) v31, n6, p30-38.

7 "Journalists Are People Too," *Architecture*

8 Padjen, Elizabeth. "Getting Noticed," *Architecture* (June 1998), v87, n6, p154.

9 See *Economic Impact subhearing rules*, U.S. Direct Marketing Today, Direct Marketing Association (1999), accessed on-line at www.thedma.org/services/libres-ecoimpact161a.shtml

10 Ibid.

11 See Stimpson, Jeff.

13 | Services On-line

"The web was doubling in size every few months. I've never seen anything outside of a petri-dish grow that fast."
JEFF BEZOS
Amazon.com, 1996

The world is changing dramatically and business is changing dramatically along with it. We are in the throes of a revolution that is based on information technology and the merging of computing, communication, and entertainment technologies. The access and use of information is altering the way people shop and, therefore, the way things are sold. This information-based revolution is creating aftershocks in its wake. It has had a direct impact on the increased rate of globalization of markets and has led to major changes in business organization.

Not surprisingly, professional services have been affected by this revolution. Information technology is, and will continue to be, a source of great opportunities for sales, relationship building, and growth.

In this chapter, we will address the following questions about the impact of the information-technology revolution upon professional services marketing:

1. What is meant by e-commerce and on-line marketing?

2. How do those who work and shop on-line differ from the general population?

3. How is e-commerce growing as a way of doing business?

Lyle DeWitt used to spend up to five days a month tracking down answers to questions on administrative minutia. The task was part of his job as controller of TriNet Employer Group, a San Leandro, California, professional employer organization. Sometimes DeWitt couldn't figure out the answers himself and he spent money for an expert. For example, one time he paid $2,250 for an immigration attorney to determine whether a foreign postdoctoral student conducting research for one of DeWitt's clients was exempt from Social Security taxes. (The answer, it turned out, was yes.) DeWitt lamented that such questions drove him crazy: He had to find the answer fast and had to get the right answer or face substantial financial penalties.

Today, DeWitt's life is easier because he is a subscriber to Ernst & Young's on-line consulting program called Ernie. Now DeWitt can type questions into his computer and get a response on each one from an Ernst & Young expert within 48 hours. Ernst & Young's Ernie is a form of on-line consulting developed to attract small companies. Traditionally, these small companies could not afford big-name professional service firms. On-line programs such as Ernie give major accounting and consulting firms the opportunity to attract small clients who may grow into more lucrative accounts later on.

Questions put to Ernie are sorted according to subject by the firm's "knowledge providers" and routed through Ernst & Young's Intranet to the appropriate professional. The firm fields questions in several categories, including general management, human resources, information technology, taxes, and corporate finance.

Ernst & Young offers two levels of service. For an annual fee of $18,000, five employees from the client company can ask an unlimited number of questions; for a $3,500 annual fee, five employees can ask a total of ten questions. Under each arrangement, the client receives unlimited access to a PAQ (previously asked questions) data base; to TrendWatch, a data base providing an overview of topical trends in various emerging growth industries; and to Mediawatch which provides articles from seven trade magazines.

Ernie's clients seem to be a largely satisfied lot with many success stories. On-line consulting allows individuals or companies that previously avoided consultants because of their high hourly rates to use a consulting base that focuses on the organization's specific goals at a reasonable cost. As one client stated, "In effect, I have a consultant available 24 hours a day."[1]

4. How has professional services marketing responded to the opportunities of e-commerce?

5. What are the stages of development that professional service marketers are hoping to pass through as they utilize e-commerce solutions?

6. What are the issues a professional market may face in implementing e-commerce?

7. What resources will be necessary to keep it going?

8. What are the benefits of e-commerce to both the buyer and the seller?

9. What are some ways that the professional services marketer can utilize this new technology?

E-COMMERCE AND ON-LINE MARKETING

E-commerce can be defined as "technologically mediated exchanges between parties (individuals, organizations, or both) as well as the electronically based intra- or inter-organizational activities that facilitate such exchanges."[2]

This definition has four central components to it. They are:

1. E-commerce is about the exchange of digitized information between parties. This information exchange can represent com-

munication between two or more parties, coordination of the flows of goods and services, and the transmission of electronic orders. These exchanges can be between organizations, individuals, or both.

2. E-commerce is technology-enabled and uses technology-enabled transactions. Use of the Internet is perhaps the best-known example of such technology-enabled customer interfaces. However, other interfaces such as ATM and electronic banking by phone also fall into the general category of e-commerce. Businesses used to manage such transactions with customers primarily through human or face-to-face interaction. In e-commerce, such transactions can be managed using technology.

3. E-commerce is technology-mediated. It is moving away from simply using a technology-enabled transaction to a more technology-mediated relationship. The place where buyers and sellers meet to transact is moving from more of the physical world of the marketplace to a virtual world of a market space. Therefore, the success of business may rest on how well screens and machines manage customers and their expectations.

4. E-commerce includes intra- and inter-organizational activities. It can affect both how business organizations relate to external parties such as customers, suppliers, partners, or competitors and markets as well as how they operate internally in managing activities, processes, and systems.

On-line marketing is conducted through interactive on-line computer systems, which link consumers with sellers electronically. There are two types of on-line marketing channels: commercial on-line services and the Internet.

Commercial on-line services offer on-line information and marketing services to subscribers who pay a monthly fee. There are numerous professional service firms that fall into this category. Ernst & Young's Ernie, described in the introductory vignette, is one example. Westlaw offers a service to lawyers that allows them to access federal and state statutes on-line, and provides access to other services for law professionals, such as receiving the most up-to-date court rulings that may serve as precedents in the lawyer's current trial. Lexis-Nexis is another example of this "push technology" data base that can be accessed on demand or structured to provide continuous, moment-to-moment reporting of information as it occurs. The on-line services of professional service firms typically provide subscribers with information (news, libraries, education) as well as dialogue opportunities (bulletin boards and forums) and e-mail.

After growing rapidly through the mid-1990s, commercial on-line services such as Westlaw and Lexis-Nexis have been overtaken by the Internet as a primary on-line marketing channel.

Internet usage surged with the development of the user-friendly World Wide Web (the Web) and Web browser software such as Netscape Navigator and Microsoft Internet Explorer. Today, even novices can surf the Internet and experience fully integrated text, graphics, images, and sound. The Internet itself is free, although individual users usually pay a commercial access provider to be hooked-up to it.

How Is E-Commerce Different from Traditional Commerce?

Before we take a look at the rapid growth of Internet usage and on-line marketing and how those who work and shop on-line differ from the general population, we should first consider what differentiates e-commerce and its subsequent strategies from the traditional business strategies that professional service firms have so long relied upon. In their book *E-Commerce*, Jeffrey Rayport and Bernard Jaworski provide at least six differences to consider. They are:

1. **Core strategic decisions are technology-based.** In an e-commerce-based business, the customer service, the look and feel of the customer experience, the content of the site are comingled with the technological decisions. These decisions relate to the selection of service providers, business systems, Web design, and so on. E-commerce-based businesses cannot separate technological choices from the strategic decision-making process.

2. **A real-time competitive responsiveness.** In recent years, many business-strategy writers have discussed the notion of speed-based competition. While the necessity of speed is present

in traditional business, the speed of decision-making in e-commerce organizations has been reduced from months to minutes. Changes in competitive strategies and decisions are often in full view of the competitors on the very public Internet platform, allowing for immediate strategic responses.

3. **The store is always open.** One's Internet storefront is expected to be open 7 days a week, 24 hours a day, and 365 days a year, now simply known as 24/7. This level of access has implications for both customers and the professional service firm. On the customer side, the client is always able to gather information, conduct product searches, and request information. As such, 24/7 has significantly changed customer notions of convenience and availability. On the firm's side, the level of access has forced businesses to adjust both tactical and strategic responsiveness to competitive moves.

4. **A technology-based customer interface.** In traditional businesses the clients conduct transactions either face-to-face or over the phone. In contrast, the customer-interface in the electronic environment is a "screen-to-face" interaction. This includes PC-based monitors, PDAs, or other electronic devices, not to mention the exploding field of wireless application protocol. Operationally, such interfaces place enormous responsibility on the firm to capture and maximize the customer experience because there is often no opportunity for direct human intervention during the encounter. If the interface is designed correctly, the client will have no need for simultaneous or follow-up conversation. If the interface is done incorrectly, it may lead to client frustration.

5. **The customer controls the interactions.** At most Web sites, the client is in control during the screen-to-face interactions in that the Internet employs a self-service model for managing commerce. The customer controls the search process, the time spent on various sites, the degree of price/service comparison, the people with whom he or she comes in contact, and the decision to buy. In face-to-face interchange the control can rest with either the buyer or seller.

6. **Knowledge of customer behavior.** While the client controls the interaction, the firm has unprecedented access to observe and track individual consumer behavior. Through various software applications, companies have the ability to track a whole host of behavior: Web sites visited, lengths of stays on a site, pages viewed on a site, purchases, dollar amounts of purchases, and repeat purchase behavior, among others. In traditional businesses, this level of customer behavior tracking is not possible in any cost-effective manner.

Rapid Growth of Internet Usage and On-line Marketing

The growth of the Internet has been phenomenal. Today there are approximately 420 million active Internet users worldwide. (*Active* means users who get on-line at least once a week for an hour.) North America has the largest regional share of the connected worldwide population, with the United States and Canada accounting for 41 percent of the global Net user population. By the year 2004 there are expected to be approximately 210 million active Internet users in the United States alone, but the percentage of North American users will drop to approximately one-third (34.8 percent) of the population. This shift is due largely to the growing saturation of the United States market along with the growth potential and patterns of the rest of the world. For example, by 2002, Europe is expected to grow to 84 million Internet users (or 30 percent of the total); Asia will grow in share to more than 60 million users; South America will have 26.6 million; and the rest of the world will have 12 million users.[3]

Furthermore, the growth of the Web, the catalyst for Internet usage, is far outstripping the growth of the population. Between 1997 and the year 2002, the world population is expected to grow 1.3 percent, while Web users are expected to increase by 45 percent. Devices to help access the Web are expected to increase 46 percent; the number of URLs, 85 percent; and the number of Web pages, 95 percent.[4] (See Table 13-1.)

This explosion of Internet usage heralds the dawning of a new world of electronic commerce, a general term for a buying-and-selling process that is supported by electronic means. Electronic markets are electronic

Table 13-1. Web Growth Indicators.

Measure (figures in millions, except where noted)	1997	1999	2002	Increase 1997-2002	Compound Annual Growth 1997-2002
World Population[1]	5,840	6,000	6,225	6.6%	1.3%
Web Users[2]	44	131	282	541%	45%
Devices Accessing the Web[3]	78	NA	515	560%	46%
Number of URLs[4]	351	NA	7,700	2,094%	85%
Number of Web Pages[5]	320	850	9,100	2,744%	95%
Terabytes of Information[6] (Note: figures are not in millions; one terabyte = one billion bytes)	2	NA	54	2,600%	93%

Notes: (1) U.S. Census Bureau; (2) *eMarketer*, 1999; (3) and (4) International Data Corp; (5) NEC Research, with interpolations by *eMarketer*; (6) Alexa

Source: *eMarketer*, 1999.

"market spaces" rather than physical "marketplaces," where sellers offer their products and services electronically and buyers search for information, identify what they want, and place orders using a credit card or other means of electronic payment.

Some industries and particular businesses will be changed totally and instantly by electronic commerce, and others will feel the impact of the Internet more peripherally and gradually. Nevertheless, there is a discernible pattern: As prospects go on-line, businesses follow—and this in turn draws more prospects on-line. And although the dynamics differ, this is as true for businesses that sell to other business (B2Bs) as for those who target consumers.[5] And it is as true for professional services marketing as it is for selling cars or toys.

On-line activities sometimes threaten and replace traditional businesses. Other times, however, the two can be coordinated to support and reinforce each other. For example, a professional service may be sold in a traditional manner through face-to-face interaction, with customer service and follow-up sales occurring on-line, off-line, or both. The Internet may also enable professional service firms to more efficiently target their selling as well as develop and enhance customer relationships. The most important fact for business people to understand about the role of the Internet in their business is that there is no turning back. As noted in *e-*

Marketer's e-Business Report in 1999, "The Web is fundamentally changing the customers' expectations about convenience, speed, comparability,
service, and price."[6]

Profile of the On-line Consumer

It used to be that when people envisioned the typical Internet user, a computer nerd with thick glasses came to mind. Later, that image may have
shifted to that of the young upscale techie male professional. Such dated
stereotypes hardly capture the changing face of the Internet user today.

In the United States, the Internet population does differ demo-
graphically from the general population. In general, the Internet user is
still relatively young, more affluent, and better educated than the general
population.

As of July 1999, the distribution of U.S. Internet-user age groups
was split roughly as follows:

- 25.7 percent are children under the age of 18
- 23.5 percent are between the ages of 18 to 34
- Nearly 30 percent are loosely defined as Baby Boomers (ages 34
  to 54 at the time)
- 21.3 percent are seniors (age 55 and older)
- 51 percent female; 49 percent male

As indicated by these numbers, the U.S. population split roughly
into quarters; however, Internet usage is weighted heavily toward younger
users, with young adults age 18 to 34 representing 28.5 percent of
Internet usage, while individuals older than 55 represent only 12.1 percent.[7] (See Figures 13-1A and 13-1B.) However, these characteristics are
beginning to shift. Once again, the shifting demographic profile of
Internet users is a result of the saturation level of more traditional
Internet segments as well as increased accessibility to the rest of the
market. As a result, the profile of the typical Internet user increasingly
resembles that of the overall population.

As with most other demographic variables, the Internet user population is also heading towards a gender balance close to that of the overall population. Presently, women represent 51 percent of the entire U.S.

Figure 13-1A. Age Group Distribution within Total U.S. Population.

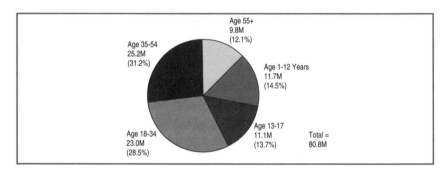

Figure 13-1B. U.S. Internet User Population by Age Group, for 1999.

population as well as 51 percent of Internet users. Web content and Web store fronts dedicated to the interests and needs of women on-line are expected to stimulate this growth and amount of time spent on-line among the group.[8] (See Table 13-2.)

Presently, the Internet consumer is financially well off. The median income for on-line users is significantly higher than that of the average American. The median household income for an American household is $37,005; the typical Internet user's household income is $58,000; and the typical Internet shopper's/buyer's household income is $62,000.[9]

Table 13-2. Shifting On-line Gender Demographics.

Gender	Population	Total U.S. Population (% Total)	1997 Internet Users	1998 Internet Users	1999 Internet Users	2000 Internet Users	2001 Internet Users	2002 Internet Users
Female	139,526,000	51%	39%	44%	46%	49%	50%	51%
Male	133,352,000	49%	61%	56%	54%	51%	50%	49%

Sources: *e-Marketer*, 1999; U.S. Census Bureau, 7/99.

Similar to income, education is a variable that is tightly connected to Internet usage, and even more so to buying on-line. Whereas only 22 percent of Americans are college-educated, 43 percent of Internet users have a college degree. Among Internet shoppers/buyers, the percentage of those who have a college degree increases to 53 percent.

The ethnic makeup of Internet users reflects the general population less than any other demographic grouping. Although the overall U.S. population is 71.9 percent white, 12.1 percent black, 11.5 percent Hispanic, and 3.8 percent Asian, the distribution of ethnic groups on-line demonstrates that both blacks and Hispanics are less likely to be wired than whites or Asians. Asians, with a 70-percent penetration, have even a higher percentage of on-line presence than whites at 58 percent.[10]

Finally, Internet consumers differ in their approaches to buying and in their responses to marketing. They are empowered consumers who have greater control over the marketing process. People who use the Internet place greater value on information and tend to respond negatively to messages aimed only at selling. And whereas traditional marketing targets a somewhat passive audience, on-line marketing targets people who actively select the Web sites they will visit and the ad banners they will click on. Individuals browsing the Net decide which marketing information they will receive, which products and services they will buy, and under what conditions. Thus, in on-line marketing the consumer controls more of the interaction. Due to the availability of information on-line, consumers are also better informed and more discerning shoppers. In fact, on-line buyers are increasingly creators of product information, not just consumers of it. As greater numbers of consumers join Internet interest groups that share product-related information, "word of Web" is joining "word of mouth" as an important buying influence. Thus, the new world of e-commerce will require new marketing approaches.

It is immediately obvious that the demographics of the on-line user are vitally important to the professional service firm. With the possible exception of the age of on-line users, the characteristics of on-line users are in line with those of individuals likely to use many professional services (architects, consultants, and certain market segment of doctors and lawyers). Furthermore, business-to-business transactions and relationships dominate the Internet. To operate effectively in the New Economy, the professional service provider must create an on-line presence.

THE GROWTH OF BUSINESS-TO-BUSINESS E-COMMERCE

In the world of physical goods, business-to-business (B2B) sales far exceed those of business-to-consumers (B2C). This reflects both the greater number of transactions and higher average expenditures.

Global trade, defined as goods and services changing hands, reached more than $80 trillion worldwide in 1999. Trade between businesses is estimated to account for $60 trillion or 75 percent of that total. In the United States, the business-to-business percentage is even higher at 85 percent of the total transactions.

In the world of electronic commerce, business-to-business also dominates business-to-consumer transactions. At present, the business-to-business sector accounts for 77 percent of the total e-commerce worldwide. By 2003, the business-to-business portion of on-line sales is expected to account for 87 percent of the total.[11]

There are a number of reasons why B2B is growing at a faster rate than B2C. The "need for speed," as well as the importance of driving down costs, have become vitally important in today's global competitive market. Consumers, for the most part, do not share in this same urgency.

The on-line magazine *e-Marketer* identifies the following eight reasons why B2B transactions will continue to dominate e-commerce.

1. Businesses are better equipped for and connected to the Internet.

2. Businesses are used to trading at a distance, particularly overseas.

3. Businesses are more cost-conscious regarding process and opportunity costs than consumers.

4. Businesses buy more frequently and in more predictable patterns.

5. The average dollar value per transaction is three times greater for business-to-business than it is for consumer sales.

6. "Network economics" make getting on-line a matter of survival for businesses that are trying to compete on a global scale.

7. There are more business users on the Web than there are home/personal users.

8. Consumer e-commerce drives growth in business-to-business e-commerce. For example, a single consumer purchase from a dot-com retailer such as Barnes & Noble or Amazon can create a cascading series of B2B transactions including those with suppliers, manufacturers, and service providers such as the postal service.

Because many professional service firms—particularly the major accounting firms, consulting organizations, and architectural firms—focus most of their time, money, and attention on the business-to-business market to keep pace with their clients, they must develop efficient and effective e-commerce capabilities.

GROWTH OF SERVICES ON-LINE

Along with the growth of business-to-business transactions on the Internet is the growth of services business as a function of that. According to Forrester Research, in 1999 services represented $22.1 billion of a total business-to-business e-commerce transactions totaling $131 billion. By the year 2003, services are expected to represent $220 billion out of a total expected business base of $1,551 trillion in e-commerce business.[12] (See Table 13-3.)

The importance of an e-commerce strategy and its subsequent penetration varies as a result of different industry drivers and competitive structures. Businesses with product and services in which information is a significant component of the total value are the most likely to embrace an e-commerce strategy. Financial services, which include banking, finance, and insurance, are some of the most information-based services. As a result, approximately 54 percent of organizations in this industry have e-commerce strategies. Twenty-two percent of healthcare organizations employ e-commerce; and in the realm of professional services, the figure is approximately 22 percent.

With regard to on-line activity, there is room to grow in many service sectors. Physicians are a good example. According to a Harris Informative poll, although 89 percent of physicians are Internet users and their average time on-line is six hours weekly, most of this is for personal

Table 13-3. Business-to-Business e-Commerce Forecasts by Sector.

Category	1999	2003
Services	$ 22.1	$ 220.0
Goods	$109.3	$1,330.8
Total B2B EC	$131.4	$1,550.8
Source: *Forrester Research*, 1999		

use rather than clinical use. This study found that only 28 percent of physicians used the Internet to access information about their patients and 52 percent reported that they sometimes use computers to receive laboratory results.[13] On the other hand, within the services segment, ten of the leading consulting firms racked up Internet-related revenues of $1.9 billion in 1998 alone.[14]

Stages in E-Commerce Strategy Development

A common expression in the Internet world is that a Web year is at best equal to three months in the real world. While such an expression cannot be statistically proven, it does provide a perspective of the speed at which developments in e-commerce occur. For reasons we have already established, professional service firms that wish to conduct business over the Internet need to move quickly. In general, companies' e-commerce experiences can be divided into four stages: (1) electronic brochure, (2) corporate expansion, (3) on-line buying and selling, and (4) integration. It should be noted that not all companies would or could go through all four stages and that transitions from stage to stage are generally gradual and overlapping. Let us look at each of the four stages in more detail.[15]

1. Electronic Brochure

Most professional service firms first stake their claim on the Web with a site that is little more than an electronic brochure. In fact, these sites are also called *brochureware* sites. Such sites include limited information about a firm and descriptions of its services. Potential clients can contact the firm via e-mail, fax, telephone, or the traditional snail mail. The Web contains many millions of such Web sites.

2. Corporate Expansion

In the second stage, firms expand their Web sites to include information about the firm, such as its history, job openings, and relevant press releases. Such sites usually focus on providing the client with as much information as possible about the firm in an effort to build customer loyalty and brand recognition.

3. On-line Buying and Selling

In the third stage, companies leap into full-scale e-commerce. They provide Web shoppers with the tools to order a product or service and pay for it. These e-commerce Web sites include on-line order forms and links to extensive data bases. Designed for convenience and ease of use, these sites focus on how to best serve the client.

4. Integration

In the final, and for most companies still future, stage of development, the customer-focused Web site is tightly integrated with all company operations. Information gathered about customers and clients on the Web site is automatically available to all company departments. The difference between a stage-three and a stage-four Web site is not immediately obvious to the client because the appearance can be the same. However, the goal of the integrated Web site is to ensure that behind-the-scene activities are conducted in such a way to ensure the smooth and efficient operation of all facets of a firm's operations.

Aligning the E-Commerce Strategy and Implementation Objectives

Most successful on-line professional service firms are much more than just electronic store fronts and well beyond brochureware sites. Their Web sites entertain and educate clients, provide customer service, and streamline information processing. An on-line business can also extend on-line activities beyond its own Web site to monitor the activities of its competitors. In order to focus its efforts effectively, an on-line service firm, just like any other business, requires a comprehensive business plan. The plan should identify the specific goals and describe the activities in which the business will engage to fulfill those goals.

Strategic Questions

The first and most important question to ask is: *Why would some-one come to my Web site?* The answer "to purchase my services" won't get you too far because plenty of other Web sites are probably offering services similar to yours. Your site must provide clients with a reason to stop by and, more important, a reason to stay, and ultimately a reason to buy and return again. A list of potential strategic questions a professional service must answer in creating its Web presence is provided in Table 13-4. The answers to these questions should be in line with one's overall corporate strategy and answered in a manner that allows the effective implementation of their Web site and on-line strategies.

Table 13-4. Sample Strategic Questions.[16]

1. What products or services am I selling?
2. Who are my customers?
3. Do people buy these products or services on-line?
4. What do customers want from my site?
5. What is the price of similar products being sold on-line?
6. Who is my competition?
7. What does my site offer that my competition's site does not?
8. What product-related interests do my customers have?
9. How can I use my Web site to better serve customers?
10. Where can I sell my products?

Web-Site Activities

Table 13-5 lists some of the principal activities for a Web site and includes some suggested methods for accomplishing these activities. These methods could well take advantage of new technological advancements related to the development of Web sites. For example, if your desire is to build branding, you would want to make sure that every page on your Web site includes a distinctive logo that loads as quickly as possible.

Table 13-5. Web-Site Activities.

Web-Site Activity	Sample Methods
Build customer loyalty	Provide live on-line help
Sell services	Securely process transactions electronically
Conduct market research	Include on-line surveys and use cookies to track where customers travel on your Web site
Create customer communities	Create discussion forums or chat rooms
Support customers	Include FAQ (Frequently Asked Questions) pages
Build branding	Customize the buying experience
Manage purchasing processes and interact with suppliers	Register corporate customers and provide one-click order processing

Web-Site Goals

Rather than creating a Web site for your professional service firm simply because everyone else has one and you "need to keep up," you should have tangible, measurable goals for what your firm intends to accomplish through its Web site. Such goals might be to increase revenue from existing clients by 10 percent; increase the client base by 15 percent; handle 20 percent of existing clients' needs via the Web site. Your strategic goals should be stated in such a way that allows the activities of your Web site to be both measured and evaluated.

Practical Considerations

Once you have answered your strategic questions, identified appropriate activities for your Web site, and established tangible measurable goals, you need to focus on practicalities. For example, can you accomplish the goals you have set up for your Web site? For example, does your firm have the time and expertise to build the site or to oversee a third party to build the site for you? Does your firm have enough money to build and maintain the Web site effectively? The answers to these questions might preclude some of the activities and goals you have planned for your Web site.

Implementing Your Strategy

Once your firm's Web strategy has been developed, it must be effectively implemented. The on-line implementation process can be divided into two phases. The first phase is to get the Web site up and running in such a manner that it supports your strategy. The second phase focuses on the continuous modification and evolution of the Web site in keeping with changes in the marketplace and within the firm itself.

The importance of a strong implementation effort cannot be understated. This is true for two reasons. First, poor execution of the organization's strategic principles hampers its chances for success. Second, and even more important, poor execution not only increases the likelihood of poor performance in the marketplace, but creates a situation in which senior management will be unable to distinguish low performance due to inappropriate strategy or poor implementation. Solid marketing strategies may be discarded as failure when in truth the failure is in the *implementation* of the strategy.

Effective implementation of on-line systems requires that the firm coordinate and focus five distinct factors on its intended strategy. These components of its implementation system include people, systems, assets, processes, and possible supply chains.[18]

1. **People.** A key characteristic of many successful Internet-based organizations is a human resource system and associated culture that places high value on the recruitment, selection, training, development, and evaluation of key personnel. Table 13-6 provides a framework for the functional areas and corresponding responsibilities one may need in order to create and maintain an on-line presence.

2. **Systems.** Systems are defined as established procedures designed to help the firm meet its goals. In the context of on-line marketing, these would include data-base systems, Web-site support systems, management information systems, and any other digitally-based approaches.

3. **Assets.** Assets can be divided into physical and information-based assets. Physical assets are those so often found in tradi-

Table 13-6. Web-Development Team Composition.[19]

Functional Area	Responsibilities
Business Management	Develop proposals, ensure that business plan goals are met, oversee project components, administer the budget.
Applications Specialists	Design and maintain the Web site, create and edit Web pages. If Web-site design is out-sourced, in-house staff might receive training in site maintenance.
Systems Administrators	Maintain the server and operating systems, and ensure secure and reliable operations. Companies that do not own a server outsource systems administration to an ISP.
Network Operations	Manage internal networks, develop firewalls (security systems), solve network problems.
Data-base Administration	Create and maintain product data bases, support transaction processing, coordinate shopping options.
Accounting	Process payments and refunds.
Customer Service	Handle e-mail requests, provide phone or on-line support, handle customer registration, develop FAQ pages, customize orders where applicable, personalize the shopping experience, handle exchanges and returns.
Content Specialists	Develop content that supports product information on an ongoing basis; frequently update content.
Marketing Consultants	Conduct usability and test-marketing studies, monitor competitors' Web sites, develop marketing materials, submit the site to search engines.

tional businesses, such as buildings, offices, or equipment. Information-based assets are constructed from data including data bases and customer behavior data. One of the most influential developments in business over the past decade has been the replacement of physical assets with information-based assets as value generators. In other words, it's not what you own, it's what you know.

4. **Processes.** Processes are defined as the patterns of interaction, coordination, communication, and decision-making that employees use to transform resources into customer value. A few of the processes that the professional service firm must establish in its implementation of on-line strategies are:

- *A resource allocation process* that formalizes and prioritizes the company's resources and opportunities it wishes to pursue on-line so they are in line with its strategies and uses its limited resources in the best possible manner.

- *Human resource management process.* The professional service firm will find that it will need to scale up quickly and adjust to keep growing with the market. Upgrading human resource capabilities is essential in a rapidly changing on-line environment.

- *Payment and billing processes.* It should be clear that without proper function of payment and billing processes, an on-line professional service firm will have difficulty producing anything other than *virtual* profits.

- *Customer support processes.* Finally, given a lack of face-to-face communication in a Web environment, it is important to have the capabilities of addressing client concerns or questions about their on-line or off-line interactions with the firm. It is essential that the professional service firm have processes designed to address these concerns in a timely manner when they arise.

5. **Supply chains.** Many professional service firms have strategic partnerships with other companies that enable them to deliver their services to clients in a high-quality manner. When implementing on-line strategies, the firm must not forget to involve

and include business partners in the development of its on-line presence.

BENEFITS AND LIMITATIONS OF ON-LINE STRATEGIES

The professional service firm that decides to implement on-line strategies will quickly find that they provide the firm with distinct benefits. However, on-line strategies also have some limitations.

The Benefits

The benefits of an on-line strategy include the following:

- *On-line strategies expand the firm's audience in local, national, and even international markets.* With minimal capital outlay, a firm can quickly and easily locate more potential customers as well as potential business partners anywhere in the world. It can also help develop the firm's service on a local level. WebMD, an on-line healthcare resource, is providing a service to physicians that allows them to connect to hospitals, insurance companies, suppliers, and even other doctors across the country. In fact, WebMD offers a free computer to physicians who subscribe to their service. In addition to using WebMD to find answers to their healthcare questions, consumers can also use WebMD's physicians list to find doctors in their area.

- *On-line strategies decrease the costs of creating, processing, distributing, storing, and retrieving paper-based information.* A professional service firm can create an on-line catalog or brochure and distribute it via the Internet at much less cost than a traditional brochure. Furthermore, this on-line strategy also provides the organization a greater flexibility, allowing it to make ongoing adjustments to its offers and its programs. For example, in mailing traditional brochures, the services, prices, and other features are fixed until the next brochure is sent. An on-line brochure can be adjusted daily or even hourly, adapting services, prices, and promotions to match current market conditions.

- *On-line strategies can support business processes and reengineering efforts.* By changing its processes, the firm can greatly enhance the productivity of its partners, sales force, and administrators. For example, one doctor's group, the Spokane Internal Medicine in Washington State, has developed an integrated computer system that contains all the patients' information and interfaces into a referral form. The form can be sent directly to specialists or the patient's health plan. According to one estimate, the system has saved the business $60 and two staff hours per referral.[20]

- *Electronic and on-line strategies can help lower telecommunications costs.* The Internet is much cheaper than VANs (Value Added Networks).

- *Electronic strategies can enable analysis of client profiles*, which may enhance the firm's cross-selling opportunities.

- *On-line strategies assist the firm in serving new clients.* Healey Baker Commercial Property, a consulting firm, attempted to identify a problem or an opportunity a potential client had and propose a solution. In addressing the problem, Healey Baker was able to use the Internet to find out a great deal about the prospective client, the market in which the client operates, and the client's competitors.[21]

- *E-strategies can help build brand awareness and brand equity.* Greg Siskind, an immigration lawyer from Nashville, Tennessee, used the Internet to build his practice from a sole practitioner to one of the leaders in the field of immigration law. He has positioned himself, via his Web site, as an on-line source of immigration law for the entire profession. When other lawyers searched the Internet for immigration law, they would be linked to his site.[22]

- *Electronic commerce and on-line strategies can be used to build relationships with clients.* The Internet can be used by a professional firm to communicate in a flexible, inexpensive, and convenient manner. It increases clients' access to the organization and gives the firm the opportunity to respond to needs as they develop.

- *The Internet can save on marketing expenditures, too.* According to Penton Research, the average cost per contact on the Net is 98 cents, compared to $1.68 for direct mail, $31.20 for telemarketing, $162 for trade shows, and $277 for an industrial sales call.[23]

The benefits to clients are also numerous, and include the following:

- *On-line strategies enable clients to interact and do other transactions 24 hours a day all year 'round from almost any location.* The clients may be able to access the organization's Intranet and obtain services and information made available on-line specifically for them.
- *On-line strategies may help consumers access the organization's services at a reduced cost.* Ernst & Young's Ernie service, described in the opening vignette, is a good example of cost-saving services.
- *Clients can receive detailed and relevant information downloaded in seconds rather than days or weeks, thereby improving their organizational efficiency.*
- *The Internet gives clients more options.* Naturally, this presents a challenge for the service firm, because as clients have greater information about and access to the competition, the firm must work harder to retain its clients.

The Limitations

The professional service firm must be aware of the fact that on-line strategies and electronic commerce are not without limitations. The drawbacks of electronic commerce can typically be grouped into two areas: technical and non-technical.

Exhibit 13-1. Missing the Technology Opportunity.[24]

In the same survey on the use of technology by professional service firms cited earlier, although 78 percent of the firms responding used a contact data base, most did not use it to its full potential. More than 70 percent used a contact data base to automate traditional marketing tasks such as:

- Marketing mailing
- Managing day-to-day marketing interactions with clients and prospects
- Communicating marketing-oriented account information between business units

Only about 30 percent of the professional service firms responding used the data base's strategic potential for data mining, which may allow the firm to:

- Gain a deeper understanding of its clients' needs
- Build historical and predictive perspectives on the similarities, differences, and shifts in clients' buying patterns
- Develop new value-added offerings to meet the demands of the marketplace

Smaller firms (fewer than 200 employees and less than $5 million in revenues) used technology at a significantly lower rate than large firms. Smaller firms:

- Appeared unwilling or unable to assign people to the support and management of marketing technology
- Didn't believe they had the capital to adopt marketing technology or update it once it's in use
- May have felt they could not absorb the loss of resources if a marketing technology doesn't bring in "results"
- Appeared intimidated by the development or use of technologies that require technical expertise and/or specialized equipment

This is unfortunate because technology provides smaller firms with a unique opportunity to gain ground competing against larger firms, because smaller firms can:

- Effectively manage data flow and access to client information
- Easily get senior-management support for a technology strategy
- Easily design and grow the quality and usability of the information in the data base

Technical Limitations

- The use of e-commerce and the Internet are still relatively new. As a result, software development tools are still evolving and changing rapidly.
- At the present time there is still insufficient telecommunications bandwidth.
- Some e-commerce software may not fit with some hardware, or may be incompatible with some operating systems.

As time passes, these limitations will lessen or be overcome. In addition, appropriate planning can minimize their impact. (See Exhibit 13 1.)

Non-technical Limitations

The non-technical limitations that may slow the spread of on-line strategies among professional service firms include the following:

- While the cost of developing a Web site may not be prohibitive, it does take a great deal of time and energy to maintain a site at the level necessary to successfully serve customers or clients. Further, a Web site must be constantly updated to give clients a reason to come back.
- Clients and customers perceive privacy matters as extremely important and have not yet come to trust e-commerce privacy capabilities. Convincing customers that on-line information and transactions are secure will require a lot of effort on the part of organizations that conduct business via the Internet.
- Because the Internet is still evolving at a rapid pace, keeping abreast of new technologies is a challenge for organizations of all sizes, particularly those with limited resources.
- At least in the foreseeable future, electronic commerce and on-line communications will never replace the value of human relationships and one-on-one interaction in person. Organizations must not rely too heavily on technology and forget that professional services are still based on human interaction.

CREATING A WEB SITE THAT WORKS

In many ways, the Internet is not a place to sell but a place to create an atmosphere to buy. Creating such an environment takes time and energy. Creating a Web presence can be accomplished in a matter of hours; however, creating a Web site that engages the client, provides useful information, and invites the client back for more is a bit more complicated. Good Web sites share some common features. Among them are:

- *Separate pages for each area.* Good Web sites are organized into areas. It is always useful to use an outline known as a site map to help in planning this design.

- *A functional and attractive home page.*

- *Current information and frequent updates.* One way to accomplish this is to have a daily message, fact, quote, or info bit to enhance the perceptions that the site is up-to-date and to encourage potential clients to visit often. It is also important to frequently update the site content and overall appearance.

- *Allows quick transfer or download* from the server to the users' computer for display. This may mean using smaller images or keeping the graphics relatively simple.

- *Uses colors for background, text, hyperlinks, and other elements* that will display and print well. Typically, this means dark text colors on a light background. An alternative is to provide printer formatted versions.

- *Allows for two-way communications.* Most sites have no immediate ability to send someone an e-mail message or ask a question. However, because questions often lead to sales, overlooking this element can be costly. If a firm's Web site enables clients and potential clients to e-mail the firm, the rule of thumb is that questions must be answered within 24 hours; therefore, along with two-way communication capabilities, the firm must have the proper support staff to communicate with clients or potential clients. An even more immediate solution would be establishing and manning an IM (Instant Messenger) account for real-time assistance.

- *Avoids frames.* A frame is a rectangular section of the screen that scrolls separately from other sections. A frame is commonly used for a table of contents. When a user clicks a link in that frame, the related contents appear in a larger frame. Not all browsers can handle frames and they take a lot of space on the screen. In addition, they are typically cumbersome, unattractive, and prone to errors.

- *Provides an internal search for large sites.* Some Web servers can build a site index automatically. When a Web site contains a vast amount of information, providing the ability to "search" the site may increase its usability.

- *Contains information relevant to its target audience.* A firm must build its Web site with the clients' perspective in mind. In addition, a firm can provide additional value to clients by enabling them to link to articles, other support services, and information about their account from the firm's Web site.

Some basic elements of a professional service firm's Web site that most clients find of interest are:

- *A summary of the firm's areas of expertise and services.* As we established in Chapter 8, one of the most important criterion in choosing a professional service firm is experience and expertise.

- *Descriptions of signature projects.* This can further establish a firm's experience base by providing information on the size and scope of the projects, their unique challenges, and how the firm handled these challenges.

- Be sure to include *e-mail links to relevant personnel.* This will help develop communication between service providers and potential clients, creating the perception that the firm is accessible and allowing for personal selling.

- *A list of all locations.* This should also include all contact information, mailing addresses, driving instructions, and general e-mail addresses, phone numbers, and Web-site links.

- *Posting of job positions.* An organization should always be looking for the best talent. Providing job postings will help the firm recruit employees and market the firm to potential employees.

- *Addresses the newest trends or happenings in an industry.* The site should provide content that demonstrates the firm's mastery of the latest trends, software, equipment, etc.; however, the content should be presented in a language clients can understand.

- *Biographical information about key personnel.* People buy people, not law, architectural, or accounting firms. Elizabeth Cordeau of the Law Society of British Columbia, Vancouver, uses head shots of each of the firm's attorneys. A picture puts a face to a name and specific accomplishments. She believes it makes a friendly or warmer presentation of information.[25]

- Finally, the information posted on a firm's Web site should *coincide with other information the firm presents to its publics.* It is important to ensure that all members of a professional organization are aware of the contents of the organization's Web site.

In developing a firm's Web site, it is important to have a long-term Web plan. Many organizations have an "Everybody else is doing it, so why don't we?" mentality about their on-line presence, but using technology for technology sake is the wrong approach to on-line marketing strategies and developing relationships with clients. Hi-tech still is not as important as high-touch. A firm's Web site is a support mechanism and in essence is part of its integrated marketing mix created to help distinguish it from the competition.

SUMMARY

On-line marketing is conducted through interactive, on-line computer systems that consumers and sellers use electronically. There are two types of on-line marketing channels—commercial on-line services such as WestLaw, and the Internet. Internet usage has surged with the development of the user-friendly World Wide Web. As a result, there is a rapid growth of on-line marketing and electronic commerce (the buying and selling process that is supported by electronic means).

Today, the typical Internet consumer or client is younger than the average population, enjoys a higher income, is more likely to have a college degree, and is most likely Caucasian. However, these statistics are expected to change in the future to more closely reflect overall demographics.

On-line business and e-commerce have been growing at a very rapid rate and will continue to grow rapidly in the future. Access and use of on-line strategies is expanding to other geographic locations and becoming more sophisticated. Presently, business-to-business (B2B) far exceeds business-to-consumers (B2C) markets both in physical goods as well as on-line.

Along with the growth of on-line business and e-commerce has come the growth of services on-line.

On-line marketing provides benefits to both the organization as well as the clients. Some of these benefits are: convenience, ease, immediacy, efficiency, and flexibility. At the same time, e-commerce does have some limitations. These include: the cost and time involved in maintaining a Web site, security concerns, and rapidly changing technology.

The professional service firm must learn how to create an effective Web site. Some practices a firm should employ are making frequent updates to the site and providing value-added services such as articles or news stories that give clients a reason to return, and building a Web site from the clients' perspective, not the firm's.

NOTES

1 Adapted from "Querying Experts by Keystroke," by Steve Kaufman, *Nations Business* (November 1, 1998), p37.
2 Rayport, Jeffrey F. and Jaworski, Bernard J. *E-Commerce.* New York: McGraw-Hill/Irwin, 2001.
3 "e-Stats Report," *e-Marketer.* e-land, Inc. (1999), p16.
4 Ibid.
5 "e-Business Report," *e-Marketer.* e-land, Inc. (1999), p14.
6 Ibid.
7 See "e-Stats Report," p27.

8   Ibid, p31.

9   "e-Marketing Report," *e-Marketer*. e-land, Inc. (1999), p36.

10 Ibid, p42.

11 "e-Commerce B2B Report," *e-Marketer*. e-land, Inc. (1999), p33.

12 See "e-Stats Report," p21.

13 "Dr. Doolittle, Online at Last," *Daily e-Stat*. e-land, Inc. (April 30, 2000).

14 See "e-Business Report."

15 Cram, Carol M. *E-Commerce Concepts*. Course Technology, 2001.

16 Ibid.

17 Ibid.

18 See Rayport and Jaworski.

19 See Cram, Carol M.

20 "E-Health: Where to Next?" *Health Line*, (August 11, 1999).

21 Marcus, Bruce. "A Gift of the Magi or Pandora's Box?" *The Marcus Letter*, accessed on-line at www.marcusletter.com/gift/html.

22 www.perton.com

23 "The Mousepad that Roared," *Marketing for Lawyers* (April 1998), v11, n12, p9.

24 Adapted from *Expertise Marketing's* "Survey on Technology and Marketing," 1999. Used with permission.

25 Beck, Paul. "Web Sites = Marketing Tool," *Building Design and Construction* (June 2000), pp. 27-28.

14

Retention and Relationship Strategies

....

"When you need a friend,
it's too late to make one."

MARK TWAIN

Retention and relationship strategies are inseparable. Every professional service organization wants to maintain and build upon its present customer base, and each would like to think that once it wins a customer or client, he or she will be a client for life. However, in order for this desire to become a reality, the service organization must constantly work at enhancing its relationship with its clients.

A professional services firm's focus on building relationships should occur at two levels, the macro and micro.[1] At the macro level, firms engaged in relationship strategies recognize that their marketing activities affect customer markets, employee markets, supplier markets, internal markets, and influencer markets such as financial and government markets. Simultaneously, at the micro level, relationship strategies recognize that the focus of marketing is shifting from completing the single transaction to building a long-term relationship with existing customers.

Relationship strategies are not built on the firm's services and products, because those come and go. Nor are they built on the magnitude of the firm's information networks. In fact, Michael Schrage, a research associate at MIT and an expert on collaborative design, has stated, "As a general rule, too many organizations have spent too much time obsessing

Patricia J. Roy, D.O., family physician in Muskegon, Michigan, has been providing school sports physicals for two school districts in her area since 1982. Even though her practice is closed to new patients, she continues to do this work. When she began, her motive was marketing, pure and simple. She was a new doctor and believed that sports exams would be a good way to get her name in front of lots of families, including teachers and administrative staff. Her strategy worked well. Many teachers and staff members became patients. Many of the schoolgirls turned to her when it was time for them to leave their pediatricians or find a new family doctor and have become her most loyal patients. She has even taken care of some of the children of the girls she saw at the beginning of her practice.

Dr. Roy has built a relationship with her patients over time based upon a number of factors. First, she enjoys the work. Second, she believes that having a woman doctor makes the physicals more comfortable for girls and removes the last barriers to athletics for some of them. Before she started providing these services in the school districts, the young women athletes needed to be examined by a male doctor, which many of the girls found embarrassing. And for the same reason girls find it uncomfortable to be examined by a male doctor, Dr. Roy believes that boys would be uncomfortable being examined by a female doctor, thus only provides physicals at the school, only for young women and not boys, even though she has been asked several times to consider the latter. Dr. Roy's services also are appreciated by parents. Because she does the required pre-participation physical in the school, parents—many of whom cannot afford the expense—do not need to take their children to outside doctors. Dr. Roy also takes a great deal of pride in making a difference in her patients' lives by picking up on previously undiagnosed health problems. Over the years, she has identified such life-threatening ailments as malignant melanoma, diabetes, and heart disease among her patients.

Doctor Roy has also developed good relationships with other physicians in the area. When she identifies a problem in an athlete, she makes the necessary notification to both the student's parents as well as her family physician and she encourages her athletes to follow whatever treatment regimes their doctors prescribe as a result of her diagnosis.

Most of all, Dr. Roy enjoys the relationships she develops with the young athletes. She begins seeing the girls as early as sixth grade and by the time they are seniors in high school, she has developed a bond with them. She says she enjoys the feedback she gets when she sees young athletes year after year and admits to being a bit proud when one of "her" athletes takes a state title or wins a college scholarship for athletics. She likes the feeling of having been involved in their success.[2]

on the information they want their networks to carry, and far too little time on the effective relationships that those networks should create and support." He goes on to say, "The so-called information revolution itself is actually and more accurately a relationship revolution . . . . The traditional economics and established markets for human relationships are yielding new cost-benefit equations enabled by new media (and technology). The coin to this new realm is not data and information; it's the value and priority that people place on the quantity and the quality of the relationships."[3]

Overall, relationship marketing emphasizes the importance of customer retention and a concern for the quality that transcends the boundaries of departments. Relationship strategies broaden the definition of the customer from "the final consumer" to "all groups" (for example, suppliers, employees, influencers, etc.) that are integral components in bringing the services to the marketplace. Efforts to retain the relationships with all these customers and clients are the core of the relationship marketing concept.

In this chapter, we will discuss the components of effective retention and relationship strategies. In particular, we will answer the following questions:

1. Why are retention strategies so important in building a successful professional service firm?

2. Why don't professional service marketers do a better job of retaining their present clients?

3. What is the relationship between retention strategies and relationship strategies?

4. What is the basis of long-term client relationships?

5. Are all clients worth having a relationship with?

6. How can a firm better manage its client relationships?

THE IMPORTANCE OF RETAINING CLIENTS

The importance of retention strategies can best be exemplified through a popular analogy referred to as the "leaky bucket theory." (See Figure 14-1.) Imagine a bucket in which someone is pouring water, but the bucket has multiple holes near its base and water is escaping through those holes. Logic would dictate that the fastest and most efficient way to fill the bucket would be to plug the holes. Now, imagine that instead of water being poured into the bucket, it is the professional service firm's time,

Figure 14-1. "Leaky Bucket Theory."

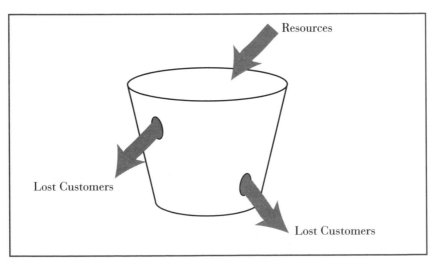

energy, and money that is devoted to attracting new clients. And instead of filling a bucket with water, the firm's goal is to grow to a certain size. The firm suddenly realizes that "there are holes in its bucket"; that as it is attracting new clients, others are leaving. The firm must plug the holes in its bucket—that is, the firm must understand why clients are leaving and must devote the time and energy to keeping them.

RETENTION AND PROFITABILITY

There are at least six reasons why keeping customers longer and more satisfied will lead to more profits.

First, existing clients represent higher probability prospects. This is due to the fact that the firm has already won the trust and confidence of its current clients, which in turn is one of the most important factors in making a decision to choose a professional service firm. Furthermore, because the firm already knows a client, it is also more likely to be able to identify his or her concerns and needs than it could with a new client.

A second reason is that the cost of satisfying an existing client is less than the cost of attracting a new client. An often-quoted statistic is that it costs five times more money to get a new client than it does to keep one.

A major part of new business development is focused on issues such as awareness building, qualifying activities, comfort building, investigatory interviews, competitive presentations, proposals, and so on. Once a firm has obtained a client, not as much effort and resources are necessary for these processes.

A third reason is that once clients have confidence in a firm's abilities, they may be more likely to employ the firm for other types of services. For example, a client may have originally hired a lawyer because of his or her expertise in real estate law and then employed the same firm for services that related more to personal injury or family practice law.

A fourth advantage is the increase in internal efficiencies within the firm. As a firm works longer with an existing client, the firm can integrate more juniors into the delivery of services to the client. By building up clients' acceptance and comfort with the firm's junior members, the hourly cost to serve goes down and profit margins go up.

Fifth, clients experience increased value as a result of the relationship. In Chapter 10 we defined value as *benefits minus costs.* Two of these costs are psychological and social. Through the development of a relationship, the client begins to experience lower psychological and social costs.

Finally, existing satisfied clients are more likely to provide referrals, which benefits the firm in two ways. First, referrals reduce the costs of obtaining new business. Second, the referred client is likely to come with a higher opinion of the practice and a degree of pre-existing trust because someone he or she trusts made the recommendation. This pre-existing trust gives the firm a head start on establishing a strong relationship with the new client.

WHY FIRMS FAIL TO FOCUS ON EXISTING CLIENTS

David H. Maister, in his book *Managing the Professional Service Firm,* has identified at least five reasons firms tend to neglect their existing clients.[4]

First, Maister believes that firms find pursuing and getting new clients to be more fun than taking care of their current clients. New clients provide the thrill of the chase in a way that nurturing existing relationships does not. Pursuing a new relationship usually has characteristics of being a well-defined, finite project, with a relatively clear task and specific deadlines. And one gets to experience the reward of landing the new client. Nurturing an existing relationship, on the other hand, has few inherent deadlines, little obvious structure, and involves many ambiguous tasks. It is, therefore, less likely to provide the adrenaline rush of a new pursuit.

A second reason lies in the firm's reward structure. Professional service organizations tend to over-reward the bringing in of new clients and under-reward bringing in new business from existing clients. Bonuses and recognition are more likely to be tied to a new client rather than developing more work with an existing one.

A third problem stems from the accounting practices of most professional service firms, which often have separate budgets for developing new business, while having no budget for developing business from existing clients. Further, all time spent on existing clients must be accounted for; therefore, time spent on activities aimed at pursuing more business from them often shows up in the accounts as extra costs, which in turn means lower profitability. As a result, members of the firm may forego the desired marketing activities necessary to increase business from current clients.

A fourth reason is the fact that different types of marketing activities are involved in pursuing more business from existing clients. When obtaining new clients, members of the firm are more likely to be involved in less high-touch, less intimate, and more detached activities. For example, reaching a new client may mean doing research on the prospect, writing proposals, giving seminars, or making structured presentations rather than dealing with the client personally, as is necessary for building a long-term relationship with an existing client. In order to develop an "intimate" involvement with the client and his or her business, members of the firm must get close to the client and develop a high level of interpersonal trust and show a personal interest in the client's needs.

Finally, Maister believes that in many professional service firms, marketing is reactive, meaning that it responds to an external impetus such as a request for a proposal. As a result, available marketing time is quickly filled with activities initiated by external stimuli. Because existing client opportunities must be actively sought and brought to the surface before the client is aware of the need, a reactive posture typically results in the under-exploitation of existing client opportunities.

In addition to Maister's five reasons firms spend more time developing new business than nurturing business from existing clients, we would like to add a sixth reason. One of the more difficult stages of the selling process is asking for the business, in other words, "the close." Many individuals feel uncomfortable with directly asking a prospective client for the opportunity to work on a specific project. It typically requires practice, a belief in the selling process, and a high level of self-confidence. Further, many professional service providers may feel that it is unnecessary to sell their services to existing clients on the assumption that if they have done a good job in the past, their clients will actively seek them out and automatically provide them with business. Such assumptions help individuals uncomfortable with asking for more business avoid the task altogether. However, such assumptions are typically short-sighted, because one rarely gets what one doesn't ask for.

BUILDING RETENTION THROUGH RELATIONSHIPS

It is human nature to seek connections and a sense of belonging, to search out and develop relationships with others. This holds true not only in our personal lives, but in business relationships and endeavors as well. Given the opportunity, most clients would like to be able to develop a stronger relationship with those who supply them with necessary professional services. Ideally, clients would like to work with an accounting firm, architectural group, a lawyer, or doctor whom they can trust and with an organization that they perceive to be reliable and to have their best interests in mind. Developing such relationships reduces the client's stress in obtaining professional services.

Developing stronger client relationships takes effort, time, and commitment and a strong foundation of the four building blocks of trust, customer knowledge, customer access, and technology. We will discuss each in turn.

Trust

A leading social scientist, Francis Fukuyama, in his 1995 work *Trust: the Social Virtues and the Creation of Prosperity*, argued that social capital represented by trust will be as important as physical capital in the very near future.[5] As our economy and economies throughout the world become more centered on services, trust is the capital by which individuals will purchase services that they cannot touch, see, feel, or inspect. Trust is what allows a patient to let a surgeon take a scalpel to his or her body, or a consultant reorganize our organization. However, trust is not something given out cheaply. It is earned and built over time. Trust is established through a professional service firm's actions and deeds. It is awarded to professional service marketers who have demonstrated their *credibility*—expertise in a given area and honesty in how they have portrayed themselves—and *reliability*, having done what they promised in a consistent and dependable manner. The New York architecture firm of Greenfield, Sawicki and Tavella has been extremely successful in establishing a trusting relationship with its clients. A full 80 to 90 percent of its work is generated from repeat client business. Employees within the firm and the client firms have changed since the 1922 founding of Greenfield, Sawicki and Tavella, but the trust and relationships have endured.[6]

Trust is also a two-way street. The professional service marketer must not only display trusting behavior but must also trust his or her clients. Many professional service marketers resist giving a service guarantee for fear that their clients might abuse it. While Technical Assistance Research Program data indicates that in the United States only 1 or 2 percent of the population may be unethical in their business dealings, firms still create systems to protect themselves from the 2 percent and ignore the 98 percent who dominate their client-base.

A firm can build client trust in several ways, including: helping clients with contacts and referring business to them; sending clients useful articles that relate to their business; providing free services such as putting on special seminars for the clients' staff, volunteering to attend the clients' internal meetings, or even offering a free day of counseling.

One good example of an organization that builds trust with clients by helping them develop their own business is the Minneapolis accounting firm of Boulay, Heutmaker, Zibell and Co., PLLP. This firm developed a comprehensive relationship marketing program designed to enhance the firm's bond with attorneys. Members of the firm developed a practice development kit for attorneys that provided advice on increasing their success in working with clients, prospects, and referral sources. The kit included a newsletter produced in-house called "Hot Tips" that provide timely updates on a wide range of subjects from taxes to marketing to business valuations. The newsletter was mailed once or twice a month to the firm's attorney data base. Boulay, Heutmaker, Zibell and Co. also has a program called Signature Marketing, which is a five-step personal marketing program for attorneys that is designed to help them make the most of their unique talents to grow their practice. Boulay distributes the kit through meetings with attorneys, group presentations, advertising, public relations, and the mail.[7]

Another way to develop trust with clients is by capitalizing on the trust the firm has already developed with present clients, employees, and other important groups. The Chicago law firm of Schiff, Hardin and Waite has been publishing an alumni directory for years. The directory keeps track of lawyers who formerly worked for the firm and is a useful resource both when the law firm needs to refer work that it cannot take because of a conflict of interest and when the firm is seeking work from an organization at which an alumnus might be employed. When giving a presentation to a client or potential client where the firm has an alumnus, it helps the firm's sales process because the client knows what the firm can do and the client knows members of the firm as well.[8]

Other law firms such as Reed, Smith, Shaw, and McClay, LLP, developed a newsletter before developing a directory. This Pittsburgh firm of 450 lawyers sends out its newsletter to former Reed Smith lawyers now working in cities throughout the nation as well as a number of foreign countries. In its newsletter the firm highlights "war stories" of life as a lawyer; profiles former Reed Smith attorneys; devotes a special column of events in alumni lives such as marriage plans, promotions, or special awards; and has a section that discusses what the firm is doing. It includes descriptions of recent work performed, new attorneys at the firm, and publications about legal issues authored by Reed Smith lawyers.[9] By actively maintaining the relationships with its former lawyers, both the firm and its alumni are developing a source of referrals that have a better chance of inspiring trust.

Customer Knowledge

The second building block in developing stronger client relationships and commitment is customer knowledge, which involves three steps. The first step the firm must take is to use marketing research to find out all that it can about its clients and the environments in which they operate. The second step is to develop organizational memory—through the appropriate procedures and data bases—so that clients never have to be asked the same question twice. The final step is for the firm to make use of the information that it obtains.

How Do Professional Service Firms Get Closer
to Their Customers?[10]

A recent study of 516 professional service firms across the United States and Canada sought to answer the question, "What strategies and tactics are professional service marketers using to become more sensitive to the marketplace and get closer to clients?" The results can provide important lessons to all professional service marketers.

A very important finding that reflects the importance of marketing research is that only 25 percent of the participating professional service firms reported having a marketing research budget. But, those firms that had a budget were:

- Nearly five times more likely to report they are effective in delivering services as a method to get closer to their clients.

- Nearly three times more likely to report they are effective in managing a change in their professionals' behavior as a method to get closer to their clients.

- More than two times more likely to report they are effective in using innovation as a method to get closer to their clients.

- Nearly two times more likely to report they are effective in employing competitive practices as a method to get closer to their clients.

Information is indeed power. At the same time only 25 percent of the firms reported using data-mining techniques to get closer to their clients. Those that were using them reported that they were:

- More than twice as likely to report they are effective in delivery of services as a method to get closer to their clients.

- Two and a half times more likely to report they are effective in using innovation as a method to get closer to their clients.

- Nearly three times more likely to report they are effective in using client-relationship management strategies and tactics as a method to get closer to their clients.

- Nearly twice as likely to report they are effective in employing competitive practices as a method to get closer to their clients.

- More than twice as likely to report they are effective in employing market research as a method to get closer to their clients.

The most commonly cited techniques to get closer to customers were:

- Delivering services to clients which included flexible methodologies (74%) and customized techniques and the use of formal checkpoints to enable client interaction (59%).

**How Do Professional Service Firms Get Closer
to Their Customers?** (*cont.*)

- Manage service professional's behavior which included training programs (67%), communication programs (47%), career-management or leadership-development coaching (44%), deeper, broader strategic planning responsibilities (41%), incentives (31%), and adapting performance measures (28%).
- Client-relationship management which includes the use of software applications for customer relationship and contact management (52%), implementing client-retention activities (52%), tracking and proactively working to build "share of customer" (47%), and using new technologies as Extranets to get closer to clients (40%).

The least used strategies for getting closer to clients were:

- Innovation which includes co-developing or piloting new services with clients (46%) and creating/improving the firm's new product development pipeline (30%).
- Using new approaches to compete against rivals such as offering free solutions to win jobs (42%) and engaging in "co-opetition" (collaborating with competitors to win assignments) (39%).
- The use of marketing research to become more sensitive to clients' desires and unmet needs which include primary client research (59%), secondary client research (43%), trend analysis (34%), and economic forecasts (33%).

We will briefly review the type of marketing research the firm needs to conduct in order to successfully develop and maintain business relationships. The firm must conduct research to obtain the following information:

- The type of business the client is in
- The types of products and services he or she offers
- External issues affecting the client's company (such as industry trends, market issues)
- Internal issues affecting the client's business (managerial structure, organization, etc.)
- The client's business goals

- The client's suppliers and his or her level of satisfaction with them
- Who the decision-maker is at the client's firm
- How satisfied the client is with the firm's past efforts

Custom Research, Inc., a winner of the prestigious Malcolm Baldrige Award for Quality, is a good example of how this process can be put to use. As part of its multi-tiered marketing research and marketing information systems, Custom Research employs what it refers to as "a client notebook." This notebook contains everything about a client—from how he or she likes to do business to the way he or she prefers reports to more personal information such as the name of the client's spouse or how many children the client has. Not only does each team member assigned to a client contribute to the notebook, but each knows its contents as well. Furthermore, when a new employee joins the team to service the client, the client notebook is used as an integral part of the training process so that the client never feels the need to re-educate others in the firm about themselves or their needs.

Custom Research's client notebook also represents a form of organizational memory. Just as it is important to remember one's wedding anniversary or the birthdays of loved ones, it is important to remember information important to a client. Whether it is in paper or electronic format, this information must be kept up to date, must be accessible, and, most of all, must be used.

Customer Access

The third building block in developing strong customer relationships is customer access—the process of making it easy for clients to do business with the firm. It involves giving clients every opportunity to communicate with members of the firm. This could be accomplished in one or all of the following ways:

- Locations convenient to clients
- Hours of operation that match the clients' schedules

- In-bound 800 numbers
- Internet and Intranet access
- Face-to-face time

Clients themselves are initiating some levels of access. For example, major corporations such as DuPont are becoming more aggressive about insisting on preferred provider relationships with law firms. They are seeking legal firms that are willing to provide better service and closer partnering in exchange for more of their business. In essence, they are searching for fewer but better relationships with their legal suppliers.[11]

At the same time, opportunities for developing client access can and should be initiated by the professional service firm itself. Beyond creating the capabilities for clients to contact the firm, the firm should do everything in its power to increase its amount of client contact. This may involve telephoning or e-mailing on a regular basis, visiting the client, scheduling business meetings with the client near mealtime that may allow the opportunity to develop a social bond, and inviting the client to the firm's offices.

Technology

Technology is the final building block in a firm's ability to build lasting client relationships. Recent years have seen constant improvements in computer memory, storage, bandwidth, software, chip speed, and processing. These improvements provide a heightened ability to improve client relations and allow the firm to develop relationships with its clients on at least seven levels. First, access to computing and communication capabilities can help a firm determine which customers to focus on. Second, technology can help determine which types of services to offer and who within the firm should provide these services to which clients. Third, technology can improve the firm's capabilities in servicing customers by providing more relevant information and accessing past evaluations and customer satisfaction levels. Fourth, technology may provide the tools to better understand the costs involved in securing, servicing, and retaining customers. Fifth, better information systems facilitate the use of financial- and accounting-based controls. Sixth, the firm may be in a better position to customize its service offerings in line with the client's desires and expectations. And seventh, technology allows the firm to focus its communication to the level of conversing one-to-one, in real time, with individuals.

Does the Firm Want Relationships with Everyone?

At some point, someone in the firm must ask the question, "Is it worth having a strong relationship with all of our clients?" The short answer is no. First, the firm may have attracted clients that the firm is not ideally suited to serve or who may not be profitable to serve. Second, if the sale to the client was made based solely upon the drive to add clients, chances are that the client will not be as satisfied with the outcome of the service and would therefore be more open to switching to a competitor. Third, weaker clients take away time from serving better clients better. For example, when Custom Research Inc. strategically reduced the number of its clients from 138 to 75, the firm's revenues increased threefold. The firm deliberately chose to work with those clients who wanted a deeper relationship, enabling Custom Research to provide better service in exchange for more of each client's business.

MANAGING CUSTOMER RELATIONS

Good relationships do not happen by chance. They are nurtured, grown, and strategically managed. This means the firm must use the information that it has to identify those clients who are not only profitable now but would be profitable in the future.

Ian Gordon, a noted consultant in relationship strategies, has developed a matrix that provides guidelines on how to better manage relationships between professional service firms and their clients. (See Figure 14-2.) Gordon classifies clients based upon their current profitability and their potential future profitability. For clients that the firm identifies as being profitable now but potentially unprofitable in the future, he recommends managing the relationships. He suggests that the firm should

Figure 14-2. Ian Gordon's Customer Segmentation Portfolio.

	Unprofitable	Profitable
Profitable	MANAGE	REWARD AND INVEST
Unprofitable	FIRE	DISCIPLINE

Customers—Current (vertical axis: Profitable / Unprofitable)

Customers—Future (horizontal axis: Unprofitable / Profitable)

identify what issues may be blocking the clients from becoming profitable in the future and then help them overcome these obstacles.

For clients that the firm deems to be unprofitable now but who could be profitable in the future, Gordon suggests a strategy of disciplining the clients. This could include charging clients extra fees for not being profitable now. If a client decides that a relationship is important and is willing to shift practices to make the service fees disappear, the firm has accomplished its task. On the other hand, if the client decides to seek a new supplier, the firm now has more time to devote to its more profitable customers.

Those clients that the firm deems to be both profitable now and in the future require a strategy whereby they will be rewarded and the relationships will be nurtured by investing the proper resources in their development. These clients have earned the firm's best efforts. They are provided the greatest access to the most important partners and are recognized for their part in making the relationships work. Finally, there may be some clients who are not profitable now and are not expected to be profitable in the future. Gordon recommends "firing" these clients, thereby allowing the firm to focus on more promising relationships. However, a note of caution is warranted here. The professional service firm should be careful to manage the firing of a client just as it would the firing of an employee. The process should be conducted in a professional manner, and there should be a dialogue between a member of the firm and the client to identify and articulate the reasons the relationship broke down. The goal is not to create enemies but to leave the door open for the possibility of future relationships.[12]

SUMMARY

One of the fastest ways for an organization to grow is not to constantly search for new clients but to grow the ones the firm already has. Focusing on the firm's current clients is likely to be more profitable for a number of reasons. These include: The fact that the firm has already won the trust and confidence of its current clients makes it more likely that the firm will be able to do future business with them; the cost of satisfying an existing client is less than the cost of attracting a new client; the cost to serve the client is reduced because the dollars invested in obtaining and establishing the relationship with the client in the first place do not need to be replicated; an increase in internal efficiencies within the firm; the client's perception of increased value as a result of the relationship; and, finally, existing satisfied clients are more likely to provide referrals.

Service firms tend to neglect existing clients for a number of reasons, including: getting new clients is more fun; rewards systems within the firm are frequently focused on client acquisition and not retention; there are no budgets specifically aimed at maintaining clients; it takes a different type of skill to maintain a relationship than to make a sale; and members of the firm assume closing techniques are no longer necessary to get sales from existing clients.

The building blocks of strong client relationships are trust, customer knowledge, customer access, and technology. Each of these blocks facilitates the nurturing, development, and growth of strong long-term business relationships.

At the same time, not all clients are worth developing into a strong relationship. A firm might be better off focusing on fewer clients but developing stronger relationships. The firm might be focusing on clients whose needs they cannot meet profitably or who demand too many

resources and cost too much to serve. Based on current and future profitability, clients may be classified into four groups and each group can be
handled in one of four ways: managing, disciplining, rewarding and
investing, and finally, terminating.

NOTES

[1] Martin, Christophe;, Payne, Adrian; and Ballantyre, David. *Relationship Marketing.* Oxford: Butterworth-Heinemann, 1991.

[2] Adapted from "Could This be Your Best Marketing Move?" by Patricia Roy, D.O., *Medical Economics*, December 23, 1996, n24, p62.

[3] Schrage, Michael. "The Relationship Revolution," Merrill Lynch Forum at www.ml.com/woml/forum/relation.html.

[4] Maister, David H. *Managing the Professional Service Firm.* New York: Free Press, 1997.

[5] Fukuyama, Francis. *Trust: The Social Virtues and the Creation of Prosperity,* Free Press, 1995.

[6] "Architectural Firm Approaches 75th Anniversary," *Real Estate Weekly* (February 19, 1997).

[7] "One Firm's Marketing Efforts," *The Practical Accountant* (February 1997).

[8] Neil, Martha. "Some Law Firms Reach Out to Touch Someone—Alums," *Chicago Daily Law Bulletin* (December 28, 1998), p1.

[9] Ibid.

[10] Adapted from a survey on "Becoming More Market Driven," by Suzanne Lowe, *Expertise Marketing* (2001). Used with permission.

[11] Haserot, Phyllis Weiss. "Lessons From Other Industries," *New York Law Journal* (April 27, 1999), p5.

[12] Gordan, Ian. *Relationship Marketing.* New York: John Wiley & Sons, 1998.

15 | Future Directions of Professional Services Marketing

"Success is never final."
WINSTON CHURCHILL

In the previous 14 chapters, we have been focusing on how the professional service marketer can compete more effectively in today's world. We have discussed the applications of marketing strategy to the professional service environment, the use of segmentation in sharpening the firm's focus on the marketplace, the benefits of understanding clients and customers, how to develop a strong service offering coupled with competitive pricing structures, better access and integrated communications, the impact of the Internet, and, finally, the importance of developing relationships as a primary means of client retention. In this chapter, we will attempt to identify variables that will affect how the professional service marketer competes in the future.

NINE TRENDS IN PROFESSIONAL SERVICE MARKETING

Every professional service organization must create a plan for the future by identifying and adapting to long-term trends in the professional ser-

The Four Levels of Marketing . . . So Far[1]

Professional service firms go through four discernible levels on their way to identifying marketing as an institutionalized business process. A level-one firm has an emerging sense of what marketing is all about. In other words, management knows it needs to do "something" but isn't sure of what that something is. As a consequence, the something tends to be social occasions such as golf outings or basketball games. Admittedly, this is not marketing, but at least the firm is making an attempt at marketing. Level two is more interesting. Here a firm usually attempts to codify a marketing program—or at least something the firm's management perceives to be a marketing program. A telltale sign of level-two behavior is hiring a marketing coordinator. The mindset of a level-two firm is that the professional service practitioner should not be spending his or her time marketing—that these tasks should be delegated to someone else, though typically that person is without charter, budget, influence, or accountability. The end result is a disappointment to everyone, particularly to the marketing coordinator who more often than not ends up unemployed.

The good news is that level two is the forerunner of level three, which is where marketing starts to be taken seriously. At level three, a professional service firm forms marketing committees and appoints a senior-level partner or manager to supervise the marketing program. Usually a marketing consultant is retained as the firm's advisor in matters of promotion and client development. Marketing events are planned and executed. Goals, objectives, and budgets are established, measured, and managed. A level-three, marketing program usually pays off with positive results. However, these results are usually not sustainable or replicable. At level three, marketing is still viewed as a series of unrelated episodes, social events, seminars, new brochures, advertising, and, of course, more golf.

Level four is where the professional service firm needs to be in its marketing mindset. Level-four firms look at marketing as a systematic process, one that makes marketing a part of the firm's core values and institutional culture. Client development is now a way of life, a continuous process encompassing all facets of the practice. Marketing is no longer seen as a distraction or time taken away from the firm's activities, but an integral part of the business itself.

In the process, the firm's culture undergoes a transformation from an inward to an external focus, one that is based on close examination of the clients' actual needs, as opposed to what the firm has historically provided.

vice environment. Much has happened to professional services since the often-cited case of *Bates* vs. *Arizona*, which gave physicians the right to advertise. Professional codes of conduct have changed to allow the use of established marketing techniques; an increase in wealth has allowed clients to pay for more services; technology has allowed services to be delivered in a more efficient manner and to more people; and increased competition is creating an even more client-focused mentality.

Trends that will affect professional service firms in the future include blurred distinctions among professions, the growth of the world economy, and cultural shifts, among others. Here we will discuss nine trends that will have a significant impact on the future of professional services.

New Models Mean New Ethics

New models of business may lead to new models of ethical behavior. There are two likely models of business. The first is the societal marketing concept that holds that the firm should determine the needs, wants, and interests of target markets. According to this view, a professional service firm should deliver superior value to clients in a way that maintains or improves the clients' and the society's well being. According to the societal concept, pure marketing concepts overlook possible conflicts between client short-run wants and clients' and society's long-run welfare. For example, in the United States, the most litigious country in the world, many critics cite the vast number of "frivolous" lawsuits that are clogging up the court system. Television ads that focus on ambulance lights and large cash returns may be the tools of lawyers who truly believe they are providing representation to individuals. Their clients might believe that contingency fees are a great equalizer in the nation's courtrooms by helping them afford to sue wealthy corporations. At the same time, one must wonder if all these suits are necessary and how many might have been avoided either through mediation or common sense. Could the nation's courtrooms be better utilized by focusing on more serious and "legitimate" cases? As Figure 15-1 shows, the societal marketing concept calls on marketers to balance three considerations in setting their marketing policies: firm profits, client wants, *and* society's interests. Originally most firms based their marketing decisions largely on short-run company profit. Eventually, marketers began to recognize the long-run importance of satisfying customer wants, and the marketing concept emerged. Now the societal marketing concept is under consideration.

A second model that is affecting ethical consideration of professional service firms is the growing adoption of business thinking and

Figure 15-1. The Societal Marketing Concept.

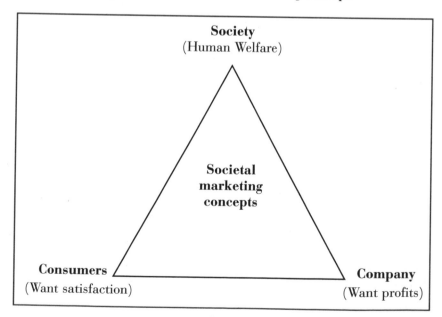

practices among professional service providers. Outside of management consultants, most professional service marketers have not studied business as part of their professional education, but the new business orientation of professionals may bring in new ways of running their practices. Consider the ethical dilemma in the following case.[2] A large group practice consisting of more than 100 physicians sold their money-losing clinic to a far-away, investor-owned, for-profit health plan from California and continued to practice in the clinic as employees of the new owner. Each physician in the clinic reportedly was paid an average of $3.3 million upfront in the form of the acquiring health plan common stock. That purchase price appears to have covered not only the physician's book of patients, but also sundry tangible assets including a 60-percent stake in a for-profit health maintenance organization that the physicians had founded years earlier. Long before the deal with the California health plan, the physicians had already sold 40 percent of their HMO to outside investors. As a result of the sale, this group of physicians came face to face with a number of difficult decisions.

The first decision focused on dealing with life as an employee in a profit-making venture. As the clinic continued to lose money, the new owners resold the clinic to yet another investor-owned company that specialized in managing primary-care independent-practice associations. This newest owner started to impose a variety of tough cost controls on the clinic that threatened the physicians' salaries and job security. As a result, the physicians voted to unionize. One physician lamented that they had ended up in a commercial world where the patient is merely a revenue stream and they were expected to make financial rather than clinical decisions. These physicians were facing a societal dilemma of balancing the patients' long-run needs with corporate short-run profitability. Furthermore, the physicians in question needed to reassess their own behavior and part in this dilemma. Were the physicians behaving in an ethical manner in selling their practice for money and then turning around and unionizing? In addition, the physicians had to make a decision as to whether they should disclose to their patients that they had sold the business in return for future cash profits that the patients themselves represent. Should the patients be told explicitly of the financial incentives the physicians received so that the patients could make more fully informed choices?[3,4]

As professional service markets become more competitive, the business models of the 21st century are likely to be increasingly adopted by professional service firms, yet professional service providers must be aware of the impact and the strengths and limitations of each of these models.

Blurred Distinctions among Professions

There is an increasing number of professional services that are crossing over and offering expertise and assistance in areas that were traditionally outside of their domain. Some accounting firms have more lawyers working for them than some law firms have; and some of the biggest players in the management consulting business are the Big Five accounting agencies. The migration of services has a number of ramifications. First, clients gain the opportunity to benefit from "one-stop shopping." Thus, a firm engaged in a merger or acquisition may find it convenient to have the same professional service firm handle the accounting as well as legal work. The professional service firm benefits by deepening the relationship with clients, increasing the profitability of their accounts, and potentially strengthening the firm through diversification. The downside of such a strategy is that it may create a "jack-of-all-trades, master-of-none" situation. Lack of focus may result in overall lower quality.

As professional service firms invade each other's space, there is an increase in competition between and among professional service firms. This in turn requires an increasingly sophisticated "business" approach to the management and marketing of the firm. This in turn increases the acceptability of a business model for running the professional service firm. A result of these shifts in how professional service firms do business is the need for business education for professional service practitioners. It is more common to see universities offering combination MD/MBAs and JD/MBAs. Organizations such as the American College of Physician Executives are offering credentialing programs in business. The changing needs of the CPA profession motivated the Board of Directors of the American Institute of CPAs to endorse a framework for educating future CPAs that emphasizes personal competencies and business skills. All these educational efforts are aimed at preparing today's professional service practitioners to succeed in an increasingly competitive world.

Migrated Marketing

Marketing is no longer only the job of a marketing department. While the marketing function ("doing marketing") belongs to the marketing department, being marketing-minded and client-minded is everybody's job. In fact, several scholars have noted that as marketing becomes an organizational responsibility, it may lose its functional identity.[5] The result could be a simultaneous upgrading of market orientation and downsizing of the formal marketing function.

A real danger of this migration of marketing is that when everyone is responsible for marketing, then no one may be responsible for marketing. However, in the majority of organizations, marketing is likely to remain a defined and powerful functional area, but its role and function might change significantly. Here are some potentially new roles for marketing:

- The marketing department may increasingly become a functional silo, the creator and repository of the firm's marketing skills and knowledge base. It will operate the firm's marketing information system, data bases, and analytical models; conduct research commissioned by its process teams or marketing units; and be responsible for environmental scanning.

- The marketing department will be a home base for marketing specialists assigned to various teams or units, to which they will rotate back periodically.

- Marketing may provide the marketing training and education of technical and non-technical members of the organization.[6]

The Growth of the World Economy

Most professional service firms limit their work to their own country. Doing business in one's own country is easier. One knows the culture, one knows the language, one knows the "rules of the game," and there is no need to disrupt family life with travel abroad. There is nothing inherently wrong with this approach; however, this mentality may be shortsighted for two important reasons. First, given the size and significance of the

American market, many foreign professional service firms will be attracted to do business in that market, which will result in increased competition in an American firm's home market. Second, professional service firms may have to focus on international markets because, to paraphrase Willy Sutton, "that's where the money is." Clients are increasingly demanding worldwide service. Through the use of technology, even small local businesses have the opportunity through alliances to reach global markets. Professions such as accounting, architecture, law, and management consulting have the capabilities of serving larger regional and international markets.

Cultural Shifts

Two fundamental changes in the marketplace are calling for increased levels of cultural awareness and competency from professional service marketers. The first is the globalization of the world economy. The second is the decline of a Caucasian dominance in the U.S. population. In both cases, professionals must become more culturally sensitive as they work with an increasingly diversified base of clients.

Cultural differences are well illustrated in the following example. One of the authors' colleagues is French and has an American spouse. The French colleague and his spouse were both equally taken back in their initial exchanges with physicians from the opposite culture. The American wife on visiting a physician in France found she irritated the doctor by asking him questions about his medical reasoning and subsequent diagnosis. The physician was not used to being questioned by a patient, especially a woman. The French husband had a different experience the first time he visited an American doctor. When his office visit was nearly completed, the doctor asked the husband if he had any questions or concerns that he would like the physician to address. Being caught by surprise and not expecting to be offered the opportunity to ask questions, he stated he had none even though he did.

To be successful in the multicultural world, professional service marketers must first be able to identify differences in cultures, then they must develop cultural empathy, an understanding of the logic behind the cultural differences. Behind every cultural norm there is some reason rooted in history; acceptance of cultural differences comes with understanding that history. Finally, one must understand that behaviors and standards are different throughout the world and that handling cultural shock brought about by these differences is an integral part of developing cultural competence.

The Increasing Importance of Relationship Strategies

Relationships will continue to be the basis of retention strategies and a core component of a successful professional service firm. Some of the customer-relationship management processes that will become increasingly important are:

- An emphasis on service quality and measurement of customer satisfaction.
- The development and delivery of valued-added services.
- Going beyond a financial and social bond to developing an integrated structural bond that fosters a partnering relationship.
- A focus on mass-customization where each client is a segment of one and receives highly tailored services.
- A focus on customer retention and loyalty versus acquisition and attraction to ensure long-term growth.
- A continued emphasis on improving relationships with one's employees as a means of enhancing client relationships.

The Increasing Importance of the Brand

"A strong service brand is essentially a promise of future satisfaction. It is a blend of what the company says the brand is, what others say, and how the company performs the service, all from a customer's point of view."[7] The firm must carefully communicate its identity and purpose in a manner that is consistent with its intended position in the marketplace. The firm needs to coordinate its advertising, publications, physical facilities, and so on to deliver a consistent positioning. These factors along with word of mouth are primarily responsible for brand image. Brand image and cultivation were found to be a principal success driver in the study of fourteen mature high-performance service companies in a variety of industries.[8] The creation of brand awareness combined with the delivery of a promised brand experience builds brand equity more powerfully than any advertisement.

More Focus on Cost-Savings

While it is important for firms to continuously improve their quality and value, their prices must remain competitive and accessible. At one extreme, small businesses are increasingly turning to do-it-yourself professional servicing to save money. For example, Nolo's Law Store, a publisher of law books, publishes books for laypeople and small businesses with forms for doing much of their own legal work without engaging a lawyer. And some small businesses are preparing their own tax or accounting statements using increasingly sophisticated, although still easy-to-use, software.

At the other extreme, high-volume purchasers of professional services are looking for less expensive services. Clients of all sizes are becoming more price conscious. As a result, some law firms are offering to cap their charges rather than bill on a cost-plus basis. All this means that firms must become more skilled in managing their costs.

The Continued Impact of Technology

Technological advances are affecting businesses along three dimensions: speed, scope, and cost. With respect to speed, information diffusion is much faster than ever before. Technology allows for information to flow faster both vertically and laterally. Firms are using such software as Lotus Notes and developing Intranets to improve access and exchange of information. Along with increasing efficiencies within the firm, the clients benefit as well because there is less "I'll get back to you with that information," and more instantly available answers to clients' questions.

With regard to scope, technology—and in particular the Internet—widen the scope of the market. Information can be collected throughout the world, analyzed, and implemented in a way that provides a broader perspective to a firm's business operations. Independent firms called *infomediaries* will emerge to manage and market information to their clients.[9,10] Technology will allow clients to better serve themselves by allowing them to access a service firm's Web site to obtain information and answers.

The Internet can also be a cost-saving tool because it presents a very efficient way to communicate with clients. However, this cost-saving only comes after a significant investment in the technological equipment and development of the data bases that will make these communication efficiencies possible. For many smaller organizations, these costs are too high and keep these technological advances out of their reach.

While technology provides substantial benefits for both professional service firms and their clients, technology can also raise client concerns about privacy, confidentiality, and the receipt of unsolicited communications. While technology can bring about better relationships and service, its improper use may result in negative outcomes or client backlash. A firm must make every effort to ensure that the use of technology enhances clients' trust and does not destroy it.

THE LEARNING ORGANIZATION

In this book, we have sought to identify those variables that will enable the professional service firm not just to compete in the coming years, but to thrive. We have discussed the importance of service quality, the use of marketing research, strategic planning initiatives, segmentation, consumer behavior, developing a strong service offering, effective pricing strategies, creating access to the service firm, integrated communications, the use of the Internet, and relationship and retention strategies. It is our belief, however, that the professional service firms that will truly thrive in this new century will be those that have actually become client sensitive and client driven. The key to being absolutely client centered is the ability to constantly learn. The clients we know today will not be the clients we serve tomorrow. Their needs are constantly changing. The marketplace continues to evolve as a result of competition, globalization, and technological innovation. Professional service firms need to seek continuous information and insight into how all these changes will affect their current and future clients.

NOTES

[1] Adapted from Martin Katz, "Law Firm Marketing is an Extended Process, Not an Event," *Illinois Legal Times*, January 1998.

[2] Adelson, A. "Physician, Unionize Thyself: Doctors Adapt to Life as H.M.O. Employees," *New York Times* (April 5, 1997), Section 1:35.

[3] Azevedo, D. "Taking Back Health Care: New Owners Drive This Group to Unionize," *Medical Economics* (1997), p194-207.

[4] Reinhardt, Vive E. "Economics," *The Journal of the American Medical Association* (June 18, 1997), v227, n23, p1850(2).

[5] Day, George S. "Using the Past as a Guide to the Future: Reflections on the History of the Journal of Marketing," *Journal of Marketing* (October 1996), v58, p37-52.

[6] Achrol, Ravi S. and Kotler, Philip, "Marketing in the Network Economy," *Journal of Marketing (Special Issue)*, 1999, v63, p146-163.

[7] Berry, Leonard L. "Cultivating Service Brand Equity," *Journal of the Academy of Marketing Science* (2000), v28, n1, p128-137.

[8] Ibid.

[9] Hagel, John, III and Singer, Marc, *Net Worth*. Boston, MA: Harvard Business School Press, 1999.

[10] See Achrol and Kotler.

Index